The World Guide to
SPIRITS
Liqueurs, Aperitifs and Cocktails

TONY LORD

The World Guide to

SPIRITS

Liqueurs, Aperitifs and Cocktails

TONY LORD

'Macdonald and Jane's · London'

A QUARTO BOOK

First published in 1979 by
Macdonald and Jane's Publishers Ltd
Paulton House, 8 Shepherdess Walk, London N1 7LW

ISBN 0 354 04378 1

© Copyright 1979 Quarto Limited
This book was designed and produced by
Quarto Publishing Limited, 32 Kingly Court, London W1
Art Director: Robert Morley
Art Editors: Martin Hendry and Clive Haybal
Editor: John Smallwood
Assistant Editor: Jane Struthers
Phototypset in England by Lowe and Brydone Printers
Limited, Thetford;Filmtype Services Limited, Scarborough
Colour separation by Scan Kolor, Ilkley
Printed in Hong Kong by Leefung-Asco Printers Limited

The author and publishers would sincerely like to thank the following for their help in providing copy, information and illustrations, or in checking the material used in the compilation of this book: Gustav Ledun, Bureau National Interprofessionnel de l'Armagnac; Jacques Bonnyaud, Syndicat National des Fabricants de Liqueurs; Louis Kriel, Oudemeester Group, South Africa; Llando Casprini and Raymond Lamothe, Italy; Peter L'Anson, Peter L'Anson Distillery Services Ltd; Tony Hart; Dr Peter Hallgarten; Robert Campbell and Peter Saunders, New Zealand; ER Bonner, Irish Distillers Group Ltd; Catherine Manac'h, Food from France; Stanislaw Mirgos, Anglo-Dal Ltd; Chris Swanepoel, Wynboer, South Africa; MJ Graille, Bureau National du Cognac; Jorge Bandirali, Mexican Institute for Foreign Trade; David Cossart, Cossart, Gordon Ltd; Clive Coates, Master of Wine; Derek Lubbock; Claude de Jouvencal, Pernod UK Ltd; Ann Barr; Teresa Wong, Association of Canadian Distillers; David Smith; Tony Beardmore, Martini & Rossi Ltd; Hilary Laidlaw Thomson; Chris Wilkinson; John Parkinson, Wine & Spirit Buyers Guide, Australia; Norman Smith, USA; Takeo Sasaki, Suntory Ltd; Eric Mayeur, Belgium; The Bundesverband der Deutschen Spirituosen Industrie; Chris Lever; Geoffrey Frankcom; Frank Ward, Sweden; Rik Cate, The Netherlands; Leif Jorgensen, Denmark; Jim Lucas, Fromm & Sichel Inc, USA; William Jaffray, The Irish Mist Liqueur Co Ltd; Keith MacCarthy Morrogh, R&A Bailey Ltd, Dublin; Michael Freeman, Latin America; Rolf Hellcx, Germany; Jack Welsch and James McManus, California Brandy Advisory Board; Paul Fletcher; Dick Kenny, Linda Watson and Michele Goldin, Counsel Ltd; Geoffrey Wormstone, Scotch Whisky Association; John Doxat and Alan McGuire, Buchanan Booths Agencies Ltd; · Derek Williams and Sarah Matthews, Odhams & Gunn Ltd; Jenny Ireland, Allied Breweries Ltd; Robin S Frost, John Harvey & Sons Ltd; Alastair Simpson, Pimms Ltd; Tanqueray, Gordon Ltd and John Tanqueray, Charles Tanqueray & Co Ltd; Alex Motsi, Cinzano UK Ltd; Peter Cunard, Durden-Smith Communications; International Distillers and Vintners Ltd; Keith Osborne, Labologists Society; John Walker & Sons Ltd; David Smith, Saccone & Speed Ltd.

Grateful thanks to Dartington Glass, Torrington, North Devon, for the loan of glassware for photography; Lockhart Catering Equipment, Reading, for loan of cocktail equipment for photography; Café Royal, London W1, for the loan of stock for photography; David Greig of the Café Royal for cocktail recipes, suggestions and advice.

Special thanks to Michael Jackson for his advice on this project, and Honor Metcalf who waited while this book became a reality.

Contents

INTRODUCTION	6
The Art of Distilling	8
Flavourings	12
The Raw Ingredients	14
The Language of Spirits and Liqueurs	16
The History of the Cocktail	20
The Cocktail Cabinet	22
Mixing Spirits	24
World Spirits/Production	26
World Spirits/Consumption	28
SPIRITS OF THE WORLD	
FRANCE	32
Cognac	34
Cognac Country	36
Creating the Great French Spirit	40
Armagnac	46
Eau-de-vie	52
A Wealth of Flavours	58
Liqueurs	62
Anis	64
Other Drinks	68
ITALY	70
Vermouth and Bitters	72
Liqueurs	78
Brandy and Grappa	80
SPAIN AND PORTUGAL	84
Spain/Sherry	86
Brandy	90
Portugal/Port	94
Madeira	100

THE MEDITERRANEAN	102
SCANDINAVIA	104
Denmark/Akvavit	106
Peter Heering	110
Sweden/Brannvin	111
Norway/Aquavit	113
THE NETHERLANDS AND BELGIUM	114
The Netherlands/Genever	116
Liqueurs	120
Belgium/Jenever	124
GERMANY	128
Korn	130
Weinbrand	132
Wacholder	134
Other Drinks and Liqueurs	138
POLAND, RUSSIA AND EASTERN EUROPE	142
Poland/Vodka	144
Russia/Vodka	148
THE BRITISH ISLES	154
England/Gin	156
Gin Production	160
Plymouth Gin	162
Flavoured Gins	164
Other Drinks	168
Scotland/Whisky	170
Malt Whisky/Production	172
Malt Whisky/The Distilleries	178
The Blends	182

The Major Companies	184
Ireland/Whiskey	186
NORTH AMERICA	194
Canada/Whisky	196
The Seagram Company	198
The United States/History of Distilling	202
Whiskey/The Styles	206
Californian Brandy	210
Liqueurs	212
The Whiskey Brands	214
MEXICO AND THE CARIBBEAN	218
Mexico/Tequila	220
The Caribbean/Rum	224
How Rum is Made	226
The Rum Islands	228
SOUTH AMERICA	232
AUSTRALIA/Brandy	234
Fortified Wines	236
Rum	238
Other Drinks	239
JAPAN AND THE FAR EAST	240
Japan/Whisky	242
China	244
The Far East	245
AFRICA/Brandy	246
The Companies	248
Index	252

Introduction

The old and the new –
an early pot still,
above, illustrating the
rudiments of the
distillation process.
The hydrometers
behind the glass of the
spirits safe, pictured
right, show the
strength of the raw
spirits.

THE ART OF DISTILLATION is an ancient one, but the distillation of spirits and liqueurs is a relatively new invention, the production of wine having started some two thousand years earlier.

Distilling originated in the Middle or Far East although no one knows exactly where and when. From there it reached south-western Europe during the early Middle Ages through the expansion of the Arab empire. In Spain, France and Italy, medical men and alchemists applied distillation first to the grape, then to grain.

Distilling spread rapidly across Europe. By the fifteenth and sixteenth centuries it had become an important commercial business and different regions were starting to concentrate on making different types of spirits and liqueurs. In Gascony armagnac was already being made, while the Charente distillers were beginning to produce the first cognacs. In parts of France and northern Italy centres for making herbal liqueurs were established, in many cases using recipes first developed in the local monasteries.

From Europe the art spread with the colonisation of the new world, often grafting itself on to existing local drinks and ingredients to give new spirits and liqueurs.

The beauty of distilling was, and still is, its versatility. Unlike successful winemaking, distillation is not dependent on a particular climate and geography. Spirits and liqueurs can be made anywhere from almost an unlimited range of fruits and vegetables – in China from rice, in Mexico from cactus hearts, in Russia and Poland from potatoes, in North Africa from dates, and so on. Add to this the hundreds of different flavourings that can be grafted on to spirits to make liqueurs, and the spirits drinker is presented with a marvellous diversity of choices.

The greatest spirits and liqueurs use grape or grain as their principal ingredient. Cognacs, armagnacs and the many other brandies that have emulated them are made from the grape; whiskies are based on grain. In addition to these, other spirits – vodkas, gins, tequilas and so on, have crossed national boundaries to become international spirits.

Each spirit or liqueur has its own history. Gin and the gin palaces were part of the social fabric of the English Industrial Revolution. The sugar cane fields of the West Indies and Caribbean which produced the molasses for rum were dependent upon the slave trade. The production of tequila developed from the Spanish conquest of Mexico; while, more recently, Canadian whisky became an important industry as a direct result of Prohibition in the United States.

Each different spirit, each liqueur, the various fortified wines and the vermouths all have their own stories. This book tries to tell some of them and show that the art of the modern distillers and blenders has a wealth of tradition and history behind it, which can only enhance the pleasure of their products.

The Art of Distilling

DISTILLATION IN ITS SIMPLEST SENSE works on a very basic principle: liquid is boiled and when it vaporises the more volatile elements come off first and can be collected and re-converted to liquid in a more concentrated, pure form. Yet the application of this art to the production of spirits came long after its discovery and use for other purposes.

Historians disagree on where and when distilling was first discovered and used. Archaeological evidence suggests the Mesopotamians used very primitive distilling apparatus as early as 3500 BC to make perfumes and essences. The ancient Chinese are supposed to have been making *alaki*, a form of raki, from rice beer, sometime before 800 BC. Other theories attribute the discovery to the ancient Alexandrians, Egyptians, classical Greeks or Romans some time before the birth of Christ. But it is quite possible that in different parts of the world at different times, from the Chinese to the Celts, the secret of distilling was found and diffused through the society.

The Alexandrians, early Egyptians, and ancient Greeks are all alleged, by different sources, to have used distillation to obtain different plant extracts for perfumes and potions. In the fourth century BC the Greek philosopher Aristotle wrote that sea water, after heating and vaporisation, could be collected as sweet water.

The Roman historian Pliny, around 400 years later, referred to wine heated with flames. But his description is too vague to be taken as the first written reference to the distillation of alcohol. What the Romans did give us is the word *distillation*, taken from the Latin verb *destillare* meaning 'to drip'.

So, while the evidence points to the art of distillation as being a relatively ancient craft, what it does not do is suggest that the ancients were distilling spirits from wine, despite the widespread consumption of wine in most parts of the ancient world.

Generally the Arabs are given credit for introducing distilling to Europe through their centres of learning in Spain and elsewhere. They gave a much greater degree of sophistication to the art they inherited from the Alexandrians and Egyptians.

Avicenna, the Arab alchemist, referred to two types of higher strength alcohol in his treatises, and Rhazes of Carthage described exactly three different distillations. They and their colleagues added to the existing knowledge the idea of distilling spirit from base alcohol, and introduced a prototype of the modern still, called an *alambic*, the name still widely used in France and other countries.

From the Arabs, too, came the word *alcohol*, to describe the end product of the alambic. The term is a corruption of *al khol*, the Arabic name for a black powder obtained by distillation and widely used as cosmetic eye shadow throughout the Arab world.

The Arab doctors and philosophers, forbidden alcohol by their religion, were only interested in its distillation for medical and scientific reasons. Over the decades they lost interest in, or just lost, the art and it was resurrected from their writings by their European counterparts.

From roughly 1100 to 1300 in northern Italy, France, Germany, Ireland and Spain, monks, doctors, philosophers and alchemists were re-discovering distillation. Some were interested in alcohol as a medicine or for extracting and infusing herbs and essences, others believed it was the secret of transmuting base metals into gold and silver. But they all believed distilled spirit was a new element, and called it 'the water of life' – *eau de vie* in French, *usquebaugh* in Gaelic, *aqua vitae* in Italian.

The French believe the lost art was rediscovered by Arnaud de Vilanova, a professor at the University of Montpellier, in the early fourteenth century. He produced a spirit-based liqueur from wine which he scented and flavoured with rose leaves, lemon essence and other flavours. His pupil Raimundo Lullio wrote the first definitive treatise on distilling spirit from wine.

Vilanova and Lullio thought they had discovered the fifth element, the elixir of life. Lullio wrote that eau de vie is 'an emanation of the divinity, an element newly revealed to men but hid from antiquity because the human race was too young to need this beverage destined to revive the energies of modern descrepitude'.

But other evidence suggests that Vilanova and Lullio were not the first to make this 'divine' discovery. Some historians believe that in northern Italy alchemists had already made a liqueur similar to the modern *rosolio* by flavouring distilled grape spirit with rose petals. And the German historian EO von Lippmann believes that *weingeist* (wine spirit) was first made in Germany sometime between 1050 and 1150, and was sufficiently established by the twelfth century for Albertus Magnus to mention the production of *aqua ardens* (ardent spirit) in his famous

Hieronymus Braunschweig's illustration of a pot still, left, featured in his Das Buch zu Destillieren, published in 1519. A detailed diagram, right, showing the stages in distilling eau-de-vie.

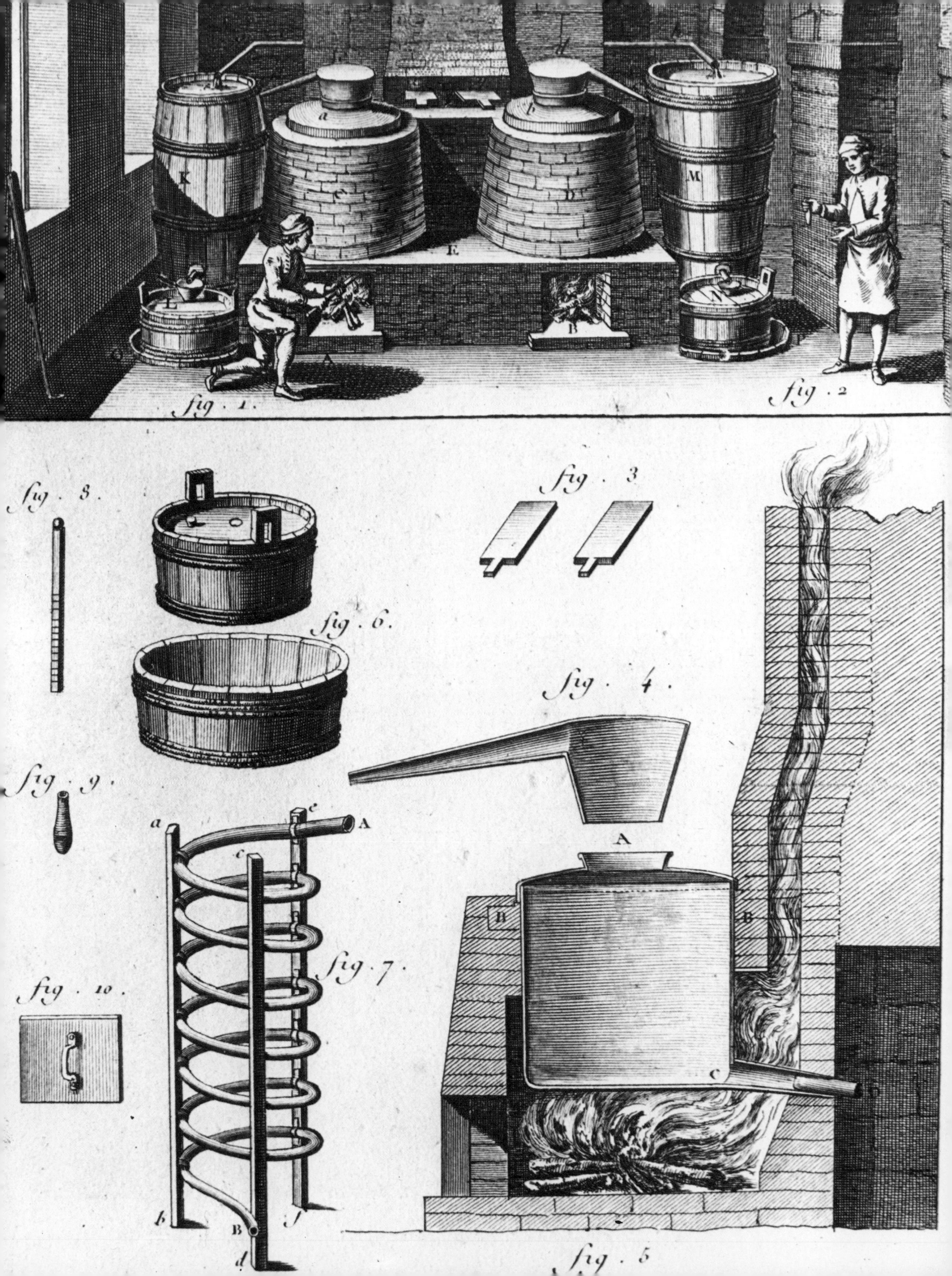

fig. 1

fig. 2

fig. 8

fig. 3

fig. 6

fig. 4

fig. 9

fig. 7

fig. 10

fig. 5

manuscript. In Ireland the production of spirits from grain is also thought to have started about this time.

From these separate but parallel developments different spirits began to evolve. Their creators realised that alcohol was neither a fifth element nor the secret of transmutation, but was valuable medicinally and it was from medicines that they developed to become popular drinks.

An existing document shows that armagnac was being made for local consumption as early as 1411, and northern Italy and Alsace already had a reputation for the production of spirits. Distilling spread into Poland, then Russia; from Ireland to Scotland; and from western Europe into the Low Countries and Scandinavia. By the fifteenth century the Germans were using corn to make *schnapsteufel* ('drink of the devil'), and this shift away from using imported wine hastened the spread of distilling into the non-vine-growing countries. The production of spirits in the

Edouard Adam, above, the man who invented the process of redistillation. An engraving showing an old distillery, right.

THE CHEMICAL PROCESS

The Pot Still

Spirits distillation is basically the separation of ethyl alcohol, the drinkable alcohol, from the base liquid – wine or a cereal wash.

At normal atmospheric pressure ethyl alcohol vapo rises at 173°F, while water vaporises at 212°F. So heating wine (with its high water content), or a cereal mash diluted with water will drive off the more volatile ethyl alcohol first and this can be collected and condensed in its concentrated form to give the potable spirit.

The final composition of the spirit is determined by the base material, the type of distillation, and the end product sought by the distiller. All alcohol contains minute quantities of substances other than ethyl alcohol. Among them are higher (or fatty) alcohols, acids, esters (which contribute to the bouquet), aldehydes, essential oils, terpenes and minor volatiles. A much higher percentage of these ingredients remain in a pot stilled spirit, giving more character to the spirit, while a continuous still removes more of them, to give the final spirit a cleaner, purer taste.

The method of distillation can affect the strength of a spirit – the first run from a pot still will only reach around 45° proof and needs to be distilled a second time to raise the proof to somewhere between 105° and 121° proof. The continuous still can reach this level and higher in one cycle.

Finally, the distiller can change the taste of the spirit by ageing the young spirit in wood or adding different flavours. With gin, for example, the juniper taste is re-added with other lesser ingredients during or after the vaporisation of the alcohol. With most liqueurs new flavours are added by soaking or distilling plants, fruits and spices in the raw alcohol. These range from cherries, oranges, peaches and plums to honey, caraway seeds and rose petals.

The pot still, the simplest of the two types of still, consists in almost all cases of a circular copper pot or kettle (1), heated by a direct gas or coal flame or by steam (2).

The alcohol in the heated wine or cereal mash rises through a long, swan-line neck (3) in vapour form and is collected in liquid form (4) after passing via a coiled tube or serpentine (5) through a water-cooled condenser (6).

Most pot-distilled spirits pass through the pot still at least twice. For even greater purity three,

even very occasionally four, distillations can be used.

The advantage of the pot still is that it retains much more of the flavouring elements in the spirit, and leaves the finished spirit with more of the taste of the base material. The basic disadvantage is the slowness of the distilling cycle which requires greater manpower to produce a smaller quantity of finished spirit than would be obtained using a continuous still.

northern countries flourished. Unlike wines, spirits gave an inner warmth and insulation from the rigours of the climate.

Until the nineteenth century all spirits were produced in more or less sophisticated versions of the pot, or alambic, still. At its most basic this was little more than a copper kettle for heating the base wine or cereal mash, with a tube taking the alcoholic vapours through a water bath for reliquification. Hieronymus **Braunschweig** illustrated this system in 1519 as the frontispiece for his *Das Buch zu Destillieren* (the Book of the Art of Distillation), and his successors only enlarged and improved on this basic principle.

In the early nineteenth century two new discoveries revolutionised commercial distillation. In 1801 Edouard Adam, working at the University of Montpellier almost 500 years after Vilanova, discovered the art of rectifying (or redistillation) to give a purer, higher strength spirit. Then, in 1826, the first working model of the continuous still was designed by Robert Stein, a cousin of the Scottish Haig family. Aeneas Coffey, his contemporary, patented an improved design in 1830 which became known as the *Coffey* or *patent* still.

The new still was cheaper to run, could be kept going indefinitely and produced a purer spirit. In Scotland it transformed the whisky industry by allowing the distillers to make a less expensive, lighter grain whisky to blend with the heavier, more expensive, lower volume malts. Blends now account for 99 percent of all the whisky produced in Scotland.

This process was quickly adopted by other spirits producers, and today gin, vodka, akvavit, white rum, some dark rums, many Canadian and American whiskies, many brandies including armagnac, and schnapps, are wholly or partly made from patent still spirits.

The pot or alambic still survives as the vehicle for the production of cognac, malt whisky, most Irish whiskies and the flavours used in liqueurs.

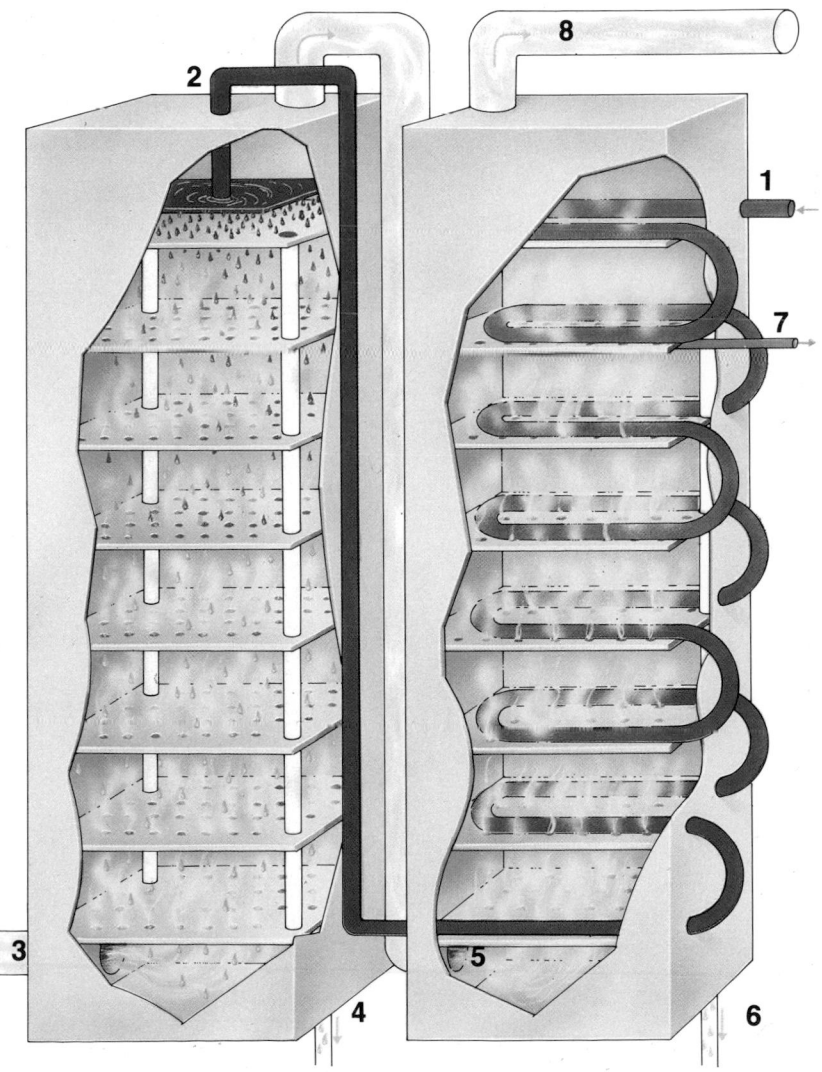

The Continuous Still

The modern version of the Coffey (continuous or patent) still consists of two columns, much taller than they are wide. Each column consists of several compartments divided by a series of horizontal perforated copper plates.

The alcohol-bearing wash enters the top of the first column (1), the rectifier, and descends down the column through a twisted pipe where it is heated by steam passing up through the perforated plates.

It then crosses over to the top of the second column (2), the analyser. The hot liquid runs through the analyser and at the bottom of the column meets superheated steam rising upwards (3). The steam evaporates the more volatile elements in the wash, including the alcohol, leaving the rest – the spent wash (4), to be drawn off at the bottom of the analyser.

The alcohol-bearing vapour passes back to the bottom of the rectifier column (5). There it rises, warming and, in turn, being cooled by the new wash descending in its pipe. The heavier volatiles quickly condense and are removed from the bottom of the column (6). The good spirit starts to condense back into liquid form about two-thirds of the way up the column and is drawn off (7).

The most volatile elements reach the very top of the column and are also removed (8) for redistillation with the elements removed from the bottom of the column.

The continuous still is much cheaper to operate, produces much more spirit, and spirit of a purer, stronger type. Used in banks of ten or twelve, it is ideally suited to the production of high volume spirits brands. The distiller has slightly less control over the cycle than the rival pot distiller, and the end product will have less of the character of the base wine or cereal mash (a desirable feature for a gin or vodka distiller).

Flavourings

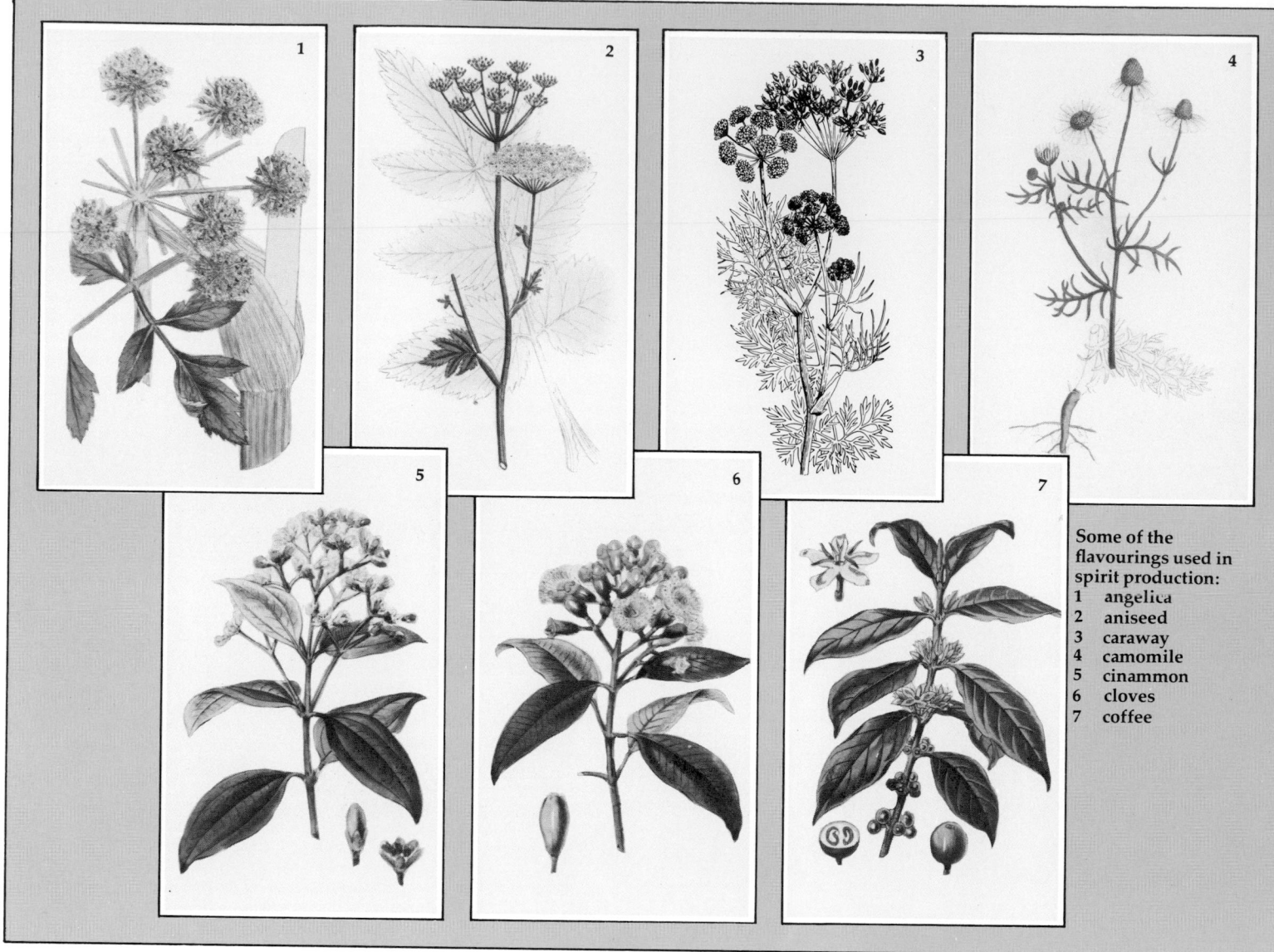

Some of the
flavourings used in
spirit production:
1 angelica
2 aniseed
3 caraway
4 camomile
5 cinammon
6 cloves
7 coffee

ALL LIQUEURS, AND A few other wines and spirits, are flavoured in some way after distillation. Indeed, liqueurs are characterised not by their base alcohol, which can range from brandy or rum to a neutral spirit, but by their flavourings. Initially, flavouring was introduced either to make a crude spirit more palatable, or to impart medicinal qualities to the drink.

There is an almost infinite variety of substances used to make flavoured wines, spirits and liqueurs. They can be broadly classified into three groups: herbs and spices, seeds and plants, and fruits. These flavourings include everything from spices such as cinnamon or cloves to almonds, honey, coffee and tea, even lavender and rose petals.

The flavours of the raw ingredients can be obtained in four basic ways: pressure (commonly used to free the juice from citrus peels, for example); extraction, using non-volatile fats, for instance, which take up the scents and flavours and are later removed by alcohol solvents; extraction with a volatile solvent, usually alcohol, which picks up the flavours; and distillation from an aqueous or alcohol solution.

The essences and flavours can be introduced or re-introduced into base alcohol in several ways. First, by the soaking or *maceration* of one or more ingredients (which have usually been crushed to release their characteristics more freely) in alcohol. If the alcohol is warmed to hasten the process, this is called *digestion*.

Percolation, which could be described as intensive maceration, is a more efficient method than digestion. This is done by continuously passing hot or cold spirit through the flavourings, or by vaporising the alcohol so that the steam passes continuously through the ingredients.

A third method is by mixing the ingredients with alcohol and distilling the mash. The condensed vapour is then both high in alcohol and has the flavour of the raw materials.

Once the essence of the raw ingredients has been merged with the spirit, *rectification*, or redistilling, can be used to remove some of the undesirable alcohol flavours.

In modern commercial times each producer keeps his recipe a secret to protect himself from imitations. A good chemist-blender could unravel the ingredients, but would be hard pressed to determine in what proportions they were used and how they were put together. The different macerations, distillations and percolations must be assembled in a precise sequence. The slightest variation can completely change the flavour of the resulting spirit. So the compounding process, or recipe, is kept a closely guarded secret.

Vermouth is probably the oldest flavoured alcoholic drink. Even before the ancient Greeks, herbs and honey were being used to disguise a harsh or old wine. Of the fifty or so herbs that are added to a base white wine (with a little grape juice and brandy) to make a modern vermouth, wormwood is by far the most important. Juniper, camomile, rose petals, orange peel and quinine are among the other ingredients used in small quantities.

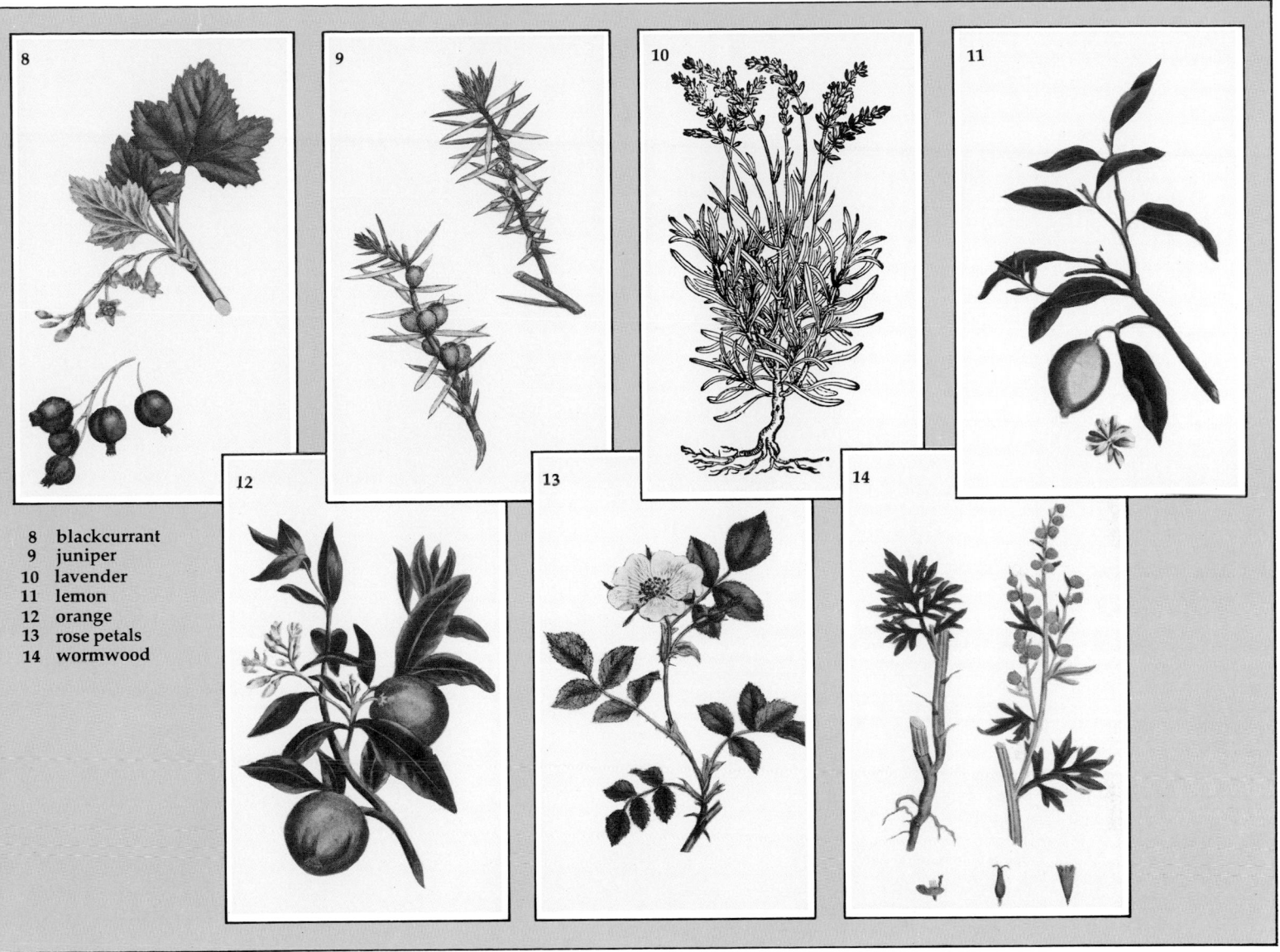

8   blackcurrant
9   juniper
10 lavender
11 lemon
12 orange
13 rose petals
14 wormwood

The many other aromatised wines, such as Campari and St Raphael, which are related to vermouth also use a variety of herbs as flavourings, each to the manufacturer's secret formula.

There are several flavoured gins available, made by steeping fruit in the spirit, but the characteristic flavour of gin itself is obtained by adding flavourings to what is a neutral base spirit. Juniper berries produce the distinctive taste, although a variety of other flavourings, including angelica, orange peel and orris root, are also added to make gin. Each distiller has his own secret recipe which can include dozens of different ingredients. Aquavit is the other well-known flavoured spirit. It is flavoured mainly with caraway seeds; herbs and citrus peel are also added.

Liqueurs flavoured with herbs and spices are frequently known by their brand names. Each drink may include up to a hundred different ingredients which may be kept a close secret by each manufacturer. Bénédictine, possibly the oldest existing liqueur, is a

prime example of this. All that can be said for certain is that 27 different herbs, plants and peels are added to a cognac base to produce this liqueur.

Chartreuse, both yellow and green varieties, is also a herb-based liqueur still made to a secret formula. Drambuie, made from Scottish malt whisky and heather honey, and Galliano and Strega are other well-known herb liqueurs.

Aniseed is one of the seeds and plants used to flavour spirits. Its distinctive flavour is added to neutral grain spirit to produce anisette. Caraway and cumin seeds are distilled in a clear base spirit to produce Kummel. Aniseed and caraway seeds are used to flavour Danziger Goldwasser – the gold flakes in the liqueur, originally believed to add curative properties, are only decoration! Crème de cacao is flavoured with cocoa beans (and sometimes a little vanilla). Tia Maria is a rum-based liqueur using coffee extracts and spices. Also using coffee flavouring is the Mexican liqueur Kahlua.

Fruit-flavoured liqueurs and fruit-flavoured brandies should not be confused. Although on many labels the terms are used interchangeably, the term 'fruit brandy' should only be applied to those spirits derived from fermented grapes or other fruits and not to fruit-flavoured neutral spirits.

Cherries, apricots and blackcurrants (crème de cassis) are among the best-known non-citrus fruits used in liqueurs. Among the citrus liqueurs, curacao, made from orange peel, is perhaps the best-known. Cointreau and Grand Marnier are examples of curaçao liqueurs. Peaches and oranges are added to a bourbon base to make Southern Comfort.

Advocaat is a liqueur that defies conventional classification, being a grape-based liqueur flavoured with egg yolks. Various flavoured advocaats are also available, ranging from lemon to chocolate. Other unusual flavourings used in spirits include rose petals; tea, which is added to a grape brandy to make a Japanese tea liqueur; and almonds, to make crème d'amandes.

The Raw Ingredients

ALCOHOL IS MADE by the fermentation of sugar with yeast – tiny organisms which naturally attack sugar in solution. To produce the alcohol for spirits and liqueurs, as well as beers and wines, a variety of raw materials can be used to supply the base sugar. And it is this base that determines much of the character and flavour of most spirits. The base ingredient may contain sugar naturally, like fruits or sugar cane, or it may contain starch, like grains, which can be converted into sugar by a process known as malting.

During distillation the alcohol is progressively purified and separated off from its fermenting base liquid or mash. Ultimately, pure alcohol – a colourless neutral spirit – would be obtained. This pure alcohol would be the same whatever base it was extracted from, so instead, the alcohol is distilled to a lower purity (or proof) and the impurities, or congeners, it contains go towards giving the spirit its character and identity. It is the congeners which distinguish a brandy from a whisky, a rum from a vodka, and so on. The distiller must use his skill and judgement with these flavouring impurities, to maintain a balance – when present in excessive quantities the congeners are unpleasant. If a spirit is rich in congeners it requires a longer period of ageing in the wood. Some cognacs are aged for up to 50 years, while the more neutral gins and vodkas are not aged at all.

Fruits and grains provide the base from which most spirits are distilled. All brandies are distilled from a fruit mash or wine, most commonly a grape mash, although there are countless other brandies made from fruits, ranging from apples and pears to strawberries and pineapples.

Malted grains are the base of all types of whisky. A Scottish malt whisky, for example, will be made almost entirely from malted barley, preferably Scottish in origin. Most whiskies on the market are blends of malts and the cheaper grain whiskies. Grain whisky makes up more than half of most blends and is produced from corn with a little unmalted barley. Irish whiskey is made from a fermented mash of barley, oats, corn, rye and wheat. Bourbon is distilled from a mash of which at least half must be corn. Rye or barley make up the rest of the mash. To make rye whiskey, over half of the mash must be rye.

Gins and vodkas are neutral spirits, produced from grain or sometimes potatoes. Both spirits are distilled to a fairly high strength to remove all congeners, vodka being filtered through charcoal to purify the spirit still further. The characteristic flavour of gin is added after distillation by juniper berries and several other flavourings.

Other ingredients used to make spirits include sugar cane and molasses, both of which are used to produce rum. Small quantities of rice are added to molasses to produce the mash from which arak is extracted. Tequila is distilled from a mash made from the heart of the agave cactus.

THE GRAPE

The Ugni Blanc grape, below, is grown in Argentina, Algeria, and Tunisia to make wine, and France, where it is also known as the St Emilion, to produce cognac. The grapes are picked before they are fully ripe to ensure that the distilling wine has an acidity.

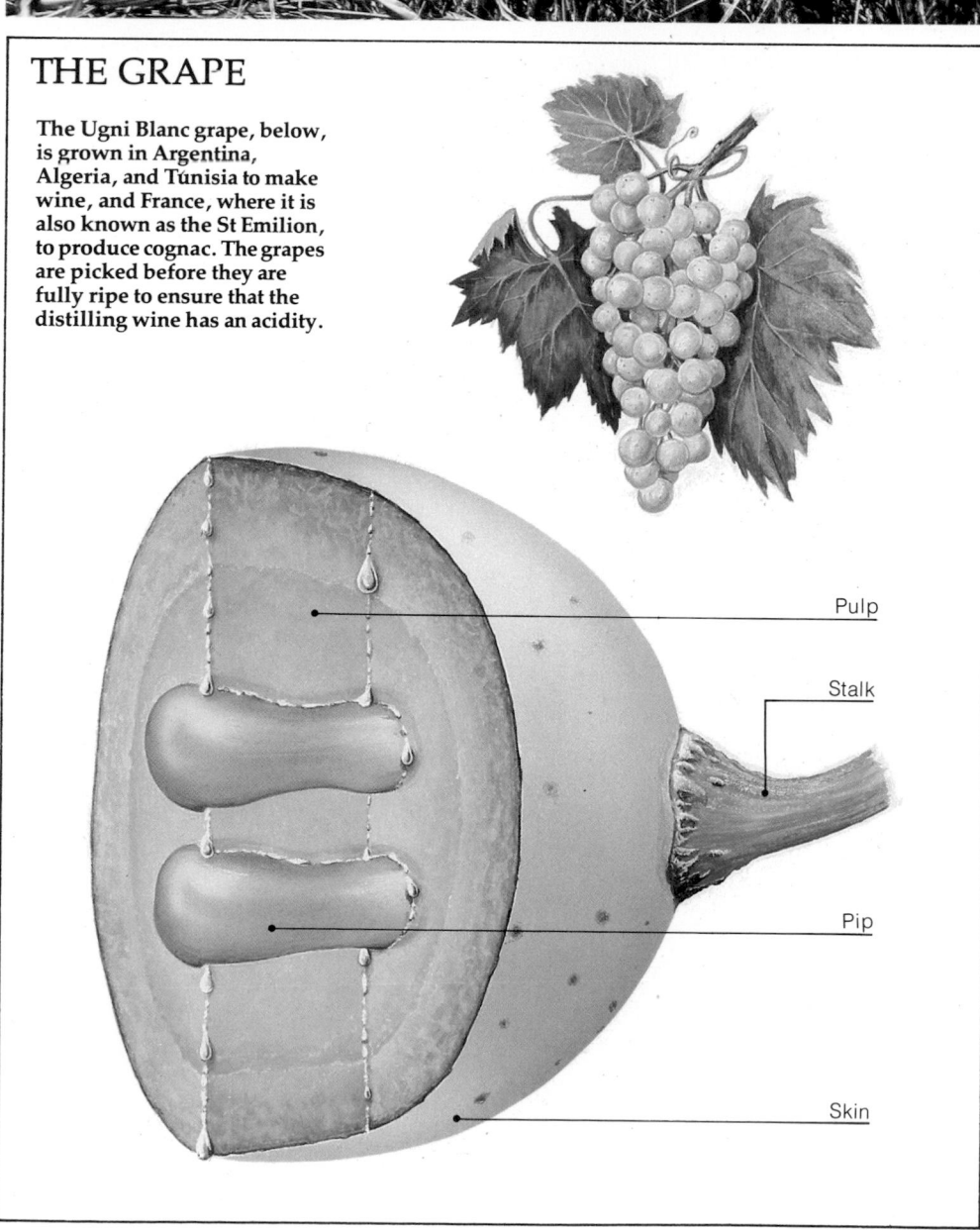

Pulp

Stalk

Pip

Skin

BARLEY

Two-rowed barley is the most widely grown of the barleys – four- and six-rowed being the other types. They are classified according to the number of rows of barley in each ear. Two-rowed barley is used in the production of malt whisky.

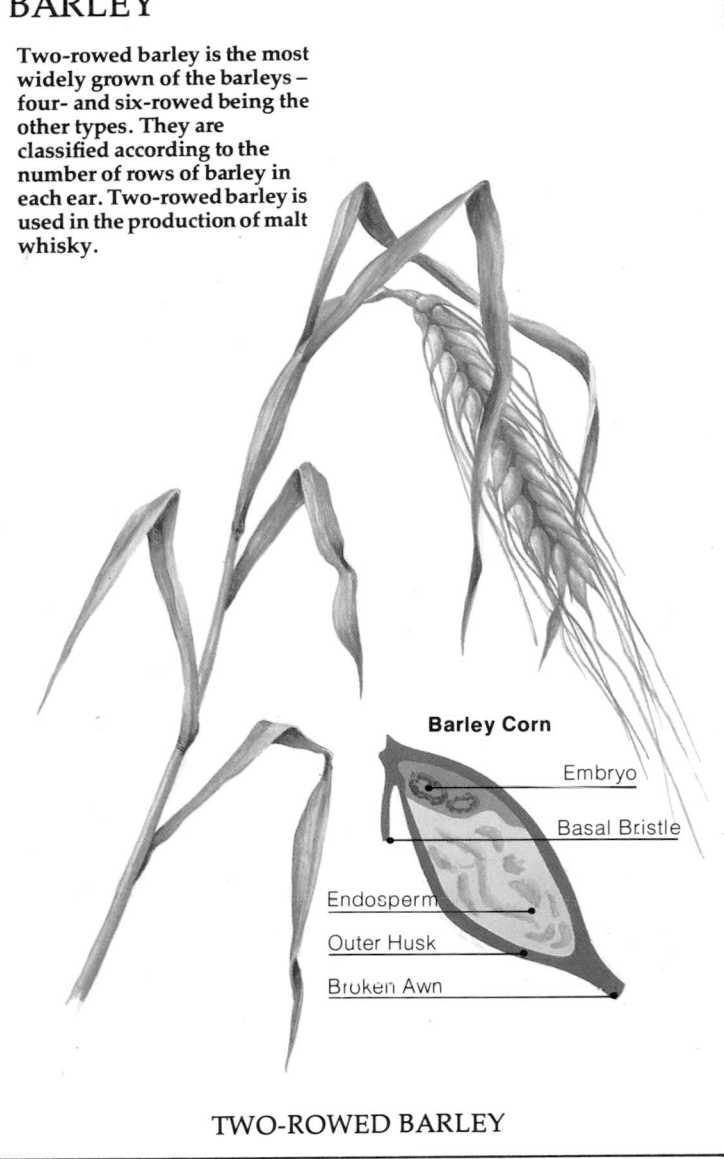

Barley Corn

Embryo

Basal Bristle

Endosperm

Outer Husk

Broken Awn

TWO-ROWED BARLEY

Spirits and liqueurs can be made from an almost unlimited variety of base materials, from rose petals to cashew nuts. Rum is made from sugar cane, opposite page; strawberries, top left, are used for eaux-de-vie and liqueurs; potatoes, centre left, for aquavit and sometimes vodka; apples, bottom left, for Calvados and eaux-de-vie; and the agave cactus, left, for tequila.

The Language of Spirits and Liqueurs

This glossary is condensed and includes all the basic terms used in the production of spirits and liqueurs.

A more detailed explanation of the major terms is given on the following pages.

Aguardiente. Spanish term for spirits, mainly brandy or whisky.
Alambic armagnacais. A modified 'continuous' still used in the production of armagnac.
Alambic charentais. Pot still used in the production of cognac.
Aldehydes. Flavour elements produced in the distillation of alcohol.
Amontillado. A dry to medium-dry Spanish sherry.
Amoroso. A sweeter-style Spanish sherry.
Apellation contrôlée. Government-enforced safeguard of the origin and standard of the finest French wines, also applied to cognac and armagnac, Chambéry vermouth and the best calvados.
Aperitif. Drink taken before a meal to stimulate the appetite.

Beer. See wash.
Bitters. Herb-flavoured drinks with medicinal origins often drunk as aperitifs or digestifs.
Bodegas. Cool, usually ground-level, warehouses where wine is converted to sherry by the catalytic action of flor yeast, then matured.
Bonne chauffe. The raw, immature cognac.
Bottled in bond. US term signifying a 100° straight whiskey, at least four years old.
Brandewijn. Brandy, literally 'burnt wine'.
Brouillis. The first cognac distillation: to produce the bonne chauffe.
Bual. A sweeter madeira.

Chais. Cellar for cognac maturation.
Congeners. Impurities, such as esters and aldehydes, in the distilled and aged spirit, that contribute to its characteristic flavour, aroma and body.
Cordial. See liqueur.
Cream sherry. Sweetened oloroso sherry.
Criadera. The 'nursery' in the sherry maturation process.
Crust. Thick deposit thrown off by port and red wines after time in the cask or bottle. Most evident in older ports.

Decanting. Transferring a wine or spirit from one container to another, frequently to remove deposits, and to let a wine breathe.
Deposit. Sediment thrown off by a wine or port in the bottle.
Diastase. The enzyme formed by the malting barley which causes the starch in grains to be converted into sugars.
Digestif. A sweet after-dinner drink to aid the digestion.

Draff. Vegetable residue in the production of Scotch whisky.
Dunder. Juice left in the still after the distillation of rum.

Eaux-de-vie ('Waters of life'). Dry colourless fruit brandies, sometimes applied to all spirits.
Esters. One of the congeners, an organic compound contributing to the flavour of a spirit.
Estufagem. Process for cooking madeira to duplicate the taste originally given to the wine by shipping it across the Equator.

Feints. Also called heads and tails, the first and last parts of a distillation which contain too many impurities and are separated off from the heart of the distillation.
Fermentation. The decomposition of sugar by yeast into alcohol, carbon dioxide and other by-products.
Fino. The best-known dry style of sherry.
Flor. A yeast that converts wine to sherry.
Fortified wines. Wines such as sherries whose natural strength have been increased by the addition of brandy.
Fusel oil. Applied generally to the higher alcohols present in all distilled spirits.

Grappa. Brandy distilled from grape pressings in Italy and California.

Head and cold mix systems. Methods of flavouring gin.
Heads and tails. See feints.
High wines. The useful spirits obtained in distillation after eliminating the feints.

Lees. The sediment thrown off by a wine in the cask.
Liqueur. Sweetened distilled spirit, flavoured with herbs, seeds or fruits.
Lodges. Warehouses in which Porto wines are stored and where madeira is stored.
Low wines. The first distillation in the production of a pot still whisky.

Maceration. Process of steeping herbs or fruits in a spirit to add the flavour.
Madeira. A Portuguese fortified wine.
Málaga. A Spanish fortified wine.
Malmsey. The sweetest madeira style.
Malting. The controlled germination of grain, usually barley, in the production of whiskies.
Malts. Unblended pot still Scotch whiskies. A bottled malt is the product of one distillery, and sometimes of a single distilling cycle.
Manzanilla. Dryest of all the sherries.
Marc. Grape skins, pips or husks distilled into a brandy in France.
Marsala. Fortified dessert wine from Sicily.
Mash. Moist grain which has been steeped in hot water for fermentation.
Must. Unfermented grape juice.

Nastoika. Flavoured Russian vodkas.
Neutral spirits. Spirits from whatever base, distilled to 190° proof or more.

Oloroso. Full-bodied, sweeter sherries.
Overproof. A spirit of more than 100° proof.

Patent still. Also called the Coffey or continuous still, used for producing most modern spirits.
Percolation. Process whereby a spirit is forced through herbs or fruits to add flavour.
Pomace. The pulp of grape skins and seeds after the juice has been extracted. Used to produce marc, grappa, aguardiente and bagaceira.
Poteen. Illegally distilled Irish whiskey. Father of moonshine and others.
Pot still. The still used in the production of Scotch whisky, cognac and other spirits, requiring the double distillation of the base wine.

Rectifying. Usually applied to the progressive purification of a spirit by re-distillation.
Reduce. Lowering the alcoholic strength of a spirit by adding water.
Ruby port. A young, deep red-coloured port.

Schnapps. German and Dutch generic term for spirits.
Sercial. The dryest type of madeira.
Solera. The system of casks used to blend sherry.
Sour mash. Process whereby mash from a previous fermentation and fresh yeast are added to the new mash to induce fermentation. Applied to whiskies, generally bourbons.
Steeps. Tanks used for malting the barley in the production of malt whisky.

Tannin. Compounds found in wood, such as grape stems or barrels, and which affect the flavouring and maturation of wines and spirits.
Tawny port. A tawny, aged port.

Underproof. A spirit with an alcoholic strength which is below proof.

Verdelho. Medium-dry madeira.

Wash. The fermented liquid before distillation usually applied in the production of Scotch whisky.
Wort. In the production of Scotch whisky, the liquid drawn off from the mash to be fermented.

Yeast. The organism which ferments sugars, breaking them down into alcohol and carbon dioxide.

THE THREE PROOF SYSTEMS

There are three main systems used to measure alcoholic content: the French Gay Lussac (GL) system, American proof, and British proof (or Sikes).

Of the three the simplest is the French system, which gives the percentage of alcohol by volume. So, 40°GL means the drink has 40 percent alcohol by volume.

American proof is also relatively simple. US 100° proof is the equivalent of 50 percent alcohol by volume; so 200° proof is 100 percent alcohol by volume, or pure spirit; and 50° proof is 25 percent alcohol by volume. (Halve the proof and you have the volume [percentage] of alcohol.) American proof can also be related to the Gay Lussac system easily – twice the GL is equal to the American proof, so 40° GL equals 80° US proof.

The most difficult of the three is the British system. The British proof system is based on the method developed by Bartholomew Sikes in the early nineteenth century of measuring alcoholic content. He determined a way of measuring what was hitherto known as proven spirit.

Before Sikes, spirit was tested by setting fire to gunpowder in solution with the spirit. If the flame burned weakly or not at all, it was underproof. If the flame burned too fiercely it was too strong. If the flame burned evenly the spirit was 'proven'. Sikes put a figure on proven spirit – 57.1 percent alcohol by volume, and this is 100°proof. On this basis pure alcohol is 175.1° proof, or 75° overproof. For each half percent of alcohol by volume above, or below, 100° proof, 1° proof is added, or deducted. So 70° proof on a bottle of London Dry gin actually means it is 30° underproof.

Fortunately most spirits are sold in different countries at around the same proof: 40° GL, which is equivent to 80° US proof and 70° British proof. For the mathematician, British proof is converted to Gay Lussac by multiplying by 4 and dividing by 7.

For the purposes of this book all measurements are given in British proof, the only reason being that it is the most commonly used measurement, even though it is the most archaic. It is now being gradually phased out, and will eventually be replaced by the percentage alcohol by volume (GL) system that the EEC has adopted as its standard.

Gay Lussac	American Proof	British Proof
10%	20%	17.50%
20	40	35.00
30	60	52.50
40	80	70.00
41	82	71.75
42	84	73.50
43	86	75.25
44	88	77.00
45	90	78.75
50	100	87.50
57	114	100.00
60	120	105.00
70	140	122.50
80	160	140.00
90	180	157.50
100	200	175.00

APERITIF

AN APERITIF TAKES its name from the French
word for appetiser, and is literally any
drink consumed before a meal that
sharpens the appetite. Anything from a dry
Martini to a pastis, a sherry to a glass of
champagne, a dry port to a dry madeira
qualifies as an aperitif.

Aperitifs have only become popular in
this century. Our forefathers would
occasionally have a glass of champagne
before dinner, but it was not customary to
start drinking before the food was served.
Sherry or dry madeira was not poured until
the soup arrived, and vermouths and
bitters were served after the dinner as an
aid to digestion. Vermouths and other
aperitif wines have now moved forward to
the pre-dinner period to act as palate
cleansers and appetite stimulators, as well
as filling in what used to be called 'The
Black Half Hour' before everyone was
settled at the dining table.

There is no one explanation for this
change in drinking patterns, but what it
has led to is a group of drinks that are now
usually considered as aperitifs.

Vermouth and other flavoured fortified
wines have almost become synonymous
with the term aperitif, but there are several
other drinks which may be considered as
aperitifs.

Dry wines, usually white, champagne,
various cocktails, gin and tonic and whisky
with water are all drunk before dinner, but
of these, only champagne is thought of as a
true aperitif. With it are the dry and
medium sherries; white port (and
sometimes red port); dry marsala; dry
madeira; French oddities such as pineau de
charente and ratafia; various bitters and
anis-based drinks; vermouth and other
related aromatic wines; Punt e Mes,
Campari, Lillet, Byrrh, St Raphael, and
Dubonnet.

FORTIFIED WINE

A FORTIFIED WINE is a wine whose alcoholic
content has been raised to 15° or more by
the addition of alcohol. Brandy is generally
used, as being a distillation of the grape, it
tends to harmonise better with the
fermented grape juice, or wine, than other
spirits. A very small number of wines reach
this high degree of alcohol naturally and
are either left as they are or 'topped up'
with a tiny addition of alcohol. They too
usually fall under the heading 'fortified
wines'.

The addition of alcohol serves both to
stop the fermentation process, and hence
leave a residual sugar in the wine, and to
increase the alcohol content of the wine.

Consequently, fortified wines invariably
have a high level of natural sweetness.
And, as sugar in a wine tends to deaden
both the palate and the appetite, these
wines are served at the end of a meal.

**Chartreuse is still made by Carthusian monks of
whom only three at any one time know the
recipe, which uses over 130 herbs.**

The foremost examples of fortified wines
are port (although white port and
sometimes the ruby and tawny styles are
drunk, chilled, as an aperitif); the sweeter
sherries (cream, oloroso, golden milk, and
even a rich amontillado); the sweeter
madeiras (bual and malmsey and
sometimes verdelho); marsala; málaga;
Commanderia St John; angelica and
Californian tokay; the *vins doux naturels* of
France; the *moscato* of Italy (both naturally
sweet); and the various port, sherry and
sweet natural fortified wine styles of
Australia, California, Cyprus, South Africa
and elsewhere.

With sherry, fortification takes place after
the flor has determined its style, and is
done progressively, with less spirit used
for a fino style (to help retain the light
freshness of the wine) and more for an
oloroso (with its deeper, richer flavour).
For port, fortification takes place while the
wine is still fermenting, to retain part of its
natural sugar. Basically, the same process is
used with marsala, madeira, málaga and
montilla (the alternative sherry-style wine
of Spain).

Each wine differs in the grape types
used, the method of vinification, and the
way the resulting wine is handled.

made from black Mission grapes fermented off the skins to give a rich white wine which is then fortified to retain the sweetness. Californian tokay, another fortified wine from the west coast of the United States, bears no resemblance to the lush tokay wine of Hungary. It is angelica given a reddish tinge through the addition of Californian port and a slightly burnt taste from a small dose of Californian sherry.

LIQUEURS

LIQUEURS, OR CORDIALS as they are called in America, are defined by Dr Peter Hallgarten as 'sweetened and flavoured alcoholic beverages'. They are also commonly called *digestifs*, particularly in France where a herb-based liqueur is often taken after dinner. Indeed, liqueurs originated and were developed through the ages as curative herbal drinks. The term 'liqueur' is also used to describe old brandies and whiskies that have taken on the smooth maturity of a liqueur through age, although lacking its sweetness.

The name liqueur derives from the Latin *liquefacere* meaning 'to melt, to make liquid, to dissolve', which in essence is the way liqueurs acquire their flavour.

The secret of a good liqueur, says Dr Hallgarten in his book *Liqueurs*, is its flavour, its perfume, the fine balance of the alcohol (which must be present but not obvious) and its cohesive sweetness – essentially it should be a smooth homogeneous liquid, of enticing and entrancing perfume and colour.

Alcohol is the essential ingredient common to all liqueurs, and its purity determines the quality of the liqueur. The purer it is, the better the liqueur and the less fusel and other pungent oils found in most spirits will mask the flavour of the liqueur.

The spirits commonly used as the base for liqueurs are neutral spirit (including grain spirit), whiskies, rums, brandies, fruit spirits, and rice spirits.

The ingredients used to flavour these alcohols fall into three basic categories: herbs and spices, seeds and plants, and fruit.

As explained on pages 14–15, the variety of flavourings is almost endless and, once extracted, their infusion into the base spirit may follow any of several different methods. The ingredients and compounding of each liqueur is a highly skilled, and often secret, art – a single liqueur may contain as many as one hundred different flavourings.

SPIRIT

THE TERM SPIRIT applies to all alcoholic beverages which are obtained by distillations. Thus, neither wine nor beer, the products of fermentation, are spirits.

Fortification is an ancilliary to the way the different fortified wines are made.

The French *vins doux naturels*, which are classified as fortified wines, can be served chilled before or after a meal. They mainly come from the southern vineyards of the Languedoc-Roussillon, have a high sugar content which is retained in part by the addition of small amounts of fortifying spirit. They are not often found outside the immediate area, the best known are Banyuls, Rivesaltes, Lunel, Frontignan, Maury, Côtes d'Agly and Côtes de Haut-Roussillon.

France also produces two other fortified wines: the *vin jaune*, which is the result of flor acting on Jura wine, and the pineau de charente of the Cognac area, which is a red or white wine fortified by the addition of cognac.

The various *muscatel* wines of France, Italy, Spain, other Mediterranean countries, South Africa and Australia, are wines made from muscat grapes, grapes which have a high natural sweetness, and which are fortified with neutral spirit or brandy. The sweetness is often concentrated in the grapes by drying them before they are fermented, thus removing most of the water and leaving the natural sugar in a concentrated form. In Italy these are called *moscato* wines, and are very rich and very powerful and lush to smell.

In California, angelica is a unique wine

The History of the Cocktail

No one knows for certain how the cocktail got its name. Of the several theories that exist, most of them delightfully fanciful, each is about as valid as the next. Expert mixologist John Doxat, the man who coined the word 'mocktail' to describe a non-alcoholic cocktail, favours the story surrounding the great English man of letters, Dr Johnson. His companion Boswell introduced Dr Johnson to a new Piedmontese wine which he (Boswell) had obtained from a merchant called Martini. On being told that this new wine was mixed with gin by the young bucks of London Dr Johnson remarked: 'Sir, to add ardent spirits to wine smacks of an alcoholic hyperbole. It would be a veritable cocktail of a drink.'

'What' asked Boswell, 'is a cocktail?' To which Dr Johnson replied: 'In parts of the country sir, it is a bucolic custom to dock the tails of certain horses of merit, yet which are not of entirely pure stock. Such animals of mixed provenance are known as cocktails!'

A second English theory also comes from the eighteenth century: 'cock-ale' was a mixture of spirits fed to fighting cocks which would also be imbibed by the wining bettors, with the number of tail feathers in the drink supposedly showing the number of ingredients in the victory cup.

American author Harold Grossman believes that the term is American in origin. He favours the explanation of the genesis of the name given by James Fenimore Cooper. It concerns the Irish landlady Betsy Flanagan who ran Betsy's Tavern near Yorktown during the War of Independence. The tavern was a meeting place for the American and French officers of Washington's army who used to go there to drink a concoction called a 'bracer'.

One evening Betsy served her customers chicken taken from her Loyalist neighbour, and when the officers went to the bar to wash down the meal with bracers, they found each bottle decorated with a tail-feather from the

'liberated' fowls. The Frenchmen in the party toasted their hostess with the cry 'Vive le cock-tail'.

Whatever the origins of the name, cocktails have come to mean mixed drinks, usually based on spirits but not necessarily so. The cups, punches, toddys and mulled drinks based on wine which were very popular in Victorian England also qualify as cocktails, as do *flips, fizzes, slings,* and the *bowlens, maibowles* and *Kalte Entes* (basically wines mixed with water or soda water) of Germany.

The cocktail had its heyday between about 1920 and 1937. Already a number of pre-mixed cocktails had been on the American market, but, naturally, they disappeared with Prohibition. Instead, the cocktail took on a new role – it was an ideal way of disguising

the often appalling, occasionally lethal, spirit peddled by the bootleggers.

To a lesser extent the popularity of the cocktail spread across the Atlantic, but America was, and still is, its real home. John Doxat estimates that something like 7,000 different cocktails were invented during this era. The cocktail era came to an end with the beginning of the Second World War and, to a certain extent, with the growth in popularity of the various mixers. The classic cocktails have survived – the Dry Martini, Manhattan, Bronx, Mint Julep, Brandy Crusta, Americano, Stinger, Sidecar and others. Newer cocktails have also emerged – Bloody Mary, Bullshot, Tequila Sunrise, and Harvey Wallbanger have helped the cocktail enjoy a modest revival in popularity in recent years.

The cocktail may be principally associated with the Roaring Twenties, but its history dates back to the time of Dr Johnson. During the American Prohibition, cocktails were drunk to mask the revolting taste of bootleg liquor.

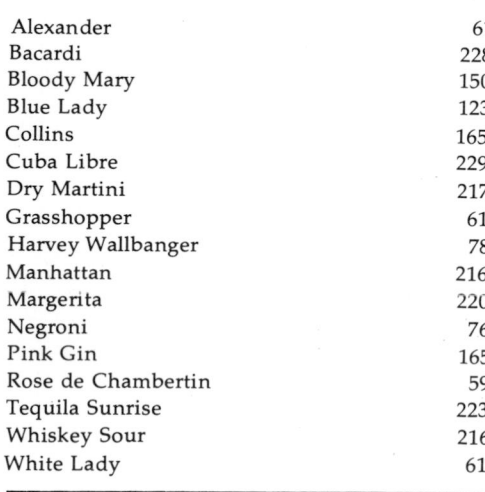

THE COCKTAILS

A list of cocktail recipes in the book.

Alexander	61
Bacardi	228
Bloody Mary	150
Blue Lady	123
Collins	165
Cuba Libre	229
Dry Martini	217
Grasshopper	61
Harvey Wallbanger	78
Manhattan	216
Margerita	220
Negroni	76
Pink Gin	165
Rose de Chambertin	59
Tequila Sunrise	223
Whiskey Sour	216
White Lady	61

VOGUE

The Cocktail Cabinet

The contents of a drinks or cocktail cabinet are entirely personal. The bottles reflect the tastes of the owner and, to a lesser extent, those of his friends. They also mirror the changing fashions.

The cocktail cabinets of the 1920s would not, for example, have featured white rum, vodka or tequila, unless the owner had very esoteric tastes and the money to indulge them.

In the same way, different countries have different tastes according to climate, availability of different drinks, differing social patterns and other variables. So, for instance, a Polish or Russian cocktail cabinet would have only different flavoured and unflavoured vodkas, with, perhaps, the odd bottle of brandy. In Scandinavia, aquavit would be an essential, in South Africa cane, in the United States a bourbon, and in Italy a bitters and a grappa.

However, certain drinks should be in the 'ideal cocktail cabinet': a blended whisky for drinking on the rocks, and a malt for sipping with a dash of water; bottles of gin, vodka, white rum or tequila, according

to taste; a mixing brandy, and a cognac or armagnac for drinking neat; a good dark rum for mixing or drinking neat.

A sweet and a dry vermouth are essentials, with perhaps a chambery for drinking on its own with a twist of lemon, and a dry sherry.

Optional extras would be a port, Campari, Dubonnet, Pernod or Ricard, Irish whiskey, a bourbon, madeira or marsala, and aquavit, flavoured vodkas and a genever (all kept in the freezer).

Apart from the Dry Martini and one or two other cocktails, all the classic cocktails and mixed drinks contain at least one liqueur. As it would be impossible to stock every major liqueur without considerable expense, the question of which liqueurs to feature in the drinks cabinet is largely a matter of personal taste.

However, some are world favourites and are used time and time again in the leading cocktails. Many of them are available in half- or smaller-size bottles. They include Galliano, Amaretto, Bénédictine, Cointreau, Chartreuse, Drambuie, Grand Mar-nier, Kahlua, Cherry Heering, Crème de Cassis, Strega, Southern Comfort, Kummel, Curaçao, Grenadine, and an alcoholic bitters such as Angostura.

In some countries, particularly the United States, a chilled dry white wine is becoming a favourite aperitif, and, of course, a Frenchman would argue that there is nothing better than a bottle of champagne, served straight or mixed with Crème de Cassis to make a kir, orange to make a Buck's Fizz, or Guinness to make a Black Velvet.

All the cocktail recipes in this book (see list, page 20) were prepared using the spirits and mixes depicted here. The bottles have been chosen to represent a well-stocked cocktail cabinet. This selection has been made by David Greig, bar manager at the Café Royal, London.

23

Mixing Spirits

THE TERM, MIXER, covers a wide range of drinks, most of them non-alcoholic, used to dilute a spirit (or occasionally a liqueur) to make it into a less potent, long drink.

A mixer can be just about anything from water, orange juice or tonic to the white wine used to make a kir (crème de cassis) or the Angostura Bitters dripped into a pink gin. But, excluding fruit juices, the most commonly used mixers, and the ones that are generally implied by someone using the term, are soda water, tonic water, ginger ale and lemonade (or 7-Up), and Coca Cola – the most recent arrival.

Soda water is the oldest of all mixers. It was originally made as a commercial substitute for the naturally fizzy spa waters popular for their medicinal properties. However, with time, soda water lost the fashionable 'health-giving' connotations that first established its market.

The idea of using mixers with spirits is basically a Victorian concept springing from the heyday of the British Empire. Expatriates in India, Ceylon, the Far East and the West Indies clung to their old drinking habits and whisky, gin and brandy were still the favoured spirits. But it needed a strong con-stitution to drink these spirits neat in the intense heat of these countries. Consequently it became acceptable to dilute spirits with mixers and serve them iced. Tonic water, in particular, was used for its quinine content, which also served to protect the drinker against malaria.

This novel way of drinking spirits was brought back to the northern countries and mixing became a fashion and then a norm. In the United States it boomed under Prohibition with the need to disguise the taste of bootleg spirits; and in more recent decades mixers had a second filip with the popularity of white rum, vodka, and tequila – spirits rarely drunk neat.

Basically, modern mixers are purified water which has been chemically treated, sterilised and filtered, then sweetened with sugar (or saccharin for low-calorie drinks) and flavoured with various essences. They are carbonated by the injection of carbon dioxide under pressure.

Different mixers have an affinity with different spirits, based primarily on sheer taste rather than any complex chemical reaction. Whisky, if it is to be despoiled with anything, should only be served with pure spring water, and never with ice which breaks down its esthers. However, a recent survey showed that the average Scotsman, despite his insistence that whisky should only be drunk neat or with spring water, more often than not dilutes his whisky with lemonade. It is a common sight in Glasgow to see a bottle of lemonade on the bar, available free to the drinkers. Soda is another commonly used additive, dating from colonial days, and dry ginger is almost as popular.

Similarly, the purist will only drink gin with still spring water (bottled, of course). But mixing with tonic water is the fashion, and the gin-and-water man is usually a seasoned member of the gin industry. Lime juice and bitter lemon are two other mixers drunk with gin.

White rums and vodkas go well with either Coke, tonic or fruit juices. The Russians, in particular, are trying to encourage a break from straight vodka drinking to help combat their alcohol problem.

Brandy is often drunk with soda, water or dry ginger, although cognac and armagnac should be drunk neat. The various types of schnapps are frequently mixed with fruit juices, while dark rums are sometimes drunk with blackcurrant, or Coca Cola.

The North American whiskies are served neat or with iced water, or mixed with Coke, soda or dry ginger. Vermouths go well with soda, orange or dry ginger.

From a Victorian fashion, mixers have developed into a highly competitive and profitable industry – no better illustrated than by the annual turnover of Schweppes, one of the biggest. Currently their world-wide sales are in the order of 2,500,000,000 bottles and cans each year.

THE STORY OF INDIAN TONIC

In 1638 the wife of the Viceroy of Peru, Count of Cinchon, was stricken with fever. The physician who cured her used a powdered bark well-known to the Indians and the Countess vowed to make her cure widely known, and the bark powder became known as cinchon.

Also called Peruvian or Jesuit's bark, cinchon reached Europe in the eighteenth century through Spain and Italy (where it is still a favourite flavouring in many drinks). The apothecaries used it to fight fevers, and the extract, known as quinine, became an important medicine used against malaria.

The modern tonic water, based on quinine flavouring, is believed to date from the days of the British Raj in India in the nineteenth century. To combat the bitter flavour of the daily dosage of quinine, prescribed for the British troops, sugar was added and the mixture diluted with water. 'Indian Quinine' or 'Indian Tonic Water' became a standard mixture, almost a patent medicine, and at some point someone decided to take his medicine and his favourite alcohol, gin, together, and created the gin and tonic.

Modern tonic water no longer contains enough quinine to claim any medicinal properties. The quinine is now used only in tiny quantities to give the unique bitterness that blends so well with the dryness of gin.

MIXERS AND ACCESSORIES

Long drinks invariably call for a mixer of one sort or another. The mixer industry is big business, and the standard types – soda and tonic waters, dry ginger, Coca Cola and lemonade or 7-Up – are international in composition and taste.

The drinks cabinet should have all of them, plus fruit juices like orange, lemon and Crème de Cassis. Many long drinks call for a twist of lemon or orange peel, a few for sugar or the white of an egg. To many of its fans, Dry Martini is not complete without an olive. Mint Julep calls for mint, and it is often added to a Pimms. Other cocktails and long drinks can be dressed with assorted shrubbery, such as borage and celery.

Angostura bitters are essential for the pink gin and other drinks, and various recipes call for Worcestershire sauce and Tabasco, such as the Bloody Mary and the Bullshot, which also requires beef consommé.

Limes or Roses Lime Juice and pineapple or pineapple juice, fresh whipped cream, peaches or peach juice, maraschino cherries, cloves, grated nutmeg and cinnamon all feature regularly in the popular mixed drinks.

Bar equipment need not be expensive. An ice bucket with ice tongs, a standard cocktail shaker, a long barspoon, a one-ounce or '5-Out' measure, a strainer with a wire edge, a corkscrew, a bottle and can opener, and a mixing jug with a pouring lip would meet most needs.

Other useful but not obligatory accessories are a cutting board and paring knife for slicing and taking the rind from fresh fruit, something for squeezing juices, a funnel, an ice pick, bottle pourers, and a wooden pestle for pulverising the mint for a Mint Julep.

There are about twenty different standard glass shapes for different mixed drinks, but it is by no means essential to have every type. The only real requirement is that the glass should not be too small. It is better to have a large glass two-thirds full than a small one filled to the brim.

A good selection of glasses, suitable for any drink, would be the sherry, brandy, old fashioned and long glasses, champagne flutes, and Paris or other wine goblets in large and medium sizes. Mugs, beer goblets and a punchbowl with accompanying cups would also be useful.

World Spirits/Production

The USSR dominates world spirits production. Reliable sources put the Russian output of spirits, consisting almost entirely of vodka, at 8,400,000 hectolitres in 1975.

The Russians are known to import sizeable quantities of vodka from Poland, but in recent years they have also heavily promoted their own vodkas on the major western markets. Major deals have been secured with leading western marketing groups to get their leading labels – Moskovskaya and Stolichnaya – on to the supermarket shelves alongside domestic vodkas, so far with moderate success.

The second biggest spirits producer is Britain, who produces mostly whisky from Scotland and gin from England.

The United States is not far behind the British output. The majority of the spirits produced is whiskey and bourbon, much of which is exported.

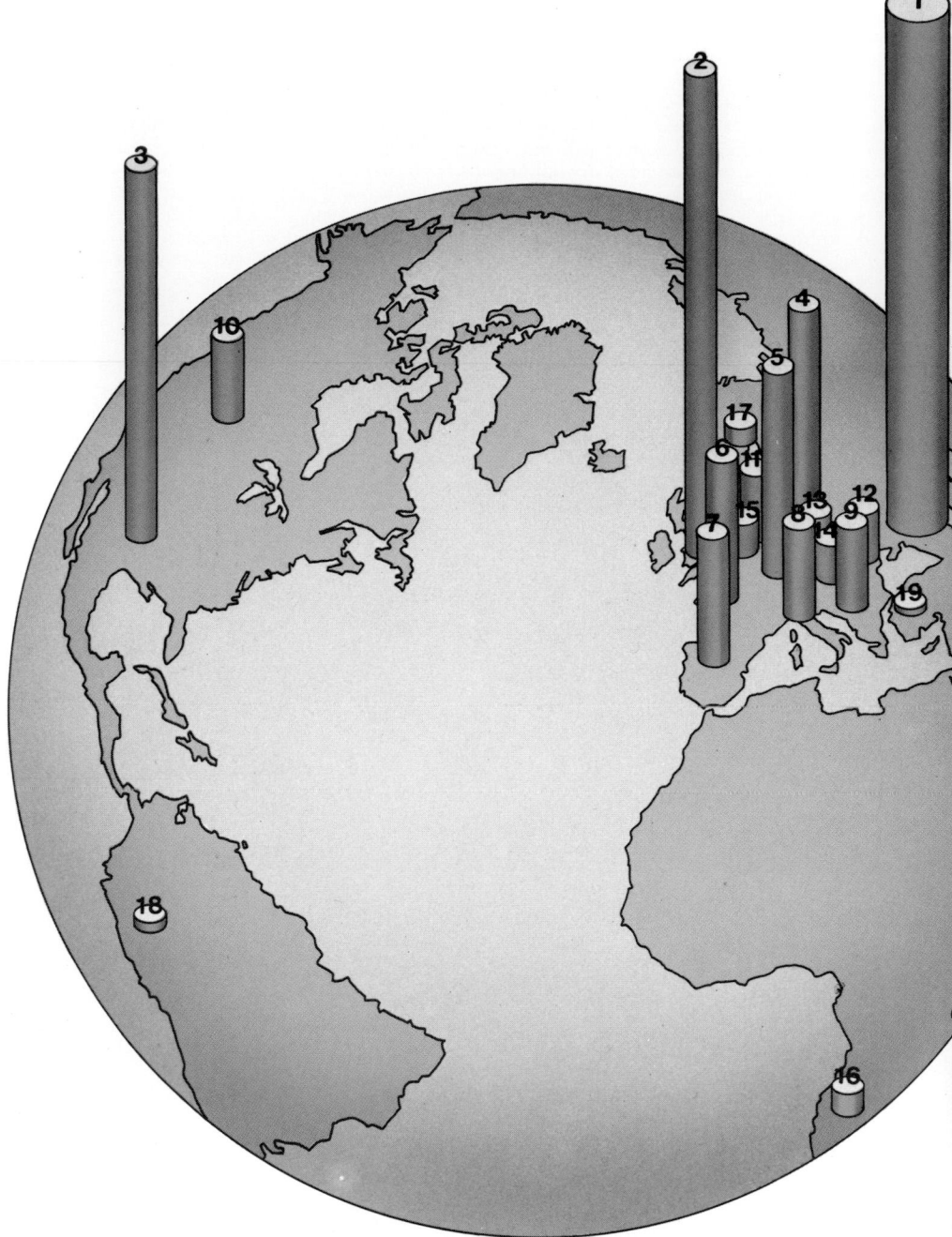

THE TOP TWENTY BEER-PRODUCING NATIONS

The major beer producing countries is led by the United States, with a massive 185,000,000 hectolitres. This is almost double the amount produced by West Germany, which leads the beer drinking nations. However, among the beer drinkers, per capita, the Americans only rank fourteenth.

1 USA	11 Mexico
2 West Germany	12 Australia
3 United Kingdom	13 Spain
4 USSR	14 Belgium
5 Japan	15 Poland
6 Czechoslovakia	16 The Netherlands
7 France	17 Denmark
8 Brazil	18 Columbia
9 Canada	19 Yugoslavia
10 East Germany	20 Austria

Production in 1,000 hectolitres

1	USSR	8.400
2	United Kingdom	3.850
3	USA	3.036
4	Poland	1.855
5	West Germany	1.347
6	France	1.240
7	Spain	1.111
8	Italy	0.815
9	Yugoslavia	0.750
10	Canada	0.744
11	East Germany	0.600
12	Rumania	0.500
13	Czechoslovakia	0.465
14	Hungary	0.435
15	The Netherlands	0.337
16	South Africa	0.268
17	Sweden	0.243
18	Peru	0.225
19	Turkey	0.200
20	Australia	0.176

THE TOP TWENTY WINE-PRODUCING NATIONS

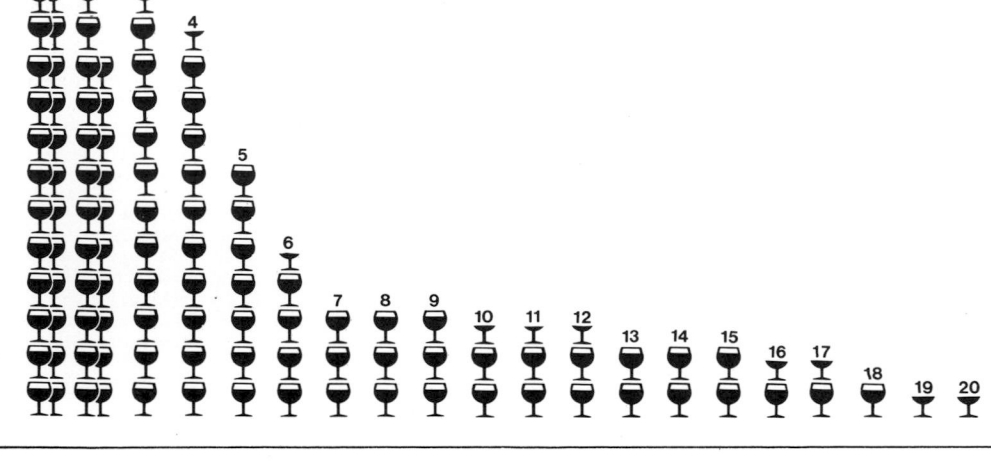

Italy is the world's largest vineyard, making just under 70,000,000 hectolitres of wine in 1975, which is about 4,000,000 hectolitres more than its rival France. However, the French consume more wine than the Italians.

Spain comes third, and the USSR, where in recent years massive new plantings and winery modernisation programmes have been authorised, lies fourth.

1	Italy	11	South Africa
2	France	12	Yugoslavia
3	Spain	13	Hungary
4	USSR	14	Greece
5	Argentina	15	Chile
6	USA	16	Australia
7	Portugal	17	Bulgaria
8	West Germany	18	Austria
9	Rumania	19	Brazil
10	Algeria	20	Poland

World Spirits/Consumption

As this chart shows, the Poles lead the world in the consumption of spirits, by a wide margin. In Poland, domestic flavoured and unflavoured vodkas account for almost all the spirits consumed within the country. In fact, the Polish authorities are worried about the high incidence of alcoholism, as these figures mean that every man, woman and child in Poland drinks a standard measure glass of spirits every third day.

They are less concerned about their substantial vodka exports to neighbouring Russia, where the authorities are equally worried about drunkenness. The Soviet authorities have run massive advertising campaigns to persuade the citizenry to cut down on the amount of spirits they are drinking, and to use mixers more. Stiffer penalties have been introduced for public intoxication.

Interestingly enough, the Canadians, seventh in the world tables, with more restrictive drinking laws, consume more spirits than the Americans.

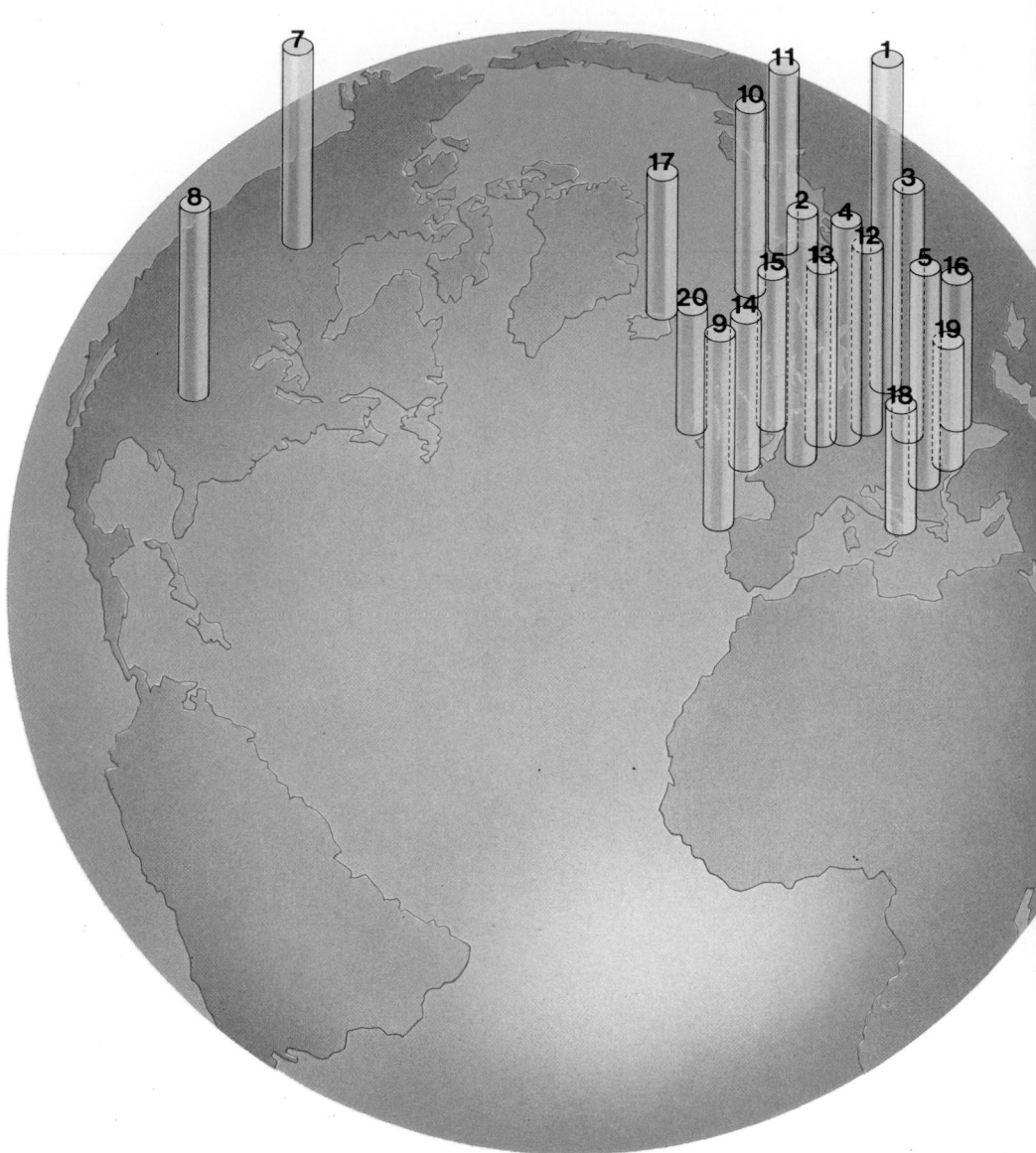

THE TOP TWENTY BEER-CONSUMING NATIONS

Not surprisingly, the West Germans have the highest beer consumption in the world – just over 150 litres a head in 1976 – followed by the Australians, Czechs, Belgians and New Zealanders.

It is, however, the tiny Duchy of Luxemburg which takes the first prize as the country which consumes the most wine, beer and spirits per head of population in the world.

1 West Germany
2 Australia
3 Czechoslovakia
4 Belgium
5 New Zealand
6 Luxemburg
7 East Germany
8 Eire
9 United Kingdom
10 Denmark
11 Austria
12 Canada
13 The Netherlands
14 USA
15 Hungary
16 Switzerland
17 Sweden
18 Finland
19 Venezuela
20 France

1	Poland	5.4
2	Luxemburg	4.1
3	Hungary	4.1
4	East Germany	3.6
5	Yugoslavia	3.5
6	USSR	3.3
7	Canada	3.2
8	USA	3.2
9	Spain	3.2
10	Sweden	3.0
11	Finland	3.0
12	Czechoslovakia	2.8
13	West Germany	2.5
14	France	2.4
15	The Netherlands	2.4
16	Rumania	2.3
17	Iceland	2.0
18	Italy	2.0
19	Bulgaria	2.0
20	Eire	1.9

THE TOP TWENTY WINE-CONSUMING NATIONS

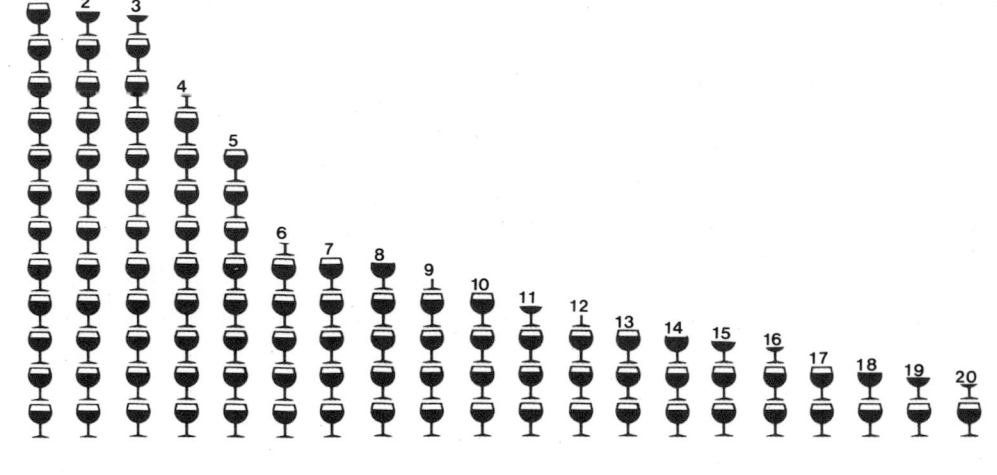

The world's two biggest wine producing countries are also its two biggest consuming countries. However, Italy, which makes more wine than France, does not drink quite as much per head of population. It is interesting to note that two important producers of wine – the United States of America and Germany, 6th and 8th on the world tables – are 31st and 15th in the consumption tables.

1	**France**	11	**Hungary**
2	**Italy**	12	**Rumania**
3	**Portugal**	13	**Yugoslavia**
4	**Argentina**	14	**Uruguay**
5	**Spain**	15	**West Germany**
6	**Chile**	16	**Bulgaria**
7	**Luxemburg**	17	**Czechoslovakia**
8	**Switzerland**	18	**Belgium**
9	**Greece**	19	**USSR**
10	**Austria**	20	**Denmark**

Spirits of
the
World

France

Such an extraordinary variety of spirits, liqueurs and fortified wines are produced in France that almost every drinker can find something to satisfy his taste. Foremost among the French potables are the brandies, distilled from either wine or fruit, and the greatest of these is, without doubt, cognac. Armagnac, cognac's only serious rival, is produced not far from the delimited Cognac region but is very different in style. Marc, a dry, colourless brandy, is distilled from grape pomace throughout France.

In addition to these grape-based distillations there are countless other fruit brandies (sometimes called eaux-de-vie, although this term is variously applied) produced in France, principally in the Alsace region.

The array of other French spirits and liqueurs range from anis, fortified wines and vermouths (rivals to the Italian vermouths and bitters), to the internationally famous liqueurs such as Chartreuse, Bénédictine, Grand Marnier and Cointreau.

Cognac

Cognac, france's premier brandy, is produced in the area that nestles on the north bank of the Gironde river, and is partly bounded by the Atlantic Ocean between Royan and La Rochelle. Apart from the ravages of war, it has always been a prosperous part of France. Gauls farmed the undulating inland areas and the lush coastal strips for wheat and other cereals. Then the conquering Romans, recognising the area's potential as a trading centre, introduced two more sources of revenue to what they called the provinces of Pagus Engolismensis and Pagus Santonensis – the extraction of salt, from the sea water, and wine-making.

Vines were planted inland from La Rochelle, and by the early Middle Ages the fresh, light white Saintonge wines were a valuable second cargo for the ships from the north loading salt at La Rochelle, Saintes and St Jean d'Angély. Sometime in the earlier part of the seventeenth century the vinegrowers in the old provinces of Aunis, Saintonge and Angoumois began to distil their wines to make the first cognacs. The vineyards had been ravaged by war in the sixteenth century

and the quality of the Saintonge wines had suffered from constant replanting and attempts to get as much from the vineyards as possible, but the change to distilling, already widespread in France, is puzzling.

Cyril Ray, in *Cognac*, advances the most plausible reason. He says the Dutch, attracted to La Rochelle by its salt trade, encouraged the local wine makers to turn to distilling to meet a growing demand from the cold northern countries for brandy wine. The Dutch dominated the sea trade at this time, and had strong ties with the Protestant

Huguenots of La Rochelle. They were shrewd traders, and knew they could find ready markets in England, the Low Countries and further north for brandy, rather than the local wine, which had fallen from favour and did not travel well. The Dutch fostered the change to brandy production, and within 60 years, around the turn of the sixteenth century, brandy had largely replaced wine as the local product.

The first cognacs, if they could be called that, were crude spirits intended to be drunk diluted with water – spirits often thought of as some kind of wine concentrate. The grape growers and distillers further inland, faced with higher costs in getting their produce to the ports, learned they could compete only by making better brandy. As a result, they gradually transformed the inland vineyards around Cognac and Jarnac into the major producing centres, turning the tables on their coastal neighbours and laying down the pattern of excellence that exists today.

In the eighteenth century cognac brandy improved, and so did its reputation. Most of the major houses were founded in this century, by both French and foreign merchants. Jean Martell came from Jersey in 1715, Richard Hennessy from Cork, Ireland, in 1765, Thomas Hine from Dorset in 1775, and the Delamains returned from Ireland after a hundred years away from the area.

Cognac enjoyed a golden era until the *phylloxera* blight between 1880 and 1890 devastated the vineyards. The replanting and recreation of the vineyards changed cognac slightly, but its traditions and its famous producing houses are essentially the same now as they were in its heyday, from 1750 to 1850.

The Charente grape harvest begins before the crop is fully ripe in order to produce the acidic wine ideal for distillation.

Cognac Country

THE COGNAC AREA, as defined by law in 1909, embraces all of the department of Charente Maritime, most of the Charente (the modern departments that replaced the old provinces of Aunis, Saintonge and Angoumois) and a few communes of the Dordogne and Deux-Sèvres departments. The river Charente meanders roughly through its middle, to meet the sea near Rochefort, via the towns of Cognac and Jarnac. The Atlantic forms the western boundary, the river Gironde the southern limit with the great claret vineyards of the Medoc on the opposite bank.

The land is flat or gently undulating. The richer parts, less suited to the vine, are used for the dairy cattle which produce Charentais butter and cheeses. The winter is mild, the summer hot and dry, and the sky often has a particular luminosity that the fanciful like to associate with a fine cognac.

The sleepy provincial town of Cognac sits almost in the centre of the growing area. It radiates outwards from an old central square, and the outskirts are dotted with the establishments of Martell, Hennessy, Otard, Remy Martin, Salignac, Polignac and Larsen. A few kilometres upriver the smaller town of Jarnac, proud of its separate identity, is home to Courvoisier, Hine, Bisquit and Delamain. The casual visitor would hardly guess that these two towns are the capitals of the vast,

The white St Emilion grapes grown in the Cognac area would make a very poor wine, low in alcohol and high in acidity. However, these two characteristics of the wine are ideal for distilling into cognac.

Outside France, the largest market for cognac is Britain, where it has long been a popular drink among the wealthy.

COURVOISIER COGNAC

NAPOLEON'S BRANDY

36

wealthy cognac industry. From a point just south of Cognac the six main vineyard areas spread outward, as laid down in the 1909 law, and confirmed with the granting of *appellation contrôlée* in 1936. These six regions were first demarcated in the wake of *phylloxera*, to protect the vineyard owners from cheap imitations while they tried to rebuild their devastated properties. As Cyril Ray writes: 'The law of 1909 provided for the territorial delimitation of appellations of origin, and that of cognac was based upon local knowledge, the customs of trade, and various official, unofficial and semi-official classifications of the component zones of the region that had been made throughout the nineteenth century, but never given the force of law.'

The finest growing area, which has the highest percentage of the prized chalky soil that gives a cognac much of its character, is also the smallest. The Grande Champagne as it is called ('champagne' referring to open land, like the Italian *campagna*) is bordered to the north by the Charente and includes the towns of Cognac and Segonzac. Its 11,500 hectares of vines yield the best, most fragrant and subtlest cognacs. They take the longest to reach their peak, and hold that peak the longest.

Second to the Grande Champagne is the Petite Champagne, about twice the size, but with only marginally more land under vine – about 12,750 hectares. The Petite Champagne sweeps south of the Grande Champagne in a semicircle. Its cognacs

The ancient town of Cognac is the heart of the cognac industry. Here the shippers blend and age the spirit. A characteristic feature of the town is the black fungus on buildings and rooftops, which lives on the cognac fumes exuded during ageing.

Since nearly all modern cognacs are blended, the term 'vintage' generally no longer applies. True vintages usually belong to the 19th or early 20th century.

37

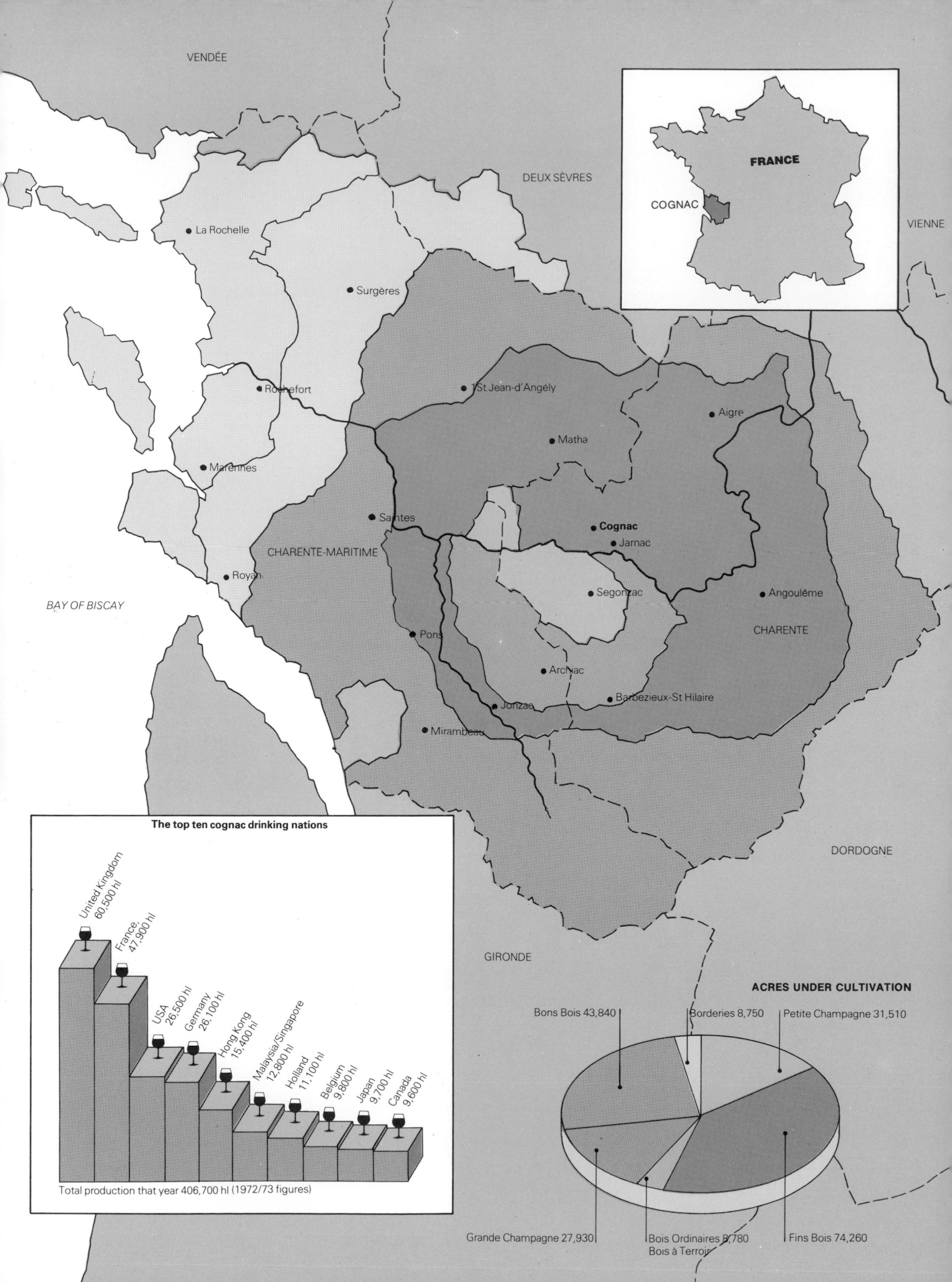

VENDÉE

DEUX SÈVRES

FRANCE

COGNAC

VIENNE

• La Rochelle

• Surgères

• Rochefort

• St Jean-d'Angély

• Aigre

• Marennes

• Matha

• Santes

Cognac
• Jarnac

CHARENTE-MARITIME

• Segonzac

• Angoulême

• Royan

CHARENTE

BAY OF BISCAY

• Pons

• Arch?ac

• Barbezieux-St Hilaire

• Jonzae

• Mirambeau

DORDOGNE

GIRONDE

The top ten cognac drinking nations

United Kingdom 60,500 hl

France, 47,900 hl

USA 26,500 hl

Germany 26,100 hl

Hong Kong 15,400 hl

Malaysia/Singapore 12,800 hl

Holland 11,100 hl

Belgium 9,800 hl

Japan 9,700 hl

Canada 9,600 hl

Total production that year 406,700 hl (1972/73 figures)

ACRES UNDER CULTIVATION

Bons Bois 43,840

Borderies 8,750

Petite Champagne 31,510

Grande Champagne 27,930

Bois Ordinaires 8,780
Bois à Terroir

Fins Bois 74,260

mature a little faster than those of the Grande Champagne, but there is not much to separate the two in quality. Together they make up the area that can be used to produce *fine champagne* cognac, a particularly fine blend that must include at least 50 per cent Grande Champagne brandy.

The third and smallest area is the Borderies, a spur that juts into the surrounding Fins Bois area on the right bank of the Charente to the north west of Cognac. For its size, it is heavily planted with just over 3,500 hectares under vine. Borderies cognacs are full bodied but mellow quickly, and are used to give backbone to lighter cognacs in a quality blend.

The fourth area, the Fins Bois (*bois* denoting woodland as opposed to *champagne* or open land), is also the largest. It virtually encircles the first three areas with the greatest parts to the north and east. Its brandies reach their peak fairly quickly and so are used to soften the hard flavour of younger, finer cognacs in a blend. Within its boundaries there are about 30,000 hectares under vine.

Around the Fins Bois is the Bons Bois. Its soils are sandier and less chalky, so only about 18,000 hectares are planted. Its cognacs have a coarseness, and some big houses will not use them in their blends.

The sixth area, the Bois Ordinaires, is sometimes split into a seventh called the Bois Communs. This classification is given in the extract from the Revue Vinicole, used by the Bureau National du Cognac as their introductory leaflet. It is the area (or areas) to the extreme west of the region along the coast from La Rochelle to Royan. Once the main growing area, it now only has 3,500 hectares under vine and produces only about three percent of the total cognac production. Its

The major cognac producers were founded in the early part of the 17th century. Hennessy's headquarters still stands in Cognac old town; Courvoisier is located on the banks of the river Charente at Jarnac; and Martell is in the centre of Cognac.

brandies have a distinct *goût de terroir* (flavour of the soil), and are mainly for local drinking and use in brandies other than those sold as cognacs.

The neat cognac vineyards throughout the whole area are planted, where possible, on slight slopes to catch the maximum amount of sun. The three main grape varieties, all white, are the *St Emilion* (no relation to the claret-producing area further south), the *folle blanche* and the *colombard*, all of which can be harvested in any quantity; plus the *jurançon blanc, montils, sémillon, sauvignon* and *blanc ramé* which can only be used to a maximum of ten percent in any cognac harvest.

Before *phylloxera* the folle blanche was the main cognac grape, but it did not take easily

to regrafting on to new root stock after the blight. It is also more susceptible to grey rot than the St Emilion which has replaced it as the favoured grape. St Emilion grapes now make up something like 90 percent of the total crop. The St Emilion also has a higher yield and a higher acidity.

A high acidity and a low alcoholic content is what the vigneron wants in his wine. The average is 8° to 8.5° alcohol, but 7° is better – compared to 9° and more for table wines. The high acidity in the wine, when it is distilled, helps the young spirit draw character from the wood it matures in. The low alcoholic content means that more wine has to be distilled to get the cognac, but gives the spirit a better bouquet.

Creating the Great French Spirit

THE CHARENTE GRAPE HARVEST starts in late September and sometimes runs through to early November. The freshly picked grapes go straight to the presses where they are gently squeezed to extract the juice. The Archimedes press is commonly used in France, except in the Charente, where it is forbidden by law and the juice is extracted in more easily regulated horizontal presses. The winemaker takes care not to use too much pressure, so a minimum amount of pectins and tannins from the grape skins go into the juice. Once it has run free, the remaining pulp is softly pressed and the last liquid added to the *vin de goutte* (first pressing). The grape juice is fermented into wine quickly, usually ready in just over a week to go to the distillery still on its lees (sediments).

To be called cognac, the wine must be turned into spirit (by double-distillation) within the demarcated Cognac region. The law also specifies the type of still, called the *alambic charentais*. Basically, this is a simple wood or gas-fired pot still (oil, which could taint the spirit, is not used), little different from those used a century or more ago, and operated in exactly the same way by both the farmer-distiller and the big companies.

The distilling cycle begins as soon as the wine is ready, and lasts through the winter months until March 31. The wine, with its lees, goes into the *chauffe-vin* (a type of holding tank) where it is warmed by the tube conducting the vaporised alcohol to the condenser which passes through the waiting wine. The wine then goes into the *chaudière*, the onion-shaped still, where it is heated to around 170°F, and vaporises. The alcoholic steam rises through the swan-necked *chapiteau*, via the chauffe-vin to the condenser where it falls through a spiral *serpentin* (tube) immersed in cold water to bring the vapour back to liquid form.

As the raw spirit emerges from the circular condenser, with its pointed 'hat', the distiller sets aside the *produit de tête* (heads) which may be a milky colour and will probably be tainted. After the first few percent that make up the heads, the spirit starts to run clean and clear. The distiller switches this into cask as *le coeur*, the heart of the spirit. Towards the end of the eight-hour distillation, the spirit starts to lose its intensity and quality, so the remainder, the *produit de queue* (tails) is put aside with the heads to go back for redistilling.

The clean spirit, about 60 percent of the run, is called the *brouillis*, or first distillation. Usually three batches are needed to get sufficient good spirit for the second distillation. The second cycle is the same, with the heads and tails put aside, and the best spirit going straight into barrels. This batch, the end of the distilling process, is called the *bonne chauffe*. It is the infant cognac, raw, about 70° proof, and uncoloured.

The infant cognac goes straight into oak casks made preferably from the trunks of 80

THE UNIQUE COGNAC OAK

Young cognac is colourless, the spirit getting its distinctive golden glow from maturation in casks made only from the oaks of the nearby forests of Limousin and Troncais, shown on the map below. This oak is used because its porousness allows the high rate of evaporation necessary to mellow the cognac, while its soft tannin produces the correct flavour and character in the matured spirit.

After cutting into staves, the oak is left to season outdoors for several years. Oak for Martell's casks, shown below, is seasoned for seven years. Only then is the wood ready to be made into cognac casks. A cognac spends at least a year and a half in the wood. After the first year, the young brandy is transferred from a new to an old cask to prevent the spirit absorbing too much tannin from the wood.

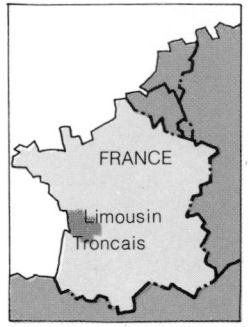

Coopering, an ancient and highly skilled craft, is essential to the cognac industry. Each year, thousands of new casks are needed to mature the new spirit, and every barrel is expected to last for up to forty or fifty years.

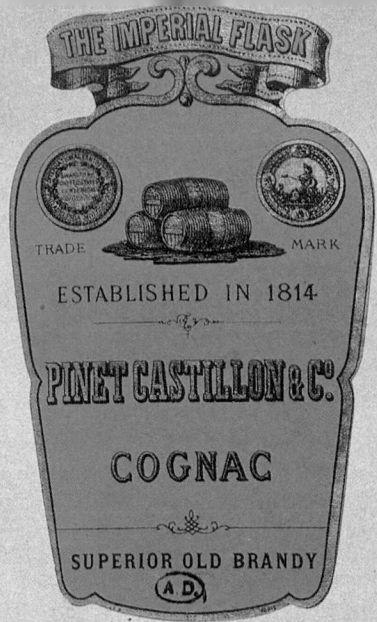

THE IMPERIAL FLASK

TRADE MARK

ESTABLISHED IN 1814

PINET CASTILLON & C?

COGNAC

SUPERIOR OLD BRANDY

A.D.

COGNAC VIEUX

QUALITÉ SUPÉRIEURE

GUITTON-FIGEROU & C?

VERY OLD BRANDY

COGNAC

COGNAC

HANAPPIER & C?

COGNAC VIEUX

QUALITÉ SUPÉRIEURE

J. PLESSAC & C?

COGNAC

CHAMPAGNE VINEYARD PROPRIETORS C?

BOUTELLEAU MANAGER

OLD COGNAC

Fine Champagne

J. GAIRÉ

A.D. COGNAC

SUCCURSALE A LONDRES - Regent Street N? 89

SOC.té INTERNATIONALE LUDOVIC CAMBON & C?

COGNAC UNIVERSEL

DIRECTEURS

BORDEAUX

Cognac labels in the
19th century were
especially florid.

HOW COGNAC IS MADE

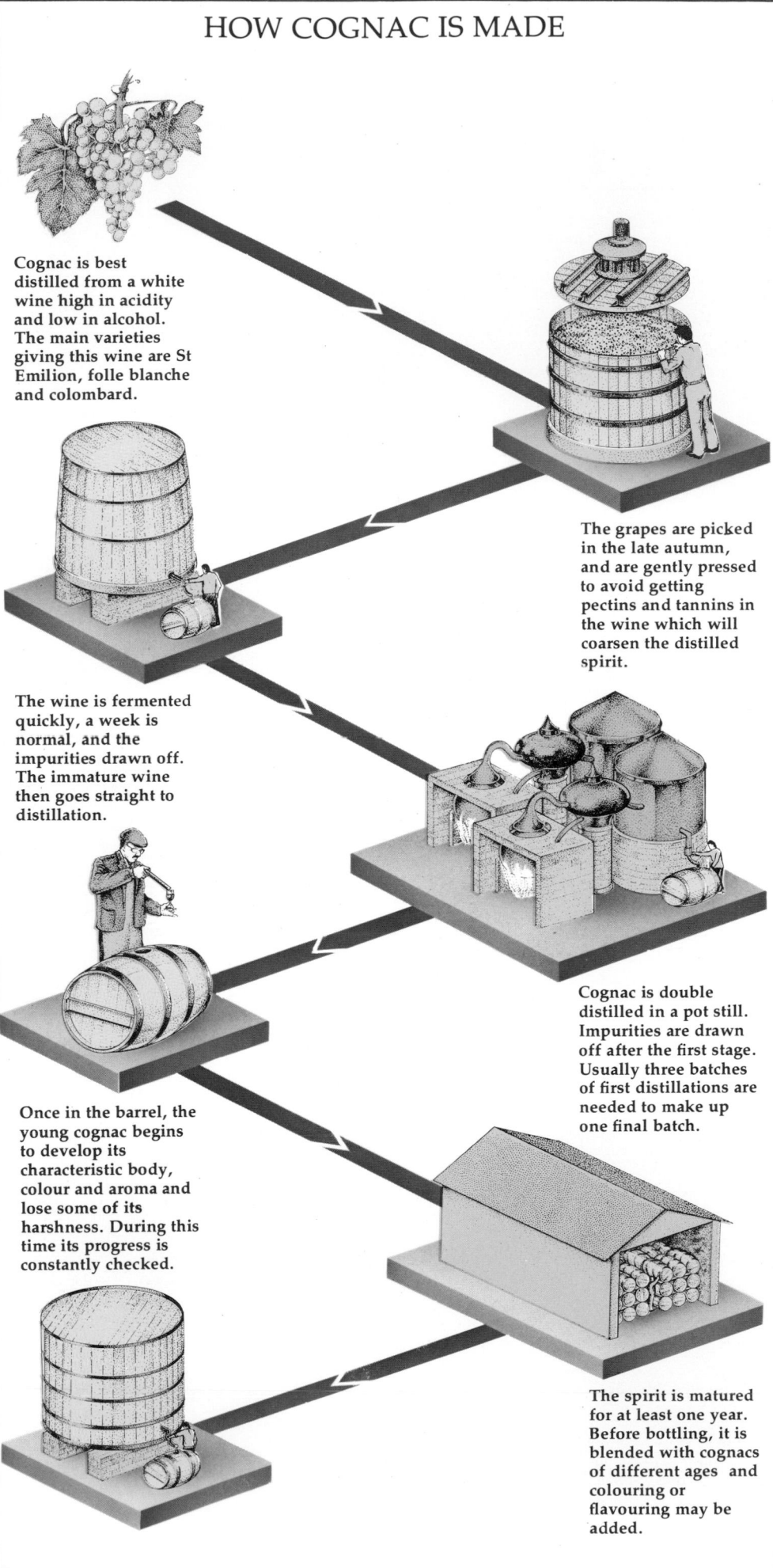

Cognac is best distilled from a white wine high in acidity and low in alcohol. The main varieties giving this wine are St Emilion, folle blanche and colombard.

The wine is fermented quickly, a week is normal, and the impurities drawn off. The immature wine then goes straight to distillation.

Once in the barrel, the young cognac begins to develop its characteristic body, colour and aroma and lose some of its harshness. During this time its progress is constantly checked.

The grapes are picked in the late autumn, and are gently pressed to avoid getting pectins and tannins in the wine which will coarsen the distilled spirit.

Cognac is double distilled in a pot still. Impurities are drawn off after the first stage. Usually three batches of first distillations are needed to make up one final batch.

The spirit is matured for at least one year. Before bottling, it is blended with cognacs of different ages and colouring or flavouring may be added.

to 100-year-old Limousin or Troncais oaks (the only two permitted sources of wood) which have weathered for four to five years after cutting.

The spirit stays in the new wood for up to a year, and then will most likely be transferred to older barrels, already used to cognac, so the tannin enrichment is not excessive. The small amount of air that comes in contact with the spirit through the pores of the wood causes a slight oxidation that brings out the bouquet. The complex interaction between the spirit and wood, still not yet fully understood, gives cognac its golden colour, much of its distinctive flavour, and its mellowness.

All cognac is blended, with the spirit from different areas and different years eventually reaching perfect marriage and the desired taste. Each cognac house has its own style, and the blending of thousands of different barrels to maintain the style is the most highly skilled of all the processes involved in the making of cognac.

The blenders must possess a highly refined palate, an almost encyclopedic memory, not only for what their own warehouses hold, but also the stocks available from all the other major suppliers. They must know where they can get a certain type of taste quickly to complete or correct an almost finished blend. They check the cognacs daily under their care to see that each cask is on its right course.

Blending starts fairly early, usually after the first year in wood, with pauses between each step to allow the different flavours to marry. As the casks mature they also give off evaporation, up to about five percent by volume a year. In the biggest warehouses it is so strong that the doors must be kept wide open, otherwise the workers inside would be overcome by the fumes. The fungus which blackens the roofs of the cognac warehouses feeds on this evaporation which the Charentais delightfully call the angel's share. Remy Martin estimate that the lucky angels get the equivalent of 12,000,000 bottles a year. The maturing casks must be refreshed to allow for this loss as the spirit ages. After suitable ageing (judged by the blender), the cognac is put in a large oak tank where the final marrying is done before the cognac goes into bottle.

The cognac houses are only permitted three legal additions to their spirit: sugar, caramel and oak chips. Sugar or sugar syrup up to a maximum of two percent can be used to soften the slight harshness of younger spirit. Caramel can be used in small quantities to maintain continuity of colour, although a deeper colour does not indicate a finer cognac, as demonstrated by Delamain Pale Dry, one of the best cognacs. An infusion of wood chips (la boise) may be used to approximate the effect of proper wood ageing. But while it will give the spirit the tannin flavour and colour, it will not impart the necessary softness. Although this is perfectly legitimate, it is practised sparingly, and is not widely talked about in the Charente.

THE COGNAC PRODUCING REGION

Three distinct groups of people are involved in the making of cognac: the vine growers and winemakers, the distillers, and the blenders and bottlers.

Hugh Johnson in his World Atlas of Wine estimates that there are something like 50,000 farmers in the Charente growing white wine grapes, and as many as one in ten have their own still. Both figures are too high. While the Charente is a patchwork of tiny vineyard, probably half of them only a hectacre (2.2 acres) in size, the number of growers is more likely to be around 30,000. The Bureau National du Cognac's own statistics show that only 3,966 stills were operating in the defined area in 1972/73. It is therefore more likely that 2,000 or less of these growers have their own still. Those with the licence to make their own cognac are known as bouilleurs de cru, and they are only allowed to work with their own wine, no one else's.

The vast majority of growers sell their wine to one of the 25 co-operatives or the approximately 250 bouilleurs de profession, the specialist distillers. Between them, the co-ops and bouilleurs de profession account for more than 70 percent of all the infant cognac distilled each year. Many have invested heavily in the stills that are their livelihood, and their reputations rest heavily on their ability to convert the young wine into good young spirit. Their art, like the art of blending, is often passed on from father to son.

Many are linked to the 250 or so cognac blenders and bottles – the big houses that either sell under their own name or to large importers who then sell under their registered brand names. As the blending and maturing of cognac is an expensive and skilled business, requiring large-scale capital investment, the birth of a new cognac house is a relatively rare event. Each group –growers, distillers and blenders- prefers to let the others preserve their traditional skills as a separate operation. Few of the big houses even own their own vineyards. Martell probably have more vines than any of the others, although they only supply a fraction of the company's total needs. Salignac, Hennessy, Bisquit-Dubouche and Polignac (a grower's co-operative with its own maturing and marketing arm) and another, rare example. Courvoisier, on the other hand, own no vineyards at all, even though they are one of the three biggest cognac shippers. Nor do Hine, Otard, Delamain or Denis Mounie.

However, when any of these houses take a sizeable part of the output of a bouilleur de profession, they will have a degree of control over the style of cognac he makes. They will also provide the technical back-up through their own laboratories and, in some instances, help with capital for expansion.

There are hundreds, if not thousands of different cognac brands ranging from those offered by a bouilleur de cru, such as Pierre Seguinot, to the Martell, Courvoisier and Hennessy houses. Most of these large, reputed houses were founded sometime between 1700 and 1850 with Augier, founded in 1643, claiming the oldest existing name. Other well-known names, apart from those already mentioned, are Gautier, Camus, Barriasson, Barnett, Exshaw, Cusenier, Castillon, Frapin and Jean Fillioux.

THE BUREAU NATIONAL INTERPROFESSIONNEL DU COGNAC governs the strict laws that fix the minimum age for cognac before it can be labelled. From April 1 of the year after the harvest, a cognac distilled in the winter months between October and the end of March is zero rated. After twelve months, on the following April 1, it is rated one, and so on up to the sixth year when it is rated five. After that, the Bureau no longer keeps a check on the age ratings but relies on the honesty of the producers.

For the French market a cognac labelled *Three Star* must have a rating of one, which effectively means it is about a year and a half old. As with all ratings under this system, it means no cognac in the blend in that bottle can be younger than that age. Any cognac designated *VSOP* must be rated four, so is at least three years old. In practice the average of all cognacs is greater than that defined by the minimum age requirements.

Regulations vary for export markets, with the United States stipulating that a Three Star cognac must be at least two years old, while Britain maintains it must be three years old. Since 1955 the minimum ages of higher grades have been fixed at a minimum of four years old for any spirit labelled *VO, VSOP,* or *Réserve,* and five years for those labelled *Extra, Napoléon* and *Vieille Réserve.* Brandy less than four years old can only be labelled *Three Star Cognac,* or *Cognac Authentique.* At this end of the scale some of the largest houses have moved away from the popular Three Star designation and use just a trade name. Martell Medallion and Hennessy Bras Armé are two examples. Others, like Remy Martin and Bisquit, do not offer a Three Star at all.

The designation *Fine Champagne* is reserved for cognacs which are blended only from Grande and Petite Champagne wines, with at least half coming from the Grande Champagne. Higher up the scale some shippers make and bottle exclusive cognacs just from Grande Champagne or Petite Champagne wines and sell them labelled as such.

Since 1962, vintage cognac has been all but banished from the Charente on the very logical grounds that all cognac is blended and therefore a vintage date is relatively meaningless. Some old bottles do appear with a date on the label from time to time, and one or two small producers do continue to make them on a tiny scale.

The final cognac style is the *early-landed* and its brothers, the *late-bottled.* Both are the result of English shippers bringing cognac over from France in cask and holding it in their own cellars to mature. Early-landed signifies the cognac has been shipped when very young, possibly only a year old, and late-bottled signifies it has been held in cask for the length of time marked on the label. The main shippers still producing such cognacs are Harveys of Bristol, Berry Brothers & Rudd and Justerini and Brooks.

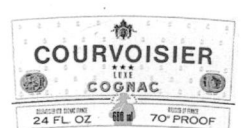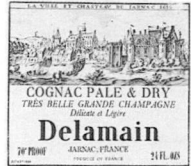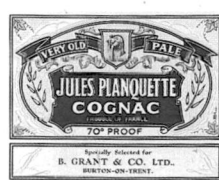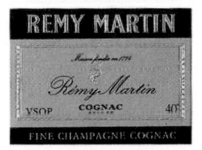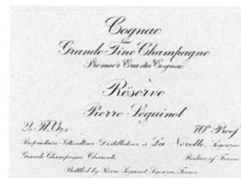

Modern cognac labels include a bewildering variety of honorifics – the different permutations referring to the age and blend of the brandy.

THE BRANDY OF NAPOLEON

One of the famous legends of the cognac trade is the so-called Napoléon brandy – a cognac with the famous N crest on it and with a vintage date around 1811. Certainly bottles do exist from around this date but they are oddities rather than anything else. The spirit is likely to have deteriorated and, if it had been bottled say 20 years after being made it would be no better than another cognac made in 1950 and bottled in 1970. Alternatively, if the 1811 cognac had been held in cask for over a hundred years, since evaporation is at the rate of five percent each year, little original spirit would remain. Those few very old bottles that do appear are historically interesting and do not, and should not, fetch extremely high prices.

Courvoisier, on the other hand, do use the Napoléonic hat and the symbol N on their labels, and call their second-best brandy Napoléon (using the Bureau National designation in its proper sense). This association between the shipper and the emperor dates from 1815 when several casks of brandy supplied by Emmanuel Courvoisier went on board the two ships Napoléon was using for his planned escape to America. Instead, the emperor and his ships fell into the hands of the British Navy, and its officers took great delight in the casks of Courvoisier cognac on board.

Armagnac

ALTHOUGH ARMAGNAC IS OFTEN compared to its great rival, cognac, it is a wholly different brandy. While cognac is admired for its elegantly smooth, soft and dry flavour, armagnac is prized for its pungent, earthy character with a strong sensation at the very end of the taste – what the Armagnacians like to call 'the dancing fire'.

Although the defined Armagnac region is only 80 miles (130 kilometres) south of the Cognac area at its closest point, the marked differences in the geography and the production methods give these two premier brandies of France their readily discernible differences in taste.

The principal vine variety of Cognac is only a secondary variety for Armagnac. Cognac vines grow in chalk, Armagnac vines grow in sand and clay, Armagnac has a hillier geography and an overall warmer microclimate than Cognac. Cognac uses the double-distillation (pot still) to make its brandy, Armagnac uses the single, continuous distillation. Good cognac is aged in lighter Limousin oak, armagnac in the black, sappy Monlezun oak. These vital differences between the two areas, translated into their respective brandies, have been officially recognised by the French government with the granting of *appellation contrôlée* status for

each area – the highest accolade and guarantee of quality.

Armagnac is regarded as the spirit of Gascony, although in fact its production is largely confined to the department of Gers with small incursions into neighbouring Les Landes. In the very southwest of France, framed by the Pyrénées, the Armagnac-growing area is still very isolated with a comparitively low standard of living. The locals have strong ties with the Basques on both sides of the Spanish-French border. Bullfighting (in Toulouse and elsewhere) is a popular summer sport, and many Gascon words are closer to Spanish than northern French.

From a flat coastal strip the area becomes hillier inland, and, south towards the Pyrénées, crisscrossed with rivers and streams. Stunted pine trees, oaks and cork oaks dot the hills, and there are heavily-forested patches which are the refuge of wild boar, deer, hare and game birds. The arable land is split into thousands of small farms. Most farmers grow several different crops, and few have more than seven to ten acres of vines planted.

Before the turn of the century, Gascony's armagnac went north to the Charente for blending with cognac, in much the same way

Several varieties of white grape are used to make armagnac, principally St Emilion. They are grown in the sandy soil of the remote armagnac region to the south of the Cognac area. Like cognac, the base wine is distilled into the young spirit by dozens of local growers. They use a special still, somewhere between a pot still and a continuous still, to produce a low strength, highly flavoured spirit.

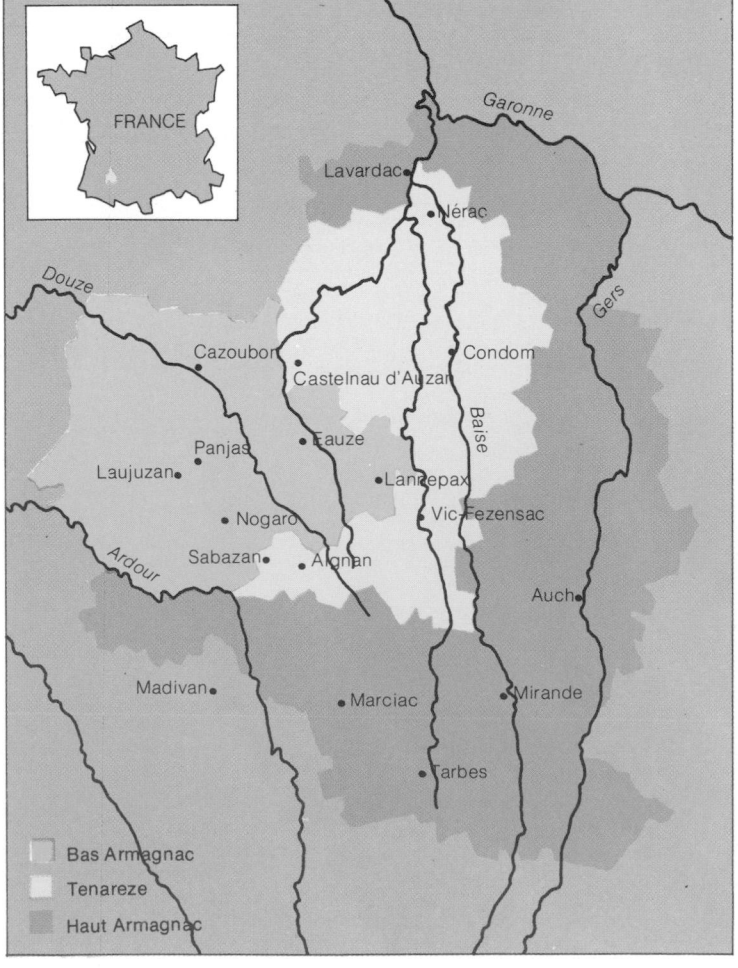

THE DECLINE OF THE TRAVELLING STILL

Armagnac is historically the oldest brandy of France. There is a written reference to it dated 1411, at least 150 years before calvados and more than 200 years before cognac, but is certainly an older spirit than that.

Vines were probably introduced to Gascony by the Romans, but armagnac owes its origins to the native Gauls, who were probably the first people to make wooden casks, and the Moors who introduced distilling to the area from across the Spanish border.

Despite its longer history, armagnac has always lived in the shadow of cognac. Today cognac still outsells armagnac by three bottles to one in France, although many connoisseurs prefer armagnac. Cognac prospered through its geographical advantage over armagnac. Near to the ports along the Gironde river, cognac was better placed to take advantage of the growing taste in Britain and the Low Countries for brandy which was carried back by traders arriving in Bordeaux to buy claret. Gascony, comparatively isolated, lacked the investment which flowed into the cognac houses.

Some of these cognac houses now have interests in armagnac, among them Martell in Janneau, Camus with Prince de Chabot and a distribution link with Marquis de Puységur, and Courvoisier who are linked to Maillac. Izarra, the liqueur company, are linked with

Cles des Ducs; Pernod to Marquis de Montesquiou; and the Bordeaux wine shippers Kressman and Borie Manoux to Kressman and De Casteja armagnacs respectively.

At the lowest level, a small number of the 14,000 winemakers also have a licence to distil. The few farmers that do not distil produce modest quantities for their own consumption or sale at the farm gate.

A number of larger producers, about 16 in all, have sufficient vines and buy in enough extra wine or spirit, to distil but do not bottle and sell under their own name. Then there are nearly 60 negociants big enough to export ranging from small family companies like de Puységur to Cognac-backed companies like Janneau, Maillac, Sempé, Cles des Ducs who mature, and in some cases distil, themselves, and sell their armagnac blends under their own name and to buyers in and outside France.

The biggest producer is the Union des Caves de Vinification de l'Armagnac, a union of ten co-operatives, which has roughly 40 percent of the armagnac production each year, and nearer 80 percent of the aged stocks of armagnac. The UCVA, one of five co-operative bottlers, sells under the Marquis de Caussade label.

Of the approximately 80 companies big enough to export armagnac, more than half are based outside Gascony.

---

as the dark red Cahors wines went to Bordeaux to give backbone to its clarets. Then in 1909 the French government defined the area of armagnac production to preserve its individuality and its status as a rival to cognac.

Within the overall demarcated region, three separate zones were created: Bas Armagnac to the west towards the flat coastal sand dunes; Ténarèze further inland; and finally, Haut Armagnac, almost encircling the other two.

Bas Armagnac, with Eauze as its capital, gets its nickname *armagnac noir* from the local dark oak and pine woods among its fields. The sandy soils produce the armagnacs with the greatest suppleness and finesse and, when some is rubbed between the hands, a characteristic scent of plums.

Ténarèze, with Condom as its capital, produces a lighter, faster-maturing armagnac, with a scent of violets, from its clay soils. The Ténarèzans have a great rivalry with their Bas neighbours. Each claim their armagnacs are the best. While the argument seems to be going the way of the Bas producers, each area makes a fine spirit, and only an experienced connoisseur could really tell the difference.

The third and largest area, the Haut Armagnac, is characterised by the chalk and limestone outcrops on its hilltops – and hence its local name *armagnac blanc*. The chalky soil, so prized in the Cognac area, has the opposite effect on the armagnac vines and gives the poorest quality spirit of the three areas. Most Haut armagnac is used for

making liqueurs and the delicious regional specialty, prunes in armagnac.

The main grape varieties for the base wine that will be distilled into armagnac are the *folle blanche, picquepoul du pays, St Emilion* (the classic cognac grape), *colomb* and *jurançon*, and half a dozen other authorised varieties. Increasing use is also being made of the hybrid Californian grape *baco 22A*. The white base wine for armagnac, like cognac, should ideally be high in acidity and low in alcohol. It makes a poor table wine, so most of the surplus each year goes north to Germany for conversion into sparkling sekt or is made into a dry sparkling white wine drunk locally and used for the Gascon aperitif – the *pousse*

The sand and clay in the soil of Gascony help to produce the best grapes for armagnac. Many of the hundreds of châteaux that dot the region produce their own labels, such as Ravignon shown here, using the skills of maturing and blending that have been handed down from father to son for generations.

rapière (an armagnac-based liqueur topped with sparkling wine).

The young wine is distilled as soon as it is practical in the distinctive *alambic armagnaçais* – a type of continuous still that looks like a giant torch with the handle pointing upward. Unlike a true continuous still, the spirit vapour bubbles through the base wine on its way to the condensers. The raw young armagnac comes out at a much lower strength than cognac – 53 percent against 70 percent – which leaves a much higher proportion of the flavouring elements in the spirit. The single distillation also means that some of the impurities (which would be eliminated in a pot still) remain in armagnac. This combination of flavouring elements and impurities give armagnac its rustic, earthy character and rich bouquet.

The alambic armagnaçais replaced the pot still late last century when the Gascon wine growers, depressed by the *phylloxera* blight in the 1870s and 1880s, found it cheaper to distil once, rather than twice in the pot still which needed more labour. The armagnaçais also yielded more spirit from the base wine.

In 1936 the pot still was outlawed in Gascony, but in 1972 the ruling was reversed and it is now making a comeback. One estimate has nearly five percent of the armagnac produced today coming from pot stills. But the characteristic original encroachments of the pot still are unlikely.

The final stage in the making of armagnac is its maturation in oak casks. The oak used comes from the nearby forests of Monlezun. This special sappy, tannic oak is always split with axes, never sawn, to preserve these characteristics for they give the finished armagnac part of its complex flavour, and its dark, nut-brown colour with golden flints, with a core that deepens almost to black.

During maturation the casks are kept in shady rooms at a cool temperature. Loss by evaporation amounts to about 3 percent annually and this is made up regularly by the cellarmen.

After about six months the young spirit falls sick, exuding a smell that resembles rotting wood. The cellarmaster cures this sickness by blending in older armagnacs. From then on the Monlezun oak matures it quickly, faster than the Limousin oak will a cognac. After about 18 months it is still young and fiery but can be drunk. With three years' maturation it begins to lose its rough edges and after blending with older armagnacs starts to reach its peak. By between five and ten years it is fully mature, ready to blend into fine armagnac. After that, it begins to soften, lose some of its fire, and change into an old brandy. Thirty to forty years after the harvest an unblended armagnac has lived its life and is nothing more than a curiosity.

Whatever its age, armagnac should only be sipped to bring out its full flavour – a flavour that perfectly complements the rich cuisine of Gascony.

D'ARTAGNAN'S DUTCH COURAGE

The patron saint of armagnac is Charles de Batz de Montesquiou Fezenzac, better known as d'Artagnan, hero of Alexander Dumas' Three Musketeers.

Born in 1611 in the château of Castelmore in the centre of the region, he epitomised the arrogant but brave Gascon figure. The Gascons will rarely claim that d'Artagnan drank armagnac, and it was not even known as such for at least another two hundred years, but the story still persists that a flask or two were in his saddlebags when he left for Paris to serve with the King's Musketeers. Dutch courage, as it were, for his interview with the formidable Captain de Tréville. D'Artagnan rose to the rank of capitaine in the King's personal bodyguard, later became Maréchal of Lille, and died in 1674 at the siege of Maestrid from a musket ball through the heart as he stormed the city walls.

In his memory, the brotherhood of armagnac producers and friends calls itself La Compagnie des Mousquetaires de l'Armagnac.

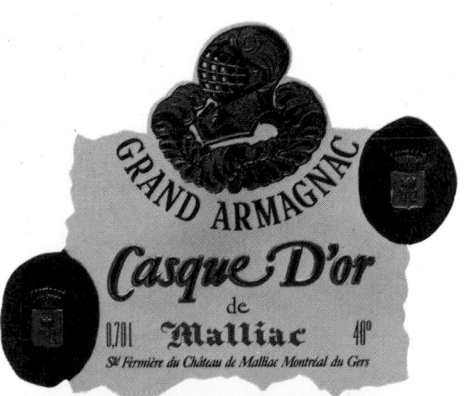

THE YEARS OF ARMAGNAC

Armagnac, traditionally sold in the flat-sided basquaise **70cl** or the 2.5 litre pot gascon **bottle**, has certain minimum ages laid down for the various grades under French law.

Any label with 3 stars, crowns, letters (XXX for example) or the like must be a minimum of one year old, which, with the beginning of the year dating from the September 1 of the year after the harvest, means at least 18 months old in practice. Designations such as Monopole, Sélection deluxe and the like indicate an age of at least one year. For certain markets such as Britain and the United States, local regulations guarantee that a 3 Star or similar designation armagnac will have had a minimum 3 years in cask, giving it an effective minimum age of three and a half years.

Armagnacs labelled VO, VSOP, Réserve and so on must be a minimum of four years old, and those designated Extra, Napoléon, XO, Vieille Réserve **or** Hors d'Age **must be a** minimum of five years old.

Very few armagnacs are blended solely from Bas Armagnac or Ténarèze distillations. Nearly all are blends of the two areas. Marquis de Puységur and Samalens, both Bas Armagnacs only, are two better-known exceptions.

A few of the largest producers offer vintage armagnacs, or spinsters as they are called, although moves are being made to end this style of armagnac – as has already been done with cognac. But vintage armagnac is still permitted under the regulations and Janneau 1939, Malliac 1928 and Marquis de Caussade 1936 are available.

In practice an armagnac from a reputable producer will contain much older distillations than required under law. And one truism applies to armagnac – a bottle will on average contain spirits of greater maturity than a comparable cognac.

The sale and distribution of armagnacs is frequently highly localised. Licensed producers will often sell their unblended spirit direct to the public from shops and roadside tasting rooms such as the converted cask shown below.

Eau-de-vie

An inn sign showing a simple pot still in Strasbourg old town is a reminder that the city lies at the heart of the French eaux-de-vie producing region of Alsace. The most famous of these fruit brandies is Kirsch, made from cherries, but nearly all are clear spirits distilled from fruit and aged in glass or stoneware jars to preserve their clean, fresh taste.

AN EAU-DE-VIE IS ONE of the very few spirits that completely captures the flavour of its principal ingredients.

In France eau-de-vie is the official name for a distillate of wine or fruit. The distillates of wine, called generically brandies, include everything from marc, made from wine lees, to cognac and armagnac. More commonly eau-de-vie on a label denotes a fruit spirit distilled from a fruit mash. The best known is calvados made from Normandy apples or eau-de-vie de cidre made from apples grown outside the defined Calvados area and eau-de-vie de poire from pears.

In eastern France, in the area of the Vosges around Strasbourg and Mulhouse, the unusually warm climate is perfect for producing many different fruits. Better known as Alsace, this fruit-growing area spills over into Germany's Black Forest and down into northern Switzerland. Pears, plums, cherries, strawberries, raspberries, blackberries, greengages, rowanberries, and a dozen other fruits are cultivated or grow wild. From them the French, Germans and Swiss make delicately-flavoured eaux-de-vie.

The process is relatively simple. The fresh, carefully selected fruit is mashed, allowed to ferment, then converted into fruit spirit in a pot still. When a stone fruit is used the kernels are crushed and added to the mash to give the resulting spirit a fine bitter tang. The only real secret about fruit spirits is the careful control of the fermentation temperature. If the mash is too cold, the fermentation takes too long to complete. If the temperature is too high, the mash loses part of its bouquet and flavour. The ideal temperature is between 20° and 22°C.

Most eaux-de-vie are about 45° proof and as colourless as distilled water. This lack of colour has earned them the French nickname *alcools blancs*. They are bottled as soon after distillation as possible to preserve their fruit fragrances, and unlike brandy or whisky are never put into a wooden cask which would colour them. If unbottled, they are stored in large glass or pottery containers.

Apart from the few specialised distillers, most eaux-de-vie are made by farmers from their own fruit in small stills housed in anything from the garage to the barn. Almost a cottage industry in Alsace, the tradition has spread throughout France with even city dwellers making their own alcools blancs from fresh fruit macerated in neutral alcohol obtained from a distiller or local chemist. It is traditional to offer a glass at the end of a meal as a specialty of the household.

The best-known commercial eaux-de-vie are kirsch (from cherries), Poire Williams (from the Williams pear – often with a whole pear grown in the bottle on the tree), mirabelle (from the yellow mirabelle plums), quetsch (from Switzen plums), framboise (raspberries), fraise (strawberries), fraises de bois (wild strawberries), mûre sauvage

C. SPINDLER

Dolfi KIRSCH D'ALSACE

THE SPIRIT OF THE NORMANS

The verdant Duchy of Normandy straddles the mouth of the Seine in northwest France. It was named after the Norsemen, or Vikings, who were given this rich land in the ninth century in a vain bid to halt their repeated sacking of the French coastal towns. When the Norsemen took this land they found parts were covered with wild apple trees. They and the native Bretons fermented the juice of these apples to make a rough cider.

Some 600 years later, in 1553, a document records that Gilles de Gouberville successfully distilled the rough cider into an apple brandy. Five years later, the Spanish galleon El Calvador, one of the Armada fleet on its way to attack the English Navy, was driven on to the Normandy coast in a storm. A town near the site of the shipwreck took the name Calvados, the Norman pronunciation of El Calvador, and over the years the whole area became known as Calvados. By the nineteenth century the name Calvados was used to describe the local apple brandy which, along with cream, butter, and Camembert, Livarot and Pont l'Evêque cheeses, has become a highlight of Norman gastronomy.

The area where the calvados apples grow is now rigidly defined and controlled by the Bureau National Interprofessionel des Calvados et Eaux-de-vie de cidre et de poire (BNICE). Roughly rectangular, it is bordered to the north by the Channel, and runs inland for about 95 kilometres from the mouth of the Seine to the base of the Cotentin peninsula – much bigger than the defined Cognac and Armagnac areas.

Under the rules administered by the BNICE, eleven separate sub areas are designated, each named after a valley or pays. The first and best known is the Pays d'Auge, a strip of land in the eastern part of the Calvados area, south of Deauville between two small rivers. Since 1946 the Pays d'Auge has been an appellation contrôlée area, singled out for its excellence, and subject to even stricter controls than the other areas. The other ten areas are l'Avranchin, Cotentin, Mortainais, Domfrontais, the Vallée de l'Orne, Pays de Merlerault, Perche, Pays de la Risle, Pays de Bray, and Calvados. Each is designated as appellation réglementée. Apple trees may be grown only in parts of each area and the distillers can use a continuous or pot still to make their brandy, whereas for Pays d'Auge a pot still only must be used. In practice the best calvados, from whatever area, is made in a pot still.

The calvados cycle begins with the farmer selling his apples to his local co-operative. The co-operative ferments the rough cider and either distils it or sells it to a local distiller who concentrates on this one part of the cycle. The distiller runs the cider once through his still, keeping only the middle of the run, the alcools de coeur. This is then distilled a second time, again keeping only the heart of the run. The rest goes back for redistillation.

The young calvados is then bought by the shipper (whose name will appear on the label). As the secret of a fine calvados is in its blending of different areas and different vintages, plus proper ageing in oak casks in cool cellars, it is the shipper who is ultimately responsible for the quality of the product.

Some calvados is sold in Normandy, for local consumption, when it is a minimum of two years old. Its rough, fiery taste can quickly deter a new calvados drinker from further tasting. Good calvados should be a blend of four, five and ten year old casks; and the very finest a blend of eight, ten, fifteen, twenty and twenty-five year old casks. Various names are used to describe these different grades of calvados. Under the rules of the BNICE a calvados described as Vieux or Réserve must be a minimum three years old; VO or Vieille Réserve a minimum of four; VSOP five years old and an Extra, Napoléon, Hors d'Age or Age Inconnu six or more years. In practice most of the calvados in a bottle carrying one of these descriptions would be a lot older than the official minimum age.

When the young calvados comes out of the still it is around 72° proof or higher. As it matures, in 600- to 700-litre casks, about 10 litres evaporate and the strength drops by about one percent each year. When blended and ready for bottling the alcoholic strength should be between only 40° and 50°. The taste should be smooth with a sharp, crisp finish, the perfume rich and reminiscent of apples.

Calvados is a vital part of the Norman way of life. They will have un 'tit Calva as a pick-me-up in the morning, and halfway through their evening meal a larger glass, usually swallowed in one gulp, which they have nicknamed the trou Normand (Norman holemaker) to settle their stomachs. Finally, they will have another glass after dinner with their coffee.

Outside the defined calvados areas other apple brandies are made. But they can only be called eaux-de-vie de cidre (or poire, if they are made from pears) de Normandie, Bretagne (Brittany) or Maine – the three main apple growing departments. They must not be called calvados, and they rarely have the same quality.

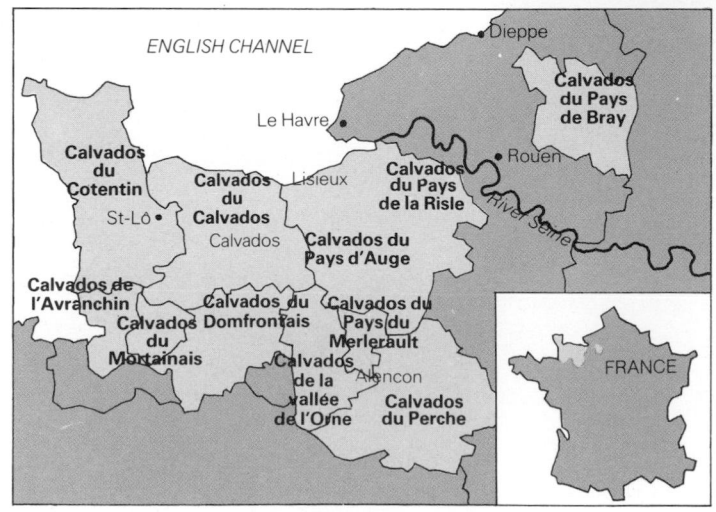

One of the ships of the Spanish Armada allegedly gave rise to the name of France's premier apple brandy – calvados. The legally defined calvados producing region consists of 11 areas clustered around the Normandy coast. Once the juice has been pressed from the apples, it is fermented before being distilled. Pot stills, right, produce the most refined calvados; in all areas apart from the Pays Auge continuous stills are also used.

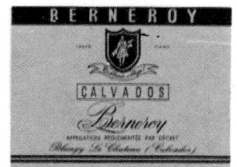

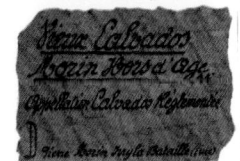

A range of
calvados labels.

THE ALPINE WATERS OF LIFE

The valleys of Switzerland rival Germany's Black Forest and the French Alsace region in the making of fruit brandies. Again, production is often on a very small scale, but some large firms do exist, such as Nebiker, left.

Kirsch, made from cherries, is the main Swiss fruit brandy. One brand is named after General Johann Sutter, a Swiss-born 19th-century adventurer who was one of the founders of the Californian wine and brandy industry.

The other main Swiss eaux-de-vie are poire (pears), himbeergeist (raspberries), erdbeergeist (strawberries), zwetschenwasser (mirabelle plums) and zwetgenwasser (quetsch plums).

Labels from some of the leading Swiss fruit brandies are seen below, alongside a map of the manufacturing centres.

Left, a friendly poste at the H Nebiker distillery in Sissach in the extreme north of Switzerland. Right, a leading Swiss brandy, Ergolsthaler, set amongst the apples from which it is distilled. The firm is based in the northern town of Ormalingen.

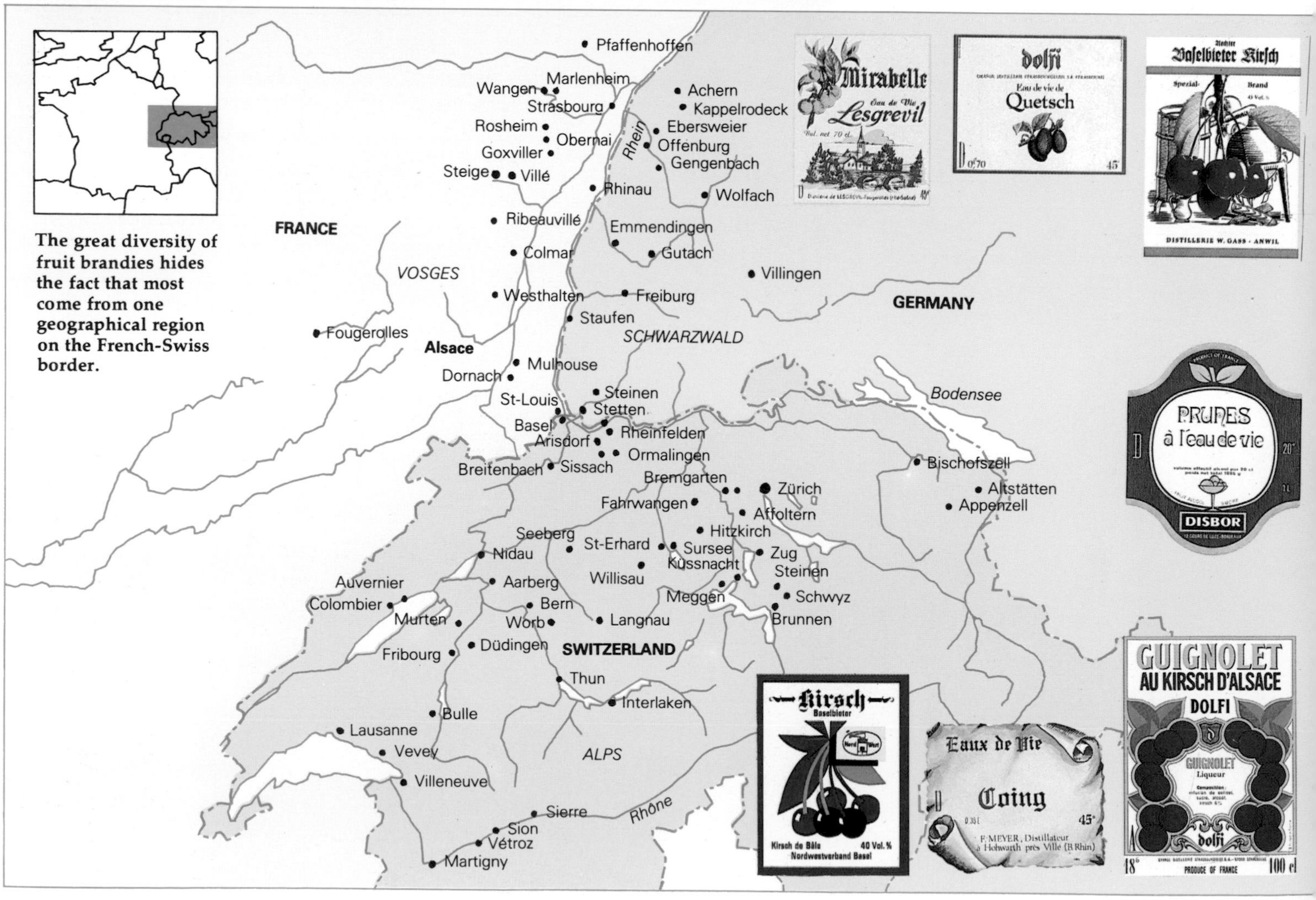

The great diversity of fruit brandies hides the fact that most come from one geographical region on the French-Swiss border.

FRANCE

VOSGES

Fougerolles

Alsace

GERMANY

SCHWARZWALD

Bodensee

SWITZERLAND

ALPS

Pfaffenhoffen
Marlenheim
Wangen
Strasbourg
Rosheim
Obernai
Goxviller
Steige · Villé
Ribeauvillé
Colmar
Westhalten
Mulhouse
Dornach
St-Louis
Basel
Arisdorf
Breitenbach · Sissach

Achern
Kappelrodeck
Ebersweier
Offenburg
Gengenbach
Rhinau
Wolfach
Emmendingen
Gutach
Freiburg
Staufen
Villingen

Steinen
Stetten
Rheinfelden
Ormalingen
Bremgarten
Fahrwangen
Seeberg
Nidau
St-Erhard
Aarberg
Willisau
Worb
Langnau
Düdingen

Zürich
Affoltern
Hitzkirch
Sursee
Küssnacht
Meggen
Bern
Brunnen
Thun
Interlaken

Zug
Steinen
Schwyz

Bischofszell
Altstätten
Appenzell

Auvernier
Colombier
Murten
Fribourg
Bulle
Lausanne
Vevey
Villeneuve
Sierre
Sion
Vétroz
Martigny

Rhein

Rhône

Mirabelle Eau de Vie **Lesgrevil**

dolfi Eau de vie de **Quetsch**

Baselbieter Kirsch Spezial-Brand

PRUNES à l'eau de vie DISBOR

Kirsch Baselbieter — Kirsch de Bâle 40 Vol. % Nordwestverband Basel

Eaux de Vie **Coing** F. MEYER, Distillateur à Hohwarth près Villé (B Rhin)

GUIGNOLET AU KIRSCH D'ALSACE DOLFI GUIGNOLET Liqueur — PRODUCE OF FRANCE

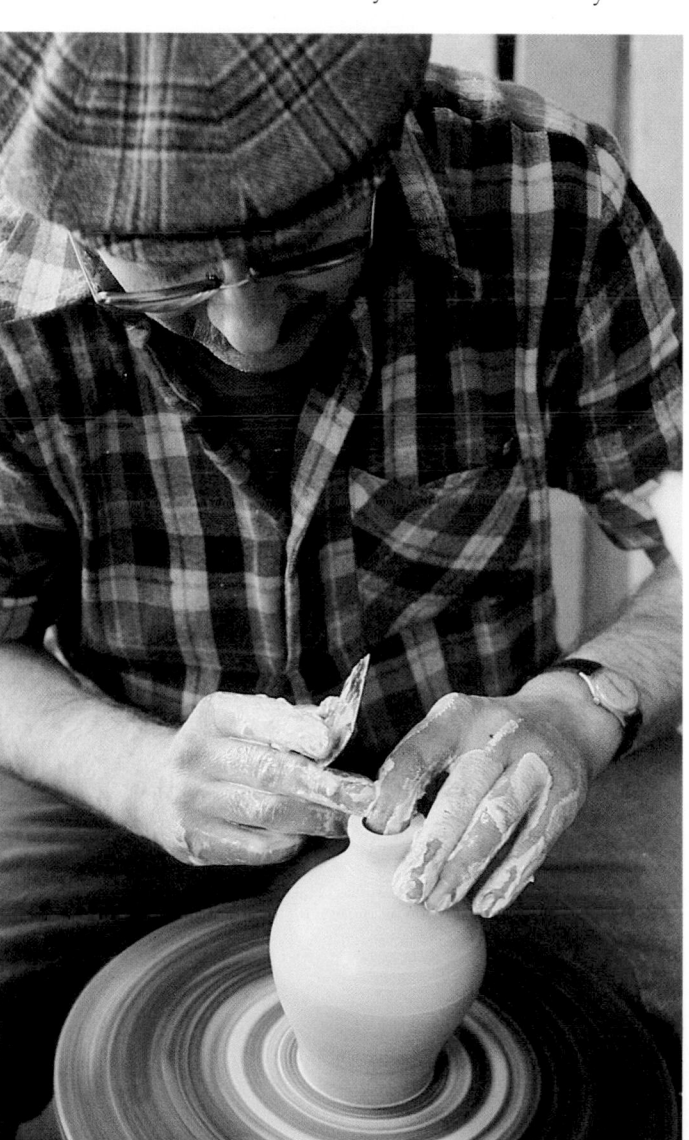

(blackberries), gentiane (from the gentian plant), baie d'alisier (rowanberries), the wonderfully aromatic baie de houx (from holly berries), myrtille (bilberries), nèfle (medlars), reineclaude (greengages), baie de sureau (elderberries), and even genévrier (from junipers – almost a gin).

Kirsch, best known of the French eaux-de-vie, has four different gradings which should, under law, be indicated on the label: Kirsch *pur*, or *naturel*, is a natural distillation from cherries with no other additions; Kirsch *commerce* is a blend of true kirsch with neutral alcohol or another eau-de-vie, with no other permissible additions; Kirsch *fantaisie* is neutral alcohol flavoured with natural kirsch and other ingredients; Kirsch *artificiel* is neutral alcohol diluted to normal strength and flavoured with the appropriate essences.

These eaux-de-vie are usually served chilled, traditionally in a chilled glass, as an after-dinner drink. Kirsch, mirabelle, and quetsch are recommended as digestifs after the rich Alsatian cuisine.

Unfortunately the vast amounts of fruit needed to make relatively small amounts of spirit means these alcools blancs are expensive, even in Alsace, and only a few distillers find it worthwhile to export. In France itself most restaurants will have at least two or three different flavours that can be tried by the glass.

Outside the main Alsace area, eaux-de-vie are also made in the Franche-Comté (south of the Vosges) from cherries, sloes, mirabelles, holly berries and greengages; in Lorraine from its famous mirabelle plums, bilberries, blackberries and fruit kernels; in the Rhône valley from Williams pears; and on Corsica from myrtle and the native arbouse berry.

To preserve their clean fruit flavour, nearly all eaux-de-vie are stored in earthenware jars or glass-lined casks after distilling. (In wood they would colour and change flavour.) Some eaux-de-vie manufacturers, like Meyblum, handmake their own traditional pottery containers and matching cups. The potter shown here works in the village of Betschdorf which is largely devoted to the production of such containers.

Liqueurs

FRANCE PRODUCES AN EXTRAORDINARY range of liqueurs – both in the diversity of flavours and brands, and in the fantastic labels and bottles used to package the drinks. Some have only one basic flavour, others can contain up to 150 different fruits, herbs and spices, with no single flavour dominating the finished liqueur. Only Italy offers a selection that comes anywhere near the varied and splendid range of French liqueurs.

Liqueur production ranges from private concoctions made by individual households to old family recipes, through the cottage industry variety for local consumption only, to the selection produced by the 90 or so members of the Syndicat National des Fabricants de Liqueurs, and in particular, the internationally-known brands made by the inner court of the Syndicat – the Groupement des Grandes Liqueurs de France.

Homemade liqueurs are common in France. Usually produced by the simple method of macerating fruits and herbs in alcohol, they are the pride of the family, to be produced for honoured guests and on festive occasions. In many of the small villages and towns the local pâtisserie or épicerie will have its own modest range of liqueurs, either made by the proprietors themselves or made for them by a small local manufacturer. Next come the regional liqueurs – those made and largely sold in a specific part of France in sufficient quantities to be considered commercial. Examples include the intensely sweet greenish, grapey Likor Kozh Bouchinot sold mainly in Brittany; the Elixir de Monbazillac; and the green and yellow Suc de Monbazillac wine and herb liqueurs (Violet-Quemin) that are a Perigord speciality; and the fruit liqueurs (fraise, poire, myrtille, verveine and framboise) made by Conçillon et Fils in the Loire, and which come in tall, elegant bottles with a crystal tree growing in the liqueur.

Some of these liqueurs would be considered exotic by any standards. For example, Denoix of Brive in the Perigord-Quercy area make Liqueur de Jus de Noix Vertes (from green walnuts), Fenouillette (fennel-flavoured), and Roc Amadour (armagnac-flavoured with juniper berries), Benoit Serres of Toulouse make Dojon (cognac and almonds), Violette (an infusion of the leaves and roots of violets), Fine Pyrénées (angelica) and Eau de Noix Serres (extract of walnuts gathered in June).

Many of the larger companies offer a wide range of fruit flavours. For instance, Marie Brizard list at least 20, while Berger (the anisette and pastis manufacturers) have a dozen including Crème de Banane and Noisettia (hazelnuts), all sold under the Fournier brand name. Briottet, Clacquesin and L'Heritier Guyot all make the famous crème de cassis from blackcurrants grown around Dijon; and Carton of Nuits St Georges make a very fine blackcurrant liqueur they call Crème de Nuits. Briottet also produce a range of fruit liqueurs including guignolet (from cherries), while Clacquesin are one of the few producers of Extrait des Pins (better known as sapindor or liqueur des pins) in which the predominant flavour is an extract of pine needles.

Dolphi at Strasbourg, Giffard in Anjou (best-known for their Menthe Pastille and Peppermint Pastille), Cazanove of Bordeaux, Disbor of Bordeaux (who make an excellent crème de cacao liqueur), Peureux in the Haute-Saone and Teissedre of Bordeaux are six other well known fruit liqueur producers. Cazanove specialise in the green and yellow Kermann liqueurs (something like Chartreuse), and Teissedre make a very good mandarine liqueur.

Fernet Branca distil their famous revitalising digestif at St Louis in the Haut Rhin, with Fleurs des Alps (a herb liqueur with crystals growing on a twig in the bottle) and Branca Menthe, their famous green mint digestif. Germain, based in the tiny village of St Florent sur Auzonnet in the south of France, make an interesting range that includes Ravanello (vanilla and coffee), Fine Lachamp (prunes and nuts), Auzonnet (lemon and mint), Gorges du Tarn (herbs) and Verveine du Rouvergue (in both green and yellow).

One of the best-known French liqueurs is Vieille Curé (green and yellow), invented at the Abbey of Cenon on the Gironde and now produced in the same town by Intermarque. A blend of brandies and more than 50 herbs, including some grown locally, Vieille Curé comes in a standard bottle or the famous flat bottle with the 'stained glass' portrait of a monk. Intermarque also produce the Cordial Medoc (claret flavoured with herbs) and Maborange orange liqueur.

Oddest of the French liqueurs is the Eau de Melisse des Carmes Boyer made by Renouard Lariviere of Paris. An elixir of alcohol, melissa, angelica, cress, cloves, lemon and spices, the liqueur is sold in a medicinal bottle and is taken in water, or as a couple of drops on a sugar cube. It is recommended for the relief of fatigue, car sickness, morning sickness, nervous tension and overwork. Eau de Melisse was first made by Carmelite fathers of the rue de Vaugirard convent in Paris in 1611 and is one of the oldest French liqueurs.

The Groupement des Grandes Liqueurs, the inner sanctum of the Syndicat Nationale des Fabricants de Liqueurs, consists of the 13 biggest French liqueur producers – Bénédictine, Chartreuse, Bardinet, Cusenier, Cointreau, Pippermint Get, Garnier, Izarra, Marie Brizard, Grand Marnier-Lapostolle, Pages, Cherry Rocher and Lejay-Lagoute.

Lejay-Lagoute, founded in 1841, have made their reputation through the cassis their founder Denis Lagoute invented, while Cherry Rocher of La Côte St André, near

HERB-BASED LIQUEURS OF FRANCE

France is one of the two major producers of herbal liqueurs, the other being Italy. Most of these liqueurs trace their origins back to the time when the preparation of elixirs and herbal cures rested largely in the hands of monks. The modern herb-based liqueurs developed from these medicinal drinks. But while liqueur makers like to promote the monastic origins of their products, in France only one liqueur is still made by monks – Chartreuse. But even with this drink, production takes place outside the monastery and the marketing and promotion is left to an independent, secular company.

🏛 Liqueurs produced in monasteries

Vienne, specialise in their cherry liqueur of the same name, together with cherry whisky, guignolet, and a range of fruit and herb liqueurs.

Izarra (Basque for star) began by producing their unique Izarra liqueur – a blend of brandies, plant extracts, and acacia honey – which is now the most important of their range of liqueurs. Likewise, Marie Brizard started with their renowned anisette liqueur, which was first made from a recipe given to Mme Marie Brizard in 1755 by a grateful patient who had returned to health, thanks to her support. Her descendants now produce the anisette in Bordeaux along with a large range of fruit liqueurs.

Verveine du Velay was invented by the Pages family in 1859 based on 33 different herbs, brandy and honey. Still made by the family at Le Puy en Velay in the Auvergne, it now comes in the stronger green style and the milder yellow form, and is considered as much an aid to digestion as a liqueur. Pages, too, have expanded into fruit liqueurs with a range of the major flavours.

Bénédictine, first made in the monastery at Fécamp by Dom Vincelli in the sixteenth century, was rediscovered in 1863 by M Alexandre Le Grand after several years of experimenting to perfect once again the lost formula. M Le Grand's success enabled him to build the Gothic fantasy castle which is now the showpiece of the company and a popular tourist attraction.

A BOTTLE OF STRAWBERRIES

Several pounds of ripe strawberries are used to make each bottle of strawberry liqueur. For the more affluent, Dolfi make a liqueur from wild strawberries (*fraises des bois*).

ROSE DE CHAMBERTIN

Cassis, the extract of blackcurrants that is a speciality of the Dijon area, is a popular cocktail ingredient. It is used in a Rose de Chambertin to add the brilliant red colour and the characteristic fruit taste of the cocktail.

Frost a medium-size cocktail glass by dipping the rim into a saucer of crème de cassis (1 & 2), and then caster sugar (3). Into a cocktail shaker with ice add ½ oz fresh lime juice (4), a dash of egg white, 1½ oz dry gin (5), ½ oz crème de cassis (6), and 1 barspoon Sirop de Gomme (7). Shake and strain into the prepared glass (8 & 9).

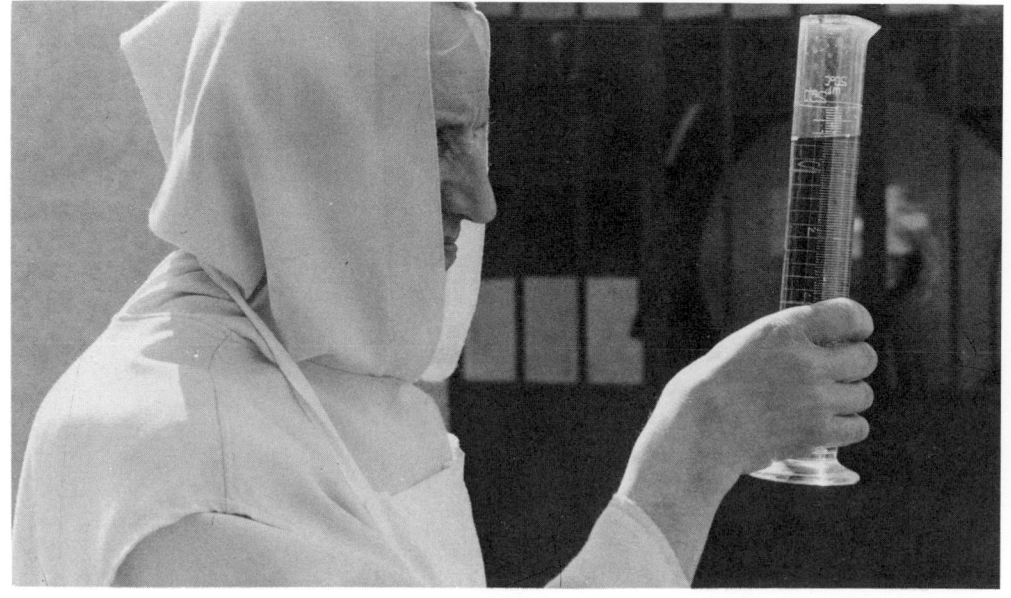

Bénédictine is a blend of herbs, some of them grown along the cliffs near Fécamp. The principal ones are hyssop, balm, angelica, coriander, thyme, cloves, saffron, cinnamon and nutmeg. American honey is another essential ingredient. Some of the herbs are distilled, some macerated, and the whole process takes no less than three years. Every Bénédictine label carries the letters *DOM*, not for Dominican Order of Monks, but for Deo Optimo Maximo, the motto of the Bénédictines. In 1938 the company introduced a second, drier Bénédictine, called B & B, which is a blend of Bénédictine and cognac.

Bénédictine also own Garnier, producers of another range of fruit liqueurs, in particular Abricotine, first made by Paul Garnier in 1872 as part of the liqueur stable he began in 1859.

Pippermint Get (now owned by the Bénédictine company) was created by Jean Get at Revel, near Toulouse, in 1796. It is one of France's two best known crème de menthes with a very intense green colour enhanced by its art nouveau-style bottle. The other famous crème de menthe is Cusenier's Freezomint, one of the extensive range of Cusenier fruit liqueurs and eaux-de-vie.

Bardinet of Bordeaux are primarily a rum company (their Negrita is France's major rum brand). However, they also make a range of 16 fruit liqueurs including peach, Parfait Amour, Kummel and Triple Sec. One of their best known is the apricot-flavoured Ardine, a name created by dropping the first and last letter of Bardinet.

Chartreuse comes from the Monastery of La Grande Chartreuse founded by St Bruno in the hills of Voiron in 1084. The liqueur recipe was given to the monks by Marachel d'Estrées in 1605 and perfected by Brothers Maubec and Antoine in 1764 as an elixir of life. Today it is still based on this recipe – a complicated distillation, infusion and

GRASSHOPPER — BRANDY ALEXANDER — WHITE LADY

GRASSHOPPER (Centre)

Pour 1 oz crème de menthe, 1 oz crème de cacao and 1 oz single cream into a cocktail shaker. Shake and strain into a medium-size cocktail glass and garnish with a little freshly-grated nutmeg.

If white crème de cacao is available, use that to give a clearer green.

ALEXANDER (Right)

Due to their velvety consistency, the Alexanders are known as after-dinner cocktails.

Pour 1 oz brandy, 1 oz crème de cacao and 1 oz single cream into a cocktail shaker. Shake and strain into a medium-size cocktail glass and garnish with a little freshly-grated nutmeg.

WHITE LADY

Harry's New York Bar in Paris claim to have created this cocktail.

Pour 1½ oz dry gin, ¾ oz Cointreau, 1 oz fresh lemon juice, 1 dash egg white and 1 barspoon caster sugar into a cocktail shaker. Shake and strain into a medium-size cocktail glass. Garnish with a little freshly-grated nutmeg.

Bénédictine and Chartreuse both have monastic origins, but only the latter is still made by monks, to the original recipe by Marachel d'Estrées, above. A stark contrast is provided by the homes of the two drinks: Bénédictine's exotic chateau at Fécamp, left, and the monastery of La Grande Chartreuse, near Voiron, right.

maceration of more than 130 herbs and spices. From the elixir came the famous Green and Yellow Chartreuses and the lesser known Orange and Myrtle flavours, still produced by the Carthusians at Voiron in a modern distillery. Green and yellow are normally sold at four years old, but 12 year old labels are also produced. However, it is worth noting that Chartreuse is the only important liqueur to age in the bottle.

Cointreau was the creation of Edouard and Adolphe Cointreau in 1849 and is still produced at Angers from the double-distillation of bitter Antilles oranges and sweet Mediterranean oranges with spirit. The water-white Cointreau is the best-known of all the orange-based liqueurs.

Made from oranges and cognac, the other great orange-based liqueur of France is Grand Marnier. It was created by the Lapostolle family in the tiny village of Neauphle le Château, between Lyon and Grenoble. Apart from its standard label the company makes a Black Label Grand Marnier in small quantities, using very fine cognacs.

For their 150th anniversary (1977) the company has also released an exclusive centenary *cuvée* made from the finest cognacs, again only in minimal quantities. It is packaged in a superb appliqué bottle.

France produces a multiplicity of liqueurs and eaux-de-vie from an almost inexhaustible list of ingredients. Some are made in tiny quantities to traditional family recipes, others are international drinks and sell thousands of bottles each year.

Because they are both made from fruit, eaux-de-vie and fruit liqueurs are frequently confused. They are, however, very different drinks – eaux-de-vie are fruit brandies distilled from fruit, fruit liqueurs are fruit-flavoured spirits. Eaux-de-vie, then, will have only one dominant flavour, liqueurs can include up to 150 different fruits herbs and spices with no one flavour dominating the finished spirit.

Many liqueurs are known simply by their generic name, such as kirsch or framboise, others have become identified with their companies' name. Crème de menthe, for instance, is usually synonymous with Freezomint or Pippermint Get; curaçao with Cointreau; cherry liqueur with Cherry Rocher. Usually the liqueur is asked for by its generic name, so if you order a crème de menthe, the waiter will usually produce either Freezomint or Pippermint Get. However, where advertising has developed a strong identity to the brand (particularly if it is a patent liqueur with no specific generic name), it will be asked for by name. Grand Marnier and Chartreuse are two examples.

Spirits with a fruit flavour
Apple calvados, perhaps the best-known eau-de-vie
Cherry guignolet, kirsch, cerise or brands such as Cherry Rocher, Cherry Marnier and Chesky (cherry-flavoured whisky)
Apricot eau-de-vie de abricot, Abricotine (Garnier is the main brand), Apry (Marie Brizard), apricot brandies (Rocher, Regnier, Cusenier)
Raspberry eau-de-vie de framboise and framboise sauvage (wild) from Pages, and Cordial Médoc with a strong cherry flavour
Yellow plum eau-de-vie de mirabelle (Jacobert, Dolphi and others)
Strawberries eau-de-vie or crème de fraises
Wild Strawberries eau-de-vie or crème de fraises bois
Blackberry eau-de-vie or crème de mûre
Wild Blackberry eau-de-vie or crème de mûre sauvage
Blackcurrant eau-de-vie de cassis or the better-known crème de cassis made by l'Heretier, Berger, Clacquesin and others
Violet Plum eau-de-vie de quetsch
Sloeberry or *Blackthorn* prunelle, eau-de-vie de prunelle or crème de prunelle
Pear eau-de-vie de poire, Poire Williams, crème de poire
Pineapple crème d'ananas
Banana crème de banane and Nabana from Cazanove
Peach eau-de-vie de pêche
Whortleberry or *Bilberry* eau-de-vie de myrtille
Quince eau-de-vie de coing

Holly berry eau-de-vie de houx
Red or Whitecurrant eau-de-vie de groseille
Rowanberry eau-de-vie d'alisier
Sorb apple eau-de-vie de sorbier
Elderberry eau-de-vie de sureau

Citrus-flavoured liqueurs

Orange sometimes labelled as just orange or fine orange liqueur, but most often curaçao (with an orange-brown hue) or triple sec (colourless). Cointreau is the best-known curaçao style. Dolfi Curaçao Orange Sec another. Cusenier and Marie Brizard are leading triple secs. Grand Marnier with its cognac content is more a curaçao style.
Mandarine Pages make a mandarine napoléon liqueur
Lemon citron liqueur is rare in France
Grapefruit also rare. Sold as pamplemousse

Spirits with a dominant flower ingredient

Rose crème de roses from an extract of the petals
Violet crème de viollettes. The best-known is Crème Yvette. Also Parfait Amour: based on citrus extracts but with a violet hue and something of the taste of the flower.
Dog rose eau-de-vie d'églantine or Gratte-Cul

Liqueurs with herbal ingredients

A whole host of liqueurs exist with dozens of different herbs making up their flavour. Most are sold under different brand names. Among them are Bénédictine, Chartreuse, Trappistine, Izzara, Kermann, La Vieille Curé, Flor d'Alpes, Sapindor, Angelica, Aiguebelle, Raspail, Liqueur des Moines, La Senancole, Liqueur d'Hendaye, Carmeline, Liqueur d'Or, Genalpy, Mazarine, Liqueur Jaune, Liqueur Vert, Verveine du Velay, Freezomint, Pippermint Get and Elixir or Suc de Monbazillac

Liqueurs with one herb predominating

Aniseed anisette. Marie Brizard is the best-known. Also edging into this category are pastis (Pernod, Ricard and others), absinthe (banned from legal production), and oxygenée
Cumin French versions of Goldwasser are known as liqueurs d'or
Mint crème de menthe as personified by Freezomint, Pippermint Get and others

Bean, kernel, nut, root and leaf

Gentian root eau-de-vie de gentiane
Pine needles eau-de-vie de sapin – Sapindor and others
Cacao beans crème de cacao (chocolate-flavoured) or à la vanille (with vanilla added)
Coffee crème de café or crème de Mokka
Almond crème d'almond
Fruit kernels liqueurs based on the extract of the stones of different fruits including crème de noyau (peach and apricot kernels; the best-known brand is from Vve Champion), prunelle (sloe kernels) and crème de noisettes (various nuts, usually hazel)

Not all French liqueurs and eaux-de-vie are produced commercially or are as distinctive as Poire Williams with a whole pear grown inside the bottle. Although many are disappearing because of the prohibitive cost of labour or the scarcity of some wild ingredients, there is still an extraordinary variety available to those prepared to seek them out.

FRANCE
Anis

THE FORERUNNER OF the modern *anis* or *pastis* drinks – absinthe – is the one spirit that cannot be made or consumed in most countries in the world. The drink itself is surrounded by a web of myths, half-truths and conflicting opinions.

It was first created by a Frenchman, Dr Pierre Ordinaire. A loyalist, he fled France in 1790 when supporters of the king were being rounded up and sent to the guillotine. He settled at Neuchâtel in neutral Switzerland, and continued to practise medicine.

The preparation of drugs from herbs was common practice at that time, and around Neuchâtel there was a profusion of wild herbs, among them wormwood. As the British herbalist Culpeper wrote, wormwood was a cure for just about everything, including drunkenness. Dr Ordinaire began experimenting with this herb and by 1792 had invented a new medicinal digestif made from wormwood (*Artemesia absinthium*) and 15 other herbs, among them anise, badiane (a second variety of anise), melissa, parsley, camomile, coriander and veronica. He further found that the effects of the different herbs, particularly the wormwood, were heightened when the infusion was steeped in 136° proof alcohol (which became the traditional strength for absinthe). Dr Ordinaire named his new digestif after its principal ingredient, and when he died a year later he left the recipe to his housekeeper, Madame Henriot.

Mme Henriot, helped by her two daughters, set up a small shop to sell Dr Ordinaire's absinthe digestif. One of her best customers was a Major Henri Dubied who, apart from appreciating absinthe's effects on the stomach, found it had another very interesting property. Taken in moderation after dinner, it was a marvellous and safe aphrodisiac. So began one of the many legends surrounding absinthe that persist to this day. The writer, Ernest Hemingway, was just one of the many who believed in the drink's erotic powers, and he mentions absinthe several times in *For Whom the Bell Tolls* – although he pointed out the erotic effect of absinthe was purely in the mind.

Fascinated by absinthe, Major Dubied bought the secret recipe from Mme Henriot in 1797 and opened the first absinthe factory in partnership with his son-in-law, Henri-Louis Pernod. Eight years later, in 1805, Henri-Louis opened a larger factory in France.

The popularity of Pernod (as the drink became known, to distinguish it from the imitations already appearing in France) grew slowly until the 1850s. Then it became a French institution almost overnight, a result of the thousands of French soldiers returning from the war of suppression in Algeria from 1844 to 1847. The soldiers were issued with a daily absinthe ration to add to their wine to fight off malaria and they carried a taste for absinthe back to France.

By the 1890s absinthe, nicknamed the green goddess, was the drink of the café and bistro society. Degas, Picasso and Toulouse-Lautrec all painted absinthe and its drinkers, and drank it themselves. The poet Paul Verlaine was addicted to it, while social reformers railed against it. It was drunk with ice-cold water, the water being added drop by drop through a special long-handled spoon with a perforated bowl.

The first concerted drive against absinthe came in 1905, after a Swiss peasant farmer named Jean Lanfray took his rifle and shot dead his wife and two daughters, and then bungled a suicide attempt. Lanfray was a heavy drinker. His normal daily intake was later revealed to be six quarts of wine, half-a-dozen brandies, and perhaps a couple of absinthes. But when it was found that his dead wife had been pregnant, the public hue and cry demanded a scapegoat. Absinthe was the victim.

Front-page newspaper stories claimed absinthe was the real killer of the Lanfray women, and when Jean Lanfray came to trial in 1906 he was judged to have been in 'an absinthe-induced delirium'. He was sentenced to life rather than executed, but hanged himself in his cell three days later. The following year the Swiss, by a majority of three votes to two, approved a national ban on the manufacture and sale of absinthe.

The French Chamber of Deputies weighed

Among the Bohemian café society in Paris around the 1890s absinthe was the favoured drink; the painting by Degas, left, is one of the many by contemporary artists containing references to the drink. Its popularity among the more colourful sections of society lent weight to the allegations of its adverse effects, which ultimately led to its banning in 1915. Today, the nearest equivalent to absinthe in most countries, is anis.

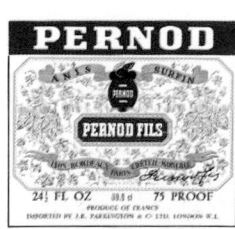

ANISETTE SURFINE

the evidence and decided not to ban absinthe in their country, but the horrifying losses of the opening year of the First World War led to a renewed, even more fervent attack on absinthe which was blamed in part for the losses. The drink was finally outlawed in France in March 1915.

Chemists had already discovered that absinthe contained two types of poisons for heavy drinkers: an epileptic group caused by the combination of wormwood, hyssop and fennel; and a stupefying group caused by the interaction of anise, badiane, angelica, oregano, melissa and mint. By this time, wormwood was no longer an essential ingredient in the manufacture of absinthe. Some French manufacturers were not using it at all, and others only in tiny amounts. However, the anti-absinthe brigade seized upon its poisonous qualities to force the government to ban it.

At the end of the First World War, the French government lifted the ban on absinthe production, but decreed that it could no longer be made with wormwood. The new drink was called anis, to distinguish it from absinthe, and Pernod were one of the first to recommence production. Their name is now synonymous with anis, a drink with all the characteristics of the old wormwood, but none of its harmful effects.

Before the 1915 ban a drink similar to absinthe had already appeared in Provence in the south of France. Known locally as pastis (from the French word for mixture), it contained wormwood and anise, but its overriding ingredient was liquorice. It too was banned for the duration of the war, and for some years afterwards, although the southern French continued to make it illegally.

When the ban on pastis was lifted, one of the first into the market was Paul Ricard, and Ricard's popularity spread rapidly northwards. When the army of occupation banned the manufacture of pastis in the Second World War, Paul Ricard retired, but returned in 1951 to build his pastis into the major French brand. He retired again in 1968, and the French press headlined the news with the words 'the harakiri of Monsieur Pastis'. In 1971 Pernod and Ricard merged, and between them they now control almost 80 percent of the 12,000,000-case French anis and pastis market.

Pernod is the only anis of any consequence on the French market. Anis differs from the pastis in that the herbal flavours are introduced into the spirit by maceration. In addition it does not include liquorice as one of its main ingredients – the flavour which most people liken to liquorice is the flavour of the anise herb, and is less obtrusive than the strong liquorice flavour of the pastis brands. A third difference is the colour. Anis is a bold yellow which turns to greenish-yellow when water is added. Pastis is brown-yellow, and goes a whitish-grey when water is added.

French café life may have hardly changed in the past fifty years, but the distilling industry certainly has. Pernod operates from uncompromisingly modern offices and distilling plants at Creteil, near Paris.

The neutral alcohol used for anis and pastis is made from either grape distillation or from sugar beet distillation by the French government alcohol monopoly. In both cases the proof is reduced, normally to 78°, at the end of the production cycle by the addition of water. The only other main ingredient of both drinks is sugar, used to stabilise the otherwise temperamental ingredient (called anethol in French) that causes the drink to change colour when water is added.

Apart from Pernod and Ricard, the other brands (all are pastis) are Pernod's Pastis 51 (named after the year it was introduced, 1951, and the ratio of water to pastis, 5:1), and Alize, a fourth Pernod-Ricard label, distributed in France by CDC Cusenier. Berger make pastis and anis blanc (a clear anis that was popular in the French north African colonies, particularly the Le Crystal brand.

This is rarely seen now and sells only in modest amounts.). Moco Tomate, Moco Perroquet and Moco Moresque are ready-mixed versions of pastis – with the addition of a small amount of fruit flavouring.

Duval (a Martini & Rossi subsidiary), Casanis (a pastis made in Corsica and also popular in Paris), PEC and Jeannot are other pastis labels.

All anis and pastis producers also make anisette (or anis liquor) at the much lower strength of 43°. Not a great deal of anisette is sold in France, but it allows the anis and pastis producers to advertise their brand names. This is because the lower strength anisette falls within the group of drinks that are allowed to be advertised, whereas the high strength anis and pastis brands may not be advertised under French law because of their high alcohol.

FRANCE
Other Drinks

EVEN AFTER COGNAC, armagnac, calvados and the fruit brandies, and liqueurs in almost endless variety, France still offers the dedicated drinker of higher strength potables an array of other drinks.

Most are confined to the areas of production, and are rarely seen or exported, outside their immediate environs. One exception is brandy. In 1920, Professor George Saintsbury wrote in *Notes On a Cellar-book*: 'There is good brandy, and there is, though it is almost a contradiction in terms, bad brandy.' In the intervening years the distinction between good and bad brandy has narrowed as commercial pressures have forced importers to look for the best possible value for money. In the last ten years both cognac and, to a lesser extent, armagnac, have increased in price, as has almost every quality product, and the sales of other French brandies have correspondingly increased to fill this gap.

Within France, it is common practice to send the surplus grape crop for distillation, often under governmental direction. Even in the cognac and armagnac areas it is not unknown for a little excess production to be sold off as 'grape brandy'. So a third brandy market has developed in many export areas with each importer selling under a brand name. The only indication of origin are the words 'French brandy' on the label, which is embellished with stars, XXXs, and various epithets such as *deluxe*, *supérieur*, even *Napoléon*, to entice the would-be buyer. These brandies are basically designed for mixing, when a quality product is not required, and would be wasted. Some are good, some are indifferent – it depends on the shipper.

The French make *marc* in just about every area where grapes are grown. A distillate of the *pomace* – the residue left after the juice has been pressed from grapes – marc is a powerful drink with a curious leathery taste, and a strong, grapey flavour. The best are Marc de Bourgogne from Burgundy, and Marc de Champagne. At the highest level, the Burgundy marcs are further qualified by area names such as marc de Nuits Georges, Romanée Conti, Chambertin, Musigny, Montrachet and Meursault. The highest quality marc is the Marc de Hospices de Beaune, reserved for and sold exclusively by the organisers of the famous annual charity auction of the same name.

These are the first growth marcs. The *crus bourgeois* are d'Auvergne du Bugey, de Savoie, du Centre-Est, des Coteaux de la Loire, des Côtes du Rhône, de Franche-Comté, de la Marne, d'Aquitaine, du Languedoc and de Provence.

Eaux-de-vie related to marc include eau-de-vie de Lie, a spirit distilled from the lees left in casks used for maturing wine: hence of indifferent quality; eau-de-vie d'Andaye, a form of marc made in the strongly Basque area round Hendaye in the very south of France; and eau-de-vie de Danzig, a liqueur spirit made by a few specialist distillers and

Every last drop of goodness is extracted from the pomace to make marc. Here, Burgundy wine pressings are boiled to produce the base liquid for distillation. Far right, the contents of a travelling still are emptied into a canal.

the French cousin of the better-known Danziger Goldwasser.

In some grape-growing areas of France, local aperitifs are made by fortifying, and sometimes slightly sweetening, young red or white wine. *Ratafia*, originally named after the liqueur which served to conclude the signing, or ratifying, of a treaty of agreement, is one example. The regions of Champagne and Burgundy are the two main producers of this odd drink that can, on occasion, taste of old rubber tyres. In the Cognac area their version is *Pineau de Charente*, both red and white, fortified naturally with cognac. Traditionally served well-chilled before meals, these aperitifs are deceptively powerful.

In other areas, particularly in the central and eastern south, the preprandial drink is likely to be a chilled bottle of lightly fortified sweet white wine, usually made from the muscat grape. Frontignac, Lunel, Rivesaltes and Beames de Venise, all around 15° (lower sherry strength) are the best known.

Although in no way a challenge to the Italians, France does have a considerable vermouth industry. Cinzano, for example, make their dry white from French grapes, and Noilly, made in Marseilles, has long had an upmarket reputation among the dry white vermouths. Noilly have recently dropped the *Prat* from their name in many of their markets.

In the Haut-Savoie in eastern France, particularly fine dry, aromatic vermouths are made by companies such as Dolin and Gaudin. They are collectively known as *chambéry* (white) or *chambéryzette* (pink) after the old Savoy city of Chambéry where the industry began. Mountain herbs are used to give these vermouths their delicious 'outdoor' bouquet and flavour, and the chambéryzette is coloured and enhanced with the juice of wild strawberries.

Dubonnet is something between a true vermouth and a patent aperitif – an aperitif made either from a wine or spirit base to one unchanging recipe. Dubonnet red and Dubonnet blonde (dry white) are usually sold and drunk as vermouth-style drinks. But the comparable French St Raphael (red and white), the dryish white Lillet, the red Byrrh,

even Cap Corse from Corsica, are made in vast quantities and sold in every bar in France in competition with the traditional anis drinks. Even Pernod, one of the two leading anis producers, now produces its own patent aperitif Suze, a rich golden-coloured, gentian-flavoured drink that is either heartily liked or loathed on first taste.

Frenchmen also have a liking for bitter aperitifs which are drunk chilled or mixed with grenadine or cassis. Amer Picon, a proprietary brand, and Toni Kola are typical examples of these.

After brandy in all its forms, the other main spirit of France is rum, or *rhum* as it is spelt there. The French taste for rum comes from its long colonial ties with Haiti, Martinique and elsewhere in the West Indies. It was the French who introduced the pot still to the rum trade and they have had an affection for both the dark and light varieties ever since. Among the many French companies who import and mature rum the two best-known are Bardinet, who sell under the Rhum Negrita labels, and Rhum Saint James.

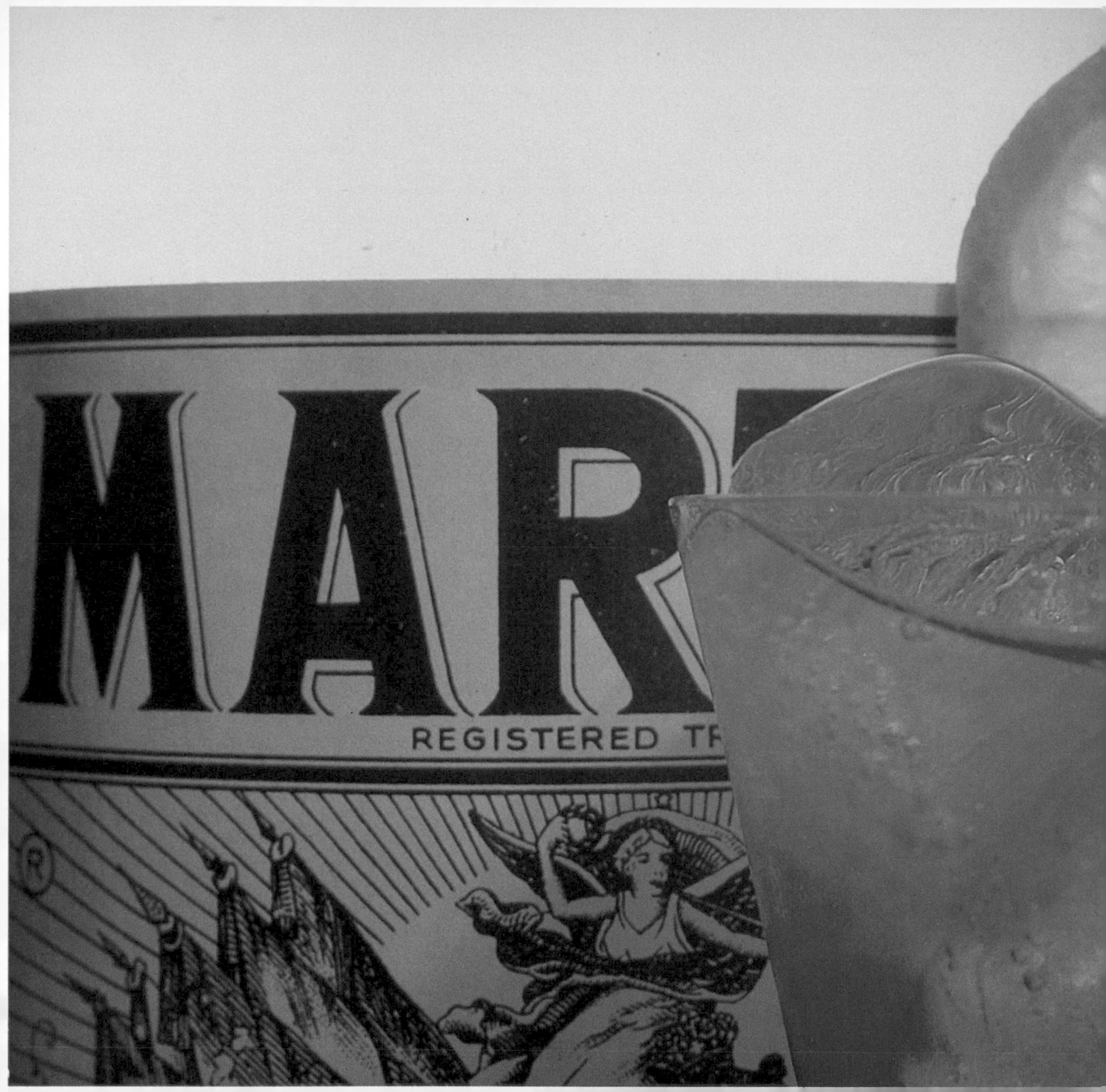
MART
REGISTERED TR

Italy

The world's largest wine producer with a large domestic consumption of wine, Italy also produces numerous liqueurs, bitters and aperitifs, ranging from the exotic and obscure to the internationally known.

Vermouth is perhaps the best known Italian drink. Although 'sweet' vermouths are sometimes referred to as 'Italian' and 'dry' as 'French', both types are produced in France and Italy. Several other aromatic wines drunk as aperitifs are also produced in Italy, notably Campari and Punt e Mes.

Many Italian liqueurs are native only to a particular region – in other parts of the country they may be almost unheard of. However, among the numerous national liqueurs, several have an international audience. Galliano, Strega and Amaretto are examples of these.

Italy produces two distinct styles of brandy. What is officially described as brandy has a sweetness which distinguishes it from a French cognac. Grappa, Italy's other brandy, is similar to a French marc and is also distilled from grape pomace.

Italy/Vermouth and Bitters

AFTER WATER AND WINE, vermouth is probably the third oldest drink in the world. Ancient Palestinian records describe wormwood – its principal flavouring – being added to wine, and Hippocrates mixed various herbs with wine to make a medicine. These, in essence, were early vermouths. The addition of a handful of herbs and a little honey helped to disguise wine that had gone off, or made a harsh wine more palatable.

The name vermouth is derived from the German *wermut*, or the Anglo-Saxon *wermod*, both meaning wormwood – the essential ingredient. Modern patent vermouths, however, originated in the late eighteenth century in northern Italy – an Antonio Carpano of Turin is sometimes credited with introducing them commercially. Most major vermouth producers were founded in the early nineteenth century, some tracing their origins even earlier.

Being a wine-based drink, domestic vermouths have proliferated in most wine producing countries. But it is the Piedmontese countryside around Turin and the alpine areas of France which are the twin centres of vermouth production and of the two countries, Italy is the largest producer.

Modern vermouths are made on a vast scale. The process is complicated but does not require the expertise of, say, a whisky blender or liqueur compounder. It begins with a base white wine of indifferent quality. In Italy it will come from the southern plains, in France from the vineyards of the Midi. When the wine has been chemically approved, it has sugar syrup or *mistelle* (grape juice fortified with brandy) added to it. It may then be processed into three main styles: rosso (sweet red), bianco (sweet

The length and slender breadth of Italy is dotted with liquor-producing villages, towns and regions and the diversity of their output is reflected on the shelves of the local bars and cafés. Among their products are vermouth, hundreds of patent aperitifs, digestif bitters and liqueurs, brandy, grappa and fortified wines.

Although the firm of Martini and Rossi has more than 20 plants in Europe and Latin America, a large part of its output comes from its headquarters at Pessione, near Turin. Like any international drinks company, Martini has to adjust the alcoholic strength of its products slightly to comply with national and state laws. The huge maturation tanks at Pessione are labelled according to the destination of their contents.

Worldwide, Martini and Cinzano are the best-known Italian vermouths, but there are scores of smaller producers. In addition to the standard rosso, bianco and secco styles, a 'rosé' has appeared in recent years.

white) and secco (dry white). All three tend to be sweeter than their French equivalents and have an alcoholic strength similar to sherry (16° to 18°). (French vermouths are almost always drier and more bitter than their Italian counterparts because they use drier base wines and a greater proportion of quinine.)

Roughly fifty herbs and other flavourings go into a vermouth. Their essences are extracted either by steeping in part of the base wine, or by maceration in alcohol or hot water. Of these herbs, wormwood is the principal ingredient, but hyssop, quinine, coriander, juniper, cloves, camomile, orange peel, rose petals, starwort, calamus root, elder flowers, gentian, ginger, allspice, centaury, forget-me-not, blessed thistle, and horehound are among the other herbs and spices used in smallish quantities.

Once the flavours are prepared they are added to the sweetened base wine and the mixture is left to blend in tanks that have special agitators to help the blending. The young vermouth is then pasteurised and refrigerated for about two weeks to separate out the tartrates and other impurities. Finally, it is filtered, bottled and stored for a few months to let it recover from its rigorous treatment before it is ready for drinking.

The white, dry vermouths are the natural colour of the wine. The slightly darker sweet white vermouths are deepened in colour by either allowing the base wine to oxidise slightly before it is used, or by the judicious addition of caramel colouring. The red vermouths get their bright ruby hue from the addition of cochineal colouring. In Italy vermouth is usually drunk neat with ice or with a mixer, such as soda or orange juice. It is not widely thought of as the classic

A label fit for medicine, a bottle shaped like an anarchist's bomb, and a solution to the social problem of over-indulgence, Unicum is a classic among the after-dinner *amaro* (bitters). It is made in Genoa, but originates from the Austro-Hungarian house of Zwack.

FROM THE AROMATIC GARDEN

As evidenced by the sign, Italian herbalists like the one below still serve a public which makes its own aperitifs, digestifs and liqueurs, as well as natural remedies. The ingredients shown here are used in a great many drinks, and typically in aperitifs and vermouths. They are, clockwise from right: wormwood, camomile, gentian flowers and root, quinine and Chinese rhubarb.

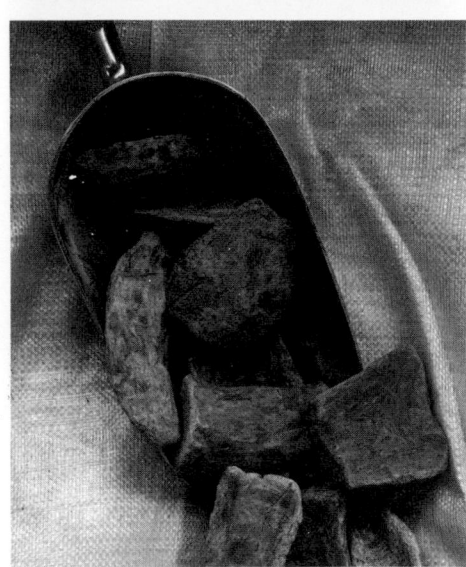

cocktail ingredient – as in the United States and Canada.

The leading vermouth producers are Martini & Rossi, Cinzano, Gancia, Cora, Barbero and Riccadonna. There are also hundreds of other labels used by shippers and retailers in specific markets.

The vermouth companies are noted for their florid labels. Originally these labels were designed not only to sell the product, but also to make it difficult for rivals to copy. This was not always successful. In their wine museum at Pessione, Martini & Rossi have one section devoted to fake labels carrying the Martini & Rossi name. More recently, the trademark laws have been a more effective way of protecting their products.

Bitters and other aperitifs

Two widely-known Italian drinks, both drunk as aperitifs but closer in style to a bitters than a vermouth, are Campari and Punt e Mes. Both are made in Milan, by Davide Campari & Co and Carpano respectively.

Campari is basically a blend of herbs, alcohol and water. It gets its bitter flavour from quinine, and bright pink colour from cochineal. Campari is sold at a strength of around 41.5°, and in Italy is often served

The combination suggested in these two posters, above and right, is one of the world's most famous couplings, but the names don't somehow sound right. The man who brought them together was a New York bartender who devised the classic cocktail. As it happened, he used French vermouth, but his name was Martini – with such luck, what company needs advertisements?

THE NEGRONI COCKTAIL

The Negroni is an example of how an extra ingredient (bitter Campari) added to a basically simple mix (gin and vermouth) can produce a truly classic cocktail.

Place several lumps of ice in a tumbler and add 1 oz dry gin, 1 oz red vermouth and 1 oz Campari. Garnish with a slice of orange and a cocktail cherry, or a twist of orange peel. Add a splash of soda water if desired.

premixed with its traditional accompaniment – soda water – from a dumpy, triangular one-glass bottle.

Punt e Mes, made only by Carpano, is a dark brown, bitter-sweet drink (the bitterness again comes from quinine). It is drunk chilled and mixed, usually with fresh orange juice. Its name comes from an old Milanese stockbroker term 'punt e mes', meaning a 'point and a half', which the patrons of Signor Carpano's bar used to describe how they wanted their drinks mixed.

Other typical Italian aperitifs include Aperol, an orange-coloured and flavoured, mildly alcoholic (6°) mixer; the non-alcoholic Bitter San Pellegrino; Bianco Sarti; and Barolo Chinato, a quinine-flavoured drink made from red Barolo wine.

Bitters have a wide following in Italy that dates back to medieval times when they were considered to have medicinal properties. They are found in two very distinct styles: those with a fruit content used as flavourings, and those based on aromatics. Almost all the popular bitters belong to the second category, and are drunk either with ice and soda as aperitifs, or neat at the end of a meal as digestive aids.

Every Italian bar stocks as many different types of bitters as it does spirits and liqueurs. They are usually a chocolate brown, slightly alcoholic and have an extremely bitter taste (usually derived from quinine extract).

The best-known of the countless varieties produced in Italy are Fernet Branca (the popular hangover cure); Laverna from Sicily; Radis made by Stock; Diesus made by Barbero; Cynar; Chinamartini; and Amaro 18 Isolabella.

A measure of herbs added to a cask of wine produces a vermouth, though it takes time and skill, too. The herb measure and the wine cart are at the Cinzano museum, in Turin. Martini and Rossi also has a museum, nearby at Pessione.

`THE HAIR OF THE DOG´

To the rest of the world, 'Fernet' has something to do with hangover cures and shuderingly-bitter drinks which make the victim feel even worse in order subsequently to feel better. To the Italian drinker, it means a classic bitter which, in the amaro tradition, may be taken on the rocks as an aperitif or, more commonly, neat as a digestif. Fernet is a branded product of the Martini and Rossi company. They claim they were the first to make such a drink for commercial sale, and to use the description Fernet. The rival Fratelli Branca company, of Milan, have their own claims to antiquity, and stress the date at which their liqueur house was founded. Fernet Branca is also made in France, at St Louis, Haut-Rhin (below), and is the better known of the two brands internationally.

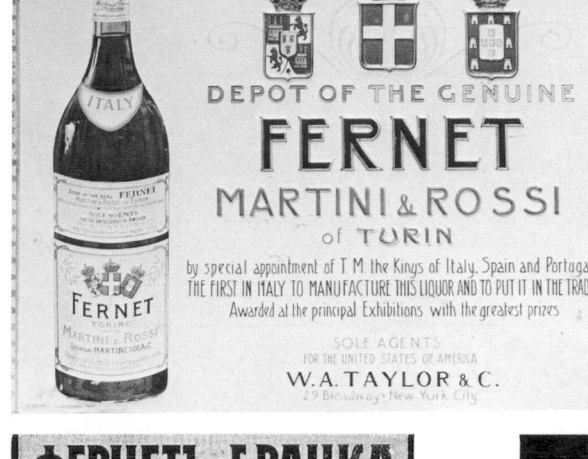

Fernet stakes its claim to originality in an ornate label which quotes the Piedmont Gazette of 1867 on the extraordinary efficacy of this speciality.

Fernet Branca was no doubt helped on the way to a worldwide reputation by some fine and consciously international poster art around the turn of the century. A mint version is also made.

Liqueurs

ITALY PRODUCES A wide variety of liqueurs, including some of the world's finest as well as some of its most bizarre and ornate.

The three best-known Italian liqueurs are Galliano, Amaretto and Strega. Galliano in its tall, fluted bottle carrying a cut-out carbiniari as a back label, is a golden herb liqueur only made by the Distillerie Riunite in Milan. It is a medium sweet vanilla liqueur, rarely drunk neat but is a classic cocktail ingredient, used, for example, in the Harvey Wallbanger.

Strega originates from the city of Benevento, northeast of Naples. Made from seventy different herbs and barks, it is one of Italy's oldest liqueurs and is served neat or over ice cream. Legend has it that this yellow herb liqueur was once made by beautiful maidens disguised as witches, as a magic drink, and that a couple who taste it together will be forever united.

Amaretto di Saronno is also a liqueur with a legend. In 1525 the artist Bernardino Luini of the Leonardo da Vinci school began painting his famous frescos for the sanctuary of Santa Maria delle Grazie in Saronno. While working on the Nativity scene, he used as his model for the Madonna a young widow who ran the inn at which he was staying.

In gratitude the poor widow took apricot seeds and fresh apricots from her garden, infused them in alcohol, and made a special liqueur – Amaretto di Saronno – for the painter. Amaretto di Saronno is made by several companies, of which Illva is the best-known. Rich and sweet, tasting of almonds and apricots, it is often served with amaretti biscuits or used in cooking.

Certosa is named after the monastery of

THE HARVEY WALLBANGER

In the last twenty years the Harvey Wallbanger has become one of the world's best-known cocktails. It is supposedly named after its inventor, a Californian surfer called Harvey, and his staggering wayward walk after drinking one too many.

Place several lumps of ice in a long glass and add 1½ oz vodka and 6 oz fresh orange juice, and stir. Add ½ oz Galliano and allow to diffuse through the drink. Garnish with a slice of orange and a cocktail cherry if desired.

The Madonna in this 16th-century fresco in the hamlet of Saronno was modelled by a young widow, who rewarded the artist with her own liqueur of apricot. Thus was born Amaretto, whose recipe has been handed down to us by generations of Saronno innkeepers.

Certosa di Pavia, near Pavia, the old capital of Lombardy. One of the two great Carthusian monasteries, the other being the Grand Chartreuse at Grenoble, its monks make a liqueur they call *Gra-Car* which closely resembles Chartreuse. The fame of Gra-Car has led commercial distillers to produce a similar liqueur, including a red version, called either *certosa* or *certosino*.

Other Italian liqueurs produced by monasteries include Gemma d'Abeto, Lacrima d'Abeto, Flora di Monteuliveto, Kummel della Val d'Aosta and Liquore Vallombrosa – all of which are hard to find outside their particular regions.

Among the better-known commercially produced liqueurs are Maraschino, a sweet, colourless liqueur made from cherries and their kernels (Drioli, Luxardo, Buton and Magazzin are the biggest producers); Doppo Cedro, a lemon-flavoured liqueur; Rosolio, a delicate liqueur made from red rose petals and orange blossom water; Mentuccia, or Menta, a mint-flavoured liqueur with a startling colour; Aqua d'Oro, a typical Italian fantasy liqueur coloured with powdered gold leaf and similar to the German Goldwasser; Alchermes, a spicy liqueur made from cinnamon, cloves, iris root, nutmeg and other ingredients; Centerbe or Silvestro, said to be made from a hundred herbs, with mint the dominant flavour; the ornate Fior d'Alpi, Alpina or Millefiori, a sweet yellow liqueur made from Alpine flowers and distinguished by the twig in every bottle on which the sugar in the liqueur crystallises – a typically ornate Italian liqueur; Amer Campari, a bitter liqueur and Cordial Campari, a strong and dryish liqueur popular with ice cream; Cerasella, a red cherry liqueur enhanced with digestive herbs – said to be a favourite of the poet d'Annunzio; Aurum, an orange and brandy liqueur made in Pescara; and Anisetta Stellata, an aniseed-flavoured liqueur also made in the city of Pescara.

Various large producers also make versions of such international liqueurs as Triple Sec, Crème de Cacao, Kummel and Mandarin.

Many Italian homes produce their own liqueurs, mainly maraschino or nocino (a nut liqueur from hazelnuts or walnuts). To do this, they simply place some fruit in a glass container with sugar and water, and let it ferment in the sun. They halt the fermentation by adding alcohol and the resulting liqueur is then allowed to mature for anything from three weeks to a year. It sounds simple, but the secret is in the timing.

One peculiarly Italian liqueur, with its sweet crystals, and some domestic liqueurs.

A RIVAL TO SHERRY

Marsala is Italy's best known dessert wine and its only recognised fortified wine. True marsala comes from three delimited areas of Sicily – Trápani, Palermo and Agrigento – and carries the governmental Denominazione di Origine Controllata (the Italian regulatory wine law, similar to the French appellation contrôlée).

Marsala is named after the town of Marsala on the west coast of Sicily. It was first produced by an Englishman, John Woodhouse, in 1773 as a rival to sherry (which it resembles in taste) and port. He formulated the curious process, still used today, of taking the strong (12° alcohol) dry white wine, made from catarratto, grillo and inzolia grapes, and adding it to heated grape must (partly fermented concentrated grape juice) to strengthen the flavour and give the wine a cooked taste. Grape juice fortified with brandy is added to stop the fermentation and leave a natural sweetness. The amount of

fortified juice that is added determines the sweetness of the marsala.

Marsala was popularised by two people: Admiral Nelson, far right, who provisioned the Royal Navy with the wine until 1800, and Garibaldi, near right. The Italian patriot toasted the landing of his 'Thousand' on Sicily in 1860 with marsala, using these words: 'This is a strong and generous wine like the people who produce it, like the men who fight with me for freedom. Here is a wine which will make its name in history.'

Marsala is available in three different qualities. Marsala fine, or IP (Italia Particolare), is the lowest grade. It must have a minimum alcoholic content of 17° and be matured in wood for at least four months.

Marsala superiore, under the labels LP (London Particular), Colli (hill wine), SOM (Superior Old Marsala), OP (Old Particular), GD (Garibaldi Dolce), must have an alcoholic strength of 18° and be aged for at least two years.

The finest quality is Marsala vergine, or virgin. It has to age for a minimum of five years, have an alcoholic content of 18° and be made without the addition of heated must.

A fourth style, Marsala speciali, includes all the flavoured varieties, including all'uovo, made with egg yolks to give a sticky yellow drink which may have developed from zabaglione (the frothy Italian dessert that combines whipped egg and marsala). Almond and orange are two other popular flavoured marsalas.

True marsala is a dark golden brown, rich and syrupy. The fine and superiore styles vary from dry to sweet, but the vergine style is always dry, nutty and rich, like an old oloroso sherry.

Dry marsala is often served chilled in Italy as an aperitif, and all styles make an ideal dessert wine. The vergine is an excellent partner to soups, but any marsala is a traditional part of Italian cooking.

The main producers are Florio, Smith Woodhouse and Ingham (all now part of the Cinzano group), Pellegrino and Rallo.

A DRINK FOR THE WITCHING HOUR

Sambuca is one of Italy's truly national drinks. Usually classed as a liqueur and drunk as such, it nevertheless has a high spirit content, with a strength of 70°, and therefore needs to be treated with respect.

Sambuca is made by the infusion of alcohol with two main herbs both regarded since antiquity as having diuretic and healing properties – witch elderbush (*Sambucus nigra*, hence the name of the drink) and liquorice which gives this liqueur its dominant taste. As such, it is related to the liquorice-flavoured *anis* and *pastis* drinks of France, the *ouzo* of Greece, the *mastika* of the Balkans and the *raki* of Turkey.

It is traditionally drunk neat or added to coffee. But, more spectacularly, it may have four fresh coffee beans floated on its surface and then be set alight. The flames are allowed to toast the coffee beans for two or three minutes to enhance the liquorice flavour.

Italy has hundreds of sambuca producers.

The blue flame after dinner serves not only to excite the attention of impressionable guests or companions, but also to roast the floating coffee beans. What else to do with coffee, and what better way to render doubly delicious the flavour of sambuca? There is even a type of sambuca which has already been flavoured with coffee, known as sambuca negra.

Star aniseed, from China and Vietnam, is an important ingredient of many drinks. Its flavour is more pronounced in the sambuca, ouzo, mastika, and raki category than in the French anis and pastis drinks.

Brandy and Grappa

WHAT IS DESCRIBED as Italian brandy can be either of two quite different drinks. The official *brandy*, subject to strict government controls, or *grappa*, which can be made by anyone with a still.

The Institue Nazionale per la Tutela del Brandy Italiano has set minimum standards for the wine used as the distillate, the distillation itself, and the length of ageing for any product calling itself Italian brandy.

The average annual production of brandy is around 40,000,000 bottles, with the big distillers based in Emilia-Romagna, Veneto and Piedmont. A handful of producers are based in Sicily and Campagnia.

The best Italian brandy is made in pot stills, and aged in Limousin oak for a minimum of two years (but generally this will be four years). It has a warm golden colour and a soft sweetness and lacks the dry, spirity flavour of a good cognac.

The producers distinguish their best brandies with such names as *vecchia*, or *vecchio* (old); *stravecchio; riserva;* and VSOP. The best-known brand is Buton's Vecchia Romagna; other leading producers are Stock (84 and Royal Stock), Carpenè Malvolti, Ramazzotti, Martini & Rossi (Vecchio Piemonte), Landy Freres (Dubac), Distillerie Camel (Fogolar), Fratelli Branca (Stravecchio Branca), Gambarotta (Brandy del Borgogne),

An ornate wooden vessel serves as mixing bowl and drinking cup for a hot Alpine punch of coffee, cognac, grappa and kirsch. During mixing, the vessel is sealed with butter. The end result is a *grolle*, a true restorative.

THE RURAL SPIRIT

Grappa is a coarse, country spirit, made by an unusual and ferocious process. The grape must ferments in a hopper, above left, until it is loaded into sealed containers like giant pressure-cookers, top right, through which steam is forced. The steam is then condensed, its alcoholic content being measured by the instrument shown left. At the appropriate strength, it is run into casks for ageing.

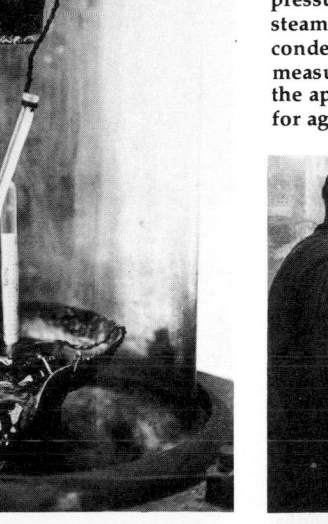

The spent must is dried and used to fuel the boilers which provide the steam. Thus this industry, itself a form of recycling, is efficient and all-consuming to the end.

Apart from its grappa, Italy also produces conventional grape brandies in the same vein as their fancy French cousins. The 15,000-litre vat on the left contains ageing brandy from southern Italian wine. The straw is used to seal cracks in the veteran vat.

'Graspa' is an old Venetian spelling. The delicate china bottle on the right once endowed grappa with a degree of sophistication in a city where nothing less would do. No doubt it contained a smooth and mellow *Vecchia* ('old') grappa.

Rene Briand SpA, Fabbri (Senor Fabbri and Cuvedor Riserva), Florio (VSOP), Schweppes Italia (Cavallino Rosso), Oro Pilla, Brandy Antinori and Contratto.

Grappa is quite different to Italian brandy and is more closely related to the French *marc* and the German *testerbranntwein*. Grappa is made from *pomace*, the compacted mass of grape skins, seeds and stems left in the press when the juice has been extracted (whereas brandy is made from young wine). The pomace is mixed with water and fermented into a rough alcoholic wash, which is distilled in a pot or continuous still.

Grappa is usually colourless, sometimes with a faint greenish hue, with a high strength (60° or more) and a slight grapey taste. It ranges from a very rough spirit, that has seen little or no ageing, to matured, smoother versions. Grappa is usually drunk in the winter months, and is often added to coffee.

As Grappa uses the by-products of wine-making, it is produced almost everywhere in Italy. It is estimated that there are more than 2,000 brands of grappa, many of which are highly regional. The best-known brands are Julia, Branca, Bocchino, Camel, Gravina, Segnana, Nardini, Andrea da Ponte, Langa Antica and Libarna.

In its simplest form, grappa is a very basic spirit, but it is also produced in a bewildering variety of other styles, most of which are highly regional. One of the most unusual is *alla ruta* – a green grappa with alleged medicinal properties from the herb plant in each bottle.

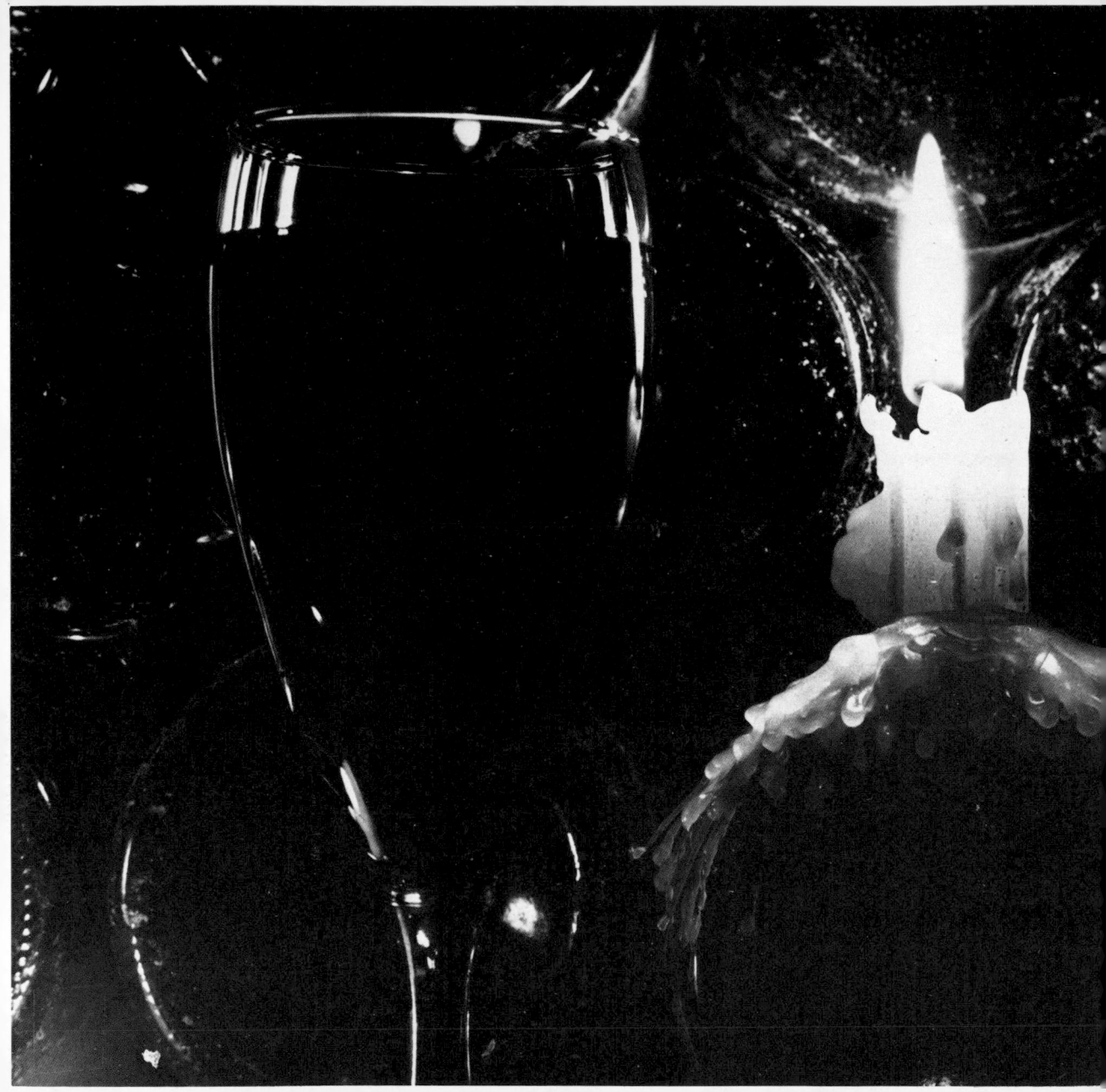

Spain and Portugal

The world's two premier fortified wines – sherry and port – originate from Spain and Portugal respectively. Both drinks are produced in several other countries, ranging from the Soviet Union to South Africa, but the two wines are generally associated with these two nations.

Two other fortified wines also come from this region – madeira and málaga. Two hundred years ago, madeira, from the island of the same name, rivalled sherry and port in popularity, but blight and disease destroyed many of the vines on the island and only now is the drink regaining a market. Málaga was also once very widely drunk, but is now regarded as being over-sweet.

Spain also produces two spirits in significant quantities: a brandy, widely drunk domestically, and a version of French marc called aguardiente.

Spain/Sherry

SHERRY HAS ONLY one serious rival as the world's finest aperitif – champagne. Fortunately they are as alike as chalk and cheese, so both can give equal pleasure.

Sherry's home is Jerez de la Frontera, in the Andalucian south-west of Spain, and it is from this city that the drink gets its English name.

Sherry has long been popular outside Spain. In England it was a favourite drink as early as the sixteenth century, and well known by Shakespeare and his contemporaries. They knew it as *sack* – probably after the Spanish word *secco*, meaning dry. Although one fanciful theory has it that the name came from the volume of sherry flowing into Britain following the Royal Navy's repeated sackings of the southern Spanish ports.

Britain has never lost its taste for sherry, it is the biggest market outside Spain. And many of the biggest producers were founded in the eighteenth and nineteenth centuries by British wine merchants – Harvey, Croft, Cockburn and Sandeman – while others such as Domecq and Gonzalez Byass are part Spanish, part English. A third group, among them Ruiz Mateos (Rumasa), Lustau, Barbadillo, de Misa and Bobadilla are wholly Spanish.

The sherry growing area is a fertile triangle stretching from Jerez to Puerto de Santa Mará to Sanlúcar de Barrameda on the coast. There are three soil types within this triangle – the chalky white *albariza*, the grey, clayey *barro* and the reddish, sandy *arena*. The main vine types – the palomino (accounting for more than 90 percent of all plantings), the

Pedro Ximenez, the mollar and the canacazo – grow in all three soils, but the albariza yields better grapes which produce a racy wine ideal for the elegant dry sherry styles.

Only white grapes are picked for sherry. The harvest starts early in September with the traditional blessing of the first grapes on the steps of the Collegiate Church in the centre of Jerez. When harvested they are crushed in the vineyards. Once this was done by Jerezanos who trod the grapes with iron-shod boots called *zapatos*. Now, more often, a mechanical crusher is used.

The fresh grape juice is poured into oak casks and taken to the *bodegas* (cellars) of the sherry shippers. In the cool, high-roofed bodegas the violent first fermentation starts, which will often shoot wine several feet into the air from the cask hole.

White grapes, mainly the palomino variety, are used to make sherry. These produce the classic sherry styles in the chalky soil of the albariza region. Here the hillsides are dotted with the dazzling white shapes of the vineyard houses.

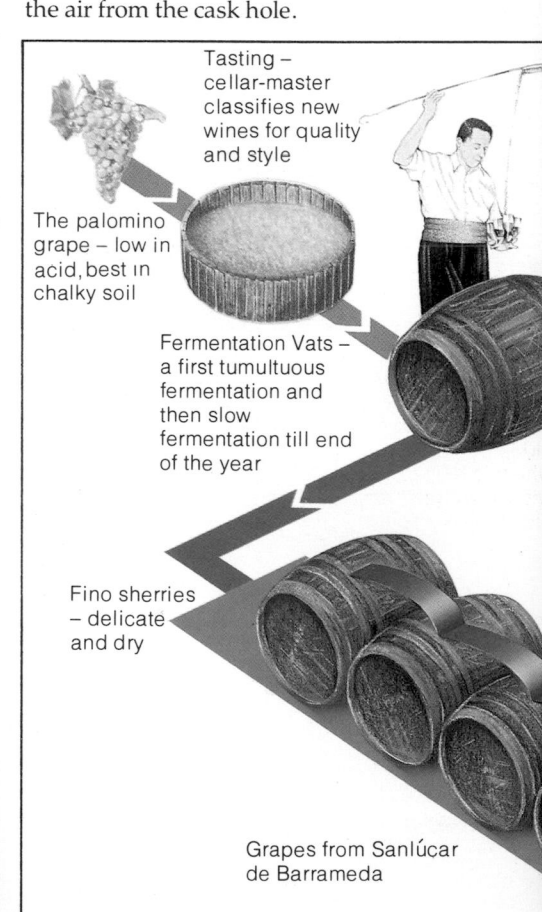

Tasting – cellar-master classifies new wines for quality and style

The palomino grape – low in acid, best in chalky soil

Fermentation Vats – a first tumultuous fermentation and then slow fermentation till end of the year

Fino sherries – delicate and dry

Grapes from Sanlúcar de Barrameda

When the vines are in leaf they make a vivid contrast to the albariza soil. 'Inocente' vineyard owned by Valdespino in the Macharnado area, shown left, is the only vineyard named on a sherry label.

The Englishman's taste for his sack is evident in the works of Shakespeare. Henry IV contains several references to the drink. Falstaff describes it as the source of 'excellent wit'.

SHERRY – THE PRODUCTION PROCESS

The principle of making sherry is very different from other wine-making processes. One grape, the Palomino, provides the two basic sherry types, fino and oloroso; one dry, the other usually sweetened. They are then treated to develop special characteristics and then ageing in the barrel develops a high degree of alcohol. The simplest sherry is the fino, dry and delicate, and mostly preferred by the Spanish: the sweeter sherries were largely developed for the British palate.

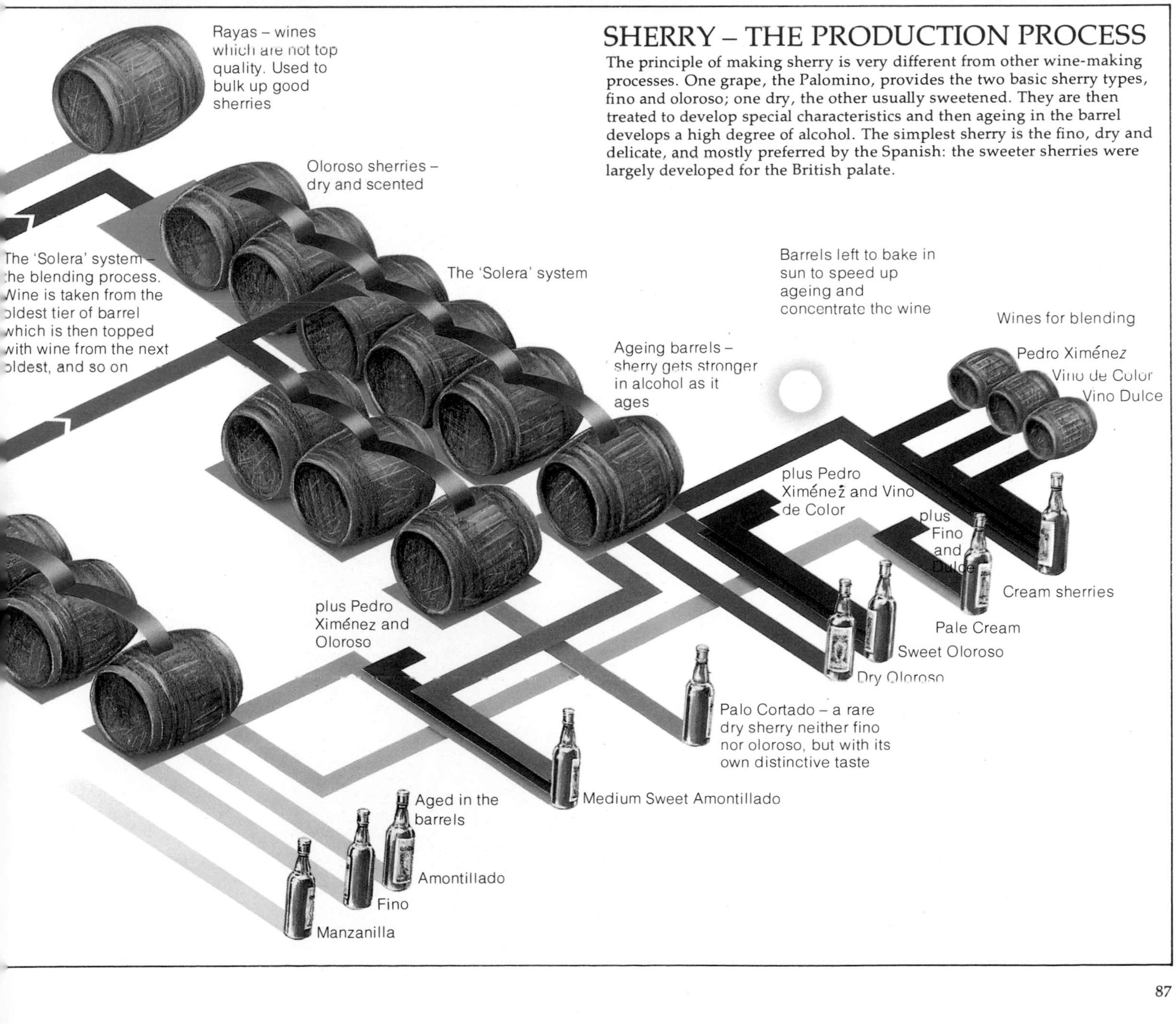

Rayas – wines which are not top quality. Used to bulk up good sherries

Oloroso sherries – dry and scented

The 'Solera' system – the blending process. Wine is taken from the oldest tier of barrel which is then topped with wine from the next oldest, and so on

The 'Solera' system

Barrels left to bake in sun to speed up ageing and concentrate the wine

Ageing barrels – sherry gets stronger in alcohol as it ages

Wines for blending

Pedro Ximénez
Vino de Color
Vino Dulce

plus Pedro Ximénez and Vino de Color

plus Fino and Dulce

plus Pedro Ximénez and Oloroso

Cream sherries

Pale Cream

Sweet Oloroso

Dry Oloroso

Palo Cortado – a rare dry sherry neither fino nor oloroso, but with its own distinctive taste

Medium Sweet Amontillado

Aged in the barrels

Amontillado

Fino

Manzanilla

Then the casks or butts are stacked up to five high, to make a *criadera*, or nursery. The quiet second fermentation begins and the famous sherry *flor*, a special strain of yeast, starts to grow into a thick white mat on top of the wine. Six or seven inches is left at the top of the cask to give the flor room to grow.

The sherry flor is unique to Jerez, although similar strains have been found or developed in the Montilla area around Cordoba, and outside Spain in South Africa, Cyprus, Australia, New Zealand, California and even in France where it produces *vin jaune*, a yellow, sherry-tasting wine, in the Jura area.

The flor converts the fermented wine into sherry, and it is one of the great mysteries of wine that no producer can tell what type of sherry the flor will make until it has started to work. Two casks made from the same grapes picked on the same day in the same vineyard can produce quite different sherries.

The two main sherry styles that have developed from the original sack are the *fino* and *oloroso*. In the spring, when the secondary fermentation is almost finished and the wine is almost completely dry, the thousands of butts of new wine are tasted by the *capataz* of the bodega, and classified into styles. The butts (casks) where the flor is fully developed will give the dry, pungent fino. Where the flor is less developed the likely outcome is an oloroso. The odd cask will be a *palo cortado*, neither one nor the other, and some, where the flor has not quite worked and the sherry resembles a coarse oloroso, will be classified as *rayas*, and left to develop to be used for blending into cheaper sherries.

When each butt is classified (and this will later be confirmed by further tasting) it is sorted with others of its type into the criaderas. In the criadera the sherry matures, taking character from the flor and the wood.

The flor dies twice a year and sinks to the bottom of the cask to form 'the mother of wine' which still imparts character to the sherry, and new flor grows on the surface. With a fino style, the flor is allowed to regenerate continuously, but for an oloroso it is stopped at the time of classification by the addition of a fortifying spirit up to strength, which stops the sherry yeast from growing. A smaller amount of fortifying brandy is added to a fino after fermentation is over.

To achieve the continuity of taste, all sherries are blended using wines of the same style. The process is best described as fractional blending, and is called the *solera* system.

A solera is a system of butts containing varying amounts of sherries that may be anything up to a hundred years old. A small amount of sherry is taken out of each solera three or four times a year for bottling, and the solera is then replenished with a similar, but younger wine. The younger wine takes on the character of the older wines in the solera and becomes a part of it.

Each solera is supported by five or six

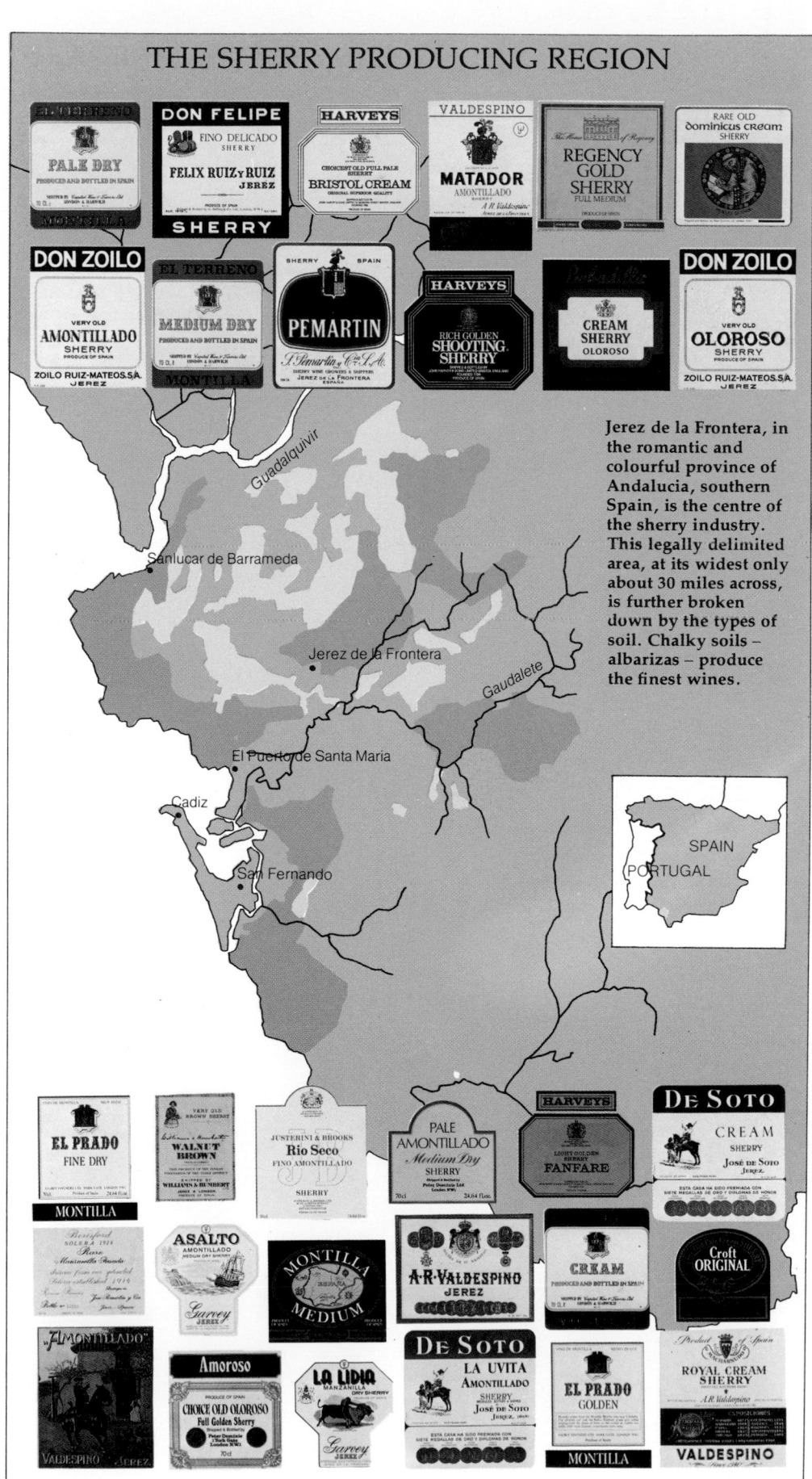

THE SHERRY PRODUCING REGION

Jerez de la Frontera, in the romantic and colourful province of Andalucia, southern Spain, is the centre of the sherry industry. This legally delimited area, at its widest only about 30 miles across, is further broken down by the types of soil. Chalky soils – albarizas – produce the finest wines.

HARVEY'S MERIENDA SHERRY
The Perfect Aperitif
JOHN HARVEY & SONS L.ᵀᴰ BRISTOL. ENG.
WINE MERCHANTS TO H.M. THE KING

In the sherry nurseries, the progress of every cask is checked at least once a year. To do this the bodega master uses a *venecia*, a silver cup with a long, thin whalebone handle. He dips the rod deep into the cask, to penetrate the flor, then withdraws his sample and whips it around his head to clear it before pouring it out.

criaderas. As the finished, mature sherry is drawn from the solera an equal quantity of the next oldest wine is added to acquire the solera character. In turn that is replaced by the next oldest wine and so on, down to the youngest criadera, wine usually only 18 months old.

Within the framework determined by the flor, the sherry maker can control the types of sherry he produces.

If he matures his finos at Sanlúcar he will make a *manzanilla* – the driest of all sherries with a slight saltiness, said to come from the sea breezes that blow through the bodegas.

If the fino is matured at Jerez or Puerto de Santa Mará it stays a fino, slightly fuller than a manzanilla, but still very dry.

If the fino is matured for ten years or so in the solera it takes a pale gold to rich amber colour from the wood, and develops a fuller, nuttier perfume and taste. This style is called *amontillado*.

All three will be 17° to 18° alcohol, although an old amontillado can be more.

Olorosos are darker in colour, almost a nut brown, with a softer perfume and fatter taste.

They usually have a lingering sweetness at the end, and will be between 18° and 24° alcohol, depending on age. An *amoroso* is an oloroso that has been sweetened and darkened with a small amount of thick dark wine made from Pedro Ximénez grapes.

The third main sherry style (apart from finos and olorosos) – the *cream* sherry – is a wholly British invention designed to cater for the British sweet tooth. It is an oloroso, sweetened to make it fuller and richer, and has been popularised as a sherry by Harveys of Bristol, the English sherry company, and copied by others.

Harveys have also led the way in *old landed* sherries – amontillados, Palo Cortados and olorosos that have been shipped to Britain and cellared for many years before bottling.

By a curious contradiction, most sherry producers in Spain call their wines simply 'dry', 'medium' or 'sweet'. But outside that country the traditional names of manzanilla, fino, amontillado and oloroso are universally used to describe the unique influences of the flor, the solera, and the butt, on the taste of the wine.

Brandy

It is not widely known, but Jerez de la Frontera, the sherry capital, produces more brandy than sherry each year. It is only very recently that this has occurred, but with the increasing consumption of brandy, both within Spain and abroad, the gap is likely to widen.

While brandy, or *coñac* as it is known in Spain to the chagrin of the cognac producers of France, is made throughout Spain, the major sherry shippers monopolise the trade in properly made and matured coñac, and account for most of the leading brands. As the main brandy buyers, using it to fortify their sherries, it was only natural that they should begin maturing and reselling the brandy under their own names. Having their own co-operages and supplies of used sherry casks, ideal for maturing brandy (and whisky), further strengthened their grip on the coñac trade.

All the leading sherry shippers now produce one or more brandy brands, following the lead of Francisco O'Neale, then Riva y Rubio in the last century. Domecq, de Misa, Vergara, Gonzalez Byass, Bertemati and others who already had their own distilleries followed, publicising their brands and fostering the market.

The grapes grown around Jerez are too valuable for making wine to distil into coñac, but almost everywhere else in Spain surplus grapes are sent for distillation.

Locally, a rough brandy, sometimes called *coñac corriente*, is often made. Quite crude, it is usually only suitable for fortifying coffee and for strong stomachs on a cold morning. More likely the white wine made from the surplus grapes will be distilled in continuous stills to give *Holandas*, a raw grape spirit of around 65 percent alcohol and with a number of impurities. This distilling is usually done in the same area as the grapes are grown (Castile and Tarragona are two of the main centres) by local distilleries or distilleries owned by the sherry shipper (such as Domecq).

The Holandas is then redistilled to remove as many of the impurities as possible, then brought down to strength with purified water. It is taken to Jerez for the *elaboración* (initial blending) and maturation, in American oak casks already used for maturing sherry. In Jerez, brandy is treated in the same way as sherry. The aged coñac is drawn from the solera for bottling, and the solera is refreshed with younger spirit from a criadera.

The Spaniards, who have quite a high per capita consumption of spirits, with brandy as the most popular, like their coñac sweetened. Many producers will also enhance the rich colour from the wood with a little caramel. The end result is therefore usually a very dark, rich-coloured spirit, thickish and sweet, with an alcoholic content of up to 60 percent. For export, the shippers keep their brandies drier and lighter to meet international tastes.

Some of the best-known brands of brandy are Fundador and Carlos (Domecq), Capa

A PAINSTAKING PRODUCT

The preparation of the herbs for Calisay is one of the most delicate stages in its production. In order to preserve the essences, some are still ground by hand in a pestle and mortar, such as the one shown right, which is over 200 years old. Ageing, sweetening and mixing takes place in oak barrels.

EXQUISITO LICOR
CALISAY
ELABORADO EN ESPAÑA POR
DESTILERIAS MOLLFULLEDA, S.A.
·ARENYS DE MAR·
BARCELONA

Anis drinks, although commonly associated with France, are also popular in Spain where they are drunk as aperitifs with water and ice. Similar, aniseed-flavoured liqueurs are made in Barcelona in sweet and dry varieties, where they would be found on the shelves of most local bars.

Negra (Sandeman), Soberano and Lepanto (Gonzalez Byass), Brandy 103 (Bobadilla), Solera 1900 and Terry 1 (de Terry), Felipe 11 (Augustin Blazquez), Gran Ducque d'Alba (Zoilo), Senor Lustau (Emilio Lustau) and Veterano (Osborne). These coñacs are occasionally called *Jerezanos* or *Jerinacs* to appease the cognac producers, but most Spaniards know them only as coñacs.

Outside Jerez, reputable and good quality brandies are made by Torres near Barcelona, Alvear in Montilla, and Larios at Málaga.

Second only to brandy, the Spaniards drink *aguardiente*. Literally, aguardiente means colourless spirit made from the left-over grape skins, seeds and stalks – a *marc* spirit. But as the Spaniards will often call anything – whether it be distilled from grapes, fruit, even potatoes – an aguardiente, the marc version is called *aguardiente de orujo*.

The Galacians often use aguardiente to make a *queimada* by pouring the spirit into an earthenware bowl, adding roast coffee beans, slices of fresh lemon and maraschino cherries, then setting fire to the spirit to burn off some of the alcohol.

Anis drinks, often called Ojen, are made all over Spain and very occasionally an illegal batch is distilled for private consumption, using wormwood, and this is possibly the nearest drink available to the outlawed French absinthe. Wormwood-free anis drinks, however, often packed in elaborate bottles, are made in every province. Anisado del Mono from Barcelona is highly rated, and the Ricard company also produces and sells

SPIRITS MEET SURREALISM

Spirits may seem to have little in common with surrealism, except perhaps as a source of inspiration, but the eccentric Spanish artist Salvador Dali, below, has produced a number of works for the spirits trade. He designed a bottle, right, for Brande Conde, one of Spain's most renowned brandies. The opaque white container was produced in a limited edition by the ceramist Cumella. Dali has also designed a dark blue bottle for a Spanish vermouth and painted 'The Fishermen' for his friend Paul Ricard.

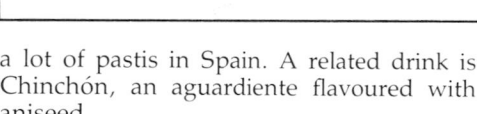

 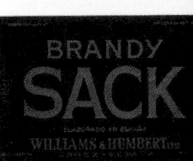

a lot of pastis in Spain. A related drink is Chinchón, an aguardiente flavoured with aniseed.

Quinine-based drinks are popular for their therapeutic and refreshing properties. The best-known is Jerez-quina, a combination of macerated cinchona bark and the bitter skins from Seville oranges blended with white wine or sherry. Calisay, the quinine-based liqueur supposedly first made in Bohemia, is a speciality of the Barcelona area, and is drunk chilled both as an aperitif and an after-dinner drink.

Other typically Spanish liqueurs are Cuarenta y Tres (43) from Diego Zamora of Cartagena, a honey yellow vanilla-flavoured liqueur, and Chartreuse in both the green and yellow versions. From 1903, when the Carthusian Order left France because of anti-clerical sentiments, to 1940 when they returned, their monastery in Tarragona was the sole source of this classic French liqueur, and now it is just as much identified with Spain as France.

Bénédictine, Cointreau and the Marie

Brizzard liqueurs are also produced in Spain under licence and, by avoiding import duties, are much cheaper than in France itself. Banana-flavoured liqueurs are made on the southern mainland using Canary Island bananas, and are sold there and on the islands as a local speciality.

Domestic gins and vodkas, many of them produced by the sherry shippers, are good and inexpensive. Gordons is distilled locally under licence with a director flying out from London to supervise the final proportioning of the ingredients for each distillation cycle. Whisky, too, is made locally.

The Spanish *ponche*, a brandy and herbs blend, is a versatile drink which fills many roles – as an aperitif, as a base for a long drink, to fortify an after-dinner coffee, or, served in a small glass, as a stomach settler. The next morning, it can be drunk as a hang-over cure and is better-tasting than Fernet Branca. The first ponche was made by de Soto, the sherry producers, in 1888, and Ponche 'Soto' is the best known. Their success has spawned a number of rivals.

The numerous varieties of brandy dominate the Spanish drinks cabinet. Also popular is ponche, a brandy-based drink, and anis-flavoured drinks.

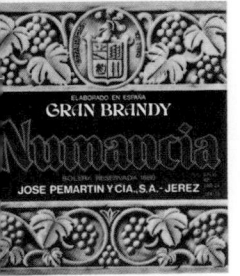

AN ANDALUCIAN SPECIALITY

Sherry aside, Spain produces one other outstanding, and once very popular, fortified wine – málaga. Like sherry, it is an Andalucian speciality, although confined to the area round Málaga on the Costa del Sol, at least four hours drive from Jerez.

The wine for málaga comes from the tiny vineyards in the high hills behind Málaga itself, many lining the road to Granada in the mountains. The wine is either made in the small cellars of the grape growers, or the fruit is taken to the bodegas in Málaga to ferment.

As the fermentation proceeds, color (a concentrate of boiled-down wine) is added to give body and a rich hue, and later the fermentation is stopped with grape brandy to leave a natural sweetness in the wine. It is then put into casks and matured and blended by the same solera system used for sherry, with the young wine taking on the character of the older vintages in the cask.

For the sweeter varieties the grapes are dried in the hot sun for a week, to concentrate their sugar content, before fermentation.

Málagas can vary from very rich, sweet dessert wines down to old, dry, almost burnt-tasting examples that can be served with soup or after dinner – their closest equivalent would be an old oloroso sherry. They were very popular in the last century, when they were often labelled mountain, referring to the geography of the region, but lost popularity in the 1920s and 1930s. Now, fortunately, málaga is starting to find a new audience, and its production is increasing again.

The official Cosejo Regulador that governs málaga production lists 16 different types, varying according to the grape variety and degree of sweetness. Pedro Ximénez and Lairén grapes are used to make sweeter examples such as the white Lágrima, Málaga Golden White, Málaga Negro and Dulce Negro, and Pajarete. Drier versions tend to come from the Jaén grape.

One of the finest málagas is the Scholtz Hermanos Solera 1885, a dry golden wine that keeps for at least three weeks after opening.

Behind these towering hills lie the vineyards that produce málaga. It is only produced around the Costa del Sol area, as indicated on the map below.

Portugal/Port

THE PORTUGUESE OFTEN call port 'the Englishman's wine'. Like sherry, it is a drink created for Englishmen by Englishmen, and if Britain now no longer drinks as much port as some other countries, the port shippers still acknowledge the debt they owe to the British taste for port.

The British first heard about Portuguese wine through the Crusaders who stopped off in northern Portugal en route to the Holy Land. Much later, during the seventeenth and eighteenth centuries, preferential duties on Iberian wines meant that Portuguese and Spanish imports became very popular.

Small doses of brandy had occasionally been added to the young red wine to help it survive the rough journey back to Britain, and elderberry juice to give the wine a richer, darker colour (a practice ended in the nineteenth century). A wine merchant, possibly one of the many who flocked to Portugal from Britain when the boom started, decided to retain some of the sugary richness of the wine by halting the fermentation with brandy. He correctly believed that this sugary version would appeal to the British taste and thereby laid the foundations of what has become one of the world's great fortified wines.

Port's success is particularly remarkable as it comes from vines grown in one of the most inaccessible, unworkable vine growing areas of the world – the upper Douro valley in northern Portugal. From Pêso da Régua, up river for almost 60 miles towards the Spanish border, the Douro twists and turns through valleys that in parts climb almost vertically upwards. In winter the area freezes. In summer it bakes under temperatures of 100°F and more, denied even occasional rain by the Serra de Marão mountains that block the rain-bearing Atlantic winds.

The vines are planted on terraces that date from the seventeenth century when they were hewn out of the granite and slate hills by hand.

The picking starts in late September, and the grapes are carried to the fermenting houses where they are dumped into stone troughs three feet deep, called *lagares*. As part of the port flavour comes from a quick fermentation, the tannin that gives the wine depth and longevity, and the other extracts, have to be gleaned quickly from the grape skins and stalks.

The most effective way, until recently, was crushing by foot. Nowadays the big shippers use closed fermentation tanks, where the carbon dioxide released naturally during fermentation agitates the wine with the skins, to give the rich ruby colour.

When the overseer decides the raw wine in the *lagar*, or tank, has sufficient body and colour, it is run off into long wooden casks, called pipes. It is here that the wine first meets the brandy.

Only top quality Portuguese brandy is used (in 1976 the shippers felt the brandy was not up to standard and forced the government to let them import brandy for mixing). The brandy is already in the pipe in a ratio of five parts wine to one part brandy.

The spirit kills the yeasts that cause the sugar in the wine to ferment, leaving some of this natural sugar that would normally be converted into alcohol, in the wine. Consequently, the vineyard owner can choose to make a sweeter port by adding more brandy. The degree of sweetness is determined by the point at which the wine is added to the brandy, and later in the blending of different pipes.

The young wine and brandy mixture is kept in the upper Douro region over the winter, when the freezing temperatures help

The Upper Douro valley, with its steep rocky terraces, is one of the most inhospitable regions of viniculture in the world. After harvesting and pressing, the wine is mixed with brandy and stored in igloo-like vats to settle. In the spring the young port is taken downstream to the lodges of the big shippers at Vila Nova de Gaia, near Oporto. Traditionally, the wine travelled in the fat *barco rabelos*, boats which could carry up to sixty pipes at a time. Nowadays they have been replaced by road and rail transport.

The prosperity of Oporto was founded in the 18th century after British demand for port had been stimulated by the signing of the Methuen Treaty. This gave preferential treatment to imports of port into Britain and successfully reduced the French wine trade.

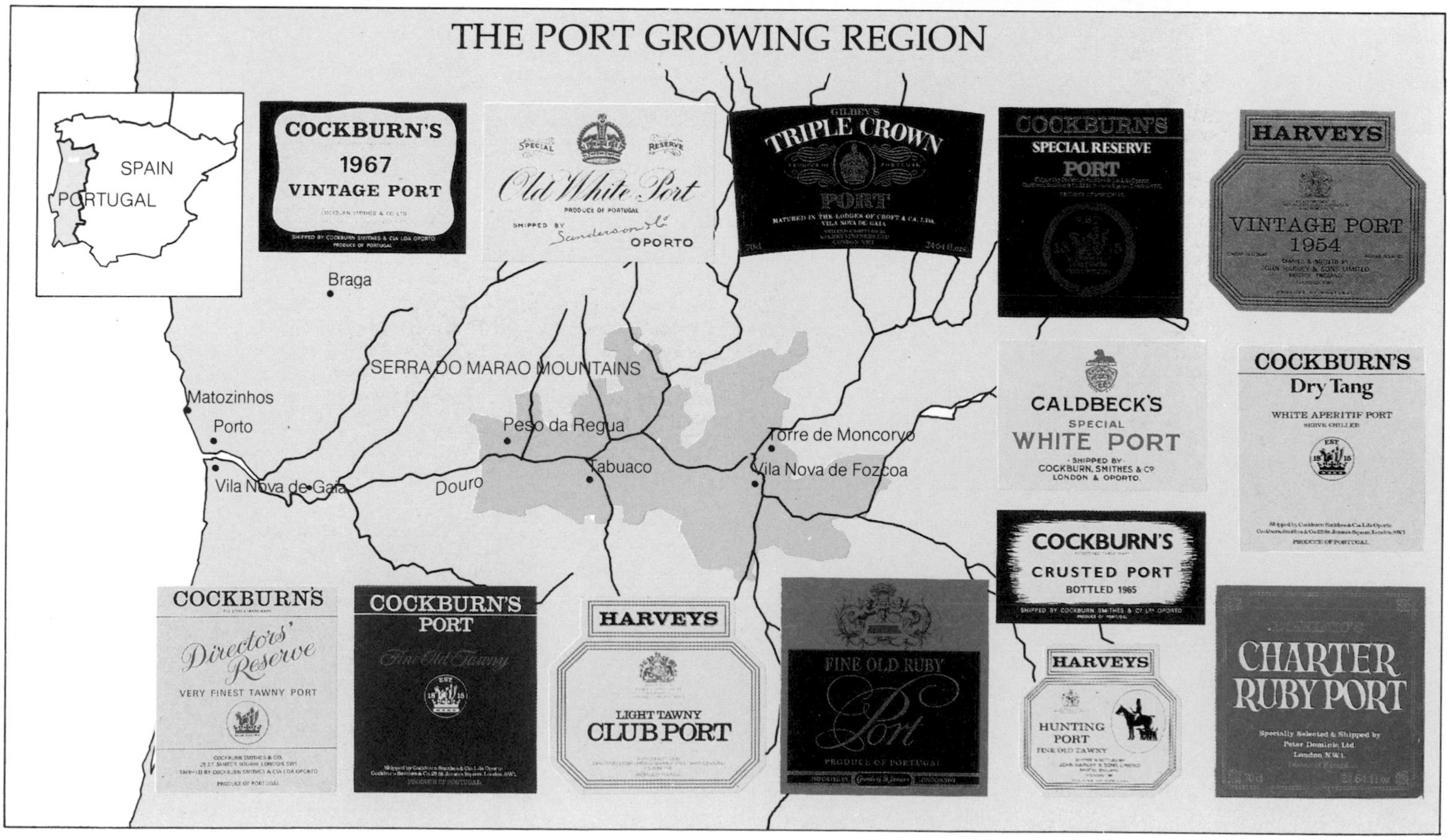

THE PORT GROWING REGION

SPAIN

PORTUGAL

COCKBURN'S 1967 VINTAGE PORT

SPECIAL Old White Port

GILBEY'S TRIPLE CROWN PORT

COCKBURN'S SPECIAL RESERVE PORT

HARVEYS VINTAGE PORT 1954

Braga

SERRA DO MARAO MOUNTAINS

CALDBECK'S SPECIAL WHITE PORT

COCKBURN'S Dry Tang WHITE APERITIF PORT

Matozinhos
Porto

Peso da Regua

Torre de Moncorvo

Vila Nova de Gaia

Tabuaco

Douro

Vila Nova de Fozcoa

COCKBURN'S CRUSTED PORT BOTTLED 1965

COCKBURN'S Directors' Reserve VERY FINEST TAWNY PORT

COCKBURN'S PORT Fine Old Tawny

HARVEYS LIGHT TAWNY CLUB PORT

FINE OLD RUBY Port

HARVEYS HUNTING PORT FINE OLD TAWNY

CHARTER RUBY PORT

the sediments settle out. In the spring, the pipes are taken down river to the shippers' *lodges* (warehouses) at Vila Nova de Gaia. Here the casks are blended and matured for anything from two to fifty years to produce the main port styles.

White port is made by a few shippers, Cockburn and Sandeman the best known, from white grapes. It is drunk lightly chilled by the Portuguese as an aperitif.

Ruby, tawny and vintage are the main red port styles. *Ruby* port is a blend of lesser wines matured in pipes for four to five years. A bright ruby colour, fruity in flavour and sometimes a little sharp, it is ready for drinking when bottled, although it will improve marginally with a year or two more in a cellar.

Tawny port is a blend of finer wines, aged in pipes for anything from five to sixty years, taking on a rich tawny gold hue and velvety consistency as it matures. The shippers signify their best tawny ports by putting 'twenty years old' or 'forty years old' on the label, showing that the youngest wine in the blend is at least that age. This labelling, like all other aspects of port production, is rigorously controlled by the Portuguese government.

Vintage port is the king of ports. Made only when the vintage has been exceptional, it is bottled about two years after the harvest.

Then it spends at least another fifteen years in the bottle, gaining its pungent, raisiny bouquet and rich, dry, spirity flavour. As it grows it throws off a sediment in the bottle. The clear, bright wine should be carefully decanted off this sediment, which can give a bitter taint to the wine.

Since the last war, the declared vintages have been 1945, 1947, 1948, 1950, 1955, 1958, 1960, 1963, 1966, 1967 (by some shippers), 1970 and 1975.

In an excellent year, but one not generally declared as a vintage year, some shippers make a *quinta* wine – a vintage port from a single top quality vineyard. It has all the characteristics of a vintage port but with a slightly burnt taste called the *Douro burn*. The main quinta wines are Quinta da Boa Vista from Offley, Quinta da Roeda from Croft, Quinta de Vargellas from Taylor, Quinta de Malvedos from Graham, Quinta da Foz from Calem and the famous Quinta da Noval of Noval.

To meet the demand for port with a vintage taste, more and more shippers are making *late-bottled vintage* ports. They are ports matured in wood for four to seven years when they throw off their sediment and take a vintage taste, but they are less intense in flavour and lighter than a true vintage port.

HOW TO DECANT PORT

Because of the thick crust thrown off by vintage ports, it is necessary to decant them before serving. Whether you are a traditionalist (and follow all the aspects of the ritual) or not, the aim is the same – to draw off the good wine from its sediment.

Before starting, the bottle should have been standing still for at least 24 hours. The two methods of decanting depend on whether the bottle was stored upright or horizontally. For both you need a clean dry decanter, a funnel (purists specify a special silver decanting funnel), a good light source (again, purists use only candlelight), a corkscrew and a napkin.

If the bottle has been standing upright you will need some clean muslin to line the funnel. Wipe the top of the bottle, then without disturbing the wine, draw the cork. Then clean the neck of the bottle before gently pouring the wine through the muslin-lined funnel into the decanter (1). The light will show you when the sediment has gathered at the shoulder of the bottle and you should stop pouring.

If the bottle has been stored horizontally it should be decanted off the edge of a table and the crust should remain undisturbed. Again, wipe the edge of the bottle before drawing the cork. Have the funnel and decanter ready to catch the wine when the cork is free (2). As the bottle empties tilt it slightly, taking care to leave the dregs and the sediment in the bottle (3). When the port has been decanted, it should be free from any sediment (4).

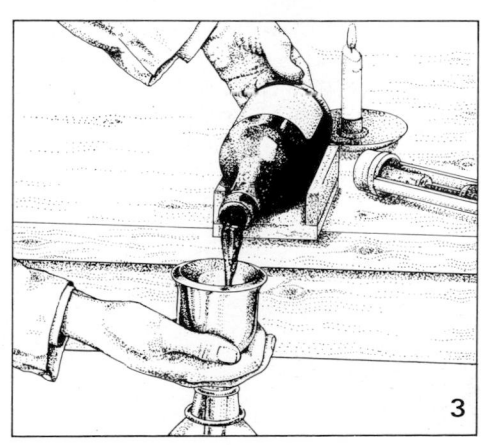
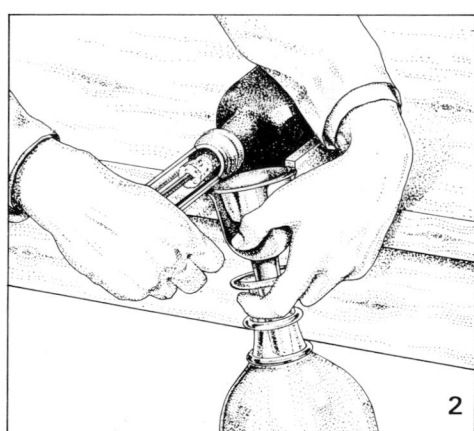

OTHER PORTUGUESE DRINKS

In Portugal, like Spain, single distillation brandies are made by most of the bigger wine makers and some of the port producers. The Portuguese call them aguardentes (a similar-sounding word to the name of the Spanish drink), or sometimes brandys or brandes. The best-known labels are Delaforce Fine Brandy, Ferriera Reserva, Antiqua from Caves Alianca, 5 Estrelas from Kopke, and Espirito from J M Da Fonseca.

The Portugueuse equivalent of the Spanish aguardiente de orujo is bagaceira, again made from the left over grape pressings, water white, and fiery to taste. Very few attain finesse.

The only liqueur of any note is Escarchado, an aniseed-flavoured drink enhanced with sugar crystals. Otherwise, most spirits found in Portugal come from outside the country.

THE BARK WHICH PRESERVES AND MATURES

Portugal is the world's largest producer of cork, which is obtained by gradually stripping the bark off the cork oak tree. Before 1750 most corks were loosely fitted and the wine did not keep. The invention of the bottlescrew, or corkscrew, meant that corks could be tightly fitted and the wine preserved undamaged by contact with oxygen.

A 100-year-old corkscrew including a brush used to clean the neck of the bottle.

Late-bottled will always say so on the label, while vintage port will show the vintage date on the bottle or cork.

The late-bottled style, if matured for only four years, will still throw a slight sediment in the bottle and will have a driven cork. An older, late-bottled will be ready for immediate drinking and is usually sealed with a stopper cork. The former will mature further in bottle, the latter will not.

Wood port is port aged, shipped and sold from the wood – a tawny with a deeper flavour. *Vintage character* port is wine from good years, matured in pipe for four to five years, where it takes on a flavour halfway between a ruby and a vintage port.

Crusted port is a 'non-vintage vintage' port. Treated as a vintage port, it is matured in wood a little longer than a vintage, then only needs seven to ten years in a bottle. Slightly lighter than a vintage, it throws off a heavy crust in the bottle, hence the name, and must be decanted off.

All red ports are served at the end of a dinner with coffee or dessert, and several cheeses can be prepared with port. In some countries, however, notably France, port is drunk as an aperitif. And, if imitation is the sincerest form of flattery, Portugal can take pride in the emulation of its finest drink by winemakers as far apart as California, Australia, South Africa and New Zealand.

Madeira

THE ISLAND OF MADEIRA, home of the fortified wine, is about 36 miles long and 14 miles wide, and stands about 400 miles off the coast of Morocco. Its wine rivalled sherry and port as a fortified wine in the eighteenth and nineteenth centuries but is now not so popular. However it retains one advantage over its rivals – it lives longer than any other wine. Bottles made in the late eighteenth century still appear in the wine auction rooms, as drinkable now as they were 200 years ago.

The Madeira archipelago was known to the ancient Phoenicians, Greeks and Romans, but the main island was not inhabited until it was colonised by Henry the Navigator in 1418 or 1419. Henry encouraged the planting of vines on the island to compete with the Genoan and Venetian merchants. The first vines to be planted were the Italian *malvasia* (originally from Monemvasía on the southern Greek mainland) which became the Madeiran *malmsey*. Later the *boal,* or *bual, cerceal* from the Rhine, which became *sercial, terrantez, listrau, bastardo* were introduced.

Winemaking flourished until the Spanish took the island in 1580 and tried to stop its sweet wines from challenging their own Canary Island wine. Portugal recaptured the island and in 1662 it was part of the dowry of Catherine of Braganza when she married Charles II of England. Three years later Charles decreed that only British ships sailing from British ports could carry European goods to the West Indies and the Americas, thereby reducing European trade with the New World. However, he exempted madeira from this, and as a result it rapidly became the wine of America, particularly in the southern states below the Mason-Dixon line.

British soldiers returning from the Colonies carried the taste for madeira to Britain. Then in 1852 mildew devastated the vines, and twenty years later the vine louse *phylloxera* struck. Madeira supplies vanished, and being unobtainable it lost its popularity, not to show any signs of recovery until the beginning of this century.

The first madeiras were just sweet wines. But in the mid-eighteenth century shippers began to fortify it with brandy to help it survive the long sea voyages. It also took on a new taste after the ships entered tropical climates. The intense heat literally cooked the wine, drying it and adding a rich, slightly burnt taste. As a result the British had their madeira shipped to the Indies and back simply to produce this taste, and the best madeira wine was always in the cask that had 'crossed the Equator twice'.

During the blockades of the Napoleonic wars the practice of shipping the wine died, but madeira was saved by a monk who found a way to duplicate the Equatorial cooking (and hence the taste) by simply leaving the wine in the sun in large glass jars.

The *estufgem* process, as it is called, has now been refined. The grapes are harvested and crushed in *lagares* (in the same way as port). The new wine, or *mosto,* ferments into a white wine called *vinho claro,* which is placed in *pipes* (casks). The brandy is already added in the pipes to stop the fermentation and retain the very high natural sweetness in the grapes for a *bual* or *malmsey* style wine. Or it is added when the fermentation is finished to produce the drier *sercial* and *verdelho* styles.

The pipes are taken to large stores, or *estufas,* which are heated to mature the wine. Over five months the temperature is gradually raised to between 100°F and 104°F and in the six month allowed to fall back to normal – reproducing what would happen to a wine crossing the Equator in a ship's hold.

From the *estufa* the wine goes through an *estagio* where it recovers from the 'shock' of cooking. Then it is blended into *lots* (much the same as a sherry solera), allowed to rest and marry, then blended again into *shipping lots* or *soleras* for export. .

THE FOUR MADEIRAS

There are four distinct types of madeira: sercial, verdelho, bual, and malmsey. All are markedly distinct in colour as well as flavour, although each producer will make his own slightly varying styles. With blends, the dominant wine may sometimes be distinguishable.

Sercial. The driest madeira, pale, sometimes a light gold colour but with a full madeira bouquet. Drunk by the Victorians to cleanse the palate after port, and can be taken as an aperitif.

Verdelho. Fuller, softer, a pale amber colour, aromatic, with a sharp, dry clean finish.

Bual. Medium rich, elegant and fragrant, with a soft sweetness. An after dinner drink.

Malmsey. The original madeira, and the popular Victorian mid-morning drink. Dark russet brown, fragrant, full bodied, luscious and rich but with the slightly burnt after-taste found in all madeiras.

Other types: Rainwater, a pale and light blend, usually of verdelhos. Vintage madeira, not generally made after the phylloxera blight of 1873 but earlier vintages still survive. Dated Solera madeira, introduced after the blight with the solera date indicating the oldest wine in the blend – usually includes more old wine than a solera sherry.

Area names such as Cama de Lobos, St Martin, or Campanario indicate wine from the best areas. 'Fine Rich' and 'Fine Dry' are blends of good wines. Some shippers still use old lot names such as 'London Market', 'London Particular', and 'East India' to denote a superior blend.

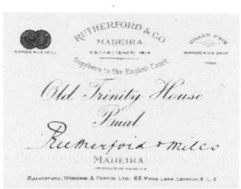

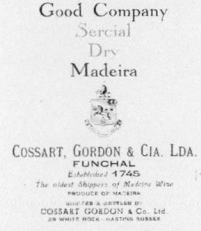

Henry the Navigator is usually credited with discovering and colonising the island of Madeira. It was he who introduced the wine to the steep hillsides of the island, but the wine they produced was not as good as the rich soil promised. It needs careful blending, maturing and the special 'cooking' process to turn it into a truly distinctive wine.

The Mediterranean

AMONG THE DRINKS of the Mediterranean countries, Cyprus sherry is one of the most recent arrivals. Cyprus also produces a brandy, similar in flavour to Greek brandies (that can be flavoured with a liqueur, with resin, or sweetened). Ouzo is a Greek aniseed-flavoured spirit, related to the French anis, which is usually drunk with water as an aperitif.

Cyprus

Cyprus and Greece are two of the oldest wine producing areas in the world. Cyprus has grown vines since Mycenean times, but the flourishing modern Cyprus wine industry is largely a result of the encouragement given in the past 100 years by successive British administrations.

Cyprus sherry is a relatively new drink, really only coming into being in about the last 30 years. The near-perfect growing weather means the grapes (usually *xynisteri*) have a high natural sugar content, and only those used for the very sweet Cyprus cream sherry need have their sugar content further increased by drying before fermentation.

Cyprus sherries are vinified in the normal way, and then chilled to stabilise the wine and throw off the deposits. Then the wine is fortified with domestic brandy and, in the case of an oloroso-style or cream, slightly sweetened with Commanderia, the Cypriot dessert wine.

The wine is matured either by the Spanish solera system, or by the local *mana* system whereby the new wine is married in a cask with some older wine (the mother, or *mana*). The younger wine picks up the characteristics of the older wine and is softened by it.

The main Cyprus sherry producers are SODAP (The Vine Products Co-operative Marketing Union), Keo, Loel, and Etko-Haggipavlu. Keo and SODAP both sell under their own labels, but most of their wine, like the other producers', is shipped and bottled under the importers' brand names. Some of the best-known of these are Emva, Lysander, Kolossi, Mosaic, Monte Cristo and Belvinta.

The main Cypriot wineries also make brandy. Much of this goes into the fortification of Cyprus sherry, but a lot is exported as pure grape spirit to Russia. Apart from the small amount sold for local consumption, a little Cyprus brandy is exported to Britain, Australia and Czechoslovakia.

A speciality unique to Cyprus is the lush dessert wine, Commanderia St John, which reputedly has the oldest tradition of any individually named wine. It was first known as *nama* and references to it can be found in texts written long before the birth of Christ.

The name is derived from the Knights of St John who took over the island in 1191, and then made Commanderia into one of the most important wines in the known world.

Commanderia is traditionally made from a blend of the red *mavron* and white *xynisteri*

grapes of southern Cyprus. The grapes are dried in the sun, which concentrates their sugar content. The juice is pressed and fermented, then goes into large earthenware jars which are sealed with pitch, vine ash and goat hair, buried, and left to mature for many years. The oldest Commanderias have such an intensity that they must be cut with young wine (which does not detract from the flavour) before they can be enjoyed.

The four main Cyprus wine producers now produce their own Commanderias by modern methods, and theirs are the ones commonly sold abroad. Some of the better-known labels include SODAP, Lysander, Saint Barnabas, Keo (who also make a Liqueur de la Commanderia) and Command.

Other high-strength drinks made on the island (invariably by one or more of the four main producers) include ouzo; mastika; vermouth (by Keo, in particular); Filfar, or Pilfar, an orange-based liqueur that resembles curacao; and Keo also produce Spécialité (another curaçao-type liqueur) and apricot and cherry brandies.

Greece

The two main spirits of Greece are brandy (as

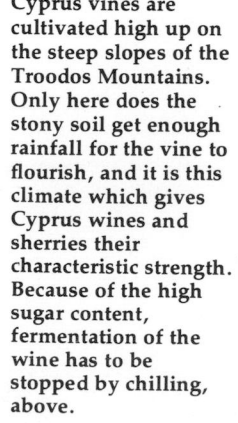

Cyprus vines are cultivated high up on the steep slopes of the Troodos Mountains. Only here does the stony soil get enough rainfall for the vine to flourish, and it is this climate which gives Cyprus wines and sherries their characteristic strength. Because of the high sugar content, fermentation of the wine has to be stopped by chilling, above.

milky white. Metaxa, Achaia Clauss, Cambas and Botrys are the main producers.

Other Greek spirits include *mastika*, or *masticha*, a resinated brandy like the flavoured wine, retsina. The gum mastic usually comes from Khios, famous for its mastika. Some of the main wineries and spirits producers also make vermouth for local consumption, and in the eastern part of Greece there is a limited production of the fiery water-white *arrack*, or *raki*, from wine alcohol macerated with figs.

Corfu makes a speciality liqueur called Kumquat from the miniature Japanese oranges (cumquats), and elsewhere in Greece a liqueur called Kitron is made by distilling lemon tree leaves in grape brandy.

Yugoslavia

Yugoslavia, despite its relatively large wine harvest, makes its national spirit from *sliva* (or *sljiva*) plums. Yugoslavia is the world's second-largest plum producer, so it is not surprising plum spirit has supplanted grape brandy. Commonly called *slivovitz*, it is also known as *slivovica, slivovitza, sljivovica*, or *rakija* in Bosnia and Serbia where it is very popular.

The true slivovitz is made from the violet-blue sliva plums gathered from trees less than twenty years old. The fruit mash, mixed with a proportion of crushed plum kernels to give the final spirit a slight sourness, is fermented in tanks for three months or more. Then the filtered mash is double-distilled to give a clear spirit around 70° proof which goes into oak casks. After a year, further selected plums are added to the spirit to strengthen the taste. The slivovitz is then either left to age or bottled.

Good slivovitz has a pale yellow colour from the oak, indicating a long ageing, but many are colourless. The best known brands are Slovin and Navip. (Juniper berries are

sometimes added to slivovitz at the first distillation to make *klevovka*.)

Maraschino was once made only in Yugoslavia, but nearly all the production has now moved to Italy and only a little is made domestically.

Turkey

Some Turkish wine production is used to make modest quantities of domestic brandy, known as *kanyak*, and as a base for raki.

Raki (also known as arrack, or arraki) is the most common spirit in the Middle East and certain parts of the Far East, such as The Philippines. (The name comes from the arabic word for *juice* or *sweat*.) It is a fiery, rough spirit, often flavoured with anis, and based on alcohol that can come from anything that is abundant locally and can be fermented – grapes, raisins, dates, palm sap, rice or figs.

The liqueurs known outside Turkey are Mersin, a Turkish version of curacao, and Pasha, a liqueur said to have the sweet spicy flavour of Turkish coffee.

Other Mediterranean countries

In Israel, Carmel, the semi-governmental wine producer is the only distiller and makes some local brandy. Sabra, once made from the *sabra* cactus, has, since the 1960s, changed. It is now a combination of chocolate and the essence of Jaffa oranges.

Egypt, Tunisia and Morocco, all Moslem countries, only have a tiny spirits production. Tunisia and Morocco once used to be moderately large spirits producers, making domestic brandies, pastis and fig and date spirits such as raki. Now, like the rest of the Arab world, they are almost completely dry.

The Egyptian Vineyards and Distilleries Co make a range of brandies from the local grapes, and sell them under the brand names Vat 1884, Vieille Recolte Fine and Vat 20.

a long drink or for after dinner) and *ouzo*, the traditional Greek aperitif.

Brandy generally comes from vines grown on the Pelopónnisan peninsula or Sámos. The principal grape used is the *savatiano*, a bigger and sweeter grape than normal brandy grapes. This, in part, accounts for the fatness and thick texture of most Greek brandies. Greek brandies are generally pot stilled, and are left for several years in cask to mellow and take on a rich golden colour.

Metaxa, the most important producer, also add a slight amount of a secret liqueur before maturation to give a distinctive taste to their brandies. They produce a three, five and seven star (the number of stars denoting the minimum age); a dry, almost French-style VSOP, which is only made for export markets; and 40-and 50-year-old labels. The Grande Fine 50-year-old is particularly dry for a Greek brandy.

The other major producers make a similar range of labels, and include Cambas, Lizas Achaia Clauss, Jupiter and Botrys.

Ouzo, a close relative of the French pastis and anis drinks, is made either from unaged grape spirit (brandy) or neutral spirit, flavoured with aniseed. In the bottle it is colourless, but when served in the traditional way over ice with water added, it turns a

THE INTERNATIONAL FAMILY FIRM

Metaxa has been family-run since its foundation by Spyros Metaxa, below, in 1888. Medals and diplomas on its labels and at its Kifissia factory testify to the quality of its products.

Scandinavia

The histories of Denmark,
Norway, Sweden, Finland and
Iceland are so closely linked that
it is natural that they should
share the same national spirit –
aquavit (akvavit in Denmark, also
known as brannvin). It is a
clear grain or potato spirit
usually flavoured in some way,
mainly with caraway seeds.
Each country produces its own
variation of the spirit using
flavourings from anis to
cinnamon, and ranging from
very dry to very sweet.

Aquavit is almost always
drunk ice-cold in one gulp,
often with a beer chaser.
Smorgasbord, the Scandinavian
traditional hors d'oeuvres
consisting of cheeses, cold
pickled meats and fish, is the
ideal partner for aquavit. The
sharp clean taste of the spirit
offsets the oiliness of the food.

In Finland, vodka – 'the spirit
of the white reindeer' – has been
made for centuries. However,
the principal brands are
unflavoured 'Western' vodkas,
unlike those produced just
across the border in Russia,
which are flavoured with a wide
variety of ingredients. Finland
also produces a unique range of
liqueurs from wild Arctic fruits.

Denmark/Akvavit

THE PARTIALITY OF THE DANES for their akvavit is legendary. In a country of just 5,000,000 people, they consume 17,000,000 bottles of akvavit annually. Traditionally drunk with beer, it accounts for over 70 percent of all the spirits sold in the country. At the Danish Distilleries, DDS, the country's main producer, one tank holding the equivalent of 4,000,000 glasses, is not enough to meet the daily national consumption.

Akvavit has been the 'Danish wine' for more than four hundred years. Archaeological evidence shows that distilling had reached Denmark by around 1400, and a method of making a medicinal version of akvavit was published in 1534.

It had become a popular spirit by 1555 when King Christian III commandeered a set of stills from the pawnbrokers to supply his own needs. Christian's son, Frederik II, had a more immoderate taste for akvavit and drank himself to death.

Frederik's son, Christian IV, also proved himself to be a legendary drinker. His entertaining at court served as a model for Shakespeare's chronicles of life at Kronborg castle in *Hamlet*.

When Christian visited his brother-in-law King James I in London in 1606, his drinking sprees became legend. After one night at the Magpie and Stump near the Old Bailey, the tavern renamed itself the King of Denmark in Christian's honour.

However, the Danish king met his match in Scotland when he was defeated in a three-day bout with the Scottish knight Sir Robert Lawrie. The victory so moved the Scottish poet Robert Burns that he wrote *The Whistle* in which he described Lawrie as 'unmatch'd at the bottle, unconquer'd at war'.

Despite his fondness for akvavit, Christian felt it was his duty to exhort his subjects to 'observe moderation, stop serving drink during church hours, the clergy to stop leading their congregations drink in hand, and the regional assemblies to begin work at seven in the morning because later in the day nobody is sober'. Christian also introduced the first akvavit taxes which, in turn, led to a rapid rise in illegal distilling.

The first attempt to curb the illicit spirits trade came in 1843. The government offered the people a moratorium – anyone who surrendered their still would not be punished, and its copper would be paid for. When the time limit ended the authorities had received 11,000 illegal stills.

In the heyday of Danish akvavit, during the last century, there were nearly 2,500 different distilleries, and Aalborg, where the DDS is based, had 100 different distilleries among a population of only 5,000 and was recognised as the akvavit capital. Later, through the DDS monopoly, the name *aalborg* became synonymous with *akvavit*. *Snaps*, or *schnapps*, are two other frequently-used synonyms.

In 1917 further stringent taxes reduced akvavit consumption and put out of business all but one of the distilleries. The only survivor was *De Danske Spritfabrikker* – the Danish Distilleries – who were given a monopoly over akvavit production in return for taking over their competitors. The DDS held this monopoly until January 1, 1973, when Denmark joined the European Economic Community and under its laws was required to allow other distillers to produce akvavit.

A few distillers have entered the market,

That 'Father's dram' in the 19th-century oil painting, far right, would have been akvavit without question. It has been the national drink in Denmark for over 400 years. One of the early distilleries from Aalborg, then as now the centre of akvavit production, is preserved at the Old Town Museum at Aarhus.

but the DDS retains more than 90 percent of domestic akvavit sales, and almost total control over exports.

Like most other *aqua vitaes*, Danish akvavit was first made from imported grains. But, by the early eighteenth century, the potato had been introduced into Denmark; its cultivation was encouraged by the government through its grants of potato-growing concessions to the French Huguenot refugees. As a result, the distillers switched from grain to potatoes.

De Danske Spritfabrikker now use potatoes from the start of the harvest, at the end of September, until April, and then switch to grain when the crop is finished. They use around 18,000 tons of potatoes each year, and estimate that 6 lbs are required to produce every standard size bottle of akvavit.

The mash, using potatoes or grain (potatoes are first steam-cooked), is fermented with yeast to turn the natural sugar into alcohol. The resulting wash is then double-distilled to remove any residual potato flavour and give a pure, high-strength spirit to which the different flavours are then added.

Denmark, unlike Norway or Finland, mainly produces flavoured akvavits, although the flavouring does not detract from their characteristic dryness. The Danish Distilleries add a variety of flavours by infusion to produce their different styles; their two best-known akvavits are based on caraway and dill and in June the fields around their distillery are carpeted with the pinky-white caraway and yellow dill plants.

Aalborg Taffel Akvavit, the best-known brand in Denmark and abroad, is a caraway-flavoured akvavit. The caraway extract is made in a pot still and infused into the spirit

Akvavit is distilled from potatoes or grain in continuous stills, right. In Denmark, the highly rectified spirit is usually flavoured in some way, mostly with caraway seeds. Akvavit accounts for around 70 percent of the spirits sold in Denmark, and of these sales, the distinctive Maltese Cross of the DDS is on about 90 percent of the bottles.

HOW TO DRINK AKVAVIT

The Danes traditionally drink akvavit from small, one-ounce glasses which should come straight from the freezer.

Akvavit is served neat, usually with food and an accompanying glass of ice cold lager to chase it down – skaling, the Danes call it.

It will be served throughout a meal, particularly with Danish smörgåsbord. The host may simply switch to another variety to serve with coffee. It can even be used to make a Scandinavian Irish coffee. The old way was to place a silver coin in the bottom of the cup, pour in coffee until the coin could no longer be seen, and then add enough akvavit until the coin was visible again.

to give a distinct flavour, although the akvavit remains colourless. The strength is 79° – about standard for a good-quality akvavit.

The oldest akvavit brand is Aalborg Taffel, first made in 1846. The slightly yellow, dill-flavoured Jubileums is the youngest. It was created in 1946 to celebrate the first hundred years of Taffel. The dill gives it an aniseedy aroma and, to a lesser extent, taste.

The other De Danske Spritfabrikker labels are Brondums Snaps (a lower-strength caraway-flavoured akvavit) and Brondums Kummenakvavit (flavoured with caraway and cinnamon). Both of these are named after a former Copenhagen akvavit distiller.

Harald Jensen Akvavit (very similar to Taffel) is named after an Aalborg distiller and arts patron of the turn of the century. Aalborg Fuselfri Akvavit is another slightly lower-strength caraway-flavoured brand, whose name dates from the 1860s when distillers found a way to remove the bad smelling fusels from their spirits.

Aalborg Esksport Akvavit (not widely exported despite the name) has a slight yellowness and burnt taste from the addition of a little madeira. Aalborg Porse Snaps (flavoured with bog myrtle) and Aalborg Akeleje Snaps (flavoured with herbs) are both sold in small amounts at 75° proof.

When De Danske Spritfabrikker lost their monopoly position in 1973 several rival brands began to appear. But so far none have made significant inroads into DDS sales. These new brands include Christianshavner Akvavit from Peter Heering; Fattigmands Snaps; Daglig Snaps and Gammelholm Snaps. They have been joined by several alcoholic bitters, among them Gammel Dansk, and Krabask Bitters.

THE SIGN OF THE MALTESE CROSS

The Maltese Cross on every Danish Distilleries akvavit label was introduced as a trademark by the Danish banker and industrialist C F Tietgen, one of the founders of the Danish Distilleries.

When the DDS was founded in 1881, Tietgen owned the Grimsby-based shipping company DFDS, who plied the route between Harwich and Esbjerg. One of the ships on this route was the S S Hengest on whose funnel was a Maltese Cross – the insignia of the original Grimsby company. Tietgen took a liking to this mark and passed it on to The Danish Distilleries when they were founded.

Peter Heering

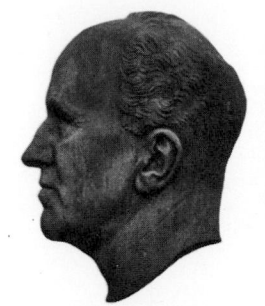

DANISH LIQUEURS ARE SYNONYMOUS with Cherry Heering. Created in 1818 by the original Peter F Heering, it is the national liqueur and the only variety that is well known outside their country.

Peter Frederik Suhm Heering was one of four children of a Roskilde tax collector. At the age of 14 he was apprenticed to a Copenhagen grocer, and it is believed to be the grocer's wife who gave Peter her family recipe for cherry brandy.

On December 1, 1818, when he was 26 years old, Peter Heering opened his own grocery shop in a cellar on Christianshavn Island in the centre of Copenhagen, selling as one of his lines his own Cherry Heering liqueur.

Among his customers were naval officers and seamen, and through them Cherry Heering spread outside Denmark. In 1833 Peter Heering built his first ship to capitalise on his export potential, and in 1838 bought a stately house on Christianshavn's Canal, which became the family home and was the company headquarters until the early 1970s.

The company expanded into shipping, trading and merchandising the Heering Liqueur, and until the commerical slump of the late 1850s it prospered. But with the decline in trade, the family concentrated on the making and selling of Cherry Heering.

The company is still run by the Heering family today, but Cherry Heering is now made at Dalby, about 40 miles south of Copenhagen.

The freshly gathered cherries are crushed along with a percentage of the cherry stones, to give a dry flavour to the liqueur. The extract is then distilled with neutral spirit and matured in wood casks. The original 3,000-gallon oak casks, carved and decorated with mythological beasts, are still used to mature a small part of the total production. Finally the liqueur is reduced to market strength, usually 43° proof.

Cherry Herring has now been renamed Peter Heering liqueur in nearly all markets (Britain still uses the Cherry Heering label), and most of the company's activities are centred at Dalby. The old family house on Christianshavn's Canal is now a museum of the Heering family and company.

Two other liqueurs are produced by Peter Heering, Cumin Liquidum Optimum Castelli, which translates as 'the best caraway liqueur in the castle', and San Michele. Commonly called CLOC, Castelli is a water-white caraway-flavoured liqueur of the kummel style which sells at 55° proof. San Michele, made from tangerine peel, is a Danish relative of curaçao.

Peter Heering also have the European licence for the manufacture of Kahlua, the Mexican coffee liqueur that is slightly fuller and sweeter than Tia Maria, its main rival.

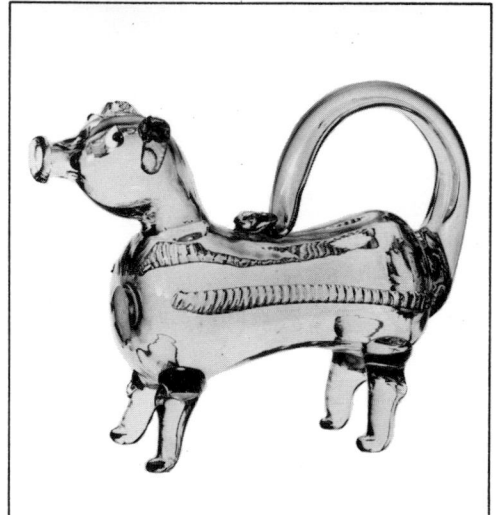

From his early headquarters on Christianshavn's Canal in Copenhagen, left, Peter Heering, top, built up the international fame of his Cherry Heering liqueur. Today the old head office is a museum containing a unique collection of glassware related to spirits. The glass dog, above, is an early 19th-century schnapps flask. Peter Heering is now based outside Copenhagen at Dalby.

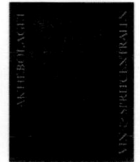

Sweden/Brannvin

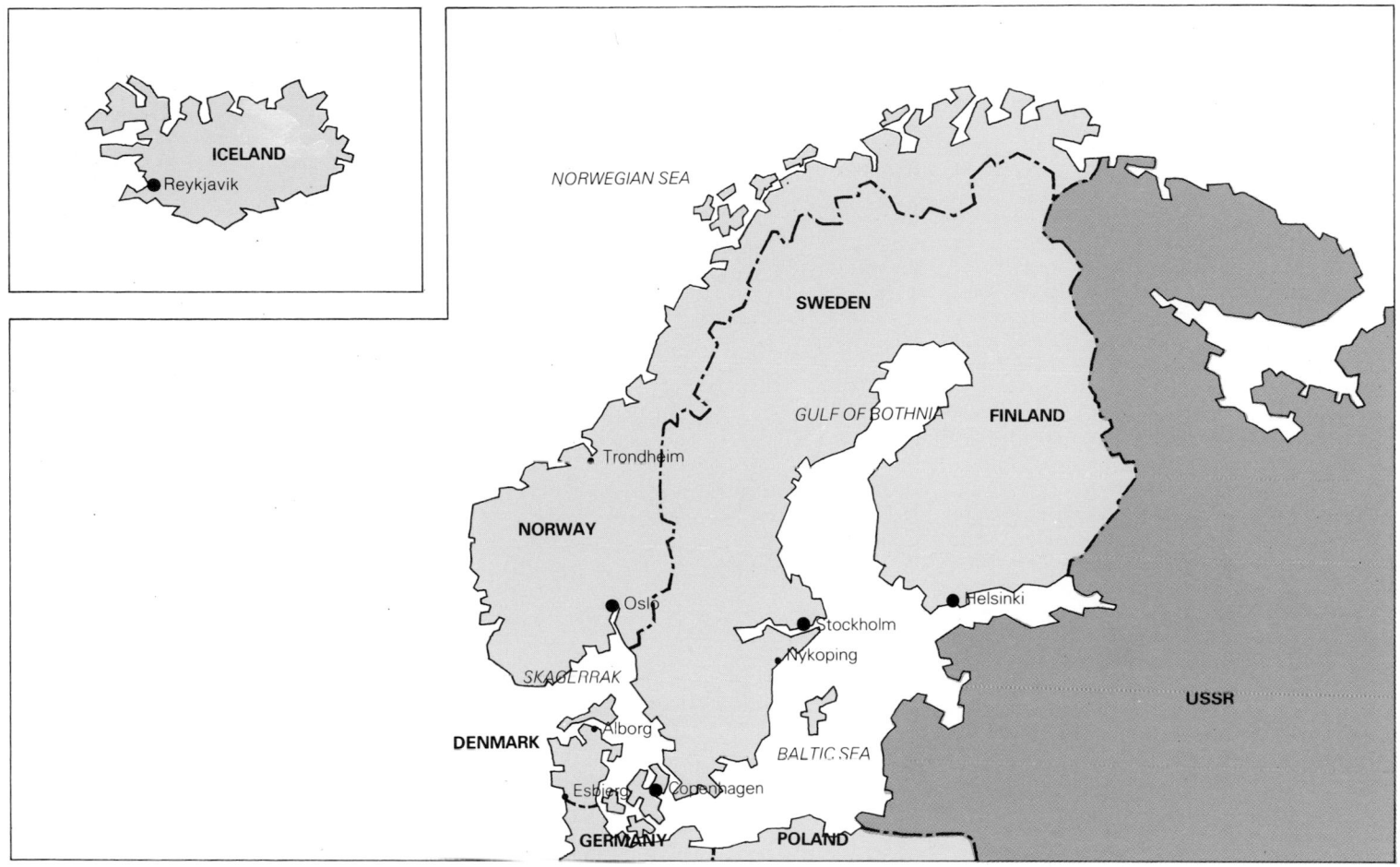

IN SWEDEN, FINLAND, NORWAY AND ICELAND the manufacture and sale of spirits is rigidly controlled. People are actively discouraged from drinking spirits by high prices and restricted supplies controlled by the national spirits monopoly. Norway has already banned spirits advertising, and both Finland and Sweden have similar legislation in hand.

Despite this, Sweden produces more akvavit for domestic consumption than Denmark itself, the Finns are widely known as heavy spirits drinkers, and in Norway so much activated yeast is sold that illegal distilling appears to be widespread.

In all four countries the favourite domestic spirit is *brannvin*, a clear spirit which may also be called akvavit, aquavit, or vödka, depending on the country and the style.

Brannvin has been known in Sweden since the fourteenth century, and has been its national drink since the following century. The first brannvin was an early form of brandy, made from distilled, imported grape juice or wine. (The name brannvin means literally 'burnt', or distilled wine.) It was first manufactured in Sweden for use in the making of gunpowder, but very soon legislation was necessary to ensure brannvin was used only for this purpose.

In the sixteenth century brannvin took on a new role, as a medicine – one contemporary manuscript cited brannvin as a cure for 40 separate diseases. Later, in 1723, it was described in the Swedish Parliament as the 'only medicament for the conservation of health' for farmers and peasants.

By this time brannvin had switched from a grape to a grain-based spirit, and its distillation was widespread. So much so that alcoholism was an acknowledged problem. Servants were often paid in brannvin, it was sold from booths outside churches, and the army was given a regular ration when it took to the field of battle.

By the eighteenth century one source estimated that there were 180,000 pot stills in Sweden, making brannvin for 'household requirements'. In an attempt to eradicate private distilling, distillation briefly became a Crown monopoly in the 1780s, with all production the prerogative of 60 Crown-owned distilleries. But by 1855, when brannvin once again became a state monopoly, the number of stills in Sweden had risen again to 152,273.

In 1911 this number had dwindled to about 100 official distilleries, and in 1917 the State Monopoly was formed to compromise with a strong temperance movement. Since the early 1970s all production has centred on one modern state-owned distillery at Stockholm, said to be the largest in western Europe. This plant supplies all of the spirits for Sweden, apart from imported brands. All, that is, except the estimated 11,000,000 litres of illegal spirit made in Sweden each year.

The best illegal Swedish brannvins are almost as good as the State's brands. Many amateur distillers leave the fusel oils in their spirit to give it extra flavour and pungency. But the State monopoly eliminates them by charcoal filtering which, they say, gives their spirits more aroma and a better taste.

The Aktiebolaget Vin & Spritcentralem, the State monopoly, makes 19 different types of brannvin. Five are plain, unflavoured spirits ranging in strength from 60° to 70° proof. The rest, usually between 70° and 87° proof, are flavoured with ingredients such as caraway, aniseed, fennel and bitter orange. Most are made from potatoes, a few from grain, by the continuous still process.

The two most important brannvin brands are Explorer and Renat, both unflavoured, which between them account for well over a third of the Vin & Spritcentralem's annual output of about 61,000,000 litres.

Most flavoured styles originate from traditional regional recipes, and they range from the very dry to the cloyingly sweet. Skane aquavit, flavoured with caraway, aniseed, fennel and other herbs, is a particularly dry brannvin. By contrast, Nyköping brannvin, using the same herbs, is particularly sweet.

Other flavours include Baska Dropper ('bitter drops') which is flavoured with an infusion of wormwood. It is the drink traditionally served with the Swedish speciality *surströmming* – fermented Baltic herrings which can release enough gas to explode their cans. Svart-Vinbärs brannvin is flavoured with blackcurrants and is used to make kir. Herrgards aquavit gets its flavour from sherry, whisky and caraway and its period of maturation in used sherry casks. O P Anderson aquavit is yellowish and flavoured with aniseed and fennel. Ahus Taffel aquavit is caraway-flavoured; Porsbrannvin is flavoured with the Lapland herb, bog myrtle. About five percent of Angostura brannvin is the famous bitters; Odakra Taffel aquavit includes coriander, caraway and fennel as its main herbs.

The Swedes drink brannvin ice-cold (usually with beer-chasers) with food – often thin crispbread spread with hard, acidulous cheese. It goes best with spicy, pickled, or salty food, all usually found in the typical Scandinavian smörgåsbord. Brannvin is also drunk with traditional dishes such as lobster cooked with dill, dill-cured salmon and pickled herrings, salted charcuterie and flambé calf's kidney with caraway.

Like the Danes, the Swedes have their own version of Irish coffee. A silver 10 ore piece is placed in the bottom of the cup and coffee added until the coin is no longer visible. Then plain brannvin is added until the coin is again visible. (Sometimes the brannvin is floated on the coffee with a spoon, and the coffee drunk through the spirit.)

One speciality made by the monopoly is a sweet, highly aromatic Swedish punch, based on arrack or rum, and first introduced by merchants trading with the East Indies in the eighteenth century. The arrack, imported at around 22° overproof, is diluted with water and blended with plain brannvin. The blend is mixed with syrup and continuously stirred for several months. Several wines are added, and the final mixture is aged in oak casks for about 6 months.

The Swedes drink this punch either cold, as a liqueur, or hot (like a true punch) with the typical Swedish dish of pea soup and diced pork fat.

There are four labels all 55.5° proof – Platin Extra Fin, Extra Gammal, Cederlunds Torr Caloric and Carlshamna.

The monopoly also makes about eighteen different liqueurs. Several of these are domestic versions of international brands. Kaptenlojtnant is a blend of Bénédictine and grape brandy. Liqueur de Château supposedly contains a small amount of the elixir made by Chartreuse at Grenoble. Tartan Nectar is a whisky-flavoured liqueur with herbs in the Drambuie style. Royal Triple Sec is a white curaçao. Anisette Classique is a domestic anisette.

Several Swedish liqueurs are based on fruit and berry flavours. Again these are generally well-known international styles, including Cherry Brandy, Crème de Bananes, Crème de Cassis and Crème de Menthe.

Illegal distilling is common in all Scandinavian countries. Home stills are used to produce a form of aquavit, also called akvavit and brannvin. Generally these home brews include much of the natural flavourings (congeners) but they may be flavoured, usually with caraway seeds, below.

Finland

In Finland all domestic spirits production, all wine and spirits imports, and all retailing is in the hands of the Oy Alko Ab, the Finnish State monopoly. However, a handful of independent companies are allowed to make liqueurs, fruit wines, beer and bitters.

The Oy Alko Ab has three modern distilling plants, at Salmivaara, Rajamaki and Koskenkorva. All three are geared to the production of vodka which is rapidly becoming one of Finland's major exports. The principal brand is Finlandia, a very pure vodka (of the Western rather than Eastern style) which is exported in a distinctive 'ripple glass' bottle that gives the clear spirit a frosted appearance. Finlandia is widely exported and the volume of production is now said to be coming close to Russia's. Koskenkorva is the second main Finnish brand.

Among the private companies, the most distinctive and popular products are their liqueurs made from wild berries. Because of the harshness of the Finnish climate their production is relatively small.

Chymos, a private company, makes a range of fruit liqueurs including the Polar cranberry, Lakka cloudberry (from cloud-berries grown in the Arctic North), and Villman raspberry flavours.

Lignell & Piispanen specialises in these wild berry liqueurs. Its range includes Karpi (from cranberries grown in the Finnish marshes), Suomurrain (their version of the bitter-sweet cloudberry liqueur), Mesimarja (made from the Arctic bramble) which is also called 'The Red Pearl of the North' and Tapio, a herb and juniper-flavoured liqueur.

A third company, Oy Suomen Marjat Ab, makes, among others, a buckthorn berry liqueur from wild berries picked on the Finnish islands. Even the Finns consider this liqueur, sold under the Tyrni brand, a speciality among specialities.

One final company, Marli, although specialising in cider, also makes several liqueurs including a cloudberry style, plus Champion bitters and Marinella fruit bitters.

Iceland

Iceland also has its own State liquor monopoly. Its main product is an aquavit which sells under the charming name of Black Death. Usually referred to as a brannvin by the locals, it accounts for much of the domestic spirits market.

Norway/Aquavit

Norway

Norway, usually thought of as a beer-drinking nation, has a healthy spirits side that is similar to Sweden's. In Norway spirits did not become popular until the early seventeenth century, but then they became part of each household. Except for the years between 1756 and 1816, each family could have its own still. (In 1830 the number of family stills was estimated at about 11,000.)

In 1845 a law transferred distilling into commercial hands, and gradually the industry developed into two large companies: Løiten Braenderis-Destillation of Kristiania and Jørgen B Lysholm of Trondheim. In 1927, faced with growing alcoholism and in increasing lobby against the production and sale of alcohol, the government took these two remaining distilleries under the control of the State wines and spirits monopoly, A/S Vinmonopolet.

The Vinmonopolet now makes a number of aquavits, flavoured and unflavoured, to sell under the Løiten (the stronger version) or Lysholm brand names. The most famous of their brands is Linie Aquavit, a pale yellow aquavit that has 'crossed the line' – the Equator – a legacy from the days it was put on board for passengers and crews of the sailing ships. The Vinmonopolet upholds this tradition by shipping the spirit in casks to Australia and back on board the Wilhelmsen cargo ships. Each cask crosses the line twice, and the Vinmonopolet labels each bottle with the name of the ship and the time of the voyage.

The fluctuations in temperature, the motion of the ship, and the influence of the salty air combine to give Linie Aquavit a softness not found in most other aquavits and brannvins. Certainly it is not found in the illegal, domestically-made aquavits which the Norwegians produce in abundance and descriptively refer to as homeburn.

Most liqueurs are imported into Norway, but one domestic speciality is the golden St Hallvard, an infusion of herbs and botanicals into neutral spirit.

The sailing ships which originally carried Linie Aquavit across the Equator may have disappeared, but this unusual method of maturing the spirit has not ended. Today, every Wilhelmsen liner sailing to Australia carries several oak casks of part-matured aquavit on the round trip.

The Netherlands and Belgium

The greatest influence of the Dutch on the world of spirits and liqueurs has been more as explorers and merchants, carriers of ideas, rather than as producers. Dutch genever, or Hollands, is by far the most important domestic spirit. Although this was the original style of gin, the English, or London Dry, style has since outstripped it in popularity internationally, and genever is rarely found outside The Netherlands.

The misleadingly named *brandewijn* ('brandy wine') is distilled from grain. The Dutch drink this neat, but it is also sold in fruit flavours and is sometimes used as a base for traditional Dutch liqueurs. The Dutch also produce a variety of liqueurs, notably curaçaos and advocaats.

The Belgian's taste for beer overshadows their wine and spirits consumption, and of the wine and spirits sold domestically, most are imported.

The Netherlands/Genever

THE DUTCH INVENTED GIN. The term itself is an English corruption of the Dutch name *genever*, and the internationally-known London Dry gins have evolved from the original *Hollands* or *Schiedam* gins.

A good genever gin has its own distinctive flavour. It has an easily noticeable aroma and a fuller and fatter taste, an intensity and thickness not found in English and American dry gins. Genever gin is a gin meant to be drunk neat and does not take kindly to mixing.

The first genever, and therefore the first gin, was made in about 1550 by Franciscus de la Boe, a professor of medicine at Leyden university. De la Boe (also called Sylvius) was seeking a cure for digestive ailments using juniper berry juice, known to have diuretic properties. The medicine he produced – a compound of juniper in *aqua vitae* (distilled spirit) – was effectively the first genever gin.

As de la Boe's medicine had a better taste than the crude alcohols already on the market, it quickly found a wider audience than the sick and suffering. By 1575 it was being commercially distilled by Bols in Schiedam as an alcohol, not a medicine.

Schiedam, the centre of the Dutch grain trade, rapidly became the genever capital. By the end of the nineteenth century it had 392 distilleries and 64 malting houses, and *Schiedam* was one name used for a Dutch gin. Hollands, Square Bottle, or simply genever were other commonly used names.

Genever (also known as *geneva* or *jenever*) now accounts for more than half the total spirits sales within The Netherlands. But the emphasis is moving towards younger, lighter, although still aromatic, styles.

Dutch genever comes in two basic forms: *jonge* (young) and *oude* (old), a distinction less to do with age and more a result of taste. An oude genever has a higher percentage of *moutwijn* or malt wine, an essential ingredient which gives greater intensity and flavour. A jonge genever contains less moutwijn and is therefore lighter.

Producers of oude genevers will usually enhance their appeal by adding names such as *zeer oude* (or ZO, meaning very old), *echte* (genuine), *graan* (made from only grain), *dubbele graan, gebeide* (distilled with juniper) and *dubbel gebeide*. However, most fine genevers qualify for any or all of these titles.

A classic genever can only be made by a long and complicated process that starts in the *mouterij* (malting house). Barley, the special genever grain, is allowed to germinate for about a week until it has developed enough *amylase* to be called malt. In the *branderij* the malt is ground with maize and rye and cooked to a *maltose* mash which, with yeast added to start the fermentation, is then left to ferment for three days.

The resulting low-grade alcoholic wash goes through three separate distillations (in pot stills for the finest quality) to produce a neutral alcohol called *moutwijn*. It is this which gives genever its body.

Moutwijn is only made in two distilleries in Schiedam, and between them they supply about 100 genever producers in The Netherlands. The largest of the two is the Mouterij-Branderij De Koning BV, a subsidiary of Ervan Lucas Bols. The other, the Branderij & Gistfabriek 'Hollandia 11' BV, belongs to the smaller Gist-Brocades NV group. A third mouterij is under construction by the Heineken brewery group, owners of several genever companies.

The last stage in making a fine genever involves distillation of the moutwijn with the botanicals (including juniper) in specially-designed stills. Most companies work to a traditional, secret recipe and will only re-distil once. If it is redistilled twice, the genever is called *moutwijnjenever*, an expensive and rare gin. Witkampff of Schiedam is produced in this way.

Nolet, another small Schiedam company, make a golden korenjenever called Proosje van Schiedam that is distilled five times. Bols also make *korenwijn* (moutwijn distilled without juniper) which they sell as Corenwijn.

With increasing economic pressures on the Dutch genever distillers, more are turning to blending their expensive moutwijn with grain spirit and then redistilling the blend in a cheaper continuous still to make their *oude*

Above: the good doctor Sylvius of Leyden found a fine medicine for mankind in the 16th century. The production of Hollands gin grew to be a major national industry, and the traditional stone crock to be as Dutch an image as the wooden shoe.
Old genever from the house of Hulstkamp, and a toast from their merchandising character, a suitably wooden-faced Hollands burgher.

HULSTKAMP'S
Oude Genever
en Fijne Likeuren
OPGERICHT
A° 1775.
HULSTKAMP
BOVEN ALLES
HULSTKAMP

Dutch liquor companies vary in size and style from the white-coated efficiency of Bols, near Amsterdam, to the city's tiny Zuijlekom distillery. Botanical flavourings may be put into a huge 'bouquet garni', or they may go loose into the still. One very special Dutch spirit is made without botanicals: the triple-distilled, all-grain, wood-aged Corenwyn, or Corenwijn (corn wine).

genever. Dutch law, while specifying that genever must be a minimum 35° alcohol, is less exact about the kind of alcohol used to reach this proof degree. Ersatz genever, usually indicated by its price, makes the odd appearance, and illegal stills are, according to one report, thriving.

The milder jonge genever was first made at the turn of the century and now commands most of the market. It is more likely to have a percentage of molasses spirit in it, and a much lower percentage of moutwijn. The cheapest brands may not include any moutwijn at all, reducing the number of distillations that are necessary, but preserving the essential genever character.

Most of the large genever producers, founded in the seventeenth and eighteenth centuries, make a complete range of gins from fine old genever to young styles. Bols, the oldest and largest distiller, sells its famous ZO Genever in traditional earthenware bottles (crocks as they are sometimes called) and also produces Claeryn, a young genever.

The Heineken brewery group have moved substantially into the genever trade through the distinguished Friesland distillery, Bokma, and Coebergh and Hoppe, two other reputable labels.

Next door to Bokma, on the same street in Leeuwarden, the independent Boomsma distillery makes fine old genever. Other major distillers include Hasekamp, Henkes, De Kuyper, Dirkzwager, Daniel Visser, Cooymans and Uto Mij. Britain's Allied Breweries have recently entered the market with Olifant and Gulden Anker.

Among the fifty or so small distilleries, ranging from one-man operations to moderate-sized family businesses, the Levert, Melchers and Verhoeven companies are the best known.

Most distillers in The Netherlands also make a London Dry style gin for mixing, and a variety of flavoured genevers. The most popular flavoured styles are *beesengenever* (blackcurrant), *citroengenever* (lemon) and *orangjegenever* (orange).

Brandewijn ('brandy wine') is a light grain distillate related to dry gin. In its unadulterated state it has less flavour than a genever. The Dutch take it neat, particularly in the eastern part of the country where they will often add a lump of sugar to the drink. Because it is made from grain, not grapes, it is not a proper brandy. However, it did give its name to brandy, through English soldiers returning from the Lowlands who corrupted the Dutch term, *brandewijn*.

Brandewijn is also used extensively to make liqueurs and there are about a dozen flavoured brandewijns, ranging from orange to raspberry.

The Dutch equivalent of French brandy is *vieux*, the second most popular spirit after genever. Vieux bears only a superficial resemblance to cognac and is made by, among others, Bols, Henkes and De Kuyper.

DUTCH DRINKING

Drinking in The Netherlands is a social activity, with atmosphere of the first importance. The Dutch put a high value on what they call gezelligheid – an intimate warmth – as personified by the café. There is an almost endless list of different cafés – neighbourhood cafés, student cafés, literary cafés, theatrical cafés, and so on. In Amsterdam alone there are more than a thousand crowded and lively cafés open each night of the week.

Genever is often drunk at the borreluur (aperitif hour) when it is served in small glasses, chilled, from the barrel, bottle or crock. Some jonge genevers are used for mixing, but they are more commonly drunk neat, and the old, pale yellow genevers will always be served this way. Outside the borreluur, a borreltje ('wee drop') is acceptable at any time, often with a pils chaser.

The old Dutch inn still serves traditional spirits in the old way. Two of the best known, both in Amsterdam, are De Drie Fleschjes (the Three Flasks) at Gravenstraat 18, and Wynand Fockink at Pijlsteeg 31, just off Dam Square. The seventeenth-century Bols Tavern at Rozengracht 106 is opposite the site where the original Bols factory stood until 1969. Bols have now moved to Nieuwe Vennap, where their museum is open to the public.

Genevers and Dutch liqueurs are customarily served in a brimming glass. The Dutchman leans over the bar to take his first sip. The inexperienced foreigner may have to adopt a more gymnastic approach, as suggested in this set of souvenir postcards.

An establishment like the Three Flasks in Amsterdam, above, is not only a convivial spot for an early-evening drink, but also a tasting room, at which Bols' products may be sampled. Sadly, the samples are not free. Once it was customary for all distilleries to have tasting rooms. The barman at the Three Flasks offers many interesting mixed liqueur drinks, and his Dutch 'cocktails' are listed on a small hanging blackboard, like a menu.

Liqueurs

THE NETHERLANDS HAS a reputation for producing distinctive liqueurs, and today there are around 100 different varieties made within the Dutch borders. Some have been widely copied, but others remain uniquely Dutch and rarely seen outside the country.

Advocaat, although classed as a liqueur, belongs in a category of its own. This most Dutch drink is also the country's most exported drink, outstripping even genever shipments by a wide margin. Three-quarters of the exported advocaat goes to Britain.

Advocaat is made in two styles: 'thick' and 'thin'. The thin version is mainly for export, while the thick style, dense enough to stand a spoon in, is for local consumption. Both are made from brandewijn, fresh egg yolks, sugar and vanilla. The blending is a critical process during which the temperature must be high enough to emulsify the mixture and low enough not to spoil it. Both versions have an alcoholic content of about 15°.

The largest Dutch exporter is the Allied Breweries-owned Warnink company, which produces nothing else, followed by Bols and the Heineken-owned van Olffen company who sell under the Zwarte Kip (black hen) label.

Bols, still the best known of all Dutch liqueur makers, produce a wide range of flavoured liqueurs, as do most of their competitors. Among them are two typically Dutch creations – curaçao orange and curaçao triple sec.

Both of these liqueurs are made from oranges, a fruit the Dutch colonists brought back from the West Indian island of Curaçao. Curaçao orange, and the drier, stronger curaçao triple sec have now been imitated in many other countries, but the Dutch distillers maintain that theirs are the authentic versions.

Apart from those drinks already mentioned and a wide range of crème de menthes, anisettes and coffee cream liqueurs, there is in Holland a type of drink that could be called 'old Dutch' liqueurs – traditional drinks associated with domestic life. *Eau de ma Tante* (Water of my Aunt) is an example – an orange-based liqueur, first made by Bols. Another is *kandeel*, made from cognac, vanilla, cinnamon and cloves. Now only made by the van Zuylekom distillery of Amsterdam, it is traditionally served at a Dutch ceremony for protecting new-born babies from evil spirits.

Other such liqueurs include *Pruimpje Prik In*, a plum based liqueur, *Naveltje Bloot* (bare navel) and *Roosje Zonder Doornen* (rose without thorns) made from the essence of roses.

Hansje in de Kelder (Hans in the cellar, or 'Jack in the box') is a classic example of these domestic liqueurs. It was traditionally served as a discreet way of announcing a pregnancy in the family. The mother-to-be revealed herself by blushing when her turn came to sip the liqueur. The Dutch even devised a special drinking vessel from which a miniature

Not only are the Dutch famous for their gins and liqueurs, but also for their advocaat, a thick concoction of egg and brandy. Its qualities were graphically depicted by the distinguished illustrator Lawson Wood in this advertisement from the 1930s. Three centuries earlier, in 1655, the original Mynheer Bols contracted to buy his premises in Rozengracht, Amsterdam, below. In 1695, the rival De Kuyper distillery, below right, was founded in the city of Rotterdam.

THE PERILS OF PRUIMPJE

A colourful and cautionary tale is spelled out by the series of nine liqueurs below, in the risqué humour of the Jordaan, the old Huguenot neighbourhood of Amsterdam. As always, it is a story of boy-meets-girl. The story starts one evening at a quarter past five (*Kwartier na Vijven*). This early-evening drink provides a momentous rendezvous for our boy and girl. It leads, in fact, to the very perfection of love (*Parfait d'Amour*), followed by two rather vulgar suggestions: From the young woman, 'the longer the better' (*Hoe Langer Hoe Liever*); from the young man, 'lift up your petticoat' (*Hempje Licht Op*). The lady being thus exposed (*Naveltje Bloot*), she makes a blushingly untranslatable suggestion: *Pruimpje Prik In*. This kind of behaviour has predictably dire consequences. In due course, a wedding has to be arranged, with the inevitable bride's tears (*Bruidstranen*). At the wedding, the bride's shape so shocks one aunt that the lady faints, and has to be given a glass of water (*Eau de ma Tante*). It is clear that the bride has, as they say, a 'little Hans in the cellar' (*Hansje in de Kelder*). In the end, of course, baby Hans is welcomed to the world with a drink, in an unusual goblet, right, made specially for this purpose. They call it wetting the baby's head.

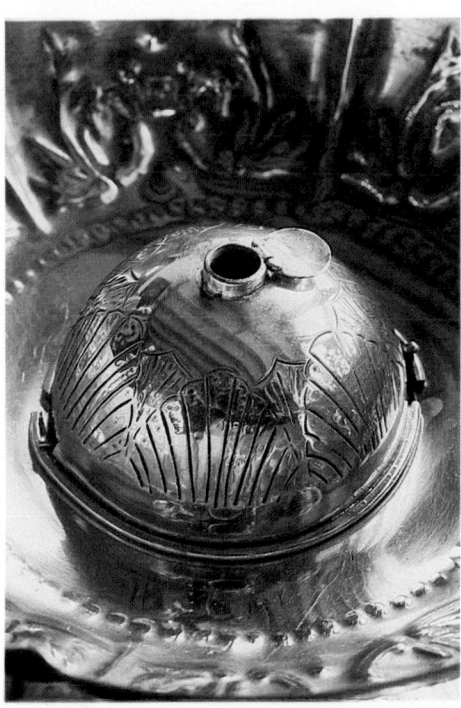

BITTER-SWEET CITY

A doubly typical Amsterdam drink is half and half, served from elegant flasks decorated with portraits of the city's mayors past and present. A bitter-sweet blend of orange curaçao and orange bitters, with cloves and other ingredients added, the liqueur is a popular mid-morning pick-me-up. The drink is said to have been created by accident at a distillery called Wynand Fockink, since taken over by Bols. However, the original tasting room still survives as an independent business, and among the many mementoes displayed, there is a set of flasks made for Amsterdam's mayors. The two shown right honour Mayors PC Hooft (1591) and Samakalden (1968–78).

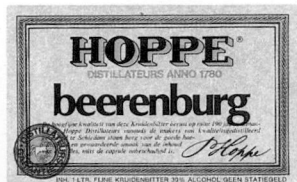
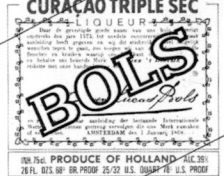

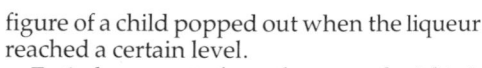

figure of a child popped out when the liqueur reached a certain level.

Entirely separate from these are the 'ship's liqueurs', supposedly developed by seagoing surgeons as medicines during long sea voyages. The two best-known are *Hoe Langer Hoe Liever* (the more the better) and *hempje licht op* (lift up your shirt).

Half om half (half and half), a blend of orange curaçao and bitters, was reputedly discovered when an apprentice accidentally poured curaçao into a cask containing bitters. It is now one of the favourite Dutch liqueurs, and one of the few known abroad.

Most Dutch liqueurs are rarely found outside certain regions. They include *Schelvispekel* (haddock 'pickler'), a brandewijn flavoured with cinnamon and other herbs, served only to the fishermen of Vlaardingen, south of Schiedam; *oranjebitter,* usually drunk as a toast to the Dutch royalty; *voorburg* and *fladderack,* two citrus-flavoured brandewijns; *hagel en donder* (hail and thunder), a Friesian sweet brandewijn flavoured with anis; and *boerenjongens* and *boerenmeisjes* (farmer boys and farmer girls), two brandewijns flavoured with raisins or apricots.

Several of the bigger distillers make proprietary liqueur brands, among them the Bols company who have three well-known examples in Bolscherwhisk (Scotch whisky and cherry brandy), Oragnac (triple sec and cognac), and Demockaat (advocaat flavoured with coffee). Vandermint, a mint-flavoured liqueur is produced mainly for export.

Dutch bitters, as personified by the Wellings, Boonekamp and Catz labels (all three principally for export), have grown in domestic popularity since 1970. Before then, bitters were popular only in certain regions.

The most popular type of bitters is *berenburg,* or *beerenburg.* Originally a Frisian drink, this style of bitters was first made by café owners in the region who gathered and tossed herbs into a pot of brandewijn and allowed them to macerate before serving the drink to their customers. An Amsterdam spice merchant who supplied ready-made packets of these herbs to the cafés gave his name to the drink. Sonnema and Boomsma both produce berenburg bitters.

The rival southern bitters are *els,* made by the Hennekens distillery at Beek, and a third, lesser known variety, *keizerbitter.*

THE BLUE LADY

This drink is called a *Marie Antoinette* at the Café Royal, but bears a strong resemblance to the Blue Lady.

Frost the rim of a medium-size cocktail glass by dipping it into a saucer of grenadine, and then into one of caster sugar. Place 1½ oz dry gin, ¾ oz blue curaçao, 1 oz fresh lemon juice and 1 barspoon caster sugar, or to taste, in a cocktail shaker and shake. Strain into the prepared glass and garnish with a cocktail cherry.

Belgium/Jenever

BELGIUM IS A BEER-drinking nation, its loyalty to beer overshadowing a taste for imported wine and its modest consumption of spirits.

In 1976 for every litre of pure alcohol consumed per head in Belgium, 7.5 litres of wine and a massive 70 litres of beer were consumed. And of this spirits intake, two out of every three bottles were imported (more than half was Scotch whisky followed by liqueurs [mostly French], genever gins, cognac, and small quantities of British gin, rums, and vodkas).

But despite this, Belgium does have its own small spirits industry which mainly produced jenever gins.

The majority of the alcohol produced in Belgium annually comes from four big distillers – Bruggeman in Ghent, Descampe in Gembloux, Koninklijke Nederlandse Gist en Spiritusfabriek in Bruges and by a Tiense Suikerraffinaderij subsidiary at Ruisbroek. But only Bruggeman actually bottle their own alcohol, the other three big distillers sell their output to other spirits and liqueur producers or to industry. Bruggeman are best known for their Herte Kamp jenever, but they also make several flavoured liqueurs.

Ghent used to be one of Belgium's main distilling centres with many farm distilleries ringing the city. At the turn of the century there were at least 25 of these characteristic distilleries left. Now there are none. But the tradition survives through the Filliers brands of jenever gin and liqueurs.

Filliers are based at Bachte-Maria-Leerne, a picturesque village on the River Leie, near Sint-Martens-Latem.

Filliers, distillers since 1863, have long since leased their original farm distillery. They now make their jenever gins from grain spirit brought in from other small producers, and liqueurs from alcohol purchased from one of the big four companies. Their jenevers range from 30° alcohol to the nine-year-old amber 50° jenever, distinctively packed in either stone bottles or small wooden casks. Production takes place between February and April or May, and is sold direct or to retailers and restaurants in the provinces of East Flanders and Antwerp.

The only surviving farm-distillery in Belgium is near the village of Balagem, half-way between Ghent and Brussels. André Vanhecke, known to his customers as Van Damme after the original distilling family he married into, distils a 31° and 41° jenever from the beginning of November to the end of May from cereals grown on his own and nearby fields.

The Van Damme distillery is more of a museum of industrial archaeology than a plant in the modern sense of the world. The steam engine installed in 1890 still powers the mill and pumps, and the warm *draff* (waste) is drawn off to feed the farm's cattle in the winter distilling months.

As André Vanhecke says, he does everything 'van korrel tot borrel' (from pellet to

The stills at Fourcroy produce a variety of drinks, but the firm is best-known for the distinctive Belgian liqueur Mandarine Napoléon. This liqueur is marketed internationally, and is especially appreciated in the Francophone world.

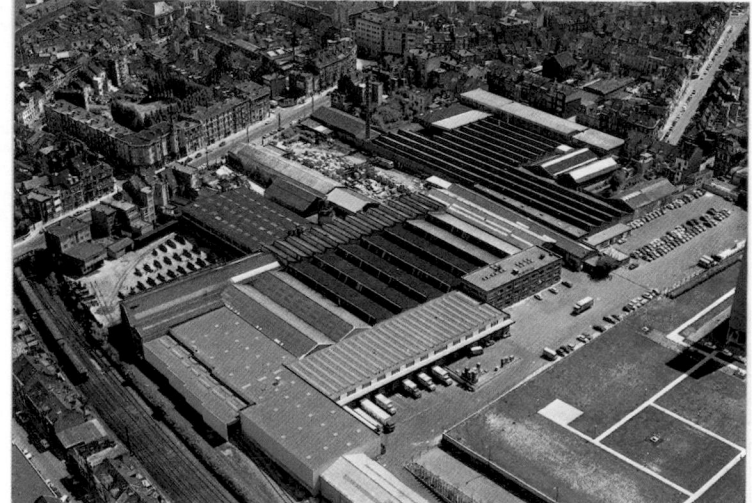

In Flanders' fields, the cattle feed well off spent grains from the tiny Van Damme distillery. In an agricultural setting, it is more a piece of industrial archaeology than a commercial distillery, but it does keep alive the distilling tradition of this district.

12 x 3/4
S.A.Q.L.C.
221-F
MANDARINE NAPOLÉON
700 ml
MONTREAL. 6631
COUPEZ ICI
Mandarine Napoléon
Mandarine Napoléon
Liqueur

ELIXIR D'ANVERS

DIPLÔMES D'HONNE
BOULOGNE s/M
25 Médailles
aux Exposition

F.X. DE BEUKELAER.

ANTWERPEN

dram). The modest quantities of jenever he makes are sold locally to wholesalers, retailers and consumers. In the village restaurant his jenevers are added to its speciality dishes.

Near the royal palace in the Brussels suburb of Laken, Alfred Fourcroy and his two sons are the third and fourth generations in a family business founded in 1862 by a French ancestor. Purveyors of wines and spirits to the King's Court, Ets Fourcroy now have subsidiaries in The Netherlands and Zaire. But in recent years they have expanded from wine and spirit merchants to producing spirits themselves. They now distil Smirnoff vodka under licence from Heublein, the American owners of the Smirnoff trade name, and their own special liqueur, Mandarine Napoleon.

More than 80 percent of the vodka produced by Fourcroy is exported (vodka accounts for more than half of Belgium's annual spirits exports).

Fourcroy's Mandarine Napoleon, produced from a blend of aged cognacs with macerated Spanish tangerines, is exported to 60 countries. The liqueur has an impressive pedigree, it has been served at Nobel Prize banquets, Queen Elizabeth II's Jubilee banquet, and at the United States' Bicentenary ball. Alfred Fourcroy is the first Belgian to be elected president of the International Wine & Spirits Federation.

The only other internationally recognised liqueur made in Belgium is Elixir d'Anvers, produced by de Beuckelaer in Antwerp since 1863. F X de Beuckelaer makes the sweet golden Elixir d'Anvers to a secret recipe from macerated herbs and spices redistilled together. The company also owns the rights to Elixir de Spa, the liqueur from the spa town in the Walloon hills.

Hasselt, in the Limburg province, is the city usually associated with jenever gin and the Belgian distilling industry. In 1610 Sampson van Horne was granted a lease to farm excises on *Wachelter water* (juniper water) in Hasselt. In 1830 there were 21 distilleries within the city walls and its 6,000 inhabitants paid 3,000,000 gold franks in duty. At the turn of the century one distillery alone was paying 12,000 gold franks a day in duty, but now only two distilleries operate there and

No doubt it was with an eye to the bourgeoisie that Elixir d'Anvers long ago spelled its home town in the French style, but the drinks of bi-cultural Belgium are predominantly in the Dutch idiom.

Brugeshas taken over as the distilling capital.

But to most Belgians, Hasselt is still the home of domestic jenever. The two companies still producing jenever there are Fryns and Smeets. The 100-year-old Fryns company make jenever and a range of fruit liqueurs, such as cherry and apricot brandies, but their importance is overshadowed by Smeets, a family business founded in 1920.

Smeets distil their own alcohol in an eighteenth-century distillery in a back street of Hasselt where once there were 17 rival distilleries. They make five types of jenever of differing alcoholic strengths and ages, fruit liqueurs, advokaat, cocktails and a domestic brandy that is used for *Hasseltse koffie* – a local version of Irish coffee.

Outside Hasselt, at Aarschot, where Limburg meets Brabant, the Geens family company make a similar range of jenevers and flavoured liqueurs. Officially called Geens Benelux, because about half their production is sold in Luxemburg, the company is still popularly known by their old trade-name, *de Torens* (the towers). Apart from spirits, Geens also sells French table wines from company owned vineyards in France.

In southern Belgium the Walloons drink less spirits than their northern counterparts and local spirits production is limited. Wine and wine-based aperitifs are preferred, along with French anis drinks.

The Distilleries Associées Belges at Jumet near Charleroi make two specialist liqueurs – Liqueur aux Fraises, from Wépion strawberries, and Sève de Sapin, flavoured with pine sap. Also near Charleroi, in the village of Chassart, a local distilling company called Chassart make their own grain-elixir and jenever sold under their own name.

Most of the jenever drunk in Charleroi and Liège comes from the Flemish north or from Holland. Most probably the taste was brought south by the thousands of Flemish textile workers who came to work in the coal mines around the two cities when their own industry collapsed in the middle of the last century. Their Walloon descendants do not ask for jenever. They call it *pequet* or *peket*, a Picardian or Flemish word deriving from *pitch* – a reminder that alcohol can be made from coal, and probably was by some poor miners.

LUXEMBURG

Luxemburg, nestling along the borders of France, Belgium and Germany, is nearest in *spirit* to the Mosel region. Right, Buff Bitter, still made according to the formulae of the naturalist Dr Boerhave, celebrated in the early eighteenth century; the Elixir de Mondorf, which originated in the nineteenth century; Père Blanc, best-known as being equally suitable before or after dinner. Above, the imposing Château-fort at Beaufort, a centre for spirits distilling in Luxemburg.

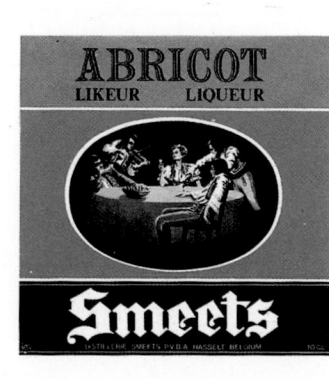

Germany

In Germany, spirits fall a long way behind wines and beers in popularity. The typical German drinks about six times as much wine as spirits and an incredible 55 times as much beer. The 60 major distillers associated with the Bundesverband der Deutschen Spirituosen Industrie account for most of the domestic spirits production.

The two most popular types of German spirits are klarers and weinbrands. Klarer is very similar to Scandinavian aquavits. Weinbrands are German brandies, usually matured in oak, which have a slightly softer, fuller taste than their French equivalents.

Wacholder is a clear spirit, frequently confused with Dutch or London gin, but distinct from both. It has a strong juniper flavour, since it is distilled from the berries, and like a Dutch gin, is drunk neat.

Germany also produces several domestic fruit brandies, similar to the French *eaux-de-vie*, notably from cherries and plums. In addition, various bitters (drunk as aperitifs and as restoratives) and liqueurs are produced.

Germany/Korn

KORN, OR KORNBRANNT or *Kornbranntwein* is usually made from rye fermented into a mash, and this may be indicated on the label by the word *Roggen* (rye). But it can also be made from *Weizen* (wheat) or *Getreide* (mixed grains). In taste it has something of a similarity to rye whiskey.

Korn was probably first made in Nordhausen, and now it is produced by up to 3,000 different distillers, most of them very small. It is the popular spirit of the northern coast of Germany and in the Ruhr and Westphalia. Two of the best-known brands are Doornkat (sometimes called 'Frisian country wine') from Norden in the north west and Furst Bismarck, made from rye and wheat only, named after the first chancellor of the Reich and still made by the Bismarck family at Friedrichsruh, south of Hamburg.

Several flavoured korns are also made, the most popular being korn-wacholder (with juniper essences); korn-genever; korn-kummel; and eiskorn.

THE NOBLE FAMILY OF BISMARCK

One of the most popular korns in Germany is Furst Bismarck, which was first distilled at the beginning of the 17th century. It is matured in ash storage vats for a year after its distillation.

Hannoverians drink their schnapps and beer simultaneously. This trick is no mean feat and requires considerable dexterity. Holding the glasses so that the smaller measure of schnapps is slightly higher than that of the beer, they are raised to the lips, the two drinks blending in a satisfying swallow.

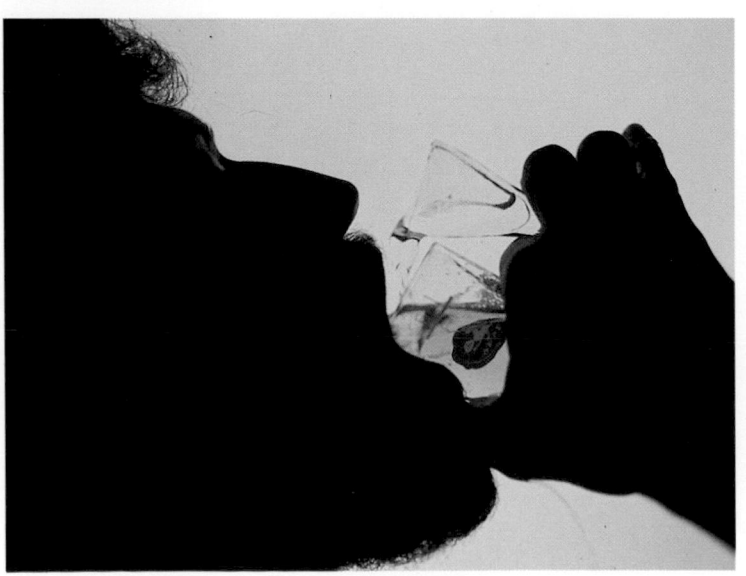

Doornkaat, founded by Jen ten Doornkaat *left*, make one of the best korns at Norden in northwest Germany. They achieve a high degree of purity in their spirit by careful malting, testing *far left* and triple distilling of the mash.

Weinbrand

Asbach, the best known German weinbrand grape brandy, was created by Hugo Asbach above at the beginning of this century.

THE GERMAN EQUIVALENT to French grape brandies are the *weinbrands* (burnt wines) which have been made in Germany since 1250. They differ from the French brandies in that they are slightly fuller and sweeter in taste. Their production is governed strictly by law. They can only be made from specific grapes, and 85 percent of the spirit must be distilled in Germany. When finished, the brandy must be blended and matured at the same plant where it was distilled. It must mature in oak (usually Limousin) for a minimum of six months (12 months if an age is to be given on the label) and the brandy must contain at least 38° alcohol. Those German brandies which do not meet these conditions can only be called *Branntwein aus Wein* (made from wine).

One of the best-known weinbrands is Asbach Uralt, distilled at Rudesheim in the heart of the Rheingau wine area, and it was Asbach who first invented the term weinbrand. Other well-known weinbrands include Dujardin Imperial and Dujardin Fine (matured for at least eight years), both distilled at Urdingen on the lower Rhine; Jacobi 1880 made in Stuttgart; Schlarlach Meisterbrand from Bingen am Rhine; Chantre made by Eckes at Neider-Olm; and Marriqcron made at Oppenheim on the upper Rhine.

The Asbach distillery at Rudesheim, above. Sometimes old German stills were mounted on cast metal feet shaped as animals. They supposedly warded off evil spirits – quite appropriate for a still. The feet visible in the picture are of a hog, a crane and an owl.

Among the advertisements that Asbach have used in the past is a postcard specially printed for WW1 troops.

ASBACH COFFEE

Asbach coffee is a rich blend of coffee, brandy and cream. Place two lumps of sugar in a cup (1). Add Asbach Uralt brandy (2) and set it alight (3). After one minute, extinguish the flames by pouring strong coffee on to the spirit (4). Add a generous amount of whipped cream spiced with vanilla (5), and sprinkle with grated chocolate (6).

Wacholder

WACHOLDER IS the German equivalent of gin, made from neutral spirit flavoured with junipers. At the lower end of the quality table it may just be juniper-flavoured kornsprit, and is known as *Wacholderkornbrannt*. At its finest it is commonly called *Steinhäger* and comes from the village of Steinhägen near the Teutoburger Wald in Westphalia. The best-known steinhägers are the Original Schilichte and Echt Schinkenhäger both made by HW Schlichte, HC Konig and Friedrich Niederstadt. The terms 'Original' and 'Echt' distinguish these steinhagers from the other wacholders.

The colourless steinhäger is usually bottled in attractive stoneware crocks (to preserve the rich juniper aroma) and it is a local tradition in Westphalia to make a type of Irish coffee with a dash of local steinhäger. The intense juniper flavour, that even defeats the coffee, comes from the direct distillation of junipers into the spirit rather than the flavouring of neutral spirit with juniper extract as in a typical dry gin or wacholder.

H W Schlichte, one of the best-known steinhäger producers, trace their origins back to the 16th century. Still a family-owned business, they use a carefully preserved recipe to make their juniper-flavoured spirit. The distillery is opposite the picturesque old village church above.

The distinctive juniper flavour of Steinhäger is achieved by directly distilling the berries into the spirit. Its other main ingredients are wheat and barley.

A BITTER PICK-ME-UP

GERMAN BITTERS ('bittere') are usually made from branntwein infused with extracts from roots, barks and herbs. Originally used as medicinal elixirs they still retain the 'pick-me-up' image and are drunk as digestifs or with one of the neutral spirits to give the spirit flavour.

The most famous bittere is Underberg made at Rheinberg. Sold in one-shot bottles, it has a sharp herby bouquet and a bitter, herby taste as well as an international reputation as a hangover cure. Boonekamp (which is also made in Holland) is another bitter and has a sweetish, aromatic and slightly sharp taste.

Underberg, the German answer to Fernet Branca, is made by steeping herbs in alcohol to give a bitter 'pick-me-up'.

THE ORIGINAL SCHLICHTE

Steinhäger is the finest type of wacholder – the German equivalent of gin. The oldest brand is Original Schlichte Steinhäger, still produced in the village of Steinhägen, in the same distillery and using the original process with pot stills, centre right . Traditionally, it is drunk neat and served well-chilled in small glasses, with a beer chaser. The Schlichte distillery bears a constant reminder of its product – a giant model of a stoneware steinhager crock, right .

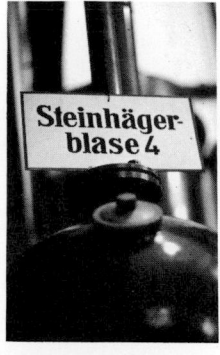

Steinhägers are bottled in stoneware crocks to preserve their juniper aroma. These are often decorated with alpine and other scenes traditionally associated with the spirit. The gentleman on the facing page was the original Herr Schlichte.

Other Drinks and Liqueurs

Some German spirits are made in private stills, like the one on the left, but the labels above all belong to commercial producers.

BETWEEN THEM, the klarers, weinbrands and korns account for well over three-quarters of the total German spirits consumption and output. Behind them are a number of speciality spirits.

Verschnitt is the generic name for different spirits blended together with one spirit giving the predominant flavour. *Rum-verschnitt* (with at least five percent rum) and *Arrack-verschnitt* (with at least ten percent arrack) are two examples of this. The word *Zuckerkulor* on the label means the spirit has been coloured and sweetened with colouring sugar.

Enzian is one of the most aristocratic German white spirits, and a speciality of the Bavarian areas. It is flavoured with an extract of the yard-long roots of the yellow mountain gentian or is distilled from fermented gentian roots to give an even greater depth of flavour. Almost half the total production comes from the Munich distiller Riemerschmied, and a second major distiller is Die Stonsdorferei of W Koerner.

Aufgesetzter (which translated means 'one put on') is the name used for pure alcohol, or korn, flavoured with blackcurrant juice. It is made only in smallish amounts to be drunk with lager. Germany also makes its own aquavits which are drunk in frosted glasses; Bommerlunder, and Malteserkreuz (from Munich) are the two main brands.

German liqueurs (*Likors*) come in a variety of shapes and forms, usually with an alcoholic content of 30° or more. *Eierlikors*, made with eggs, is produced by Verpoorten and others. *Fruchsaftlikors* are spirits flavoured with

An unusual bottle for unusual liqueurs. The Thienelt distillery near Dusseldorf markets their kroatzbeere, a deep red bramble-flavoured liqueur, and their kakao coffee liqueur together, in a bottle containing both spirits. They are meant to be drunk together, with the kroatzebeere poured into the glass first, and the kakao resting on the top. The reason for this spirituous conjuring trick is that the kroatzbeere is a heavier liquid, having a higher specific gravity.

AUSTRIA

In Austria, liqueur is the most important spirit manufactured. The taste of the strawberry and apricot liqueurs (labels, top and bottom, far right) are testament to the well-known national penchant for sweetness. The label in the middle is a coffee liqueur, a drink which bypasses the famous custom of having coffee with liqueur. Consumption of liqueur and coffee is seen, near right, in one of many famous Vienna coffee houses, dating from the best days of the Austro-Hungarian empire. In some places, the waiters calculate their tariffs by counting the number of accompanying empty water glasses.

THE LONG-ESTABLISHED FIRM OF SCHLADERER

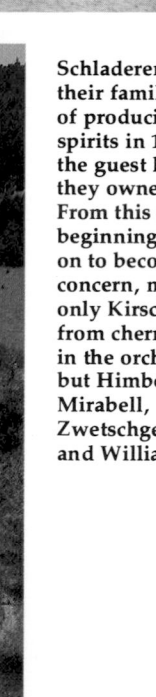

Schladerer began their family business of producing German spirits in 1844, from the guest house which they owned, above. From this modest beginning, they went on to become a major concern, making not only Kirschwasser, from cherries grown in the orchard, left, but Himbeergeist, Mirabell, Zwetschgenwasser, and Williams Birne.

extracts from a single fruit with certain additives, while *Fruchtaromalikors* do not contain additives. Some of the best-known examples of these fruit liqueurs include Meisterlikor from Scharlachberg of Bingen; Kroatzbeere (flavoured with brambles) from the Thienelt distillery at Düsseldorf; Edel-kirsch (mascara cherries) from Eckes (who also make Klosterberg and Sechsamtertropfen herb liqueurs). Other fruit flavours are made by Jacobi, Fugger, Lehment.

Set aside from these fruit liqueurs are the German eaux-de-vie made in the Black Forest area from cherries, plums, mirabelles, apricots, peaches, bilberries, raspberries, blackberries, strawberries, rowanberries, pears and apples, with the spirit distilled from the fruit mash in just the same way as across the nearby French border. So, for example, kirschwasser is the German equivalent of kirsch; zwetschgenwasser of mirabelle; zwetgenwasser of quetsch; Williamsbirnen-brand of poirc Williams; himbeergeist of framboise; and erdbeergeist of fraise. (The German distillers use *-wasser* to distinguish a fruit spirit made by distilling fermented fruit mash and *-geist* for spirit made by macerating the fruit in alcohol and then distilling it.) Of these German eaux-de-vie probably the best range comes from Schladerer who distil in the Black Forest area.

Kernobstbranntwein is used to describe a spirit made from either apples or pears, and *Honiglikor* for a liqueur flavoured with honey. *Krauterlikors* or *Klosterlikors* are herb-flavoured liqueurs, usually made to secret recipes of which Jagermeister, the dark red herb drink, is a classic example. Others include Ettaler klosterlikor, made at the monastery of Ettel in the Bavarian alps in both yellow and green forms (both of which taste like Bénédictine); Echt Stonsdorfer; and Sechsamtertropfen.

Black Forest cherry cake, one of Germany's most famous desserts, is traditionally laced with Kirschwasser, and decorated with cherries.

Swedenpunsch is a spicy cordial based on rum or arrack and drunk either in small glasses as a liqueur or with hot water as a punch; and *Allasch* is a kummel-flavoured distillate.

Two classic German liqueurs are Danziger Goldwasser and Silberwasser. Originally both were made in the old port of Danzig by Der Lachs from 1598 onwards. When the old Der Lachs distillery was destroyed in the last war production moved to West Berlin, retaining the original formula.

The Goldwasser, made from spirit flavoured with white aniseed and caraway, was distinguished by flakes of gold floating in the water-white liquid. Similarly, the Silber-wasser had silver flakes, both probably added originally to give the two liqueurs medicinal as well as alcoholic virtues.

A HOME-DISTILLED SPIRIT

Among the many locally distilled liqueurs to be found in Germany is Friesengeist, manufactured by Johann Eschen for use in his hotel. The liqueur, containing mint, is placed in a glass, flambéed, and topped with coffee and whipped cream.

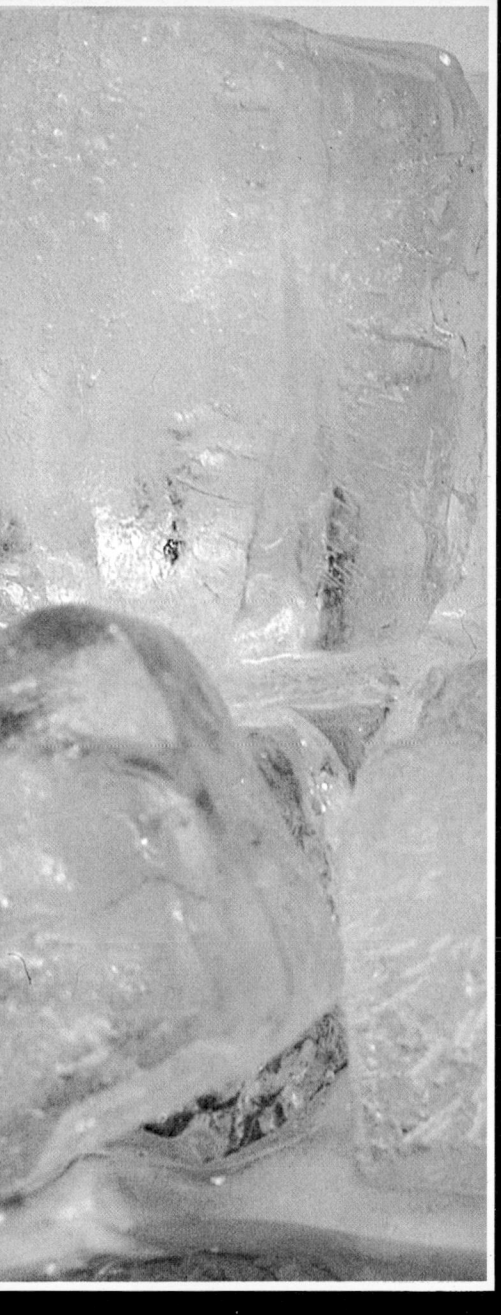

Poland Russia and Eastern Europe

What we have come to know as vodka is very different from the spirit which has been drunk in Poland and Russia for the past 1,000 years. Western vodkas have no marked taste. In contrast, Russian and Polish vodkas have a distinctive flavour and body and are never drunk mixed. Also unlike Western vodkas, some Eastern vodkas are aged for a few years in the wood.

Flavoured vodkas, very popular in the Soviet Union, and more especially Poland, are produced in such a range of flavours that together they can almost provide substitutes for any other international spirit.

In other Eastern European countries, vodka is not so predominant, and grape and fruit brandies are most commonly distilled.

Poland/Vodka

DISTILLING WAS KNOWN IN POLAND as early as the eighth century AD when, the Poles believe, the first vodkas were made. But it is likely that those early distillations were based on wine, not grain, and therefore the end result would have resembled a crude brandy rather than a pure spirit such as vodka.

By the eleventh or twelfth centuries Poland, and probably Russia, were making vodkas, commonly known as *gorzalka*. The vodkas, low in alcohol, were used only as medicines. In both countries, its production was the privilege and jealously-guarded right of a handful of nobles, monks and apothecaries.

In the fifteenth century vodka became popular as a drink, and by the sixteenth century it was commonly distilled from rye and other grains, and called, to distinguish it from gorzalka, *okowita* (the Polish derivative of aqua vitae).

Vodka was firmly established as the Polish national drink when King Jan Olbracht passed a law in 1546 allowing every citizen to make and sell spirits. Families developed their own special recipes based on different flavourings.

In 1572 the country's rulers gave the gentry exclusive rights to the production and sale of vodka. Vodka became a major source of revenue for the squirearchy and the Crown. The Polish Sejm (parliament) further imposed a *czopowe* (tap-tax) on the sale of vodka, beer and mead. Yet, despite these financial penalties and restraints on production, vodka drinking reached such levels that one contemporary writer said: 'distilleries have sprung up everywhere, and had decocted (sic) not only grain but also whole villages and towns'.

As distillation techniques improved in the seventeenth century, Poland began to export vodka, with Poznań and Kraków already

The old and the new. Vodka drinking still plays a large part in Polish life, even if customs have changed. The elaborately carved chair from Danzig, left, shows tavern drinking scenes probably dating from the 17th century. Today the vodka bottle is most commonly seen on a meal table.

Kraków, below, and Poznań, below right, are the original capitals of the Polish vodka industry. Both are still major distilling centres, a legacy of four centuries or more.

established as major production centres. In the eighteenth century *wodka*, taken from the Polish *woda* in the diminutive, meaning 'little water', became the common name.

Just after the end of the First World War, the production and marketing of Polish vodka became a state monopoly, with control in the hands of the Pabstwowy Monopol Spirytusowy (commonly known as Polmos). Their proudest achievement has been making Russia into the biggest export market for Polish vodkas. Even Smirnoff, the brand that pioneered vodka-drinking in the west, originally came from L'vov in Poland, not from Russia as many believe.

The three main distilling centres are Poznań, Kraków and Gdańsk. In the late sixteenth century, Poznań already had 49 'distilling pots' within the town walls, and the city is still the major production centre. Kraków comes second only to Poznań; and Gdańsk on the Gulf of Danzig has developed into a producing centre in its own right from being a port for vodka exports.

All vodka is basically unaged distilled spirit made from a fermented mash filtered through vegetable charcoal and diluted to proof with distilled water. The mash can be made from almost anything. In Poland most fine vodkas are now made from grain – rye is the principal variety, with maize, barley and, infrequently, wheat sometimes used as substitutes. The potato, which had its heyday in the nineteenth century, is now only used for specialist vodkas. A few vodkas are also made from sugar beet molasses.

The fermented mash is distilled in pot stills at least twice (for Polish vodka) to give an absolutely pure spirit. The spirit is filtered through activated charcoal further to cleanse it, and then brought down with distilled water to bottling strength.

Unlike their Western counterparts, both Russian and Polish vodkas have a discernible flavour and aroma. The bouquet of a clear Eastern vodka is spirity with a slight oiliness. The liquid, when poured into a glass, seems denser and thicker than a Western vodka, and the flavour is strong, spirity and almost 'green'. There is none of the neutrality that has been the basis of many Western vodka advertising campaigns.

Well over two-thirds of all the vodka made in Poland is clear vodka. But while the manufacture of clear vodkas has steadily increased from 66,000,000 litres (based on 100° proof) in 1960 to 116,000,000 in 1975, there has been a dramatic increase in the production of flavoured vodkas – from just under 8,000,000 litres in 1960 to 50,000,000 in 1975. The Poles have transformed the traditional domestic production of flavoured vodkas into a large-scale commercial operation, and are now the world's leading producers.

The best-known clear Polish vodkas are Wodka Wyborowa Red Label (65.5°) and Wodka Wyborowa Blue Label (73°) – the two Polmos export brands made from rye and both thought of in Poland as top-quality vodkas. Luksusowa (79°) is the principal vodka still made from potatoes (it is rectified three times to give a very smooth, mellow flavour). Krakus (70°), a fourth important label, is made from selected rye.

The flavoured vodkas range from the very lightly aromatised styles to richly-flavoured, strong-tasting vodkas. The former are typified by Zytnia (70°) and the higher-strength Special Zytnia (79°) – both dry vodkas with a yellowish tint from modest additions of aromatic fruit, cherry and apple brandies. Tatra Vodka Tatrzanska (79°) – a third light vodka, is light green in colour and has a herby flavour. It is a speciality of the Kraków area, and uses herbs, particularly archangelica, from the nearby Tatra mountains.

The best-known traditional flavoured vodka is Zubrowka, first made in Eastern Poland along the Russian border. In this part of Poland the government has created the Bialowieza National Park to protect the wild European bison that roam the area along with wild horses, deer, boar and wolves. The bison graze on clumps of *Hierochloe odorata* grass which the peasants used to flavour their vodkas, to give them 'the strength of the bison'.

The Polmos have maintained the tradition and put a blade of bison grass in every bottle. The grass gives Zubrowka a translucent greenish colour, and a delicate flavour. Zubrowka is sold at two strengths – 70° and 88° proof.

The golden-brown Starka vodka is a second traditional Polish drink. Traditionally, the better-off families laid down oak casks of this vodka when a daughter was born, and when she married the casks were opened and served throughout the three-day wedding celebrations.

Polmos now make Starka 88° from rye spirit, aged for at least ten years, and slightly flavoured with Spanish málaga wine to bring out the rye taste. It is the modern vodka that comes closest to the old Polish gorzalka.

Among the other flavoured vodkas are Jarzebiak (70°), a golden-coloured dry vodka infused with rowanberries; Soplica (70°), vodka flavoured with brandy and apple spirit; Orzechowka (79°), flavoured with green walnuts to give a bitter, nutty taste; Wodka Mysliwska or Hunter's vodka (79°), flavoured with rectified juniper distillates, herbs and lightly sweetened; Jarzebiak deluxe rowanberry vodka at 75° proof; Sliwowica (79°), a potato vodka flavoured with plum spirit; Passover Slivovitz (122°), a plum spirit flavoured vodka matured in oak casks and bottled at natural strength; Wisniowka (70°), semi-sweet cherry vodka and Dry Cherry Vodka (70°), with a lighter cherry flavour; Delmonico (52°), a Polish ready-mixed vodka appetiser made from spirit, herbs and fruit flavourings; Krupnik (70°), a traditional honey-flavoured liqueur vodka; and Ratafia (61°), a fruit-flavoured vodka that bears no relation to the ratafia of France.

Polmos also make 100 percent pure spirit at 100°, 140° and 168°, along with a wide range of liqueurs such as Ziolowy (herb-flavoured), Goldwasser, Cherry Liqueur, Cacao Choix, Cassis, Advocaat, Blackberry and Honey Cherry brandy.

Vodka and vodka drinking is so woven into the fabric of Polish life that a set of social customs have grown up around it. First, vodka is never drunk in Poland without food. To offer a guest food without drink, or drink without food, would be unthinkable.

In the past, each family took pride in its vodka, made to a secret recipe, and it is some of these recipes that are now used to make the Polmos flavoured vodkas. The tradition of home vodkas is still important within Poland,

and the government has obliquely encouraged it by giving families, including those living in the cities, small plots of land where they can grow trees, flowers and fruits.

The fruits, such as red and blackcurrants, strawberries, raspberries, cherries and apples, are picked and dried. Then, each family infuses them in clear vodka. The fruits are left in the spirit in large glass or earthenware containers for a year or more, then the flavoured vodka is poured off and, commonly, a second batch of spirit is added to give a lighter-flavoured vodka. The finest, first infusion vodka is kept for the guests of the house, and the Poles traditionally call it *nalevka*, to distinguish it from State-made vodka. Both vodkas are sold through Government shops and delicatessens.

Clear vodkas are usually served with a meal, though some of the lighter-flavoured varieties like Zubrowka can also be used. The flavoured vodkas are used as aperitifs, with snacks or with desserts and coffee. Whatever the style, it is always served at almost freezing temperature which brings out the slight oiliness and releases some of the spirit esters while inhibiting others. The higher strength of the Russian and Polish vodkas means they can be kept without solidifying.

Unlike the Russians who drink their vodka in one gulp, the Poles sip it from narrow-necked glasses with a small bulb at the base which can be stood in ice to keep the spirit cold. It is said that Polish (and Russian) vodka is less likely to give the drinker a hangover than whisky, brandy or gin. Scientific tests have shown that the eastern vodkas have fewer congeners than other spirits – and it is congeners that cause headaches.

As their vodkas come in so many flavours, and styles (some are almost the equivalents to gin or brandy), the Poles find little need for other spirits. Beer and mead are the only two other alcoholic beverages they drink in any quantity. Their consumption per capita of spirits is one of the highest in the world at about 5.5 litres per head per year, much higher than the 3.3 litres for neighbouring Russia. Currently the government is trying to encourage mixing drinks in bars through advertising campaigns.

THE GRASS THAT FLAVOURS

A national bison park may seem to have little in common with Poland's national drink, but the grass on which the bison feed is used to flavour a Polish vodka. Close to the Russian border at Bialowieza, a park has been created to preserve the last surviving herd of European bison – descendants of the ancient herds which once roamed the Earth. Their natural habitat of dense forest once reached as far as the Mediterranean from the Baltic Sea. Now only 140,000 acres remain as a sanctuary for the small herd – a unique insight into the past. Wild bison had been destroyed by 1919 due to relentless hunting, but were re-established in 1929 when animals were taken from private zoos. By 1952 they were back in the forest, but now their main threat is from infection – living in such a protected environment, they have no resistance, and foot and mouth disease could wipe the herd out. To ensure that the bison do not catch any disease that might be carried by tourists, they are herded together in a part of the forest which is not open to the public.

Distilleries

BISONS SVM, POLONIS SVBER,
IGNARI, VRI NOMEN DEDERANT.

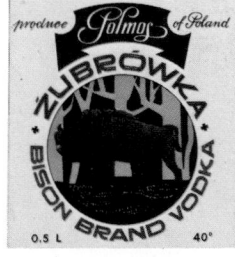

A bottle of vodka containing a blade of grass? Strange as it may seem, Zubrowka vodka is flavoured with an extract of the grass on which the famous Bialowieza bison feed, and a blade of this grass is placed in every bottle. Some may even like to think that the drink will give them the strength of the bison.

STRONG STUFF

In the far north of both Poland and Russia, the winter temperatures drop so low that all normal drinks freeze instantly. The only drink that survives in liquid form to warm the inhabitants is 168° proof vodka, possibly the strongest drink legally obtainable.

147

Russia/Vodka

THE NATIONAL DRINK of Russia – vodka – was first produced there in any quantity in about the twelfth and thirteenth centuries. Yet to Westerners it has always carried a certain enigma. Perhaps this is because the first imports did not reach Britain until after the First World War and Smirnoff, the first 'Western' vodka, was not distilled in the United States until 1934, and in Britain not until 1952. Even so, it was not until the mid 1960s that vodka really became a spirit of both the East and the West.

Historical references show that vodka consumption was an integral part of Russian life from the fourteenth century. Vladimir of Kiev told a Muslim delegation seeking to convert his people to Islam that the 'Russians are merrier drinking – without it they cannot live'. Peter the Great is one of the more notable patrons of the drink. He invented a modified still that produced a better vodka; and, never a moderate man, he wrote to his wife from Paris to complain when he had only one bottle left.

Since 1925 all Russian vodka production has been in the hands of Prodintorg, a state monopoly. Distilling is done very much on a regional basis mainly for regional consumption. Vodka distilling and drinking is concentrated in the central, north and eastern parts of the USSR; the southern republics of Georgia, Armenia, Azerbaijan, Moldavia and the southern Ukraine are more wine producing and drinking areas. The spirit produced in these parts of the Soviet Union tends to be brandy.

Again, while Russian vodka is traditionally made from grain (hence its historic name, *bread wine*), it now tends to be distilled from the most abundant raw material. Byelorussia (White Russia) vodkas are often made from potatoes, a principal crop of the region. Ukrainian vodkas from molasses, as this republic grows around 80 percent of the USSR's sugar beet production. Vodkas from

Russian nobility considered the making and selling of vodka part of their birthright. Count Karol Radiziwil is shown left distributing vodka in 1843 in Byelorussia. Peter the Great, below, was a renowned vodka drinker.

Russian silver drinking vessels – the beaker in the foreground is inscribed 'Livadiya 1911' and probably came from the summer residence of the Tsars. The inscription on the bowl-shaped vessel reads 'Drink out of it'. A selection of bottles, left, shows the wide variety of vodkas available in Russia.

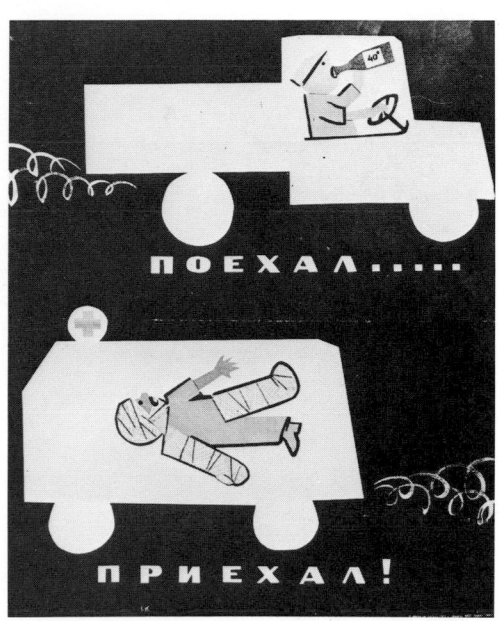

Both the Polish and the Russian governments are concerned at the high incidence of alcoholism in their countries. In the two posters above citizens are advised to seek medical help against alcoholism; the poster far right warns of the perils of drinking and driving.

the Russian Federation (European USSR up to Vladivostok) are made from grains.

Within Russia, most of the unflavoured vodkas are simply labelled vodka. They come at three standard strengths – 70°, 88° and 98°. The different regional vodkas may have their source also mentioned on the label – *donetskaya vodka* from Donetsk, and *zhitomiraskaya vodka* from Zhitomir, are two Ukrainian examples.

The brands best-known in the West – Moskovskaya, Stolichnaya and Krepkaya – can be found in the USSR but most production is sent for export by Sojuzplodo-import, the Soviet foreign trade organisation established in 1966.

In the Arctic and sub-Arctic from Archangel northwards, vodka is almost the only drink available – not out of choice but necessity. The temperatures fall so low that beer and wine, even if it could be delivered, would freeze. Even vodka, which takes very low temperatures to solidify, sometimes solidifies. When this happens the only alcohol available is pure spirit at around 168° – unpleasant to drink but the only alcohol that can survive the extremely harsh conditions.

Russia produces a variety of flavoured vodkas, although they are not exported as widely, nor considered as important domestically, as their Polish counterparts. Some, like Shasha (a clear Georgian vodka made from grapes) or Kulgan (a Ukrainian speciality flavoured with ginseng root), are considered only regional drinks.

Others are more widely known. These

THE TARTARS' FERMENTED MILK

The semi-nomadic Tartars, ranging across the Russian steppes up to the northern borders of the Himalayas, made their own special kind of strong drink from milk – the most readily available raw material – from mares, sheep, cows, even camels.

The Tartars must have added either a lactose (milk sugar) or grape juice to the milk to start the fermentation. Distillation of the fermented milk was then done in earthenware pots over slow fires with the alcoholic vapours passed through wooden tubes to the cooling receiver, probably another earthenware pot. The efficiency must have been remarkably low, and at least two or three distillations were needed. The product, however, was remarkably potent.

This milk alcohol has several names. *Koumiss* or *kumiss* (meaning milk) are the main ones.

BLOODY MARY

This classic cocktail is an excellent pick-me-up at any time, but is especially recommended by John Doxat as a hangover cure. The first recipe given below is for a single measure, and the second is for a bottle of the seasoning, which should make up to 30 cocktails if added judiciously to vodka and tomato juice over ice, in a long glass.

For one: **Place a few lumps of ice in a long glass and add 2 oz vodka, 4 oz tomato juice, 1 teaspoon Heinz tomato ketchup, 2 drops Worcestershire sauce, 1 dash Angostura Bitters, 1 dash Tabasco sauce, 1 shake celery salt, ½ oz lemon juice, and 2 dashes fresh orange juice, if desired. Stir, and serve with a stick of celery or a slice of cucumber.**

For a bottle of seasoning: **Into a clean, empty 26⅔-oz whisky bottle, pour 12 oz Heinz tomato ketchup, 6 oz fresh orange juice, 1½ oz Worcestershire sauce, ¾ oz Angostura Bitters, 1 teaspoon Tabasco sauce, 4 rounded teaspoons celery salt, and top up with fresh lemon juice. Shake well. This mixture can be stored for several weeks in a fridge.**

A rather different scene from one you might find today – a bottling room in a Russian distillery at the turn of the last century.

include Zubrowka from Byelorussia; Yubilevnaya, flavoured with brandy and honey; Kubanskaya, a colourless, bitter vodka flavoured with an infusion of lemon and tart orange peels; Starka old vodka infused with the leaves of the Crimean apple and pear trees and with brandy and Russian port added; Okhotnichya (Hunter's vodka) flavoured with ginger, cloves, black and red peppers, tormentil, ashweed and five other ingredients; Limonnaya infused with lemon peels and slightly sweetened with sugar.

Pepper-flavoured vodkas traditionally date back to Peter the Great who is said to have seasoned his vodkas with cubeb. Among the modern descendants of this, the most famous is probably Pertsovka, a dark brown spirit with a full aroma and burning flavour. Cayenne, capiscum and cubeb are the three flavouring peppers infused into Pertsovka.

Aside from Moskovskaya (70°), Stolich-

WORCESTER'S FAMOUS SAUCE

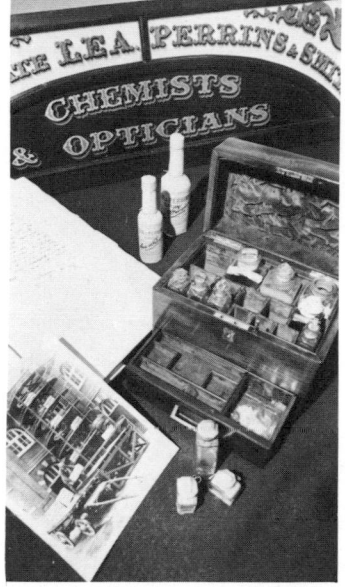

That vital ingredient of the Bloody Mary, Worcestershire sauce, was created in 1823, in the city of Worcester. A local nobleman, who was once the Governor of Bengal, asked two chemists from the city, Mr Lea and Mr Perrins, to make up a sauce from an Indian recipe. The chemists made more of the mixture than had been ordered, and stored it. The mixture matured, and tasted delicious. It was an instant success.

A collection of bottles, some containing imitations of Lea & Perrin's sauce, below.

OTHER EASTERN EUROPEAN DRINKS

A healthy tradition of illicit distilling exists in Eastern Europe as in every other part of the world. The engraving left shows Wallachians, from Rumania, making slivovitz.

WHILE RUSSIA AND POLAND concentrate almost exclusively on the production and consumption of vodkas and vodka-based flavoured spirits, the other Eastern European countries have a broader range of spirits.

In the wine-growing countries – Hungary, Bulgaria, Rumania, and to a lesser extent Czechoslovakia, together with the Georgian part of Russia – there is a reasonable production of local grape brandy for domestic consumption. Bulgaria is the main producer among these countries.

In Hungary the predominant spirit is Barack Palinka, an apricot brandy distilled from fresh apricots picked in the orchards of Kecskemét, towards the Rumanian border. Dry and unsweetened, it comes in traditional or long-necked Hungarian *fütyülös* bottles. In the same area, the Kecskeméti Barack liqueur is made from apricots. Rounded, it has a rich scent of the fruit. Other Hungarian fruit brandies are made from plums (Szilva Palinka or Szilvorium), pears (Császarkorte) and cherries (a local version of maraschino). Hungary also produces some rum (usually called Casino) and Hubertus, a form of bitters.

Tokay, the famous restorative dessert wine made from grapes grown in the extreme northeast of Hungary, very occasionally reaches an almost fortified wine strength, but without fortification. This is achieved by adding dried rotten grapes to the wine.

The *tokay-furmint* grapes are attacked by *botrytis* disease and become *aszu* (rotten), they are allowed to shrivel and are put into buckets, or *puttony*.

When normal wine is ready to ferment, the dried grapes are worked into a grapey dough and

Tokay is produced from grapes grown around the tiny Hungarian village of the same name. It will mature almost indefinitely.

added to the wine. The number of puttony added will determine the sweetness of the wine. The more added, the sweeter it will be, and the final wine is graded on the label by the number of puttonyos used – three puttonyos, four puttonyos or five puttonyos.

The richest tokays resemble fine sauternes, and although they both come from the action of 'noble rot' *(botrytis)*, each is special in its own way. The Hungarians proudly call their tokay 'The King of Wines'. The Czechs, across the border from Tokai, try to make a similar wine, but without the same success.

Bulgaria produces plum brandy which is known there as *slivovo,* some mastika, and a range of rakis from sloes, apples, grapes and plums.

An informal al fresco lunch in Uzbekistan. The tall glasses contain vodka.

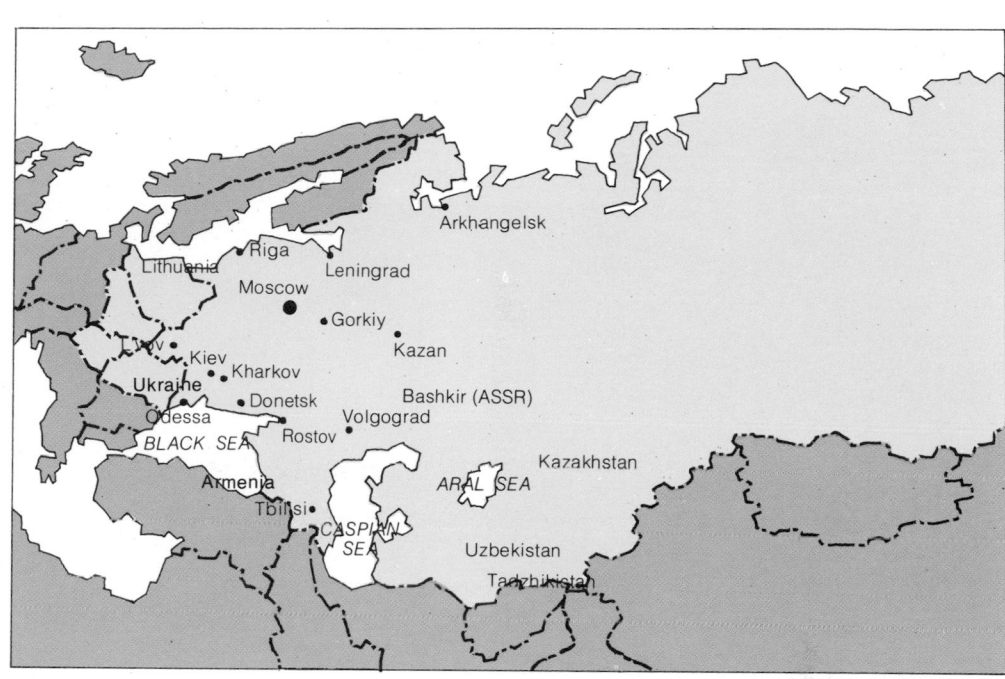

INTERNATIONAL VODKAS

Vodka is produced all over the world, from Spain to South Africa. One of the most famous brands is Smirnoff, which was first brought to America in the 1930s. For many years it was the only vodka made in the United States, and it began a new fashion in drinking.

naya (also 70°) and Krepkaya Strong (98°) clear vodkas, the other better-known international brands are Russkaya (70°), Kristal (70°) made in Riga, Stolovaya (88°), and the Estonian Viru Valge (70°).

The final group are what the Russians call *nastoika* – heavily-flavoured vodkas that border on liqueurs and in some cases are made from a different spirit base. These are typified by the Russky Blazam, dark brown strong alcohol that is both bitter and spicy; Wana Tallinn, a dark brown orange, cinnamon- and vanilla-flavoured spirit that has a rum-like taste; and three based on cherries and alcohol – the sweetish Spotykach, Cherry brandy Vichniovaia, and Zapekanka.

Despite their old *zapoi* (drunken) image, the Russians now treat vodka drinking as an event, rather than an everyday occurrence. From 1914 to 1925 its production was banned, and the vodka drinking habits changed. The modern Russian only opens a bottle with friends – either in a restaurant or home.

The Russian equivalent of the British pub or the American bar only serves beer. To drink vodka outside his home a Russian would have to go to friends or to a restaurant where he would have to wait to be served and then order a meal at the same time.

The lone vodka drinker, in the home or outside, is considered an alcoholic. Vodka is drunk in company and with food. In a restaurant the host orders it in grams – 100, 200 or 500 grams, or by the bottle – to go with dried fish, boiled potatoes, bread, vegetables, even as an aperitif with caviar, and will then continue dinner with vodka or change to wine and beer. Brandy is becoming the popular Russian post-dinner drink.

153

The British Isles

Within Great Britain, there is a clear distinction between the alcoholic traditions of England and its Celtic neighbours. England makes gin, but does not in any circumstances make whisk(e)y. The Scottish make whisky; Scotch comes only from Scotland. The Irish make Irish whiskey (spelt with an 'e') on both sides of the border. The Welsh produce very little of any alcholic drink.

English gin is a clear, highly rectified unaged spirit which is generally drunk mixed. The terms 'English' or 'London Dry' on a label describe the style of gin rather than its provenance. Nothing could be further from the truth with the best Scotch – the malt whiskies. Every malt whisky is a unique product not only of a particular region, but of a particular distillery. Malts were the original Scotch whiskies, but what most people refer to as Scotch is in fact a blend of malt whiskies with the lighter and cheaper grain whiskies. Irish whiskey is malt-based.

England/Gin

GIN FIRST REACHED ENGLAND in the late sixteenth century via British soldiers fighting in the Low countries and sailors and merchants trading. The soldiers already knew the primitive *aqua vitae* (or aquavit), but found gin – essentially the same spirit flavoured with juniper berries – more to their liking. The expression 'Dutch courage' arose from the aquavit, and later gin, they drank before battle.

In The Netherlands gin was called *Hollands* or *Schiedam*. But the English word 'gin' was derived from the common language between the Dutch and British – French. The French word for juniper is *genièvre* which the Dutch pronounced as *genever* or *jenever*. In turn this was corrupted by the English to *ginever* and finally *gin*.

Gin first reached the English seaports – Bristol, Plymouth, and Portsmouth – then London and the big cities. By the first decade of the seventeenth century English distillers were making it primarily for London where gin was challenging the sales of rum and brandy.

In 1688 William of Orange and his wife Mary succeeded to the English throne. One of their first acts was to implement a petition designed to protect and support English farmers by banning imported brandy and other foreign spirits, and encouraging the use of English grain for distilling. The act did not specify which spirits the English distillers should make, but the only one familiar to them was gin.

Within a very short time gin became established as the major spirit drunk in England. In 1690 gin consumption was around 500,000 gallons; by 1727 it had increased to nearly 5,000,000 gallons; and in 1733 London, then the principal gin distilling city, made 11,000,000 gallons. Not only was it patriotic to drink, but gin was also a cheaper and quicker way to oblivion for the urban poor than ale.

The nation's rulers, who preferred their smuggled brandy, claret, rum and port, grew alarmed at the rampant drunkenness and alcoholism among the working classes – not because they were severely damaging their health through gin, but because drunkenness reduced their work rate and led to civil disorder.

So in 1736 Parliament passed the first of the notorious Gin Acts, designed to reduce the number of gin shops and make the spirit too expensive for the working classes to drink. It forbade the selling of gin in quantities under two gallons, introduced a £50 licence to sell spirits, and put a tax of £1 a gallon on gin.

But, although thousands went to jail, the Act was impossible to enforce. In some areas there was rioting, but generally the Act was ignored and illicit distilling flourished. The London poor flaunted Parliament by renaming gin 'Parliamentary brandy' and by publicly selling the spirit as anything but gin.

The 1736 Act was repealed in 1743. Instead of diminishing, gin production had soared to

The widespread concern with the effects of drink, in particular gin, on the lower classes in the early 19th century is reflected in the caricatures of George Cruikshank, above. The engraving shown right warns patrons of the Gin Shop of the dire consequences of gin drinking: destitution, madness, jail or the hangman's noose. Death, ever present, waits to claim his victims.

The *GIN* Shop.

THE GIN PALACE

Hogarth's Gin Lane, above, was a powerful attack on the growth of gin drinking among the poor. Moral and material ruin, and finally death, are the terrible consequences of over-indulgence. In contrast, Beer Street, above right, is a place of health and good cheer.

In the early 19th century the glittering and ornate Gin Palace replaced the squalid gin shop. A perfectly preserved example is the Red Lion Inn, right, near London's St James's Square.

In the 1750s, when Hogarth painted Gin Lane, it was estimated that in the poor parts of London every fourth or fifth house was selling gin. Gin was being sold by apothecaries, barbers, tobacconists, grog shops, booze dens, merchants and pedlars and even street poets, who offered a free glass of the liquor with each tract they sold.

With the Industrial Revolution, the grog shops and booze dens began to be replaced in a Cinderella-like transformation. At the crossroads of the burgeoning industrial towns the Gin Palaces began to appear. These magnificent gaslit taverns, with gleaming mahogany and superb mirrors, catered for the new urban factory workers with wages to spend. They wanted somewhere better to socialise than the ale house and booze den, but could not afford the coaching inns, frequented by their betters. Rather than send a child out for a quart of gin on Saturday night, the worker could take his wife and children to drink at a Gin Palace.

These Gin Palaces, named after the devotion of the urban masses to gin, also sold other, less intoxicating drinks. But with all their splendour, not even Dickens could find merit in them as a retreat from the cramped homes and appalling conditions of the working classes.

Nor, in the 1870s, could Prime Minister Gladstone. In 1871 he tried to abolish half the public houses in England and Wales. His bill was defeated by a House of Lords, zealous of the rights of the common man. A bishop thundered his opposition to the Prime Minister's intolerance: 'I would better see England free than England sober'. At the ensuing election Gladstone was defeated, 'borne down on a torrent of gin', as he said.

The English pub evolved from the Gin Palace, and particularly in London, the name is still used to describe a certain type of public house. The very brewers who not long ago were demolishing the Victorian pubs are now rebuilding modern versions, pale shadows of the originals, and there is a big export trade in fake 'olde Englishe' pub fitments.

20,000,000 gallons, most of it distilled in London and consumed by its 500,000 citizens.

In 1751 Parliament introduced an improved Act that placed a reasonable tax on the distillers and encouraged them to make better gin. By then London was, as it remains, the biggest gin distilling centre in the world.

But gin was not yet respectable. Hogarth's famous Gin Lane shows all the horrors of gin's grip on lower London. Over the door of the Southwark grog shop in the lower left of his painting he had the slogan 'drunk for a penny, dead drunk for tuppence, clean straw for nothing', which summed up the attitudes of the day.

By the beginning of the nineteenth century, the Industrial Revolution was attracting thousands of families from the depressed rural areas to cities to work in the factories and mills. These new urban workers wanted somewhere better to spend their wages than the grog shop or ale house. The answer came with the elaborately ornamented fantasies of the Gin Palace, where neighbours could escape from their squalid surroundings.

At the same time, gin was gaining respectability in the better homes. Womenfolk mixed it with cordials, lemon juice and sugar (even to a recipe provided by Mrs Beeton). Members of the British Forces brought back from the Colonies a taste for the medicinal quinine (tonic) water mixed with gin.

To everyone in the 1850s gin still meant Hollands – a pungent, sweet distillation, sometimes flavoured with lemon, or heavily sugared and called Old Tom. But around this time distillers began to produce an 'unsweetened' gin with which we are familiar today. There are no records to show when the first 'unsweetened', or 'dry', gin appeared but by the 1870s many distillers were advertising their sugar-free gin.

John Doxat, writing in Stirred, Not Shaken – The Dry Martini, suggests this change from sweet to dry resulted from the idea that sweet drinks and foods were bad for the health. Other theories are that the invention of the Coffey (patent) still in the 1830s resulted in better quality gin, so that the distillers had less need to disguise the flavour with sugar. Certainly at this time there was a general change in taste from heavy to lighter spirits – a similar change happened with Scotch whisky.

By the turn of the century all London gin had become dry gin, and 'London Dry' on the label was the synonym for excellence. Today, although gin distilled in London retains its eminence, the 'London Dry' style is distilled the world over.

London Dry, partly because of its lighter taste, and partly as a result of changing fashions, was acceptable to all classes. And with the Cocktail Age from the mid-1920s to 1930s gin reached world wide popularity. In Britain today, despite the challenge from vodka, white rum and tequila, gin is still second only to Scotch whisky as the favoured spirit.

REDRUTH TEMPERANCE HALL & COFFEE TAVERN,

IS AN IMPOSING BUILDING ERECTED BY PUBLIC SUBSCRIPTION FROM THE DESIGNS OF Mr HICKS, ARCHITECT. IT WAS OPENED MAY, 13TH 1880, BY LADY JANE VIVIAN, AND IS OF COMMANDING APPEARANCE. THE GROUND-FLOOR IS FITTED UP AS A COFFEE TAVERN AND TEMPERANCE RESTAURANT ON THE NEWEST PRINCIPLE, WHILE THE UPPER PORTION OF THE BUILDING CONSISTS OF A SPACIOUS HALL OR LECTURE ROOM, CAPABLE OF SEATING NEARLY 200 PERSONS.

By the last quarter of the 19th century gin was not the only drink under attack from reformers. The powerful Temperance Movement aimed to restrict severely or prohibit sales of all alcohol. They established dry coffee 'taverns', such as shown left, as alternatives for the working man to the licensed inns and pubs.

Gin Production

THE FIRST STEP in the production of London Dry gin or any good gin is the distillation of a highly *rectified* (purified) neutral spirit, usually in a continuous still. For London Dry gins the *base*, or *wash*, is either maize or molasses, which yields grain or cane spirit respectively. Elsewhere rice is sometimes used as a base.

Some leading gin authorities believe cane spirit makes the finest gin (and vodka, as it too is neutral spirit), but the base spirit in a quality gin is almost indistinguishable.

The rectified spirit leaves the still at a very high proof – around 160°. At this proof it has had all or most of its natural *congeners* (the taste and aroma elements in a spirit) removed to leave a wholly neutral flavour.

The next stage is the infusion into the neutral spirit of botanical flavourings which give gin its distinctive taste. The various mixers used with gin will mask variations in taste, but there are distinctive differences in flavour between the leading gins. These come from the different quantities of botanicals each distiller uses in his secret recipe, and the way flavour is reintroduced into the spirit.

All gin contains juniper – its alleged medicinal value first led to the discovery of gin. The other invariable ingredient is coriander, but most gin will contain small proportions of angelica, cassia bark and orris root. Some distillers will also use calamus root, lemon peel, orange peel, liquorice and cinnamon.

There are two main ways of flavouring the neutral base spirit.

The traditional system is to distil the botanicals with *liquor* (water) and neutral spirit either by placing the botanicals in the still or enclosing them in a *head* (mesh cage) on top, or in the neck, of the still so the alcoholic vapour passes through them and absorbs the flavours on its way to the condensers. Beefeater, for example, use this method for their gins. As the flavoured spirit runs into the receiving vat, neutral spirit from a rectifying still is added in the correct proportions, thus yielding gin in one operation.

The second system is the *cold mix* system.

JUNIPER

JUNIPERUS COMMUNIS

The principal flavouring in gin comes from the blue-black berries of the evergreen juniper shrub.

Every batch of gin is nosed by the head distiller for any contamination. The aroma can betray impurities that go undetected by instruments.

The heart of a modern gin distillery is the huge stills, left. However, it is the spirits safes, above, which play the most significant part in ensuring the consistent quality of the finished gin. During the flavouring and rectifying stages, samples of the alcohol are taken from the safes for nosing. Other tests are also carried out on these samples. The density is checked, for example, by taking the specific gravity of the gin, right.

The head method is now giving way to the cold mix system, without any apparent loss of quality. The botanicals (about 2 kg for 100 litres of proof spirit) are *steeped* (soaked) in a small quantity of rectified spirit and then distilled in a pot still to give a strong flavour. This is diluted with unflavoured neutral spirit until the correct proportion between ingredients and alcohol is reached.

Whichever method is used, the craft of the distiller largely centres on making sure the final gin conforms to the brand formula.

The head distiller in a major gin firm constantly noses the product as it flows from the flavour still. His instruments describe the temperature, strength, rate of flow, but only his nose and palate can measure the quality.

During a day's run through a still, the distiller must separate the *heads* and *tails* (feints) from the rest of the re-distillation. At the beginning the flavoured spirit comes through too harshly for a reputable gin. At the end of the day it gets weak and uninteresting. In a quality gin the feints are separated and run into separate vats. The good spirit they contain will later be recovered through a rectifying still.

There is an element of truth in the old saying that 'you can make gin in the morning and drink it in the afternoon'. Gin, being a rectified spirit, does not require – legally or technically – maturation in wood. However, a good gin distiller will marry several distillations to get absolute conformity of flavour.

Once this is achieved, the gin is reduced to the correct strength for the market using demineralised water; and finally, before bottling, it is intensively filtered.

Plymouth Gin

Each gin distiller has his own secret gin recipe. But certain ingredients are common to nearly all gins, among them juniper berries (the principal flavouring), lemon and orange peel, orris root, angelica, cardamom seeds and coriander.

PLYMOUTH GIN IS historically associated with the Royal Navy. It is said that a British naval officer, probably a ship's surgeon, decided to make the Angostura Bitters, used at sea to treat all manner of ills, more palatable by adding gin. The result was *pinkers* (pink gin), subsequently the favourite drink in the Navy wardrooms. Indeed, whether a true pink gin should only be made with Plymouth gin, and not with a London gin, is a matter of debate among connoisseurs. Certainly, using more aromatic Plymouth gin, the spirit is more likely to dominate the taste of the bitters.

When gin first reached England in the latter part of the sixteenth century it came via the sea ports, Plymouth among them. The Navy, which used port with the merchant fleet, adopted the spirit. Ships sailing from Plymouth would take on board 200 cases or more for the officers, which, tradition has it, were usually finished by the time the ship reached Gibraltar.

Apart from the Navy's appetite for gin, Plymouth had a second advantage for distillers – the softness of the water from the Devon moors. This water was already supplied to Plymouth through a *leat* (duct) designed and built by Sir Francis Drake.

The first major distillery to capitalise on these twin advantages was opened by the Coates family in 1793 in a former Dominican monastery. The records do not show whether or not they were the first gin distillers in Plymouth, but from that date they have been the only distillers making Plymouth gin, and still operate from their original site in the oldest part of the city.

Plymouth gin is flavoured in the traditional way – by placing the botanicals straight into the still with the neutral grain spirit. But, unlike the London distillers, Coates dilute their gin down to bottling strength with water direct from their source on Dartmoor (which does not need demineralising).

This water gives their Original Plymouth Gin its characteristic softness and smoothness. During the last war, the company was forced to use very poor cane spirit as the basis for their gin and even unaccustomed Plymouth drinkers noticed the difference in taste.

The original Coates recipe, which gave a heavy aromatic gin, has since been changed to a drier, lighter style more akin to London Dry gin but retaining the characteristic softness. Only two ex-Royal Navy men wrote to the company to complain about the change.

The name 'Plymouth gin' has been protected by law since the late nineteenth century when a London distillery began making its own version of 'Plymouth'. Coates obtained injunctions in Chancery on March 13, 1884, and February 10, 1887, stopping the production of Plymouth gin outside Plymouth itself. They are now the only gin distillers south of London. In recent years they have become part of the Whitbread brewing group.

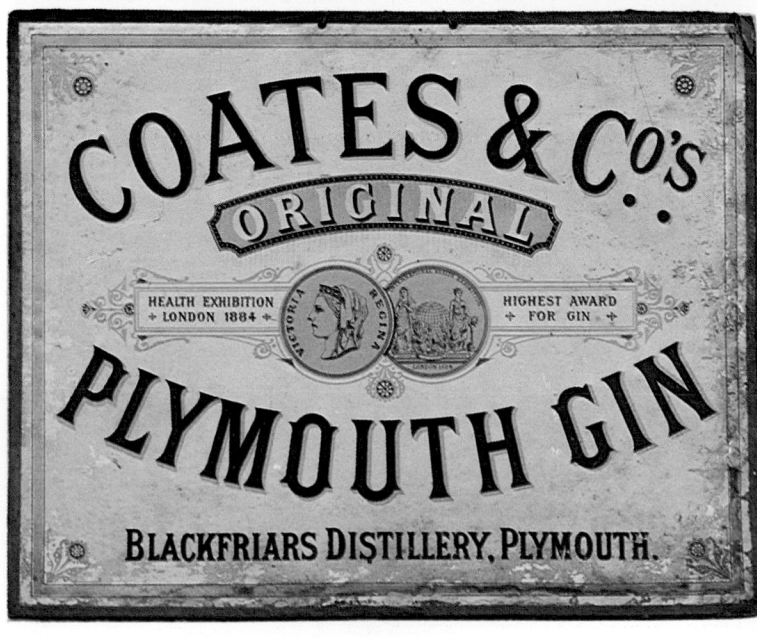

PLYMOUTH GIN

The Black Friars Distillery in Southside Street is the home of Plymouth Gin. The oldest parts of the building, including the historic refectory with its timbered ceiling shaped like the upturned hull of a man o' war, were completed in 1425 by the Dominican order of Black Friars.

The monastic Black Friars used the old buildings until Henry VIII dissolved the monasteries in 1536 and the buildings were taken over by burghers of Plymouth. The refectory became the town meeting place, and in 1620 the Pilgrim Fathers are said to have held their last meeting and slept the night in this room before sailing to America.

Later it was a debtors' prison, then a refuge for French Huguenots, and in 1793 it became the Coates & Co distillery.

The company has restored the old buildings and housed its modern still rooms alongside them. Protected from demolition or rebuilding under the Ancient Monuments Act, the Black Friars distillery is now open to the public on weekdays and Coates, in recognition of its original use, have a Black Friar on the label of their Original Plymouth Gin.

Flavoured Gins

TANQUERAY GIN

What do Isaac Walton, Emmanuel Swedenborg, Daniel Defoe, Guy Fawkes and Nell Gwynn have in common? They all frequently took the spa waters at Finsbury, London, which have been used to produce gin by the Tanqueray family since the 1740s.

Tanqueray gin is still a family-run business today. P J Tanqueray, right, the current head of the firm, is the great, great grandson of the founder.

Tanqueray gin was only introduced into America in the 1950s but since then sales have soared, and by the late 1970s more than 1,000,000 cases were being sold there each year.

Tanqueray gin is still produced to the original recipe. The contents of the 19th-century flagon, left, found in Kingston harbour Jamaica, would have been very similar to the modern gin sold in the distinctive bottles modelled on 18th-century London fire hydrants.

FLAVOURED GINS HAVE been made in England since gin itself became a national spirit. At first, flavours were introduced to disguise the harshness of the raw spirit and make it more palatable.

When the major gin distillers began in the eighteenth and nineteenth centuries they continued the tradition, although their flavoured gins were, and still are, made with quality spirit. But in recent years there has been little demand for flavoured gins and they are now only made by a handful of English distillers as a sideline to their unsweetened, juniper-flavoured London Drys.

The best-known flavouring is obtained from sloeberries. Sloe gin is currently undergoing a modest revival in popularity. James Hawker of Plymouth, who have specialised in the making of sloe gin under their Pedlar label, continue a tradition going back some 400 years. Gordons have also produced their own sloe gin in their London distillery for a century or more; Nicholsons who made a sloe-flavoured gin up to the last war have reintroduced their Liqueur Sloe gin; and Lamb & Watt, the Liverpool spirits producers, also produce a sloe gin.

Each brand has its own recipe. Mauget, for example, is made by cold compounding West Country sloeberries with gin. Nicholsons use Irish sloes which they partly infuse in 40° overproof gin (known as *strong gin* by the distillers) and then blend with sloe juice ex-

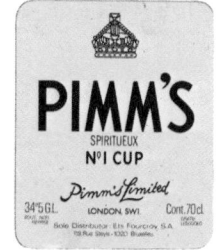

tracted from other berries to the right balance. Gordons steep eastern European fruit in 40° overproof gin before bringing it down to strength. All four sloe gins are about 45° strength, and are slightly sweetened with sugar syrup before bottling. The sloeberries picked are simply left in the gin to give the flavour. Making sloe gin in the home is popular in some parts of England where wild blackthorns dot the country lanes.

The basic commercial method is to steep the sloeberries in 40° overproof gin until the flavour is taken up by the spirit, usually about three months. Other flavourings are then added and the gin is sweetened slightly and reduced to bottling strength with distilled water – about 45° is standard. However, Nicholsons varies slightly, they infuse part of the required amount of sloes and then extract the juice from the remainder and blend the two to obtain the right flavour.

Old Tom is another traditional flavoured gin – flavoured in that it is sweetened, usually with sugar syrup (from between two and six percent). This drink is supposedly credited to Captain Dudley Bradstreet who had a gin shop advertised by the sign of a cat. During the Gin Acts he served gin to customers in the street through a pipe under the paw of the cat, and was paid his penny or two through the cat's mouth. Bradstreet changed his address frequently, with the parish soon learning where the cat had its

PINK GIN

Shake several drops of Angostura Bitters into a wine or similar glass. Roll the Bitters round the glass and shake out any surplus. Pour in 1½ oz gin and add ice, water or soda water according to taste. The gin must be added to the Bitters, not the other way round.
From Booth's Handbook of Cocktails & Mixed Drinks by John Doxat.

COLLINS

Place several lumps of ice in a long glass and add 1½ oz dry gin, 1½ oz fresh lemon juice, 1 dash Angostura Bitters and 2 barspoons caster sugar, or to taste. Top up with soda water, stir, and serve with straws and a slice of lemon.

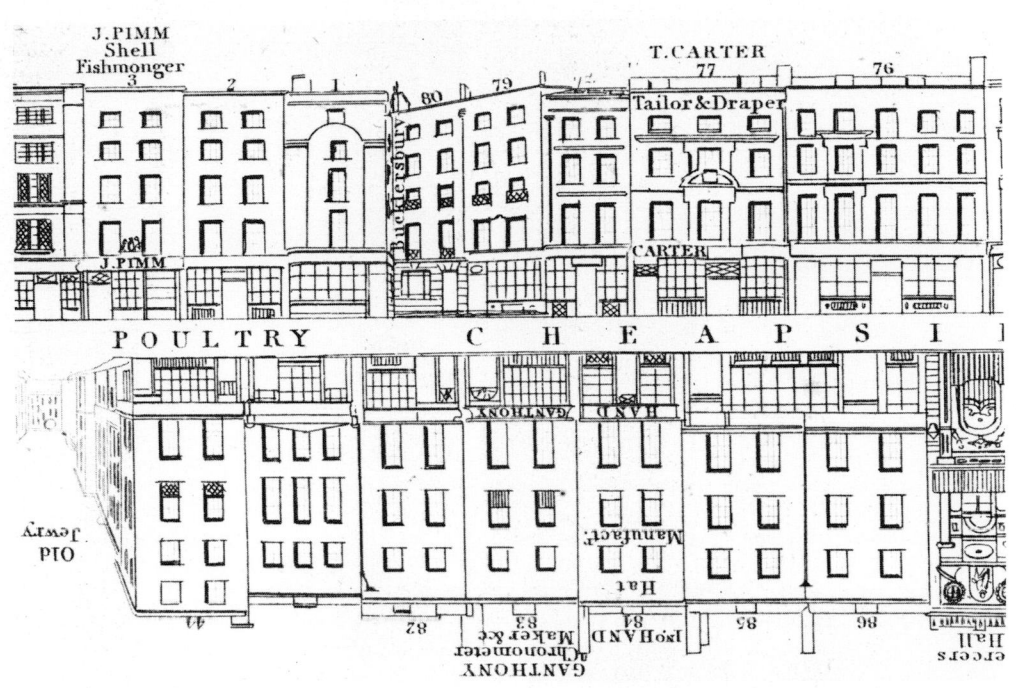

Strangely enough one of the best-known gin-based cocktails, Pimms, originated in a fish restaurant. However, as the bottle, left, shows, Pimms No 1 has been spread far and wide since then.

PIMMS

new house. Locals, probably impressed with this shifty wisdom, may have called Bradstreet's gin 'Old Tom'. John Doxat also suggests in his *Booth's Handbook of Cocktails and Mixed Drinks* that Old Tom was named after one Thomas Chamberlain of Hodge's distillery – an early experimenter with flavoured gins.

Old Tom is still made in small quantities for export only at Boords and at Tanqueray, Gordon distilleries in London. It is used as the base for the Tom Collins cocktail; the John Collins cocktail is made with dry gin.

Lemon, orange and, very infrequently, blackcurrant gins are also made for export. Tanqueray, Gordon produce both lemon and orange, and a ready-made Dry Martini cocktail.

The other famous gin-based product is Pimms No 1 gin sling, the long drink traditionally decorated with fruit. Pimms is named after James Pimm, who in the 1800s had a fish restaurant in Poultry in the City of London. At first he invented his gin sling for his customers, but found that demand grew to such a level that he could begin commercial manufacture. No 1 was followed by Pimms No 2 (whisky-based) and No 3 (brandy-based), and later came No 4 (rum), No 5 (rye whiskey) and No 6 (vodka) – the last in the line.

Numbers two to six were dropped recently, but Pimms, now a part of the Distillers Company Ltd, have brought back No 6 for the British market only. The original No 1 is basically gin compounded with herbs and essences, and enhanced with a European liqueur. The flavourings are kept secret, and there is an unconfirmed story that every Pimms employee has to sign a document swearing that they will not reveal the recipe should they accidentally find out what it is.

It seems that the most usual way of serving a Pimms is with a garnish of a fruit salad. Not so, say the makers, who maintain that the correct way to serve this refreshing drink is very simply, with a slice of lemon and cucumber rind.

Place several lumps of ice in a ½-pint tankard and add 1½ oz Pimms No 1 Cup or Vodka Pimms. Top up with lemonade, 7-Up or ginger ale. Garnish with a twist of lemon peel and a sliver of cucumber rind.

Other Drinks

  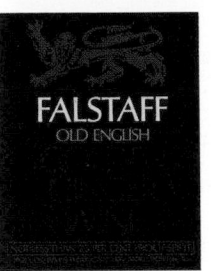   

THE ENGLISH DISTILLING industry is best known for its London Dry gins. But this is only one section, albeit a substantial one, of the English industry. To it must be added a long list of other spirits, liqueurs and fortified wines, produced mainly for domestic consumption.

Every gin and grain whisky distiller creates a supply of neutral spirit which, with little work, can be converted into vodka. British vodkas, like their American counterparts, are colourless, odourless and tasteless.

Gilbey Vintners first produced vodka in Great Britain when they began distilling Smirnoff under licence from the United States in 1952. At their Harlow distillery, north of London, they make Smirnoff red (65.5°) and Smirnoff blue (80°) for the British market. Their largest competitors are G & J Greenall who make Vladivar at the same distillery in Warrington, where their Bombay and 1761 gins are produced.

Other major labels are Cossack from Buchanan Booths (who produce Black and White whisky and High & Dry gin); James Burrough with Borzoi (alongside Beefeater gin); Allied Breweries with Romanoff; Seagram with Orloff; Nicholsons with 1812 and Wolfschmidt, originally an imported vodka.

Less important are a long string of proprietary brands, among them Balalaika, Baronoff, Czaroff, Karloff and Popoff.

The high humidity levels in many English warehouses make them ideal for maturing rum (and cognac and whisky), so several companies blend and mature rums originally imported in bulk for the domestic market and re-export. The best-known dark rums are Captain Morgan and Old Navy (both Seagram); Lamb's Navy, Black Heart and Lemon Hart (all United Rum Merchants); Windjammer (Mackinlay-McPherson); and Mainbrace (Allied Breweries).

Bacardi, Appleton, Dry Cane (Courage Breweries), Caroni, Cabana and Santiago are the main white rums. Lamb & Watt also make two blackcurrant-flavoured rums – Black Coral and Island Cask.

Green ginger wine (usually between 24° and 25°) is made by three large companies.

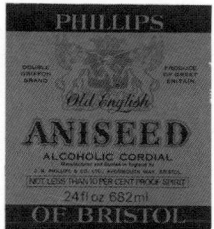

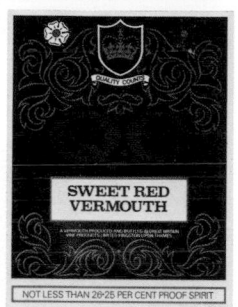

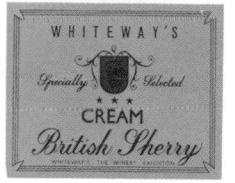

The English distilling industry produces a surprising selection of potables apart from gin. They range from ginger wines to the more obscure bitters – produced by Phillips and Can-y-Delyn, a Welsh whisky-based liqueur.

Manchester United football team have their own special whisky-based liqueur – Redalevn.

Matthew Clark produce Stone's Green Ginger; J R Phillips make Crabbies; and Cadbury Schweppes make Schweppes Green Ginger Wine. It can be drunk neat, but it is also widely used to lace Scotch whisky as a warm winter drink, called a *whisky mac*.

In the late 1960s the J H Wham company introduced the first premixed whisky mac under their Scotsmac brand name, and its success bred several rivals, among them Clan Dew, Stone's Mac, King Fergus Mac, The Real McCoy, Minstrel Mac, and two brands using British wine, instead of ginger wine – Dr Cameron's and King Duncan.

British wine, as distinct from English table wine made from grapes grown in English soil, is wine reconstituted from grape musts imported from Cyprus, Argentina, Yugoslavia and elsewhere. In the same way, British sherries and British port-style wines are made from mainly Cypriot and Spanish musts. This results in lower duties and hence lower prices. The main producer – Vine Products of Kingston-upon-Thames – has one of Europe's largest wineries, although it is miles from the nearest vineyards because its products originate from imported concentrates. It makes and sells thousands of gallons of British sherry each year under the brand names VP, RSVP, QC, Lord Ducane and Hudson & Cooper. Of their two rivals – Matthew Clark & Sons sell Old England; and Lamb & Watt have the Vine Leaf label.

Vine Products also make port-style wines and Votrix, a British vermouth, from imported musts; while Matthew Clark use the same principle to make Tosca, a British equivalent to Campari.

Mead, the historic English honey-flavoured drink, is made commercially by several companies, the main ones being Lamb & Watt with Elizabethan; Merrydown Wine Co with Merrydown and Lindisfarne; and the Cornish Mead Co, producing Edouard Robinson.

English liqueurs include Grant's Morella Cherry brandy, Trotsky cherry brandy from Davis & Co (who also make Trotsky kummel and curaçao), Rawlings Morella cherry brandy, Keelings Old English advocaat, a range of egg-based drinks including Maldano Egg Flip, Green Goddess, Late Night Final, Damson Cream and Crazy, all made by J Townend of Hull, and the highly regarded kummels sold by Wolfschmidt and Mentzendorff. A Yorkshire-based company makes Brontë honey liqueur as a regional speciality named after the Brontë sisters.

In north London Dr Peter Hallgarten makes what are probably the best-known English liqueurs. The success of his first creation, Royal Mint Chocolate liqueur, has led to half a dozen more flavours – Royal Raspberry Chocolate, Royal Cherry Chocolate, and orange, lemon, banana and ginger. He also created, to a secret recipe, Can-y-Delyn, a Welsh liqueur; and Redalevn, a Scotch whisky-based liqueur sold only to the Manchester United Football Club.

In the south of England a range of flavoured alcoholic cordials are drunk locally as digestifs and hangover cures. The only producer is Phillips of Bristol, with their Shrub, Lovage, Pink Cloves, Blackcurrant, Peppermint and Aniseed labels.

Scotland/Whisky

THE SCOTS ARE LOATH to admit it, but the roots of their whisky distilling industry most likely lie in Ireland. The art probably crossed from Ireland to the Scottish Western Isles with early invaders and settlers in the fifth century and spread with them eastwards through the Highlands. Some date the arrival later, in the early Middle Ages, when distilling was certainly established in Ireland.

There is no real evidence to support this theory, and one German authority even denies the early reputation that the Irish have as distillers. Other historians have suggested that it was introduced into Scotland from The Netherlands; or that it was accidentally discovered by a Scottish farmer looking for a way to get rid of his surplus grain. But the Irish connection is the favoured explanation.

The first official mention of distilling in Scotland appears in the Scottish Exchequer rolls for 1494 which record the provision of malt to a certain Friar John Cor to make 'aqua vitae' – the Latin equivalent of the Gaelic *uisge beatha*, or 'water of life', the still-used Scots epithet for whisky. Friar John Cor was provided with enough malt to indicate that he was going to make a good quantity of whisky, so distilling must have been firmly established in Scotland by that time.

By the sixteenth and seventeenth centuries whisky had become the true spirit of Scotland. However, it began to attract the attention of the authorities as a potential source of revenue. In 1644 the Scottish Parliament introduced the first excise tax on whisky to raise urgently needed revenue to pay the army. From this point on, the history of whisky became inexorably linked with the taxes imposed on it. The development of the industry marched in time with the various Acts regulating it, financially and otherwise. After the Stuart Restoration in 1660 the tax was allowed to lapse altogether, partly because of the extreme difficulties in collecting excise duties in the Highlands.

Excise duty was reimposed in 1693, and in 1707, following the union of Scotland and England, a Board of Excise was set up with whisky as one of its main targets. In 1713 the British Parliament, on the advice of the Board, imposed a malt tax on Scotland, but at a lower rate than the same tax in England. This tax was aimed at the raw material, not the whisky, supposedly an easier tax to collect.

The 1713 tax, above all others, encouraged illicit distilling, particularly in the remote Highland areas. And, according to whisky expert David Daiches: 'made certain that illicit whisky was of better quality than the legally distilled since the legal distillers, to minimise the malt tax, used a high proportion of raw grain.

From the second half of the eighteenth century, whisky taxes grew from moderate levels to increasingly penal financial burdens. Illegal stills flourished, particularly in the wild Highlands, making a better quality untaxed product than the licenced Lowland

About 200 years ago illicitly distilled whisky was the source of the best Scotch, and illegal production was common in the Highlands. Following the rise of the modern industry and government action, it has now almost died out.

distillers. The local communities regarded whisky as their drink and moonshining was generally accepted. Further increases in taxation only made illicit distilling even more attractive. Legal Lowland distillers complained of the competition from their illegal Highland counterparts and, under pressure, Parliament responded with a two-tier tax system favouring the Lowlanders. When that failed, a second uniform tax of 1786 placed a higher duty on all whisky, and in 1788 the level was raised even higher.

In Scotland only the aristocracy drank claret and brandy, the rest of the population was in the grip of whisky.

An impression of the part whisky played in the life of a typical Highland village in the early nineteenth century can be gained from Elizabeth Fletcher's description of Balfron: 'Balfron was a most lawless village. There was a cotton mill in it, and the workers in it were among the best people there. It was illicit distillation that demoralised the district. The men of the place resorted to the woods or to the sequestered glens among the Campsie hills, and there distilled whisky, which their wives and daughters took in tin vessels in the form of stays buckled around their waists to sell for a high price in Glasgow.'

The wily Scots even managed to turn the efforts of their foes the excisemen to their own advantage. The Government had offered a £5 reward for anyone reporting the whereabouts of an illegal still. At that time the most expensive part of a still was the copper worm through which the alcoholic vapours passed to be condensed into spirit. As Sir Robert Bruce Lockhart explained in his book *Scotch*, the illegal distillers found a second use for the worm: 'When the copper pipe was

worn out, the smugglers would dismantle their still, taking care to remove whatever might be of further use to them, but leaving the worn-out worm and other minor implements to show that a still had been there. One of the smugglers would then go to the gauger (excise policeman), report that he had discovered a still, and collect the £5 reward.

The late eighteenth and early nineteenth century was whisky's romantic era, with the smugglers against the excisemen and the few legal distillers in the middle. Parliament introduced a succession of ineffective laws and it was not until 1823 that an act was passed which effectively put an end to widespread unlicensed distilling and changed the face of the whisky industry. Illegal distilling was at its height. In that year excisemen confiscated 14,000 illegal stills in Scotland.

The shape of the Act was largely the work of the fourth Duke of Gordon, one of Britain's largest landowners with vast estates in Inverness-shire and Banffshire, two of the great whisky counties. He argued that the Highlander would not stop illicit distilling unless the legal production of whisky was encouraged by reasonable taxes, and better whisky could be made more profitably. If an act could do this, there would be no place for the illegal distiller. The 1823 Act followed the Duke's suggestions, and with the other Scottish lords he began to encourage the legal production of better whisky.

Illegal distilling did not disappear overnight, even now small quantities of moonshine are still made. But the number of illicit stills fell drastically over the next twenty to thirty years, smuggling declined, and in its place came the rise of the distillers and merchants, the fathers of the modern industry.

"Say WHEN, Man !!"

Malt Whisky/Production

SCOTCH WHISKY IS PRODUCED in three forms: malt whisky, grain whisky (rarely sold alone) and blends of malt and grain.

Malt whisky is the original of the three. Until the 1830s malt was the only whisky, then a new distilling process gave rise to the grain whiskies, and they in turn led to the blends. Whisky is tailored to the demands of the Scots climate – a climate David Daiches describes as damp, alive, fragrant, rarely numbing, a climate bound to produce a spirit which appeals primarily to the nose. He writes: 'With a climate cold enough for the national drink to have to be a warming one but not so cold as to drive people to any alcoholic expedient in order to find inner warmth or even oblivion, and with the countryside making continuous olfactory demands on the inhabitants, Scotland, one could argue, was bound to produce a spirit of rare and subtle aroma.'

A malt is the unique result of the effects of malted barley, Scottish water, pot distilling, and wood maturation in the damp air.

Scotland possesses 119 malt distilleries, each producing relatively modest amounts, but to an experienced distiller or blender each malt is as distinctive as a thumb print. Some malts are bottled as they are – single whiskies showing their own particular characteristics – but the majority of malts are used wholly or in part to give character to the almost neutral grain whisky that forms the main part of any blend.

Unlike the grains, malt whisky is only made from barley. Much of the barley used to come from the Continent or as far afield as California and Australia, and was generally considered better than the home-grown barley because it had a lower moisture content. Now, to reduce imports, it is more likely English or Scottish, harvested in September or October.

The conversion of the harvested barley to the wash is the first main cycle in the production of a malt whisky. The distillation of the wash is the second cycle.

Malting and producing the wash

Ideally the barley should be fully ripened, fat, dry and with the correct protein content. Dryness is vital, otherwise it will turn mouldy and will not germinate properly at the start of the malting process. The moisture content should be around 10 percent and English and Scottish barleys, with their moisture content of around 20 percent, are usually cleaned and dried in kilns and stored in towers warmed by hot air.

Malting is simply the germinating and drying of the barley. Nearly every distillery used to have its own malting house, but nowadays most obtain their malted barley from companies that specialise in this part of the whisky cycle. First the dried barley is soaked in water in large tanks (or *steeps*), for between 48 and 70 hours, depending on the time of year and the quality of the grain. The water is then drained off and the wet barley spread out up to two feet deep on the cement or stone floor of the malting house, and left to germinate. The grain will start to sprout, 'breathing' in oxygen and 'breathing' out carbon dioxide and giving off heat. To encourage the process the barley is turned continuously by maltmen using long-handled wooden shovels or *skips*. The barley is turned at least once a day, a hard, boring job that is gradually being taken over by mechanical agitators, rotating the grain in large drums, or by the Saladin box, a box with revolving forks to keep the grain moving.

After two to three days the barley sprouts rootlets, which in another four to five days

Two of the essential elements in the making of a good malt are the peat and the grain. Before fermentation can begin, the grain must be malted, above. This is done by germinating the grain, right, and then drying it initially over fires made from local cut peat, far right.

WHISKY PRODUCTION

The production of malt whisky is an exacting process, requiring skills and knowledge which have been built up over the long history of distilling.

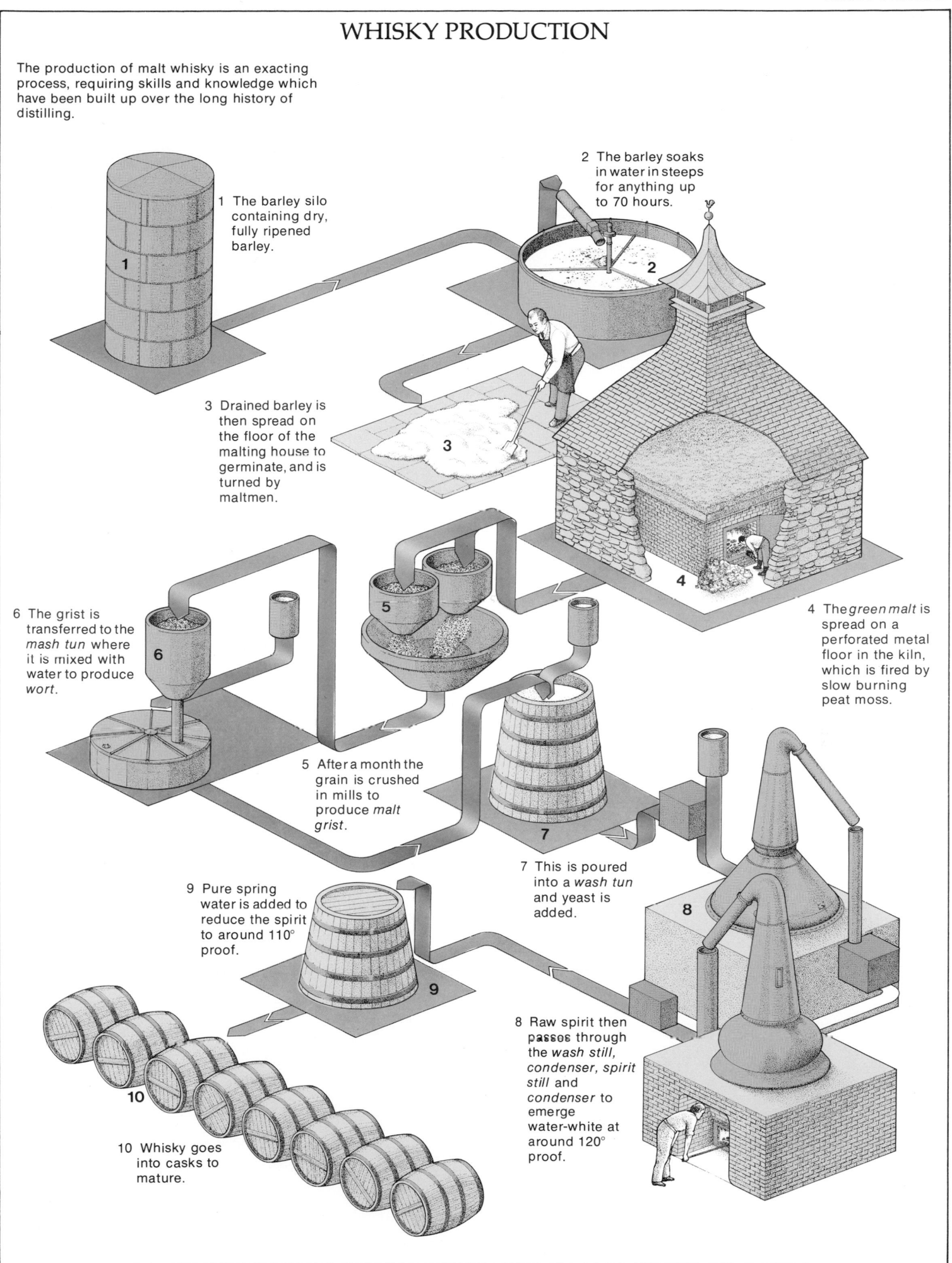

1 The barley silo containing dry, fully ripened barley.

2 The barley soaks in water in steeps for anything up to 70 hours.

3 Drained barley is then spread on the floor of the malting house to germinate, and is turned by maltmen.

4 The *green malt* is spread on a perforated metal floor in the kiln, which is fired by slow burning peat moss.

5 After a month the grain is crushed in mills to produce *malt grist*.

6 The grist is transferred to the *mash tun* where it is mixed with water to produce *wort*.

7 This is poured into a *wash tun* and yeast is added.

8 Raw spirit then passes through the *wash still*, *condenser*, *spirit still* and *condenser* to emerge water-white at around 120° proof.

9 Pure spring water is added to reduce the spirit to around 110° proof.

10 Whisky goes into casks to mature.

The characteristic peaty flavour of a malt is produced by smoking the *green malt* over peat fires above. Peating rooms at a malt distillery have distinctive pagoda-like chimneys, left.

A huge vat called a *mash tun*, right, produces the base liquid for fermentation from the malted grain. Fermentation takes place in the *wash tun*, below, and may last between 36 and 44 hours.

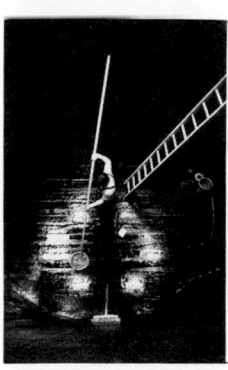

start to wither. It is then considered malted. The *green malt*, as the barley is now called, is soft, straw-coloured, floury and moisture-laden. It goes straight to the kiln for spreading on a floor of perforated metal plates or wire mesh. Ten or fifteen feet beneath this floor is a fire fuelled by slow burning peat moss. The burning peat gives off a pungent, earthy smoke with its own particular fragrance which permeates the green malt. This gives the finished spirit the prized *peat reek,* or peaty aroma, and part of the spirit's distinctive taste.

When the green malt has absorbed sufficient peaty flavour, coal and anthracite are added to the fires to raise the temperature to around 160°F. The malt dries out into crisp, crumbly, fragrant grain quite different from the original barley.

It is then left to rest for a month or more, the withered rootlets are removed and sold as malt *culms* (combings) for cattle food, and the remaining grain coarsely crushed in mills to give the *malt grist*.

The grist goes into the *mash tun* in a carefully measured quantity and hot water is added. A giant circular arm stirs the grist with the hot water, extracting its solubles, particu-larly the enzyme maltose. The water is changed three or four times and each time its temperature increased. The first two washings are run off and form the *wort,* a semi-transparent, sweetish liquid. The third and fourth washings (the *sparge*) are kept to one side to make up the first and second washings of the next batch. The thick, porridge-like mash at the bottom of the tun is removed and later sold as cattle food, like the malt culms.

The wort is poured into a giant vat called the *wash tun* where yeast is added. Its enzymes convert the maltose in the wort to *dextrose,* and then into alcohol and carbon dioxide. The wash back is continuously stirred, and the mixture bubbles and froths as the gas escapes. After a day and a half, sometimes a little longer, a clear liquid remains – the *wash*. It consists of water, yeast, and about 5 percent of alcohol by volume.

Distillation

All malt whiskies are made in pot stills. Each distillery has several copper stills that look like an upturned wine funnel, with a bulbous circular base tapering off to a long, almost swan-like neck. The capacity of the distillery depends on its number of stills, and with the increasing world demand for Scotch whisky they work all year round the clock, except for a couple of weeks in the summer when they are cleaned and maintained. The stills are the heart of the operation. So important are they that when one is damaged or replaced, the repaired or new still is modelled exactly to the shape of the old. Every bump and dent is duplicated to a minute fraction of an inch. The stillmen are the brains of the distilling operation. As the young raw spirit starts to flow, a minute can make the difference between a batch of pure spirit and one with the slightest hint of contamination. It is a skill that can only be gained through experience.

Each batch of malt whisky requires two pot stills to produce the finished spirit: the *wash still* and the *low wines still*. The first half of the cycle takes place in the wash still. The wash is pumped in and heated by coal or oil fire until it vaporises. The vapour rises up through the neck of the still to the condenser where it passes through a twisting copper pipe – the *worm* – immersed in cold water, where it condenses back to liquid form – the *low wine*. From the *low wines charger* (holding tank) it passes into the low wines still, where the cycle is repeated to produce a spirit with a higher degree of purity and alcoholic strength.

The key part of both distilling stages is the separation of the impure spirit at the beginning and end of each run from the clean spirit in the middle of the run. As the spirit starts to flow from the wash still through the condenser into the *spirits safe*, the highly impure first part, the *foreshots*, is run off into a *receiver*. When the spirit starts to flow cleanly, the stillman turns a tap and the pure spirit passes into a second receiver and from there to the spirits still. The final part of the run, the *feints*, is also impure and is cut off like the fore-shots Both are returned from the receiver for redistillation.

The same process of separation is repeated as the spirit emerges from the low wines still. As it flows into the spirits safe, a glass box kept sealed by Customs and Excise, the still-man watches the spirit looking for a slight blueness which signifies impurity. He can also test the spirit within the box by adding a few drops of distilled water. If the spirit turns cloudy it is still contaminated. If it stays clear it is the *heart* of the distillation and is run off. The spirit can now properly be called whisky. Again, the foreshots and feints are returned for redistillation.

The residue left in the wash still, the *burnt ale*, is removed and used for fertiliser or animal food. Several distilleries now have separate plants to process this and their other wastes into useable cattle food. The residue in the low wines still, the *spent lees*, is little more than hot water, and is run off and dispersed, producing the clouds of steam seen rising from the back of many distilleries.

The new whisky emerges from the still as a water-white, very pungent fiery spirit around 115° to 120° proof. The only people with the stomach to drink it seem to be the hardened distillery workers themselves. It is reduced to around 110° proof with pure spring water and put into oak casks to mature.

Different malt whiskies reach maturity over a different span of time. Some are ready after five years in wood, some eight, some ten, some twelve to fifteen, and it is generally accepted that a malt whisky does not get any better after about fifteen years, and may start to lose quality.

The traditional Scottish cask is the 110-gallon butt. Smaller casks can be used to hasten the maturation, but most whiskies still go into butts. Since the early years of the last century, these butts have come from Jerez in Spain where they have been used to mature sherry. The sherry has taken much of the woodiness (tannin) from the oak and left part

The still houses at the Longmorn-Glenlivet distillery, left, where the water comes from a local spring and the peat from Mannoch Hill.

The spirits safe, shown right, from the Laphroaig distillery, is always kept under lock and key. It is here that the still-man separates the impure *foreshots* and *aftershots*, or *feints*, from the *heart* of the run.

of its own character in the wood that in turn contributes to the mellowness, colour and, on a very small scale, the taste of the matured malt. The sherry butt is still widely used, although the modern scale of production often forces the distillers to substitute other oak butts when Jerez runs short of stock.

In the wood the malt whisky softens, loses a lot of its pungent character, and takes on its colour – anything from a pale straw to a honey gold. Although the damp climate inhibits evaporation, it does help the whisky lose some strength.

When the whisky has reached its optimum maturity it is bottled as a single malt (after spring water has been used again further to reduce the strength, normally to 70° proof for the home market, 75° for export), or it goes into one of the many blended whiskies. Very occasionally the malt is sold at a higher strength than 70°. Examples include Glen Grant Highland malt, Highland Park Island malt, Strathisla and Macallan Highland malts which are part bottled at 100° proof; Glenfarclas Highland malt is obtainable at 105° proof – almost natural strength.

During maturation the barrels are stored on racks in the distiller's warehouse. Samples are taken regularly, as this early picture from the Ardbeg distillery shows.

Malt Whisky/The Distilleries

EACH MALT WHISKY to a greater degree than each grain whisky, has its own stamp of individuality. No two are really alike. Even two distilleries using the same water, peat and barley will not make the same whisky. The differences result from the way the barley is malted, the water and peat used, the shape of the still, the temperature of distillation, the length of maturation and the casks used.

This combination of variables is what makes malt whisky unique, and impossible to produce outside Scotland. Several other countries have tried, notably Japan. (Where a town was even named Aberdeen to lend a greater authority to their whisky.) One of the favourite stories of the whisky makers concerns a party of Japanese who visited one of the famous Highland distilleries. Each had a camera, and hundreds of photographs were taken of the distillery and its equipment. About a year later an exact replica of the distillery had been built in Japan, but sadly for its owners, the resulting whisky had little in common with the product of the original distillery. Had they but asked they would have been told that even the owners of a new Scottish distillery do not know what sort of whisky they will get until the first batch has matured. They can only hope that all the variables will combine together to give them a top-quality whisky.

Because each malt whisky has its own distinctive character, it is difficult to make generalisations about different areas – even more so as the vocabulary used by the distillers and blenders to describe different malts is limited. However, the blenders do have a system of classifying the malts. Most use a geographical system, separating the malts into Lowland, Islay, Campbeltown and three subdivisions of Highland malt. Some, particularly Chivas Brothers, grade them into firsts, seconds, and thirds, based on flavour, depth, and interchangeability. But, even the head blender of Chivas admits that this is generalising about something that by its nature cannot be generalised about.

Using the geographical system, some very broad comments can be made about the malts from the different areas of Scotland, taking as examples some of the single malts that are bottled in part as single malts and which do not wholly disappear into the whisky blends.

Islay malts
Islay, the southernmost of the outer Western Isles, has eight distilleries. They produce malts which are traditionally very heavily peated to give a pungent whisky with a deep flavour and an almost medicinal character. Some whisky experts also say they can detect a slight saltiness from peat. In a blend they are used to give depth and aroma to the whisky. No one tasting an Islay against a Highland malt could fail to notice the peaty character of the island's whiskies.

Laphroaig is often picked as the best of the Islays. It has a very strong flavour and pro-

An old advertisement for Bowmore, one of the Islay malt whiskies, bottled at eight years.

The Laphroaig distillery, built in 1820.

THE MALT WHISKY DISTILLERIES

The malt whisky distilleries of Scotland listed by the Scotch Whisky Association are:

Campbeltown malts
1 Glen Scotia
2 Springbank

Islay malts
3 Ardbeg
4 Bowmore
5 Bruichladdich
6 Bunnahabhain
7 Caol Ila
8 Lagavulin
9 Laphroaig
10 Port Ellen

Lowland malts
11 Auchentoshan
12 Bladnoch
13 Glenkinchie
14 Inverleven
15 Kinclaith
16 Ladyburn
17 Littlemill
18 Lomond
19 Rosebank
20 St Magdalene
21 Moffat

Highland malts
22 Aberfeldy
23 Aberlour-Glenlivet
24 Allta' Bhainne
25 Ardmore
26 Auchroisk
27 Aultmore
28 Balblair
29 Balmenach
30 Balvenie
31 Banff
32 Ben Nevis
33 Ben Riach-Glenlivet
34 Benrinnes
35 Benromach
36 Ben Wyvis
37 Blair Athol
38 Braes of Glenlivet
39 Caperdonich
40 Cardow
41 Clynelish
42 Coleburn
43 Convalmore
44 Cragganmore
45 Craigellachie
46 Dailuaine
47 Dallas Dhu
48 Dalmore
49 Dalwhinnie
50 Deanston
51 Dufftown-Glenlivet
52 Edradour
53 Fettercairn
54 Glen Albyn
55 Glenallachie
56 Glenburgie-Glenlivet
57 Glencadam
58 Glendronach
59 Glendullan
60 Glen Elgin
61 Glenfarclas-Glenlivet
62 Glenfiddich
63 Glen Foyle
64 Glen Garioch
65 Glenglassaugh
66 Glengoyne
67 Glen Grant-Glenlivet
68 Glen Keith-Glenlivet
69 Glenlivet, The
70 Glenlochy
71 Glenlossie
72 Glen Mhor
73 Glenmorangie
74 Glen Moray-Glenlivet
75 Glenrothes-Glenlivet
76 Glen Spey
77 Glentauchers
78 Glenturret
79 Glenugie
80 Glenury-Royal
81 Highland Park
82 Hillside
83 Imperial
84 Inchgower
85 Isle of Jura
86 Knockando
87 Knockdhu
88 Linkwood

89 Loch Lomond
90 Lochnagar
91 Lochside
92 Longmorn-Glenlivet
93 Macallan-Glenlivet
94 Macduff
95 Mannochmore
96 Millburn
97 Miltonduff-Glenlivet
98 Mortlach
99 North Port
100 Oban
101 Ord
102 Pittyvaich-Glenlivet, The
103 Pulteney
104 Royal Brackla
105 Royal Lochnagar
106 Scapa
107 Speyburn
108 Speyside
109 Strathisla-Glenlivet
110 Strathmill
111 Talisker
112 Tamdhu-Glenlivet

113 Tamnavulin-Glenlivet
114 Teaninich
115 Tobermory
116 Tomatin
117 Tomintoul-Glenlivet
118 Tormore
119 Tullibardine.

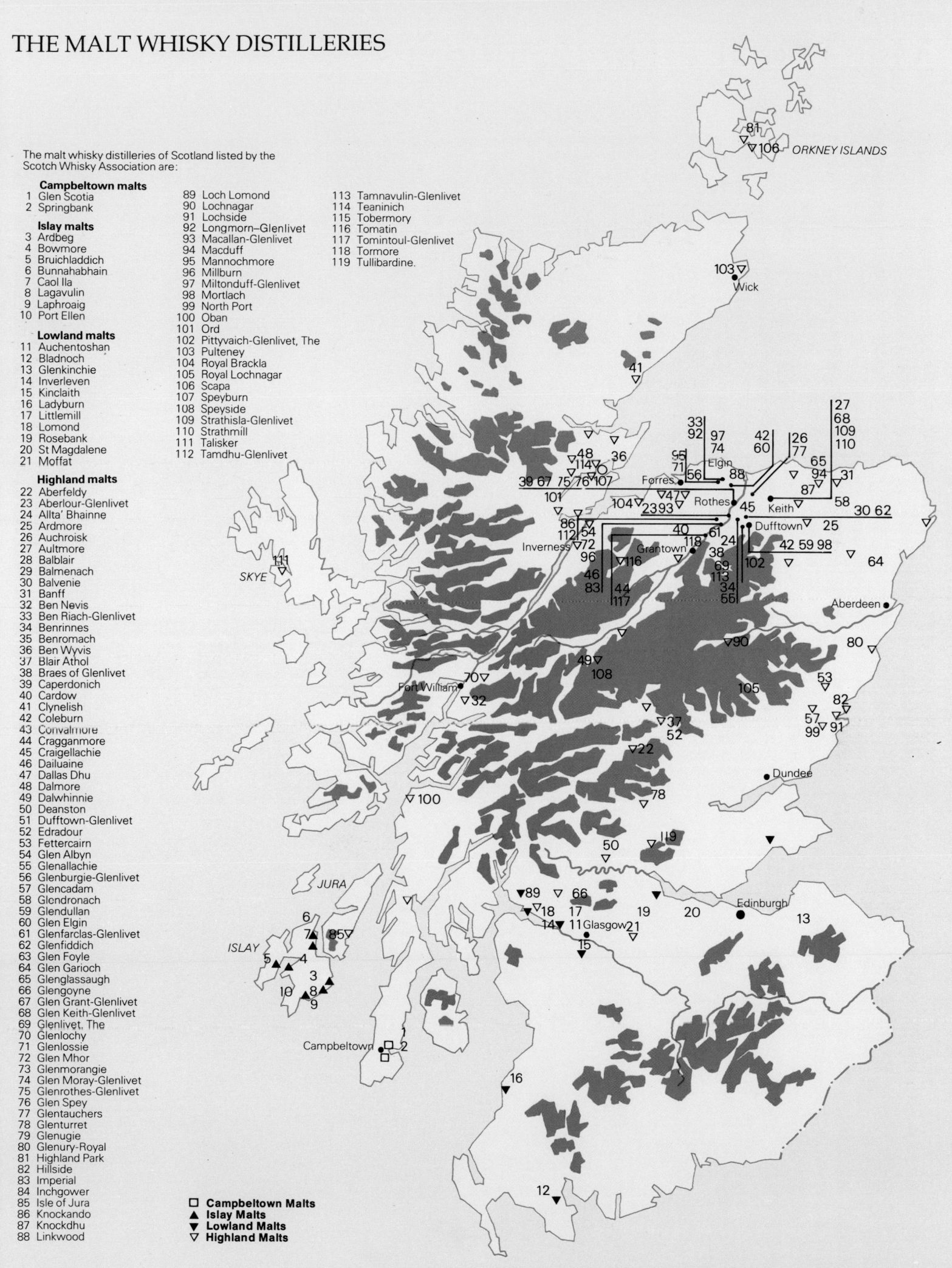

□ Campbeltown Malts
▲ Islay Malts
▼ Lowland Malts
▽ Highland Malts

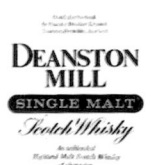

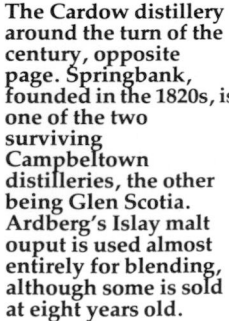

The Cardow distillery around the turn of the century, opposite page. Springbank, founded in the 1820s, is one of the two surviving Campbeltown distilleries, the other being Glen Scotia. Ardberg's Islay malt ouput is used almost entirely for blending, although some is sold at eight years old.

nounced peatiness. Lagavulin is robust but with a less obvious peat flavour. Bruichladdich is also rich but less peaty; and Bowmore is the least obvious Islay with a deep flavour.

Jura, the island just north of Islay, has the Isle of Jura distillery making a good light-flavoured malt. Skye has the Talisker distillery making a lightish, peaty whisky which, when fully matured, is one of the best of the single malts. Some experts find it has a smoky flavour. Highland Park, one of the two Orkney malts, is also highly regarded. Rich and robust, it has a characteristic peatiness. The other Orkney distillery, Scapa, is almost wholly used for blending.

Several other malts come from the Scottish islands, but they are grouped with the Highland malts because they resemble the Highlanders rather than the Islays.

Campbeltown malts

Campbeltown on the Kintyre peninsula, opposite Islay, has two distilleries. Springbank, where the foreshots and feints are redistilled separately, makes a light, mellow, almost sweet malt. Glen Scotia, by contrast, makes a heavy, pungent malt distinguished by something akin to a touch of woodiness.

Lowland malts

The eleven Lowland malts are mostly used as filler malts to give weight to a blend. As they tend to lack distinctive malt character they do not add all that much to a commercial whisky. Rosebank is considered the best, and R J McDowell in *The Whiskies of Scotland* describes the flavour as 'light, somewhat reminiscent of Glenmorangie'. Tiny quantities of Auchentoshan, Littlemill and Bladnoch are also sold as single malts, and are liked for their 'brandy' flavour.

Highland malts

All the other malts are made in the Scottish Highlands, legal successors to the illicit whiskies of 200 years ago. Perhaps the name Glenlivet is most associated with Highland malts. Twenty-three distillers use the title Glenlivet in their name, although some are a long distance from the Livet valley. Most of these are usually known by their main distillery name, only one distiller can use the name Glenlivet without further qualification and that is The Glenlivet. Properly called Smith's Glenlivet, it was the first distillery to get a proper licence after the Act of 1823, and since 1880 has, by common consent, had sole right to the unprefixed name.

Ask a Scotsman which is the best malt whisky and he will invariably reply The Glenlivet. Ripe, rich, mellow and with an outstanding malt bouquet, it has every claim to call itself the king of the malts.

Glen Grant-Glenlivet is almost as old as The Glenlivet and is very popular amongst malt drinkers. Pale and very smooth, it is sold at more than one age.

Of the other Glenlivets, Glenfarclas is a

typical full flavoured Highland malt; Longmorn is recognised for its outstanding bouquet; Macallan is smooth and rich; Tormore is very rich without being peaty; Tamdhu is well-balanced; Cardow is quite robust; Tomatin is light-bodied and peaty; Glengoyne is sweetish and smooth. Others bottled as singles include Fettercairn, Blair Athol, Glen Rothes, and Linkwood.

Around Dufftown and Keith a second group of distilleries challenges the Glenlivets for prominence. Heading the group is Glenfiddich, the distillery and the brand that has done more to popularise single malts than any other. Glenfiddich is the best-known and biggest selling malt of these. Pale, peaty, but very smooth, it is one of the best Highland malts. Nearby, Balvenie comes at very high strength and is a more robust malt. Dufftown-Glenlivet is also peaty; Mortlach is very full and rounded. Strathisla-Glenlivet at Keith claims to be the oldest operating distillery in Scotland. Founded in 1786, it makes a rich, assertive malt, much of which goes into the Chivas Regal blend.

North of the Spey a further group of distilleries producing Highland malts stretch from Inverness almost to John O'Groats. Foremost among them is Glenmorangie, a very delicate, flowery, soft malt; in complete contrast Clynelish is very peaty but mellow and almost comes up to an Islay malt for distinctive flavour. Pulteney, the most northerly distillery, has a strong character; Dalmore is dry, heavy and slightly peaty; while the light-bodied Balblair has some peat flavour and a fine aroma.

The gamut of Highland malts, from light and delicate to robust and masculine is the drinker's pleasure and the blender's challenge. More single malts should appear on the market as the demand grows. Several companies have introduced a third element into the whisky profile – a vatted malt which is a blend of single malts. These malt blends include Royal Culross (from A Gillies & Co), Strathconon (Buchanan), Glenleven (Haig), Dewars 12-year-old vatted, Glendrummond (Saccone and Speed Int), and Findlater's Marlodge.

The Blends

WHAT MOST PEOPLE describe as Scotch whisky is in fact blended whisky. Apart from the sixty or so malts sold as single malt whiskies under the distillery name, and about another twenty sold as branded malts, everything else is blended whisky.

No one knows just how many different blended whisky brands there are. Estimates vary from 2,000 to 5,000. The brands range from internationally-known names like Johnnie Walker, Dewars, Haig, White Horse, Teachers, Bells, Famous Grouse, J&B, Cutty Sark and Chivas Regal to obscure brands blended for an importer in a particular market and not sold outside that market. Some of the biggest selling brands in one market may be hardly known in another. For example, Usher's Green Stripe, Bulloch & Lade and Inver House, all major brands in the United States, are almost unknown in Britain; and Bells, the major brand in Britain by several hundred thousand cases, is only a newish name in America.

Credit for producing the first blended whisky is usually given to Andrew Usher & Co of Edinburgh. In 1853 the company blended several different Glenlivet whiskies to produce Usher's Old Vatted Glenlivet, a malt blend. Ten years later grains began to play their role in the standard blend. Now blended whiskies are so important to every big whisky company that the head blender is invariably on the board of directors, and on his expertise a brand stands or falls.

Whisky blending is an art. The aim is to maintain a consistency of colour, aroma and taste. To do this the blender must know intimately the character of every single malt and grain whisky – which are compatible, which can be substituted if one component of a blend becomes unobtainable, and where the substitute can be found in sufficient quantities, often at short notice. To further complicate his job, the blender must anticipate demand for his blend and order his whiskies accordingly for anything up to five or ten years in advance, to allow for maturation. No company produces all the whiskies it needs for its blends, and the head blender must also be adept at exchanging whiskies and buying from rival companies.

Each company has its own secret recipe for its blends. No two blends are really alike – even though the average Scotch whisky drinker would find it hard to detect differences. Every blend has a malt content of somewhere between 25 and 40 percent, and this can represent anything from 20 to 50 different malts. According to one leading blender, using less than 20 different malts does not leave enough room to substitute alternatives should one or more become unavailable.

The top blender uses only his nose to select the whiskies that compose the blend. Only very rarely, when there is considerable doubt about a particular sample, will he taste it. The different whiskies are chosen from samples

Fortunately, the testing and quality control in the production of a blended Scotch is far less haphazard than Heath Robinson would have us believe, far right. At the centre of the complicated process is the head blender who noses a sample of each whisky in the blend.

sent up to the blending rooms. Here a small amount of each is put into tulip-shaped glasses. The blender noses each, choosing some to give colour, some to give aroma, and some to give depth to the final blend.

The required quantities of the component whiskies in the blend are put into casks which are then drained into a long trough that leads to several giant vats. The different whiskies are then 'stirred' by compressed air to make sure they are well mixed and then left to marry, usually for six months or more. The final maturation of the blend takes place in oak casks.

The final step, before bottling, is the judicious addition of tiny, measured amounts of caramel colouring to ensure continuity of colour in the blend.

Since the last war the growing preference for lighter spirits, particularly in the United States, has seen the major blends move towards a lighter colour and a drier, less malty taste. In some markets the proof has been reduced to bypass import duties based on alcoholic strength. But otherwise, the blends remain the same from year to year. The cheapest brands usually have the highest percentage of grain whisky in their make-up, while the deluxe whiskies cost more as they have a higher proportion of older malts.

GRAIN WHISKY

Grain whisky is a result of the invention of the patent still by Robert Stein in 1826 and the improved version produced by Aeneas Coffey in 1830. Now commonly called the Coffey still, it was and is a totally different process to the traditional pot still.

The Coffey still works on a continuous basis, needs far less manpower to operate, produces much more spirit in the same space of time, and does not need to be sited near a good supply of fresh water (one of the main determinants of a malt distillery site).

Most grain distilleries are grouped in the south of Scotland where most of the big whisky blenders have their warehousing and bottling plants. The Scotch Whisky Association lists 14 grain whisky distilleries. They are Ben Nevis, Caledonian, Cambus, Cameronbridge, Carsebridge, Dumbarton, Girvan, Invergordon, Lochside, Moffat, North British, Port Dundas, Strathclyde, and North of Scotland. Despite their massive output and contribution to the total production and profitability of Scotch, it is only possible to buy one make bottled as a single – Choice Old Cameron Brig from the DCL-owned Cameronbridge distillery in Fife.

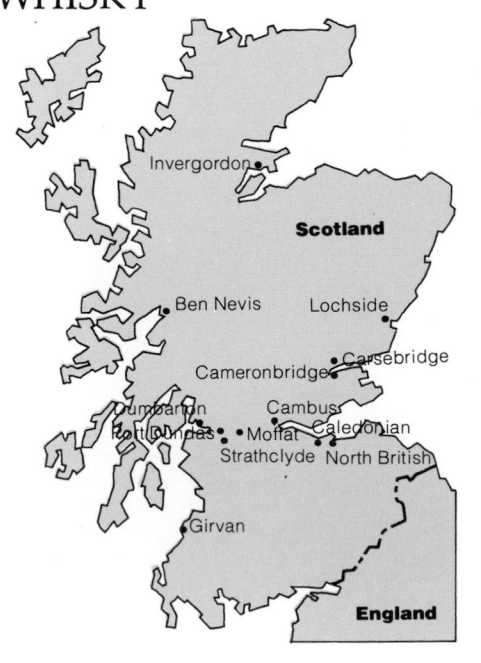

W. HEATH ROBINSON.

The Major Companies

TODAY'S BIG WHISKY companies are the result of the strong-minded enterprise and flair of a handful of Scotsmen in the early part of the nineteenth century. They first created the important blends, changing the emphasis from malt whisky to blends.

The Haigs justifiably call themselves the oldest of the modern whisky families. As early as 1655 a Robert Haig is recorded as being in trouble with his local church for distilling on the Sabbath. But the Haig brand was created by John Haig, one of several Haigs in the distilling business, after he built the Cameronbridge distillery in Fife in 1824. In 1826 his cousin Robert Stein invented the patent still prototype which John Haig installed at his distillery and thereafter used his grain whisky to build the Haig brand.

John Walker, one of the first pioneers of blends, began as a grocer and wine and spirit merchant in Kilmarnock in 1820, which led him to blend his own proprietory whisky, hence the company slogan: 'Born 1820, still going strong'. In the 1850s, his son Alexander built the blend into a major brand by selling Johnnie Walker to ships sailing from Glasgow, and to merchants coming north to buy carpets and textiles in Kilmarnock.

John Dewar, like John Walker, started as a grocer and wine and spirit merchant. In 1846 he set up his own company in Perth and introduced Dewar's White Label.

White Horse was the creation of James Logan Mackie, an Islay distiller who turned merchant. He founded his own company in 1883 to sell his White Horse blend which he based on Lagavulin, one of the Islay malts.

James Buchanan first entered the whisky business as London agent for Mackinlay whiskies. Predicting the blended whisky boom, he founded James Buchanan & Co in 1884 selling whiskies he bought in Scotland under his own name.

Bells was begun by T R Sandeman who started trading as a whisky merchant from a small shop in Perth in 1825. In 1851 he took on Arthur Bell as a partner and by 1865 Bell controlled the business. When Bell's two sons joined in 1895 the company took the name Arthur Bell & Sons, and the whisky became known as Bells. Still independent, Bells is now the largest single brand in Britain, with annual sales of over two million cases.

Cutty Sark, one of the two biggest selling brands in the United States, is a modern brand. It was created in 1933 by the St James's wine shipping firm of Berry Brothers & Rudd, with a characteristic light taste designed to appeal to the post-Prohibition American market. Cutty Sark's main rival in the United States, J&B Rare, is named after the wine shippers Justerini & Brooks, whose headquarters are just a few doors from Berry Brothers. J&B is now owned by International Distillers & Vintners.

VAT 69 was first produced by William Sanderson in 1882. From a hundred different vattings (blends) his friends chose vatting

The malt whisky produced by the Ardbeg distillery on the Isle of Islay is principally used for blending, like most Islay malts. This old photograph shows the barrels of whisky from the Ardbeg distillery being loaded on to a steamer to transport them to the mainland.

WHISKY LIQUEURS

The few liqueurs produced in Scotland are all whisky-based. By far the most important is Drambuie, internationally recognised as one of the premier liqueurs.

Drambuie is made by the Mackinnon family, who first came by the recipe in the 18th century. In 1745 the rebellion of the clans in support of Bonnie Prince Charlie ended in a massacre on Culloden Moor and the Prince was forced into hiding. He found refuge with Mackinnon of Strathaird, who hid the Prince on Skye and found him the safe boat that took him back to exile in France. In gratitude the Prince gave Mackinnon his own secret liqueur recipe. The Mackinnons kept this recipe for their own use until 1906, when the family began the commercial production of Drambuie.

According to the company, Drambuie is made from more than sixty different whiskies, mostly malts, which are aged for 8–20 years. After blending, a secret essence is added in a ratio of one gallon to five thousand of whisky. Finished Drambuie is rich but quite dry with a light liqueur texture, and hints of honey and herbs.

The oldest rival to Drambuie is Glen Mist, made by Dr Peter Hallgarten, who describes it as the driest of the whisky liqueurs. He uses much the same formula as Drambuie – whisky blended with honey, herbs and spices. A third, relatively new whisky liqueur is Glayva. It is slightly sweeter and fuller than Drambuie. Lochan Ora, made by Chivas Brothers, is sold by Seagram mainly in the United States. It has a lovely honey flavour and some of the peatiness of a malt whisky. Of the Scottish liqueurs it is the one that comes closest to Atholl Brose, a Scottish 'cocktail' made with whisky and honey, and occasionally cream and uncooked oatmeal.

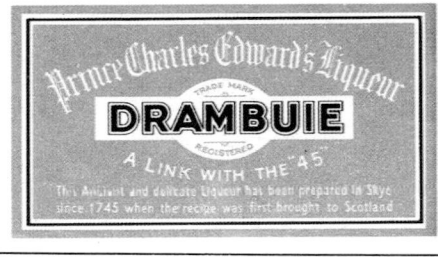

number 69 as the blend they preferred.

Bulloch & Lade, an important brand in the United States, dates back to 1856; Crawford's 'Three Star' to 1860; McCallums to Edinburgh innkeepers Duncan & John McCallum, who founded their whisky company in 1807; Abbots Choice was the creation of Perthshire farmer John McEwan.

Matthew Gloag & Son was founded in 1814, and in the last decade their Famous Grouse brand has grown to become the second most important blend in Scotland. The company is now owned by Highland Distilleries, who through other subsidiaries also own Langs, Red Hackle and Scottish Cream blends.

Queen Anne is the main brand of the Edinburgh-based Hill Thomson group; Mackinlay's of Scottish & Newcastle Breweries; Highland Queen of Macdonald & Muir and Long John, named after Long John Macdonald, the nineteenth-century founder of the Ben Nevis distillery, is owned by Long John International, part of the Whitbread brewery group.

The major brand of Stewart of Dundee, formed in the middle of the last century, is Cream of the Barley. William Whiteley of Leith make both House of Lords and King's Ransom. Standfast and Clan MacGregor are the two blends made by William Grant & Sons, producers of the famous Glenfiddich single malt.

The major companies

Well over half of all the whisky to come out of Scotland comes through various subsidiaries of The Distillers Company Limited, commonly called The DCL. Formed in 1877 by the amalgamation of six Lowland grain distillers, with John Haig & Sons as the leading participant, the original DCL was aimed at protecting its six members from Highland competition.

In the early part of the present century The DCL moved into blended whiskies through a series of takeovers and mergers, and following the boom in blended brands established itself as the biggest single whisky company and one of the ten biggest spirits companies in the world.

It now consists of 42 separate and relatively autonomous subsidiary companies. Between them, these subsidiaries operate 45 different malt and five grain distilleries – just under half of all the distilleries in Scotland. They include Talisker, Caol Ila, Lagavulin, Port Ellen, Cardow, Glenkinchie, Rosebank, Oban, Clynelish, Ord, Glen Mhor and Glen Albyn, Glen Elgin and Glenlossie, Mortlach, Aultmore, Linkwood, Dallas Dhu, Benrinnes, Dalwhinnie, Banff and Craigellachie.

The major DCL brands include Johnnie Walker, Buchanans, Haig, White Horse, Vat 69, Crawford's, Bulloch & Lade, George IV, Macallum's, Abbots Choice, The Antiquary, Black and White and Usher's, plus a number of single malts and lesser-known blends.

Among the independent companies, the largest are Seagram, Hiram Walker, Bells, International Distillers & Vintners, Berry Brothers, and Highland Distillers.

Second to the DCL in number of distilleries is Seagram. Since its takeover in 1978 of The Glenlivet Distillers Ltd, it now has nine distilleries including The Glenlivet, Glen Grant-Glenlivet, Strathisla, Glen Keith, Braes of Glenlivet and Longmorn. Its main brands are Chivas Regal, Royal Salute, 100 Pipers and Passport.

The rival Canadian-based Hiram Walker owns the Glenburghie, Interleven, Miltonduff, Pulteney, Glencadam and Scapa distilleries. Its main brands are Ballantines, Old Smuggler, Antique, Rare Old Highland and The Mackintosh.

Ireland/Whiskey

No one knows whether the Irish discovered distilling. Some theories suggest that it was introduced to Ireland by monks returning from pilgrimages on the Continent, the fanciful even going so far as to say that the art was a gift from St Patrick.

However, it is very likely that Ireland was the first country to distil from cereals rather than wine, although when this began is again subject to speculation. This skill was probably introduced to Scotland from Ireland and in many respects the distilling industries in the two countries have grown in tandem.

Spirits were probably distilled in Ireland for medicines as early as the tenth century. Two centuries later, when the English under King Henry II invaded the country, they found the Irish drinking *usque-baugh* – Gaelic for whiskey. However, whiskey was probably not commonplace until the fifteenth century. Certainly, by the sixteenth century whiskey was a popular drink in Ireland – so much so that an act was passed in 1556 to curb

drunkenness, and in 1580 the English Government in Ireland numbered among undesirables 'the makers of aqua vitae'.

Laws against the makers and purveyors of whiskey would, even in those times, have been almost impossible to enforce. Innkeepers had their own modest stills to supply their needs, independent distillers catered for those who did not wish to bother. Many households ran their own still – making a new batch of whiskey was a part of family life. In 1633 a chronicler wrote that the 'Irish eat raw meat which boyleth in their stomachs with aqua vitae which they swill in after such a surfeite, by quarts and pottles'.

In the early seventeenth century the first taxes were imposed on whiskey. Licences were issued giving the holders a monopoly over production in a certain area and from then on Irish whiskey was subject to changing systems of taxes and controls that were at times harshly enforced, frequently abused and very often even ignored.

The seventeenth and eighteenth centuries saw a succession of acts and laws aimed at controlling the production of Irish whiskey and raising revenue for the English Parliament and Monarchy. Invariably those appointed to administer the laws and collect the taxes benefited most and the distillers and drinkers of Irish whiskey suffered.

The laws and taxes were bitterly resented by the Irish and they resorted to producing their whiskey illicitly. More restrictions followed. In 1779 a law was passed which placed licence duty on each registered still. In the following year the still tax was raised, and of the 1,228 distilleries about a quarter disappeared. By 1790 only 246 survived.

The long-term effect of the new tax was to sort out the strong from the weak, for despite the greatly decreased number of whiskey producers and the stronger competition from the illegal distillers, the volume of legal whiskey production was actually increasing. Dublin and Cork were the two legal distilling

centres – among those who weathered successive changes to the 1779 Act were the Dublin-based Jamesons and the Powers.

In 1823, the 1779 still tax was repealed. It was replaced with a reasonable system of revenues which should have given the legal distillers freedom to expand and make better whiskey. The new law corresponded to one introduced in Scotland in the same year. The Scottish law was designed to eradicate illegal Scotch whisky distilling by giving the legal distillers an incentive, through reasonable taxes and duties, to make more and better whiskey. In Scotland the act worked. In Ireland it had the opposite effect.

During the 40 years before the 1823 act, as the number of still charges increased, competition between the legal distillers intensified, and it became a matter of survival rather than profit. Quality was secondary to quantity, and fraudulent practices were forced on distillers.

Few legal distillers survived, and those that

The Old Bushmills distillery, above, is the oldest operating distillery in the world. First licensed in 1608, it is still producing one of the best Irish pot still whiskies. The massive water wheel at the old Midleton distillery, right, is a reminder of earlier times.

Traditionally, Irish whiskies were served across the bar from oak casks. Today, however, they are nearly always poured from the bottle.

THE MYSTIQUE OF POTEEN

Illicit whiskies – poitin or poteen (pronounced pocheen with a short o) – has been made in Ireland ever since whiskey distilling became commonplace. It is the father of all other illegal whiskies, including the American moonshine which grew out of the methods introduced by Irish immigrants.

Until the early seventeenth century, when Irish whiskey was first taxed, most homes of any size had their own still for making the family whiskey. With the introduction of taxation and the efforts of the government to control whiskey distilling, poteen production moved out of the home and into hiding.

Poteen, being illegal, had to be made secretly – an exercise that tested Irish ingenuity to its fullest. Stills were hidden in caves, false rooms in the family house, hollow stacks of peat, remote sea coves, on the banks of quiet streams, in fact anywhere the distiller thought his activities would go undetected.

Their equipment was very basic. A kettle to heat the wash, the worm to pass the vapours through, and a barrel to hold the water to cool the vapours back to poteen ('the little pot'). The worm was the most valuable part of the still, the rest was designed for its disposability but the greatest danger arose when the illegal whiskey was being transported and sold.

Modern poteen makers, and there are still quite a few, now use increasingly sophisticated equipment, and a lot of their brewing is now done in the cities using the readily available town gas and oil heating. The ingredients to make the mash have also changed. At its heyday in the early nineteenth century, when poteen was widely considered to be a better whiskey than the legal 'parliament' whiskey, malted barley was considered the only basis for a good whiskey. Now the modern poteen makers use anything from sugar and treacle to potatoes and beets, depending on price and availability.

Poteen is basically a strong, colourless spirit with the raw taste of an unaged whiskey. Brendan Behan was no fan, he once said 'No matter what anyone tells you about the fine old drop of the mountain dew, it stands to reason that a few old men sitting up in the back of a haggard in the mountains with milk churns and all sorts of improvised apparatus cannot hope to make good spirits.' Thousands of his contemporaries and his ancestors would beg to differ. Poteen was, and is, part of their life. In 1977 a campaign was launched to legalise its production in Ireland, and in America the name has been registered for use on a legal whiskey bottle. The poteen makers would be horrified.

did produced increased quantities of blended whiskey. The introduction of the patent (Coffey) still from Scotland had permitted an even bigger production of grain whiskey for blending with the original pot still whiskies (thus preserving something of the original flavour).

In 1860, the 1823 Act was modified, and in 1880 finally rationalised into a sensible law that survived in its original form until 1952. The number of legal distilleries continued to decline, by 1900 only 30 existed, but those that remained were able to operate sensibly and at a profit.

Of the 30, seven were in Dublin; six in Belfast; four in the Cork area; three in Londonderry; two in Coleraine; and one each in Galway, Wexford, Dundalk, Limerick and the counties of Kildare, Westmeath and Londonderry.

Amalgamations and closures in this century have further reduced the number of distilleries to a handful, and the number of companies to one – the Irish Distillers Group Ltd, which now accounts for almost all the spirits produced in Ireland. Their only real rivals being the various small companies that produce Irish liqueurs.

Among the famous distilling companies that have disappeared are the Royal Irish Distilleries, once one of the biggest and best known of the companies, which finally closed in 1936; The Dublin Distillers, itself formed by a series of amalgamations including what was once William Jameson & Co; the Phoenix Park Distillery, set up on the banks of the Liffey by the Scotch whisky giant The Distiller's Company Ltd, and which enjoyed a colourful history to match its name; the United Distilleries Company of Belfast and Londonderry which finally died in 1929; The Glen Distilleries of Cork which folded in 1925; and Comber Distilleries based in Belfast, which closed as recently as 1953.

Production

Irish pot still whiskey is made in a similar manner to Scottish malt whisky, but it is the differences which give Irish whiskey a lightness and less of a peaty flavour.

Unlike Scottish whisky, the mash is made from a mixture – malted barley mixed with unmalted barley and small quantities of wheat, oats and rye. The malted barley has been dried, but not over the peat fire that gives Scotch malt whisky its distinctive peaty or smoky taste.

The wash is triple distilled, compared with twice in Scotland, which gives a final spirit with a much higher alcohol content (about 50° overproof compared to around 20° for a malt) and less of the congeners which give Scottish whisky (and other spirits) their flavour. The different mash and the triple distillation both contribute to the 'lightness' of Irish whiskey.

By law Irish whiskey must be matured for a minimum of five years (three in Scotland)

Above: tourists and local inhabitants sampling poteen straight from the still. Left: an illicit still, hopefully concealed from the prying eyes of the local police force.

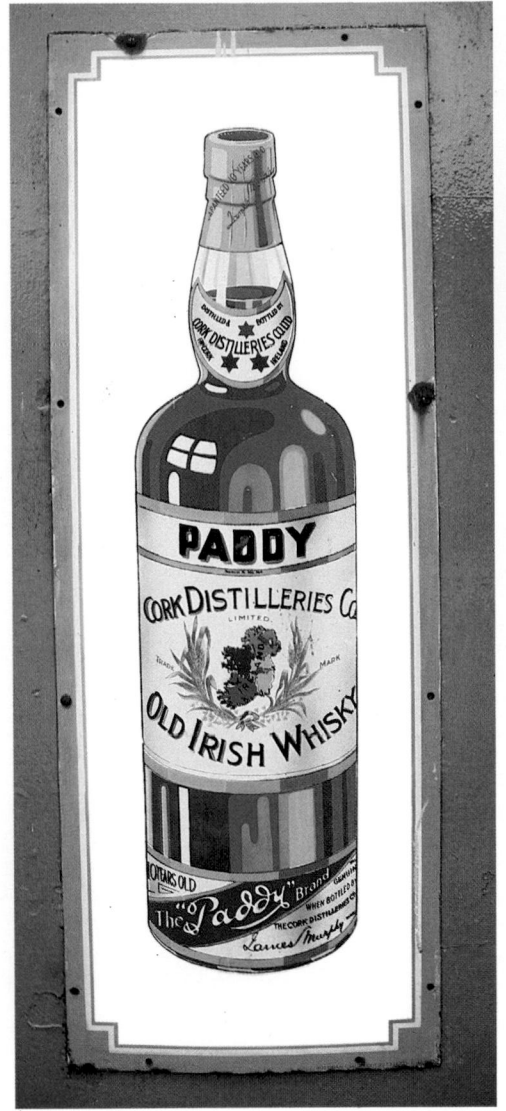

Irish bars are an institution that has been exported to many other countries by Irish immigration. Much of the social and business life in an Irish town revolves around them, and very little that happens locally is not discussed in their bars. Originally some served only whiskey or stout and, though most now offer a wider range of drinks, they have retained their atmosphere.

before bottling. In practice the best get ten, twelve or even fifteen years before they are considered ready. A fair proportion of the recognised Irish whiskeys are blends of pot and continuous still whiskies in the manner of a Scotch blend, although the degree of blending, required to maintain continuity, is nowhere near as great as in Scotland.

The companies

The Irish Distillers Group Ltd control the Irish whiskey industry. It grew from the amalgamation of three of Ireland's biggest and oldest distillers who in 1966 decided to pool their resources to tackle the giant United States and European markets.

The three included John Jameson & Son, founded by the Scot John Jameson in 1780 when he took over a small distillery on Bow Street, Dublin. Jameson led the way in the export of Irish whiskey. John Power & Son, the second member, was founded by the innkeeper John Power when he built his first, modest distillery in John's Lane, Dublin. Power were one of the first to bottle their

whiskey, and it was they who introduced the miniature to Irish whiskey. John Power also brought into the new amalgamation the Tullamore distillery.

The third party, the Cork Distillery Company, itself came into being in 1867 through the amalgamation of five Cork distilleries – North Mall, Watercourse, the Green, Daly and the old Midleton distillery – the largest in the group. It produced such brands as Paddy, Murphy's and Dunphy's.

Since 1972, the Irish Distillers have owned the oldest distillery in the world, Old Bushmills, on the road between Royal Tara of the Kings and Dunseverick Castle in County Antrim, Northern Ireland. First licensed by the Crown in 1608, it is still operating. The group also own one of the newest, a vast complex built around the old Midleton distillery, which began production in 1975.

All Irish Distillers production is now based at Midleton excepting the pot still whiskey made at Old Bushmills and the grain whiskey made at the nearby Coleraine distillery.

Midleton has both pot and continuous

(column) stills, and since its opening the production of both Jameson's and Power's has been moved from their traditional homes in Dublin to Midleton. The old Dublin premises have been phased out, although the character and flavour of both brands, as with all the other Midleton-made whiskies, have been carefully preserved.

The brands

Irish Distillers now make sixteen different whiskies. Bushmills' Three Star is a light blend of Old Bushmills' pot still whiskey and Coleraine grain. Bushmills' Black Label is a premium whiskey, matured in sherry casks for seven or more years, with a rounded flavour and bouquet. It is made mainly from Bushmills' pot whiskey, with a small amount of Coleraine grain whiskey. Coleraine is a very light blend mainly of Coleraine grain whiskey, with some Bushmills added to give it extra flavour.

Jameson is a blend of different pot still whiskies matured in charred American oak barrels to give it a light but positive character.

The old and the new at Midleton, near Cork. The giant copper stills at the new Midleton distillery produce the majority of the whiskey in Ireland. Nearby the old Midleton distillery is still operating, and contains many relics of its past including the old fire engine, below.

Jameson Crested Ten is a blend of older, sherry cask matured pot still whiskies. The premium Jameson 15-year-old is a pure pot still whiskey also aged for at least fifteen years, in sherry casks.

Tullamore Dew is a blend made at Midleton to the light, rounded character of the original Tullamore whiskey. Paddy, the second largest selling brand in Ireland, is a blend of three whiskey types – a straight pot still malt from the old Midleton distillery, a pot still malt/barley whiskey from the same distillery, and a grain whiskey element.

Hewitts is a blend of pot and grain whiskies, from the old Midleton distillery. Dunphy's is a blend of light pot still whiskey and Midleton grain, matured in charred American oak barrels. Uisge Beatha is Tullamore Dew packaged in a crock bottle.

Murphy's is an export blend of Midleton light pot still whiskey and grain whiskey, matured in the same way as Dunphy's. Midleton Reserve is a third blend produced at the Midleton distillery.

The leading whiskey in Ireland – Power's Gold Label (sold in some export markets as Power's Irish) – is made from Power's own style of pot still and grain whiskies.

Irish liqueurs and other spirits

The Irish Distillers Group also make a range of other spirits. At Midleton they produce Power's Special Dry and Cork Dry gins, Huzzar and Nordoff vodkas, and Kiskadee white rum. The group also make two liqueurs – Gallweys Irish Coffee and Irish Velvet. Gallweys is a smooth dark brown rich coffee liqueur made from whiskey flavoured with coffee, honey and herbs. Irish Velvet, a new brand, is made from coffee and Jameson whiskey. It is, in effect, a pre-mixed Irish

coffee – to one part of Irish Velvet you add three parts of boiling water, and with cream floated on top you have instant Irish coffee.

At Tullamore, a traditional distilling town up until the mid-1960s, the Irish Mist Liqueur Company makes a herb and honey liqueur based on Irish whiskey to an ancient Irish recipe. This recipe, for 'heather wine', was supposedly created by the Celts and was the drink of their warriors. The recipe for making heather wine, kept between father and son, was lost in the passing of time. One myth has it that the recipe for this Celtic 'wine' was

taken back by the Irish gods as punishment for its excessive use.

One man refused to believe the heather wine recipe had been lost. Daniel Williams, owner of the Tullamore Distillery in the early nineteenth century, reasoned that the disappearance of the recipe could be traced back to the time of Elizabeth I (who was known to like her 'caske of usque baugh'). Following the crushing defeat of the Irish by the English armies in the seventeenth century, thousands of Irishmen left their homeland to fight on the Continent. Daniel Williams be-

IRISH COFFEE

Although it looks otherwise, this is an easy and impressive drink to make, only requiring patience and a steady hand. The most difficult part, pouring the cream (either single or double) on to the coffee, should be practised before it is performed in front of an audience! Scotch whisky, Drambuie, Irish Mist liqueur, Galliano, Tia Maria and brandy are some of the spirits that can be substituted for Irish whiskey.

Prepare the coffee, sugar, cream and Irish whiskey.

Pour freshly-brewed coffee into an Irish coffee glass.

Add 2 teaspoons demerara sugar.

Stir well until it has completely dissolved.

Add 1½ oz Irish whiskey.

Gently pour fresh cream over the back of a silver spoon.

Sprinkle a few grains of fresh coffee over the surface.

lieved that during this exodus the secret had been taken from Ireland to Europe. He began experimenting at Tullamore with different blends of Irish whiskey, heather honey and herbs – believed to be the original ingredients of heather wine. At the same time he began the seemingly impossible task of trying to find the lost recipe among the descendants of the exiled Irish.

He did not live to see the final result of his searching and experimentation but his family continued his work. In 1948 an Austrian refugee arrived at the Tullamore distillery with a recipe for a liqueur based on heather honey and whiskey. It had been in his family for generations but the source was undoubtedly Irish. The recipe was found to be very close to what the Williams family's research had already discovered. It was put to the practical test and produced a liqueur that surpassed the previous family efforts, and the Celtic heather wine was reborn in this century as Irish Mist liqueur.

Tullamore is also the centre for the range of liqueurs made by the Royal Irish Liqueur Company. Under the Royal Irish label they make coffee, crème de menthe, advocaat, and chocolate mint flavours.

The most recent Irish liqueur, Bailey's Irish Cream, was launched in 1975 and has been such a success that it is still rationed in some of its export markets. Made by R & A Bailey of Dublin, a subsidiary of International Distillers and Vintners, Irish Cream is a combination of whiskey, fresh double Irish cream, neutral alcohol and natural flavourings such as chocolate. It resembles advocaat in texture, with a nutty, creamy taste. Its makers claim it is the only liqueur made with double cream.

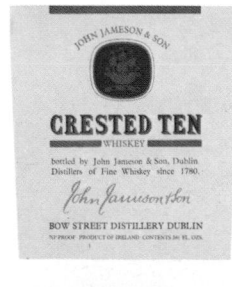

North America

The first commercially distilled spirits in North America were rum and applejack (a similar drink to calvados). It was not until the late eighteenth century that whisk(e)y, now the major spirit of both Canada and the United States (where it is spelt with an 'e') began to be produced in any quantity. Since that time its popularity has not been challenged.

Straight American whiskies (as opposed to blends) are very different from their Scottish and Irish cousins. Like a good malt or Irish whiskey, they are intended to be drunk neat or with water and ice. Canadian whisky, often overlooked in comparison to its Scottish, Irish and American counterparts, has a lightness which has increased its popularity in recent years, and it remains the best-selling whisky in the United States.

One other major spirit is produced in America – Californian brandy. Despite the interruption during the Prohibition years, it has grown in stature to become a highly regarded brandy.

Canada/Whisky

THE ONLY TRUE Canadian spirit, and the most widely produced and consumed spirit in Canada, is Canadian whisky. Around 85 percent of all the whisky consumed in Canada is Canadian whisky, yet nearly three-quarters of the total production is exported, largely to the United States, which now consumes in the vicinity of 50,000,000 gallons of Canadian whisky annually.

Canadian whisky (spelt like Scotch without an *e*) legally must be made from 'a mash of cereal grains or cereal grain products'. It must be wholly produced in Canada (although it can be bottled elsewhere), and the only legal additions to the spirit are flavouring whiskies and caramel.

Most distillers use corn as their main mash cereal because it is cheap and yields a high return of reuseable starch at the end of the mashing process. Rye, the other main cereal, is used in a ratio of about 7:1 to corn. Sometimes small quantities of other cereals, mainly barley, are also added.

All Canadian whisky is blended, and the vast proportion is made in continuous stills. The pot still is a rarity among commercial Canadian distillers.

The distilling cycle starts with mashing the corn and rye to convert their natural starch into fermentable sugars. When ready, the mash goes into fermentation vats where special strains of yeast are introduced and left to ferment for three to five days to give what the distillers call *the beer*.

The beer then goes to the stillhouse where it is fed into the top of the tall column of the continuous still. As it falls it is met by rising steam, vaporised at between 160° and 180°F. The steam vaporises the beer and strips out its alcohol, and is then brought back to liquid form in the condenser.

The alcohol in the condenser is called the *high wine*, and some Canadian moonshine has been sold in this form. Modern distillers reduce the high wine down from its 180° or 190° proof, distillation with water, and then rectify it – redistilling the high wine to give an absolutely pure spirit. A spirit almost totally free of the *congeners* (impurities) that give part of the character to Scotch whisky, cognac or armagnac.

In the second rectification of the high wine the *heads* and *tails* are run off for redistillation and only the central cut, the pure neutral spirit, is retained. This comprises about 85 percent of each distillation, and because of its purity it could be equally used to make gin or vodka. The purity gives Canadian whisky its characteristic lightness, which has made it such a successful spirit.

Once the distillation is finished, the new spirit goes into old bourbon barrels, or sometimes new white oak barrels. By law, it must be matured for a minimum of three years – unlike neutral grain spirit in the United States which can be used for blending unaged.

In the wood the spirit mellows, losing its rough edges and gaining some bourbon

flavour. After maturation the spirit is still very light and pale in colour, so up to ten percent rye whisky is added to the final blend to give it extra body and flavour, and a tiny amount of caramel goes in to give the blend a deeper, more traditional colour.

The whisky can then be bottled and sold, or sent back to the barrel for further maturation. Some Canadian distillers offer whiskies of up to 18 years old, but the optimum is generally six to eight years. Two distillers – Alberta and Acadian – market 100 percent rye whiskies. But, almost always a Canadian whisky will be almost entirely neutral grain whisky.

Most Canadian whiskies are sold at 70° proof, but in recent years a few distillers have introduced lower strength 65° labels in response to the growing international demand for even lighter spirits.

The companies

Commercial distilling started in Quebec in the 1790s when small quantities of rum were made, but whisky soon became the favoured spirit. By the 1840s Canada had at least 200 principally licensed distilleries making whisky, and countless more untaxed private stills.

The whisky industry was pioneered in the

Whisky sales in the United States as well as Canada are led by the lighter Canadian-style whiskies. Among the numerous labels in Canada, one company dominates – Seagram – and one of their brands – VO – outsells all the rest. Seagrams, with all other liquor distillers and importers in Canada, operate under the strict supervision of the Liquor Control Boards in each province.

early nineteenth century by John and Thomas Molson, James Morton, Richard Cartwright, and the partnership of Gooderham & Worts, who began at the historic Windmill at York, near Toronto, and who even managed to export their popular Toddy and Old Rye labels to London and Liverpool.

The years between 1850 and 1870 saw the growth of big distilling families and companies under such figures as Joseph Seagram, P J Wiser, Henry Corby and Hiram Walker.

The largest of them all was the Seagram Company, founded by Joseph Seagram, and today the largest drinks company in the world. Now owned by the Bronfman family, Seagram has at least a quarter of the Canadian whisky market with its VO brand alone. The company also produces Crown Royal, 5 Star and '83' (to commemorate Joseph Seagram's acquisition of his distillery in 1883).

Through subsidiaries they control an even larger share of the market. One, Thomas Adams Distillers Ltd, markets Antique, Private Stock, Gold Stripe and Homestead. A second subsidiary, Canadian Distillers Ltd, makes Canadian Lord Calvert, Canada House, Canadian Double Distilled and Heritage. A third, Hudson's Bay Co, makes Beaver Bottle, Royal Charter, Fine Old FOB and others. Other Seagram affiliates are Fort Garry Ltd, La Distillerie Montmorency Ltee, Robert Brown Distillers, Atlantic Distillers and the British Colombia Distillery Co.

Among the domestic gins and vodkas produced by the Seagram group are King Arthur, Seagram's Extra Dry, Collins lemon gin, Pickwicks, Natasha and Kolomyka.

Second only to Seagram is Hiram Walker & Sons, founded by the Massachusetts-born Hiram Walker, a descendant of English migrants. First a grocer and grain merchant, he started distilling in 1858. Walker leached his raw spirit through charcoal, added colour

and sold it the next day. In *Canadian Whisky*, the author William Rannie writes, 'Raw and harsh Walker's whisky might be by today's tastes, it was immediately recognised as a superior product by 1858 standards.'

Hiram Walker now make Canadian Club (their flagbearer), plus Carleton Tower, Imperial, Gold Crest, Special Old and 58. A subsidiary, Jas Barclay & Co, produces Barclay Square, Royal Canadian, De Luxe and Gold Label.

Other spirits made by Hiram Walker in Canada include the Crystal, Buckingham and White Swan gins, Rimski and Bolskaya vodkas, and Maraca rums.

Third in importance among Canadian distilleries is Gilbey Canada Ltd. They produce Number Eight, Golden Velvet, Black Velvet, Triple Crown, Old Gold and Red Velvet labels, plus Colony House, Manor House, Golden Special and other labels through their Palliser Distillers subsidiary.

The other major Canadian whisky distiller is Canadian Schenley Distilleries Ltd, who produce Order of Merit, OFC, and Five Thirty labels. Royal Command, Three Feathers and Three Lancers are produced through the subsidiary Canadian Park & Tilford; and Noblesse, 909, PM and Bon Vivant through Canadian Gibson Distilleries.

Schenley also produce a number of domestic flavoured liqueurs under the Henkes and Ross labels, including an example of the indigenous Maple liqueur.

These four companies have their Canadian whiskies listed by all the provincial liquor boards that control liquor sales in their respective areas. But some of the smaller distillers have strong local markets for their spirits. Acadian, for example, is important in the Atlantic provinces, the Manitoba Distillery supplies much of the whisky that is sold in Manitoba, and Potter is prominent in British Columbia.

The Seagram Company

THE SEAGRAM COMPANY LTD is unquestionably the world's biggest producer and marketer of distilled spirits and liqueurs. The company reckons it wholly or partly owns more than 200 different brands, so many that even they are uncertain about the exact number. With each brand selling in a multiplicity of strengths or flavours, and with different labels for different markets, the number of Seagram labels is estimated to run into the thousands. For example, its American-based Leroux liqueur subsidiary makes more than 40 different liqueurs alone for the American market, and imports others under its own name from Austria, Denmark, Italy and France. Apart from Canada and the United States, through its various subsidiaries, Seagram produce spirits and liqueurs in Austria, Argentina, Brazil, Costa Rica, England, France, Germany, Ireland, Israel, Italy, Jamaica, Japan, Mexico, Puerto Rico, Scotland, Switzerland, Turkey and Venezuela.

The two foremost Seagram brands, on which the company's fortunes are founded, are Seven Crown American whiskey, the top-selling spirit in the United States and the leading American whiskey brand for three decades, and VO Canadian whisky, the leading imported whisky in the United States market. Among the other Canadian whisky labels belonging to Seagram are Lord Calvert, Crown Royal (launched in 1939 to celebrate the visit of King George VI to Canada), Five Stars, Masterpiece, Hudson's Bay, James Foxe and Harwood.

In the United States the company has the Antique, Benchmark, Henry McKenna, Mattingly & Moore and Eagle Rare bourbons. Wilson, Calvert, Gallagher & Burton, Galaxy, Four Roses, Kessler, Paul Jones and Carstairs whiskies to back up Seven Crown. And the

LABELS OF FORTUNE

Although they are hardly known in Europe, Seagram's VO and 7 Crowns are the two biggest-selling whiskies in Canada and the US.

A festive advertisement showing the wide variety of brands that Seagram's offered, even 30 years ago.

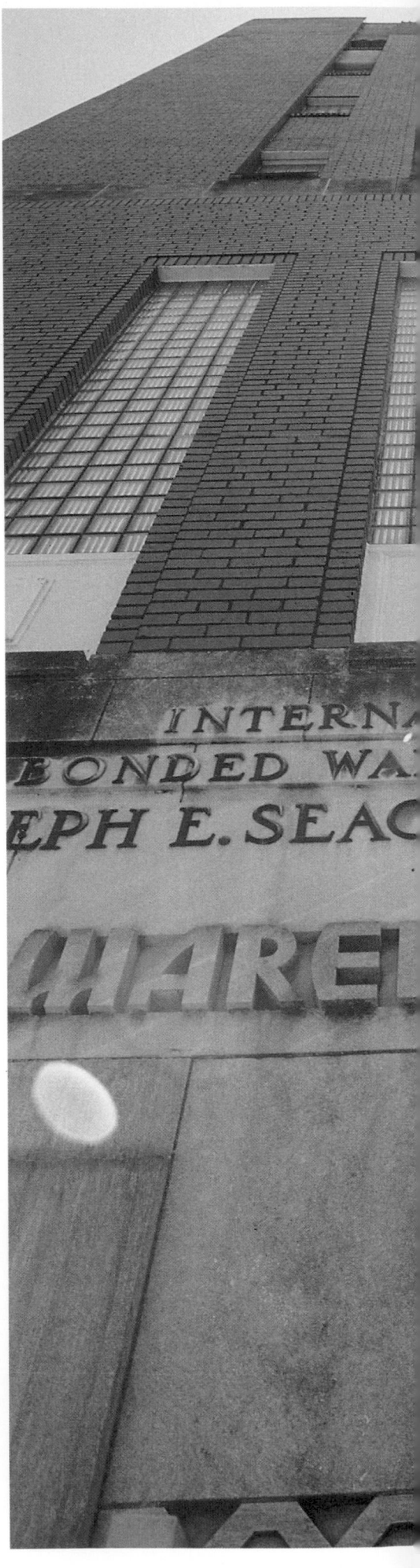

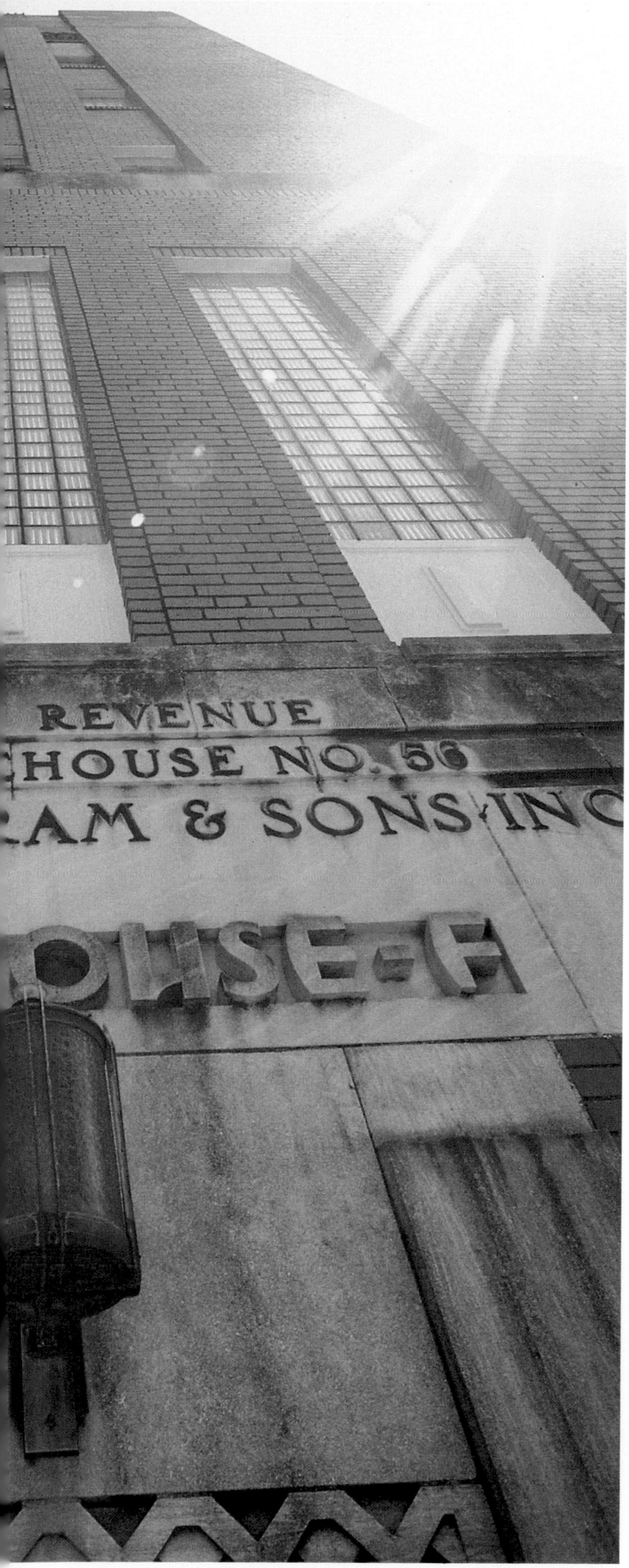

A COMPANY WITH A CONSCIENCE

We who make whiskey SAY: "DRINK MODERATELY"

ON one point all thoughtful men have always agreed. On one point all connoisseurs in the art of enjoyable living have always agreed.

The lasting enjoyment of the pleasures of life depends on *moderation.*

A few weeks will **mark** the anniversary of Repeal. We think it is appropriate that we who make whiskey should emphasize, to you who drink whiskey, the desirability of moderation.

For a situation exists today which requires us both to take an honest, serious look at the future.

Our own stake in that future is clear—our part in an industry in which we have held an honored position for 77 years.

Your stake is of vital concern.

It involves not only your health, your money expenditures, and your enjoyment of life—but a principle which is the very core and fibre of American history and tradition—your personal liberty.

The Threat to Liberty

When Repeal came, most brand names were unfamiliar. People lacked experience. They didn't know how to choose.

Many bought unwisely. And drank unwisely, too. Because this new whiskey was inexpensive, it was consumed freely. Because of its rawness and harshness, it could not be consumed as whiskey should be—for mellow warmth and flavor.

If we both think honestly and speak frankly, we must admit this condition is not in the tradition of fine living. It is not what any thoughtful person could desire.

What Common Sense Suggests

There is nothing new about drinking whiskey.

Through generations, it has always occupied a natural place in gracious living.

The House of Seagram believes that whiskey, properly used, is deserving of that position. Seagram's has always felt that the proper use of whiskey suggests a pleasure in its aroma, its flavor, its mellowness.

However, these characteristics are *found only in whiskey that has been properly distilled and then brought to full mellowness, full wholesomeness, by aging.*

The real enjoyment which whiskey can add to the pleasures of gracious living is possible only to the man who drinks good, aged whiskey and drinks moderately.

Therefore, the lesson of generations of experience is not inapplicable to problems of today. The principle of moderation is not at variance with what common sense suggests as the right course for us today.

Drink moderately... Drink better whiskey.

Whiskey is a Luxury

Whiskey cannot take the place of milk, bread or meat. The pleasure which good whiskey offers is definitely a luxury.

On our part we feel so strongly that we say—*the House of Seagram does not want a dollar that should be spent for the necessities of life.*

And even to those to whom whiskey does not mean actual deprivation, we say—treat whiskey as a luxury. A pint of good, aged whiskey will bring you more enjoyment, more satisfaction, than a quart of whiskey of dubious quality.

We feel sure that you will agree with us that the desirable way of life is thoughtful, informed by experience, guided by common sense. Realizing this, we feel sure that you will prefer moderation in the enjoyment of the finest to the empty satisfaction that follows upon profusion of the second rate.

THE HOUSE OF **Seagram**

FINE WHISKIES SINCE 1857

Caution. Do not mix.

A great many people are surprised to learn that they can become noticeably, even seriously, intoxicated on only one drink if they have recently taken certain types of medication.

The drugs to be particularly careful about are tranquilizers, antihistamines, amphetamines and barbiturates.

If you have taken both drugs and alcohol, it can be exceedingly dangerous to attempt to drive a car or other vehicle.

We don't want to sound preachy, but we have always believed that the right way to enjoy any beverage alcohol product is in moderation. Mixed with drugs, however, even moderate drinking is out of place.

If you suspect the medication you're taking is not compatible with beverage alcohol, you would be wise to consult your doctor, your pharmacist, or the government Department of Health.

Seagram's
Distillers Since 1857

In 1934, after the end of Prohibition in the United States, Seagram opened a campaign aimed at encouraging moderate drinking. This has not just been aimed at the general problem of alcoholism. In 1937 they began a series of advertisements against drinking and driving with the slogan 'Drinking and driving do not mix'. More recently, their advertisements have warned of the dangers of mixing alcohol and drugs.

Leroux liqueurs; Crown Russe, Nikolai and Wolfschmidt vodkas; and the Calvert, Frankfort, and Seagram Extra Dry gins. Ronrico, Ron Llave and Palo Viejo white rums are shipped for Seagram from Puerto Rico; Myers dark rums from Jamaica; Olmeca tequila from Mexico; Ron Montilla rum from Argentina; and Ron Anejo Cacique rum from Costa Rica.

Outside the Americas, Seagram and the Japanese Kirin Breweries launched a joint venture in 1972 that resulted in Robert Brown, a local blend for the Japanese market, in 1974. A second Japanese whisky, Dunbar's, has since followed.

In Ireland, Seagram have a share in the Irish Distillers Group, producers of John Jameson, Power's, Paddy, Tullamore Dew liqueur and Gallwey coffee liqueur. Through this group they also have a stake in the Old Bushmills Distillery, the oldest distillery in the world, dating back to 1608, and the best-selling whiskey internationally. In England the company makes Boodles, Calvert and Sir Robert Burnett's White Satin gins; Captain Morgan, Wood's Old Navy and Old Charlie dark rums; Tropicana white rum; and Orloff vodka. In Scotland Seagram are the largest independent distillers. They own the Strathisla-Glenlivet distillery, founded in 1786 and the oldest continuously operating whisky distillery, also Glen Keith-Glenlivet, and two new Seagram-built distilleries – The Braes of Glenlivet and Allt-A-Bhainne. Whiskies from these distilleries form the backbone of the company's prestige Chivas Regal whisky and the rationed 21-year-old Royal Salute deluxe blend, as well as 100 Pipers and Passport standard blends; and Lochan Ora whisky liqueur.

In 1978 Seagram gained control of the Glenlivet Distillers Ltd, owners of The Glenlivet, Glen Grant-Glenlivet, Caperdonich, Longmorn-Glenlivet and Benriach-Glenlivet distilleries. And the Seagram Company bottles the prestigious The Glenlivet malt, the Glen Grant and Longmorn malts, and Something Special and Queen Anne blends.

In Europe, Seagram own Weischler GmbH of Austria who make fruit spirits and brandies; Augier cognac in France; Polar rum in Germany; and Cherri-Suisse liqueur in Switzerland; plus Pasha coffee liqueur in Turkey; and Sabra orange liqueur in Israel.

Seagram also own, or have a substantial share in, a number of leading wine producers, among them Paul Masson of California, Julius Kayser in Germany, Barton & Guestier and Mumm champagne in France, Brolio and Tonino in Italy, a grower's consortium in Chile, Bodegas Palacio in Spain, and Montana in New Zealand.

In recent years Seagram have diversified into petroleum and gas through the Texas Pacific Oil Co, but the distilling and marketing of spirits, and to a lesser extent wines, still make up most of their revenue. In 1977 the Seagram turnover worldwide stood at a massive $US2,184,000,000.

SEAGRAM – THE FAMILY BUSINESS

From small acorns . . . the discreet advertisement, above left, dates from 1883 and was one of the earliest for the products of Joseph Seagram, left, one of the founders of the modern multinational Seagram Company.

White Wheat whiskey was one of the first labels to be produced at the original Seagram distillery at Waterloo. By 1918 production had expanded at the distillery; the bottling room, below, looks like a modern production line.

The Seagram Company is the result of the combination of the talents of two families, the Seagrams and the Bronfmans. Octavius Seagram and his wife Amelia migrated from Bratton in Wiltshire, England, to Canada in 1837. Both died young, leaving two sons, Joseph and Edward. In 1869 Joseph married and, through his wife, became a partner in the Granite Mill and Waterloo Distillery.

At first distilling was ancillary to the grinding of grain, but by 1883, when Joseph had bought out his partners, whisky was his main concern. He launched '1883' brand to celebrate his takeover, and it quickly made him a wealthy man able to indulge in his passion for horsebreeding and racing. His black and yellow colours were carried by many winners. In 1911 he incorporated his company as Joseph E Seagram & Sons Ltd , and around five years later conceived the famous V O brand. In 1919 he died, leaving his business to his sons.

The Bronfman family came to Saskatchewan from Bessarabia in the 1880s. After two years unsuccessful homesteading they moved to Brandon, where Ezekiel Bronfman graduated from horsetrading to the hotel business with his four sons, notably Abe and Sam. From hotels, the brothers moved to liquor distribution and then their own distillery at Yorktown. This development was predestined by the family name, which a Yiddish translation gives as 'whiskyman'.

DISTILLER.

MILLER.

Joseph E. Seagram.

Waterloo, Ontario, Canada.

In 1919 the brothers formed the Canada Pure Drug Company to import large quantities of Scotch and produce their own rye, bourbon and Canadian whisky. In the 1920s, with the provincial governments of Canada taking control of liquor distribution in their respective provinces, Sam steered the family to distilling quality spirits at LaSalle in Montreal to sell to these various boards. The brothers formed the Distillers Corporation Ltd, a similar name to the giant British Distillers Company who granted the brothers distribution rights in Canada for several of their leading Scotch brands. In 1928 the family took over Joseph E Seagram, and the new company was renamed Distillers Corporation – Seagram Ltd. The acquisition gave the Bronfmans two prestigious Canadian brands and a second distillery.

In a typically sentimental gesture Sam Bronfman had the yellow and black Seagram colours hung around the neck of every VO bottle. In the same way, in 1971, when he had seen the Bronfman distilling and marketing empire grow a hundredfold, he transferred its registered headquarters back to Waterloo to Joseph Seagram's original offices.

The company's centres are now in Montreal and New York, and Sam Bronfman, who died in 1971, has been succeeded by his sons Edgar and Charles who today run The Seagram Company Ltd (so renamed in 1974), producers of almost every conceivable international spirit.

Seagrams' distillery at Waterloo, Ontario, today, above, is a far cry from the plant at the turn of the century. The shape of the modern company owes much to the work of Sam Bronfman, left.

The United States

AMERICA IS ONE OF the younger distilling nations. Its spirits industry dates back little more than 200 years. Within this brief span however, the United States has grown into the world's largest spirits market with an industry to match.

Distilling and drinking spirits were brought by successive waves of immigrants, with each nationality bringing its own distinctive styles and drinks. Rum was the first American spirit, distilled by the early settlers in the New England states, along with *applejack*, the American version of calvados (apple brandy).

As the settlers moved inland they turned to the most readily available raw material for their source of alcohol – the corn and other cereals they grew to feed themselves and their livestock. For them, home-distilled alcohol replaced the rum made from the imported molasses or the wine and brandy imported from Europe to the coastal seaports.

Many of the early settlers were Irish, Scottish and Dutch, no strangers to domestic distilling. From their own homegrown corn, rye, barley and wheat they began to distil the first, albeit crude, examples of bourbon, corn, rye and other whiskies. These were highly saleable commodities that, unlike the raw grain, could survive the long and often difficult journey to the markets in the bigger towns. In Pennsylvania and Kentucky, the twin cradles of the American whiskey industry, the number of farmers making and selling whiskey slowly consolidated into an industry. Whiskey was becoming a valuable commodity, so much so that during the American Revolution it was a more acceptable form of currency than money.

The first of the two great watersheds of the American distilling industry came in 1791 when George Washington, the new president, introduced the first tax on whiskey to raise desperately-needed revenue for his administration. The revolt of Pennsylvania distiller-farmers against this iniquitous tax, known as the Whiskey Rebellion, established the centre of whiskey distilling. Washington was forced to send in the militia to maintain law and order and make sure the tax was collected. The distiller-farmers responded by moving further west, where the government would find it much harder to tax and control their whiskey-making. They followed the limestone belt that begins in western Pennsylvania, proceeds through Kentucky, Indiana and southern Illinois, then disappears to re-emerge near Baltimore in Maryland. This limestone mantle was the source of the pure water that the farmers considered the key ingredient for making their whiskies. Incidentally, this is the water that shaped the famous Kentucky caves which are the centrepiece of Mark Twain's *Tom Sawyer*.

With modern technology a distiller no longer needs to be near a water source, but it is estimated that four-fifths of legal distillers

in the United States are still based in the old 'whiskey belt' which spread across the five original whiskey-making states.

In the nineteenth century, the whiskey-making industry escalated as the population increased and the advent of the railroads opened up the country. By the turn of the century the total annual whiskey production was rapidly approaching 100,000,000 gallons – a large and commercial industry by any standards. Then came the second great turning point for the industry, the Volstead Act, passed in October 1919, which in the next year led to Prohibition. Despite the opposition of a large proportion of the population, the anti-drink forces triumphed and America went dry. Overnight the whiskey producers, like other distillers, were told they could no longer make and sell their spirits.

Some distillers moved to Canada, where they could continue to operate legally, and let the bootleggers run their wares across the border. Others went underground or just locked up their doors. For the next 13 years the Americans continued to drink, illegally, while the law and the Prohibitionists tried to stop them.

Prohibition changed the American whiskey industry in many ways. It gave the large Canadian distillers their dominant place in the American industry, closed down many of the traditional companies for good, saw the birth of new companies when it ended, established organised crime as an integral part of the United States' liquor industry and changed the drinking habits of the American nation. For the whiskey makers this change in taste was a trend to lighter-style blends, to match the new tastes formed during Prohibition when whiskey usually meant smuggled Scotch or heavily-cut local rotgut.

Prohibition ended in 1933. Since then, the whiskey industry has grown in a steady upward curve. It now has almost 30 percent of the total domestic spirits market, selling each year something in the order of 44,000,000 cases of this domestic product in the face of competition from imported Scotch and Canadian whiskies and, more recently, the challenge of the white spirits.

Prohibition

AMERICA'S LONG THIRST

The Long Thirst, or Prohibition as it is better known, began on January 16, 1919, when the 18th Amendment to the United States Constitution was passed by 282 votes to 128, to the great surprise and consternation of a considerable proportion of the American public. A year later it became effective when a majority of states passed ratification laws.

The 18th Amendment, often known as the Volstead Act after Congressman Andrew Volstead, banned 'the manufacture, sale and transportation of intoxicating liquors within, importation thereof into, or the exportation thereof from the United States and all territory subject to the jurisdiction thereof'.

The Act was a victory for the anti-drink lobby which had worked since the early nineteenth century to get just such a statute on the legislative books. As in many other countries, the American Temperance Movement was born out of a changing public opinion that liquor, particularly spirits, was less of a medicine and more of a social evil.

The first Temperance Society in the United States was founded in 1808 in Saratoga County by the First Congregational Church of Moreau. Its 40 members pledged themselves to 'use no rum, gin, whiskey, wine or any distilled spirits, except on the advice of a physician, in the case of actual disease, and exempting wine at public dinners'. From small acorns do great trees grow.

Other church groups followed suit, among them the Connecticut Society for the Reformation of Morals, led by the Reverend Lyman Beecher. His tracts against alcohol (and gambling) were widely distributed, and had such impact that by 1826 he had founded the American Society for the Promotion of Temperance, soon to become the American Temperance Union – the first big group to aim for anti-drink legislation.

By 1829 the Maine legislature passed laws allowing each community to regulate or forbid the sale of liquor if it so wished, and other states, including New York and New Jersey, followed.

In the 1830s the Laingsburg (Michigan) Temperance Society, one of the many that had sprung up, offered its members two types of pledge, the old pledge, or OP, where they promised to drink only moderately, and the total pledge, or T pledge, where they vowed to abstain from all forms of alcohol. Each member of the society sported a badge denoting whether they were an OP or a T. The hardliners got the nickname 'teetotalers' which passed into the vernacular as a name for anyone abstaining from all alcoholic drink.

By 1851 the teetotalers had forced the Maine legislature to pass the first prohibition law covering a whole state, and by 1890 five other states had gone completely dry – Kansas, North Dakota, New Hampshire, Vermont and South Dakota. Berated by such militant anti-drink groups as the Prohibition Party, the Women's Christian Temperance Union and the Anti-Saloon League, and such redoubtable figures as Carry Nation, the hatchet-wielding saloon smasher, more than 40 percent of the total American population found themselves living in dry areas by 1906.

Yet despite this partial prohibition and the

strong opposition to drink right across the United States, the 18th Amendment might never have reached the statute books if it had not been for the First World War. The temperance groups seized on liquor as the tool of the devil and the forces of evil, as personified by the Germans (well-known as brewers and distillers) and the anti-drink forces as those on the side of God and all things good. Whipped up into a wave of near hysteria, the anti-drink sentiment swept across the country, leading to the 18th Amendment and 13 years of ostensible abstinence.

In fact quite the reverse was the case. Consumption of spirits alone soared from 140,000,000 gallons in 1921 to 800,000,000 gallons in 1930. Speakeasies mushroomed everywhere, at first selling genuine smuggled liquor, and later 'bathtub' gin and other rotgut, often highly poisonous, which killed off several thousand Americans during the 13-year ban. The laws were impossible to enforce, as honest policemen, ranging from the men on the beat to Eliot Ness and his crimebusters, quickly found.

An 'experiment noble in purpose', the 18th Amendment introducing Prohibition, polarised the American public. Bootlegging became more than just a quaint method of smuggling a bottle or two and developed into a nationwide crime. Despite the efforts of the Federal Agents in capturing stills, destroying illegal liquor and patrolling the coasts and borders, alcohol consumption increased almost fivefold during Prohibition.

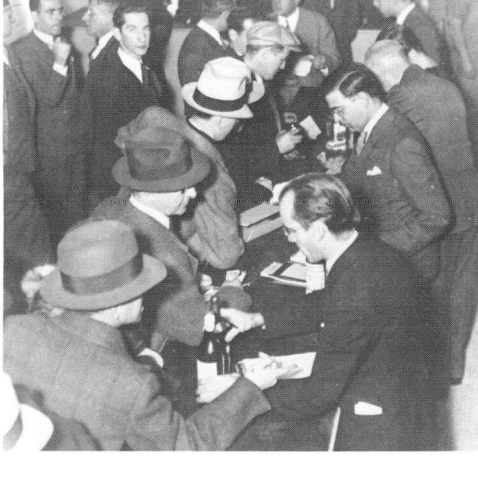

was said to be bringing in Al Capone, the king of Chicago, something like $60,000,000 a year. In New York gangsters like Boo-Boo Huff, Legs Diamond, Dutch Shultz and Mad-Dog Coll ran the liquor business, with the shadowy chiefs Arnold Rothstein and Frank Costello.

All transactions took place in cash, and so much was at stake that it led to the gang wars, including the notorious St Valentine's Day massacre when Al Capone's men shot seven members of the rival 'Bugs' Moran gang. The vast amounts of cash flowing into the coffers of the gangs led to the downfall of two of the biggest crime leaders – Al Capone and Frank Costello – ironically both were jailed for tax evasion.

Costello was particularly unlucky. He gave his social-climbing wife several thousand dollars in cash each week to run their exclusive Long Island home. As all her friends had cheque accounts, Mrs Costello decided to open her own, unbeknown to Frank. The revenue men pounced, and her husband, unable to account for the money, went to jail.

Prohibition also stopped the growing American table wine industry and thousands of acres of vines were pulled up and replaced with other crops. It was not until the 1960s that the industry re-established itself. Prohibition also saw most of the leading distillers switch their operations to Canada, where they could legally operate, and today many of the largest distillers continue to be Canadian-based.

Finally, the dry years profoundly changed American tastes for spirits. With so much watering-down and cutting of rotgut and the genuine spirits, either by mixing into cocktails or just plain dilution with water, the post-Prohibition Americans were left with a taste for much lighter spirits. Hence the continued dominance of the market by the lighter Canadian whiskies and the trend to the lighter Scotch whiskies such as J&B and Cutty Sark. The move toward light white spirits in the 1960s can be seen as a result of Prohibition.

Only five weeks after Prohibition became law, five men from the specially-created Treasury Department to enforce Prohibition were arrested for taking bribes from bootleggers; and not much later New York's Mayor La Guardia estimated he would need an extra 250,000 policemen to stamp out the consumption of illegal liquor in his city alone, plus another 250,000 men to watch the first 250,000. There were something like 13,000 speakeasies in New York at the height of Prohibition, selling alcohol day and night.

Bootlegging, so-called after the late 1880s Midwest practice of carrying a flask of illegal whiskey in the top of the boot, became almost a national pastime. It spawned such characters as Captain Bill McCoy who ran illegal liquor from his offshore ship. McCoy guaranteed to supply only the genuine stuff, hence the expression 'the real McCoy'.

By the late 1920s public figures, originally with the anti-drink lobby, were beginning to call for the repeal of Prohibition. In the 1928

election the Democrats began to identify with the so-called 'wet' faction, while the Republicans remained with the dry brigade. It helped the Democrats win the 1930 election, and repeal became part of their platform in 1932. They won, and considered the victory a mandate to reverse the 18th Amendment. In February 1933, led by President Franklin D Roosevelt, the Senate and House adopted a joint resolution proposing the 21st Amendment to the Constitution to repeal the 18th Amendment. On December 5 that year, Utah became the 36th state to ratify the 21st Amendment, creating the majority required to make it law. In 1961 Mississippi, the last state to ratify the 21st Amendment, finally ended Prohibition in the United States.

While Prohibition had a marked effect on America during the 13 years it was generally in force, there were lasting consequences. Among them was the penetration of the liquor industry by organised crime. Bootlegging and control of the speakeasies became such big business that it

THE EARLIEST AMERICAN WHISKIES were produced wherever possible from the most readily available raw material, usually in the cheapest, crudest apparatus. As whiskey replaced rum in popularity, whiskey makers began to label their wares in a more definitive way. So they became 'corn whiskey', 'rye whiskey', 'Kentucky whiskey' or 'Tennessee whiskey'. This was intended to indicate theirs was a better brew than a bottle labelled simply Old Bustard or Tomahawk. Different areas began to specialise in making different types of whiskey – Tennessee its sour mash and Bourbon County its distinctive corn whiskey.

Much later, with the introduction of the patent still, the art of blending and the change to lighter tastes, the blended whiskey added further to the multitude of different label descriptions. Guidelines had already been laid down defining the different types of whiskey, and in 1964 the 38th Congress designated bourbon as a generic type of whiskey (in the manner of Scotch) and ratified the other widely-used descriptions in a whiskey coda.

Under American law, anything that calls itself whiskey must be distilled from a grain mash to a proof less than 190° US (166° British), so it retains the taste, aroma and characteristics of what is generally accepted to be whiskey. Above 190° US proof it will lose these characteristics. The spirit must then be stored in oak (corn whiskies are not bound by this rule) and bottled at not less than 80° US proof (70° British). Within this basic definition the different categories for whiskey fall, and each must meet certain requirements before the respective descriptions can be used on the labels.

There are two main categories under the government coda. The first includes *bourbon whiskey*, *rye whiskey*, *wheat whiskey*, *malt whiskey* or *rye malt whiskey* (the last three are rarely, if ever, seen or used). These whiskies must be distilled to a proof not exceeding 160° US from a fermented mash containing a minimum 51 percent corn, rye, wheat, malted barley or malted rye respectively. The spirit must then be stored in charred new oak barrels at not more than 125° US proof.

The second category covers *corn whiskey*. This must be made from a mash containing not less than 80 percent corn grain, distilled to not more than 160° US proof, and stored at not more than 125° US proof in new or used uncharred oak containers. Treatment in charred barrels is not permitted. (The same rules apply to corn whiskey blends.)

These two categories of American whiskey could be described as generic whiskies because they retain the integrity of their base material in the same way as Scotch malt whisky does. Any of those whiskies that have been aged in charred oak barrels (uncharred for corn) for at least two years can in addition

Throughout whiskey production, rigorous tests are carried out to check the quality of the spirit, from the still rooms, far left, to the fermenting laboratories, above. Sour mash whiskey is stored in charred oak barrels, left.

call themselves *straight whiskey*. So *straight bourbon*, *straight rye* and *straight corn* are matured whiskies.

The same term, straight, can be used for whiskies made from less than 51 percent of the designated grain but which have been aged in charred barrels for more than two years, or for a mixture of different straights made by one distiller in one distillery and aged for at least four years. In practice, most straights are either bourbon or rye.

If a distiller decides to blend his straights he must label them as *blended straight whiskey*, and if the blend is all of one type of straight, say rye, he calls it *blended straight rye whiskey*. Actually, only tiny amounts of blended straights go on to the market: most blended straights are used, like malt whiskey, to give backbone to the ordinary blended whiskies which make up a large proportion of the brands on the market.

An American blended whiskey must, by law, contain at least 20 percent 100° US proof straight whiskey. The remaining 80 percent must be other whiskey or neutral spirit of a minimum 80° US proof. If the blend contains 51 percent or more of one type of straight, say rye, on a proof gallon basis, it can call itself *blended rye whiskey* or whatever. Blended whiskey has the advantages of being lighter in flavour, cheaper to make and easier to keep to a certain style. Like a Scotch blend, the secret lies in the art of the blender.

The poorest type of American whiskey is the *spirit whiskey*, a whiskey made from neutral spirit which needs only 5 percent whiskey of whatever kind in the blend. It is distinguished by its very rough, poor taste and is rarely seen.

The final widely used description found on US whiskies is *bottled in bond*.

Bottled in bond whiskies are withdrawn from the supervised warehouse after their ageing requirements have been met and tax is

paid at that point. It is a kind of credit facility for the distillers as they do not have to pay tax while the whiskey is maturing. The term can also be used on other types of American spirit providing they meet the requirements, but it mostly appears on whiskey labels. Many American spirits drinkers think this is a guarantee of excellence. In many cases it is, but this is by no means necessary. Basically, bottled in bond can be used on a label when a straight whiskey is held under bond (i.e. without the tax being paid) for a minimum four years, then bottled at 100° US proof. The straight must be from one distillery and the product of one season or year. However, some variations have been allowed in recent years, such as the mixing of one type of straight, bourbon for example, as long as it was made in the one season, or topping up of an old whiskey with a younger whiskey (although the four years dates from the youngest whiskey's year of production).

Jack Daniels

THE SOUR MASH OF JACK DANIEL

Jack Daniels Tennessee sour mash whiskey has been described as 'even more American than mom's apple pie'. Jack Daniels, the company and the product, has a unique place among American whiskies and within the American way of life.

The Jack Daniels distillery at Lynchburg, Tennessee, is the oldest registered distillery in the United States. In 1972 it was put on the National Register of Historic Places by the Department of the Interior. It is the pride of Moore County, smallest of all the Tennessee counties, and employs nearly every adult in Lynchburg (pop 361 at the last census).

The distillery stands at the end of a long, narrow gorge on the outskirts of the town. At the end of the gorge a cave set in a limestone cliff spills out the fresh spring water which, the company says, is one of the secrets of Jack Daniels.

Jasper ('Jack') Newton Daniel was born in 1848 just five miles from the Hollow (as the gorge is called by the locals). When he was 12 years old he went to work for Dan Call who was making whiskey at a nearby distillery. In three years, when he was just 15, Jack Daniel became Call's full-time partner. Just after the Civil War, Call, who was a Lutheran, was ordered by his church elders to stop making whiskey. Call complied and his distillery was taken over by his partner.

In 1866 Jack Daniel, already with a powerful local reputation for his sour mash, bought the Hollow and the 500 surrounding acres and built his own distillery. As a 'foot washin' Baptist he had none of the religious pressures or prejudices of his former partner Call.

The present Jack Daniels distillery stands on exactly the same site. Any additions or modernisation carried out in the last 130 years have been carefully designed to harmonise with the existing structures and to retain the identity of the original distillery. In the same way, the company has renovated and restored many of the old buildings in Lynchburg to give the town the character of a hundred years ago.

Jack Daniel himself died in 1911 after seeing his whiskey win many medals at international wine and spirit exhibitions and contests. He was succeeded by his nephew Lem Motlow, who commissioned the life-size statue of his uncle, dressed in his favourite knee-length frock coat, high-rolled planter's hat, vest and broad bow tie, which stands outside the mouth of the cave spring today.

Every bottle of Jack Daniels sour mash whiskey is made at Lynchburg and, despite modern technology, many parts of the production cycle still employ the original method. The sour mash whiskey is made in batches rather than in one continuing process, starting with cooking the cornmeal. Ground a little coarser than that used for bread, the cornmeal is heated to boiling point with water from the nearby cave spring. It is then cooled to around 156°F and a small percentage of rye is added to give the mash more starch and flavour. The mixture is then cooled to 146°F and barley malt added. The mash is transferred to the fermenter, where yeast and up to 25 percent of strained stillage (the residue from the previous consignment of sour mash) are added to the new batch. When the yeast has fermented it into alcohol, the beer goes into the

top of copper column stills. As it falls it meets rising steam, vaporises and is taken off to the doubler, a second still, where it is revaporised to give greater purity. Then it goes to the condenser to be returned to liquid form.

The new (clear) spirit is then charcoal mellowed. This part of the cycle to a large extent gives Jack Daniels its characteristic smoothness and its almost nutty flavour. The spirit is dripped through 12-foot high vats filled with finely ground sugar maple charcoal, made from sugar maple logs burnt and ground at the distillery. Charcoal mellowing, a leaching process that used to be called the 'old Lincoln County process', was first used by the slaves making illegal whiskey in the hills. The charcoal leaches out the corn taste, and gives a smoother flavour which distinguishes Tennessee whiskey from Kentucky bourbon.

Jasper (Jack) Newton Daniel went into the whiskey business at the age of 12. By the time he was 18, he owned his own distillery, which, although still operating, is a historic monument.

Once the young whiskey has percolated slowly through the charcoal, it is collected and put into charred white oak barrels (also made at the distillery) and is left to mature and gain its golden colour for a minimum of four years for green label, five for black.

Despite the worldwide demand, Jack Daniels is made on a very modest scale by modern distilling standards. The company only has two stills, for example. It comes in only two forms: the 78° proof strength green label which is made in very small quantities and is sold largely within the southern States, and the black label Old No 7 for the whole domestic market and the export, also at 78° proof. Jack Daniels is the only sourmash distillery in Tennessee apart from the George A Dickel Cascade Distillery near Tullahoma, Coffee County, which also makes a Tennessee whiskey.

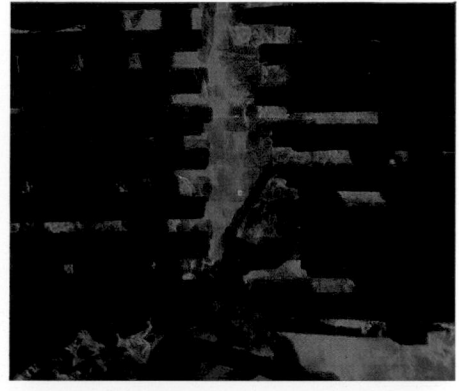

The Jack Daniels distillery has hardly changed since its inception in 1866, and neither has the sour mash process. Logs are charred (top right), and the spirit is leached through the activated charcoal that this produces (above). This gives Jack Daniels its distinctive taste. In his office, which has been preserved as a museum, stand bottles of whiskey, such as Old No 7, and original documents.

Californian Brandy

BRANDY IS ONE OF the three major spirit in the United States, with total sales o about 5,000,000 cases a year. Three out o every four bottles are domestic brandy, produced within America, and nearly every bottle comes from a small area of California where the total production of over 10,000,00(proof gallons a year is now said to exceed the brandy production of France.

The art of brandy-making reached California over two centuries ago with the Spanish missionaries spreading northward from Mexico. They carried with them the ubiquitous Mission vine to give them table and sacramental wine and small quantities of brandy. Documents show that as early as 1774 they were distilling enough brandy from their Mission grapes to start shipping casks back to Spain via the Horn.

By the early to mid-nineteenth century the acreage of vines in California had considerably increased, and the Mission grape, which yielded a poor wine, was used to make a mediocre brandy. General Vallejo in the Sonoma and Captain John Sutter at Fort Sutter on the American river were just two distillers who profited when the '49 Gold Rush escalated the demand for spirits.

The Californian brandies improved as European grape varieties were imported into the state, including the 100,000 rooted French vines transplanted to Californian soil by the Hungarian nobleman Agoston Haraszthy. The brandy distillers turned mainly to the *folle blanche* and *colombard* varieties, used in the making of cognac, and,when France's brandy vineyards were ravaged in the 1870s and 1880s by the *phylloxera* louse, Californian brandy was shipped to France to fill the gap until the French vineyards were revitalised by grafting local vines on to *phylloxera*-resistant American rootstock.

The watershed for Californian brandies came with Prohibition in 1919. The distilleries shut down, many of the vineyards were grubbed up, and the industry died. With the end of Prohibition smallish quantities of poor to indifferent brandy reappeared based on substandard or surplus grapes. Throughout the war years the quality gradually improved. In the mid-1950s the industry began to centre on the San Joaquin Valley, now its home.

Along a 200-mile corridor from Lodi in northern California, about an hour-and-a-half's drive from San Francisco, south to Kern County and Bakersfield nearer to Los Angeles, the rich soils of the valley yield the grapes for the brandies. Bounded on the east by the High Sierra, and on the west by the Coastal Range, the valley is watered and protected from excessive temperatures by the surrounding mountain ranges. The grape yields are often high but even so, with the boom in table wines of recent years, some distillers have had to turn to Arizona and Mexico for extra grapes.

Over the years something like 125 different grape varieties have been used for making

Californian brandy, but attention has now focused on two – the *Thompson seedless* and *flame tokay*. Both give clean, neutral base wines without any strong character that could flavour the distillate. There are no rules governing which grapes can be used, but few others find their way into the base wine. Minor amounts of *emperor, grenache, palomino, malaga, petit syrah*, and *mission* are occasionally used, in some instances to give the resulting brandy a specific character.

The vast percentage of California brandy is distilled in continuous (patent, or Coffey) stills which have rapidly replaced the traditional pot stills employed by the early brandy makers. Pot stills are retained by some distillers to give added flavour to blends, but they are the exception rather than the rule.

Once distilled, the brandies are aged in American white oak barrels (in many instances first used for maturing bourbon) usually from Arkansas or Tennessee oaks. They must be aged for a legal minimum of two years, but the standard is four, and can be as high as ten. The resulting standard Californian brandy is light, clean and fruity with a wine-like aroma, although longer ageing will deepen the colour and flavour. Certain additives are permitted, the main ones being sugar syrup to give a touch of sweetness and a smoother flavour, and caramel to deepen the colour of younger types.

The majority of Californian brandies are blended, though a few distillers such as Guild Wineries and the East-Side Winery also offer straights in which there are no additives. The straights, as a consequence, tend to be drier, and harder when young. The normal proof at bottling is 80° US (70° British). If bottled in bond they must be 100° proof (87.5° British) and have been distilled as

a batch within a six month period, then aged for at least four years.

Since 1971 the industry has been under the auspices of the California Brandy Advisory Board, and only brandies made from California-grown grapes distilled within the state can be labelled as California brandy. The Advisory Board now has 14 members – all the major producers – who, together with a handful of small wineries who make their own brandy and a number of distributors who buy in from Board members for their own labelling, account for the 300 or so California brandy brands sold in the United States.

By far the largest single brandy producer is The Christian Brothers, a monastic teaching order founded in France in the early eighteenth century, which raises its funds for teaching from its wineries and brandy stills. At their Mount Tivy winery, where brandy has been made since 1945, the brothers have the largest stock of ageing brandy in the western hemisphere.

The Brothers led the change to the light, fruity, slightly sweet brandy that epitomises the California style and have reaped the reward by capturing about a third of the total California brandy market. They operate both continuous and pot stills, and standard Christian Brothers brandy includes around 8 percent pot brandy. Roughly four years old, the brandy has a nutty bouquet with a sherry-like touch, and a grape taste with a smooth, sweetish finish. Their premium Christian Brothers XO Rare Reserve, first introduced in 1972, is now considered one of the finest California brandies. It is half pot still brandy of about eight years old and half continuous still brandy aged from five to eight years, and is richer, fatter, more complete than the average California brandy.

Paul Masson, one of California's largest wine producers and part of the giant Seagram Group, has another large part of the domestic brandy market. The standard Paul Masson brandy is about four years old with a pot still element, and is considered one of the grapier styles. Masson also sell Apothecary brandy in an apothecary style jar, in which the pot still content is higher giving a fuller flavour.

Schenley Distillers, one of the larger liquor groups in the United States, have a number of different own labels, among them Louis California, Jean Robert, Monastery, Certified, Coronet Special Reserve, J Bavet, Park and Tilford, and Schenley. Their premium label is Coronet VSQ, a light, very mixable brandy.

The California Growers Winery, based at Cutler in the southern part of the valley, have Growers Old Reserve as their main label, and have recently introduced the premium Setrakian brand. Named after Robert Setrakian, President of California Growers, it is a straight, column still brandy about six years old, fruity and aromatic. California Growers also sell brandy to a number of other companies who bottle under their own names, among them E & J Gallo, the largest American wine producer, who are now starting to make their own brandies.

The East-Side Winery Co-operative at Lodi at the top of the valley first began distilling brandy in the early 1930s. All their brandies come from continuous stills with Royal Host, straight or blended, as their main label. Mission Host and Gold Bell are younger blends for mixing, while Royal Host six year old and Conti Royal are at the other end of the scale. Royal Host Six is a light straight brandy, while Conti is a straight with an average age of ten years. It is said to be one of the best brandies to find the green-spicy touch that the American white oak imparts to the spirit.

Also based at Lodi, the Guild Wineries and Distilleries is the largest growers' co-operative in the United States' wine industry. They have both column and pot stills and bottle under a number of brands including Guild Blue Ribbon, St Mark, Roma Director's Choice, Citation and Winemasters' Guild. Their two top labels are Ceremony, sold as straight five- or eight-year-old brandy, and old San Francisco, a straight with an average age of ten years.

The California Wine Association, based at Delano and originally a grouping of different wineries, is now controlled by the Perelli-Minetti family. They offer a number of labels and sell to other bottlers. AR Morrow, named after one of the association founders, also comes as a bottled in bond six year old, while the slightly older, premium Aristocrat is the flagship of the group.

The Franzia Brothers Winery at Ripon, near Lodi, uses continuous stills to make the blended Franzia and Louis V. The giant United Vintners, also based at Lodi, use both types of still to make such brandies as Jacques Bonet and Hartley, the higher priced Petri, and Lejon and Italian Swiss Colony brands.

A number of large liquor companies buy from these distilleries to sell under their own brand names, and several of the smaller wineries such as Bounty, Le Blanc and Cresta Blanca make brandy from their own grapes.

Outside California, local brandies can be found in Washington, New York, Oregon, Connecticut and New Jersey; and occasionally *grappa* or *grappo* is made from grape musts.

Brandy making was first introduced into California by Spanish missionaries, an influence still operating. Since then, California brandy has grown, despite the setback of the Prohibition years, to become an internationally recognised brandy. All production is supervised by the California Brandy Advisory Board who make sure that each of the over 300 labels conform to a standard quality. Most of the brands are continuous still brandies with a pot still element. Christian Brothers dominate among the producers.

Liqueurs

THERE ARE AN ESTIMATED 16,000 different distilled spirits brands in the United States (including imports) but the same diversity does not apply to liqueurs – the number of generic American liqueurs is very small. Almost all the liqueur labels on the American market are imports, or domestic versions of those imports.

Both Southern Comfort and Wild Turkey can be drunk as straight spirits, mixed in long drinks or, more commonly, drunk as liqueurs. Both are based on bourbon and are classified as liqueurs. Southern Comfort sells almost 1,000,000 cases each year, pushing its 100° proof and 'bourbon' image; Wild Turkey aims more for the liqueur market.

Southern Comfort, almost always selling at a lower price than the premium Wild Turkey, is, according to one expert, more like a sweetened bourbon than a liqueur, whereas Wild Turkey has more of a Grand Marnier taste. Southern Comfort is flavoured with peach liqueur and freshly pitted and peeled peaches, plus small quantities of citrus extracts, which are left to marry with aged bourbon in barrels for six to eight months to soften the flavour and give the characteristic taste. Wild Turkey is flavoured with a secret recipe of herbs and spices.

Southern Comfort, by far the better known of the two brands internationally, was first made in New Orleans in the last century. The name Southern Comfort was coined by Louis Herron, a bartender in St Louis, Missouri. Before 1875 the drink was commonly called 'Cuff and Buttons' meaning 'white tie and tails'. The Southern Comfort Corporation attribute its creation to 'a gentleman distilling-genius' who first made the liquor for himself and his friends. Presumably this was Francis E Fowler, whose family still own the company and make the drink to their 'secret' recipe. Its commercial success outside New

Orleans came largely through the riverboats that plied the Mississippi. According to old tales, the captains would race their paddle steamers with the victor getting an agreed quantity of Southern Comfort, sometimes the whole cargo. The passengers too, spread the taste into Missouri and Ohio, then further afield. Today Southern Comfort is made in St Louis, one of the favourite finishing posts for the racing riverboat skippers.

Rock and Rye, and Forbidden Fruit are two well-known domestic liqueurs. Both are

made by a number of different producers so the names have taken a generic rather than a brand role, in much the same way as curaçao.

Rock and Rye gets its name from the rock sugar (candy) that is added to the base spirit, usually rye whiskey or neutral spirit, as a sweetener and which crystallises inside the bottle. Various flavours are added to the sweetened spirit, usually citrus extracts. Leroux, one of the oldest and perhaps the biggest US liqueur producer (with four dozen different labels, mainly domestic versions of

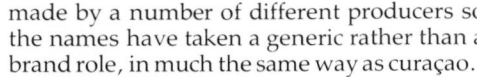

Southern Comfort and Wild Turkey, both bourbon-based liqueurs associated with the South. Based at St Louis on the Missouri, the early history of Southern Comfort was closely linked with the riverboat trade.

popular European liqueurs), use lemon, orange and cherry flavourings. They also make a version of the blend called Irish Moss which is flavoured with Irish moss, a type of seaweed. Arrow, another producer, add honey to the blend.

Forbidden Fruit is an old home-made American liqueur that has become a commercial style. Originally it was made from shaddock (an obscure relative of the grapefruit) and honey and orange infused into American whiskey, or brandy, to give a strongly citrus-flavoured, bitter-sweet liqueur. Now other citrus flavours are generally substituted for shaddock.

Other liqueurs of note (although not really peculiar to the United States) are Hawaiian pineapple liqueur; oxygenée (an absinthe-style drink also made in France on a very limited scale); Coffee Sport (a version of crème de café); the herby Claristine; and a chocolate cherry liqueur, both from Leroux; and a variety of Galliano substitutes.

A wide variety of domestic gins, vodkas, white and dark rums, tequilas and so on are produced by the big American distillers, plus lesser quantities of two quasi-generic spirits – fruit-flavoured brandies, with blackberry the most common, and applejack, once a popular pioneer drink, now more of a novelty than anything else. Applejack is the American version of calvados. Most examples have a high neutral spirit content to lighten the taste, although at the same time lessening the rich apple flavour that characterises calvados. Laird's and Spea's are the two main brands.

The Whiskey Brands

To the tastebuds of most whiskey drinkers, American whiskey is epitomised by bourbon.

In 1842 the American author Washington Irving introduced bourbon to Charles Dickens in Baltimore. Dickens wrote that the pair of them shared an enormous mint julep and that 'it was an enchanted julep and carried us among innumerable people and places that we both knew'. Another famous bourbon fan was Lady Randolph Churchill, mother of Sir Winston, who created the Manhattan to celebrate the election of Samuel Tilden as governor of New York State. She named her bourbon-based cocktail after the exclusive New York City club, the Manhattan, where the election victory party was held.

Bourbon takes its name from Bourbon County, Kentucky, where, in 1789 the Reverend Elijah Craig is said to have distilled Kentucky's first whiskey. Craig, seeing no disparity between his heavenly responsibilities and earthly pleasure, named his whiskey 'Bourbon County' and the name caught on when farmers followed his lead and distilled their corn whiskies to his basic recipe.

By 1810 there were 2,000 stills at work in Bourbon County alone, and bourbon distilling had spread through Kentucky and into neighbouring Indiana and Tennessee as the distillers followed the pure water of the limestone belt. Kentucky became, and still is, the home of bourbon, and the hub of the American distilling industry. One authority estimates that more than half of the licensed distilleries in the United States are based in Kentucky. In the early days the Allegheny Mountains stood as a solid barrier between bourbon and its big markets, mainly on the eastern seaboard. To get round this, the whiskey was shipped down to New Orleans on paddle steamers and rafts and trans-

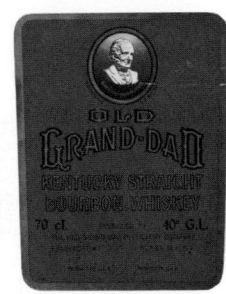

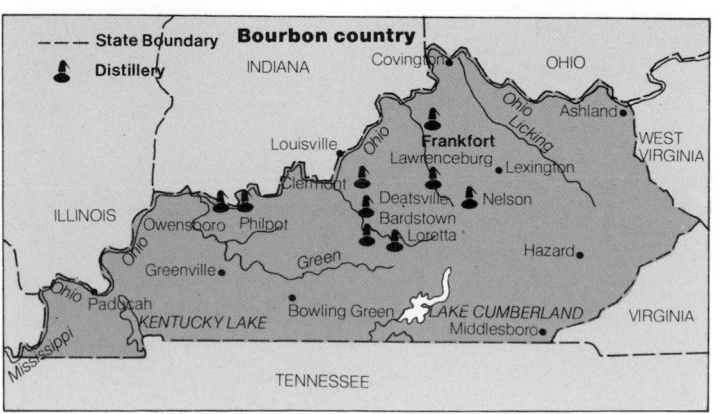

ported from there back to the thirsty east coast.

Bourbon now accounts for something like half of all the whiskey produced domestically and consumed in the United States. It dominates the straight whiskies, with the ryes accounting for almost the rest. It also accounts for almost all the American whiskey wearing the bottled in bond tag. The most popular brand, by a wide margin, is Jim Beam, followed by Early Times, Ancient Age, Ten High, Old Crow, Old Grand-Dad, Old Taylor, Old Forester, Old Charter, J W Dant, Old Sunny Brook, Bourbon De Luxe

(National Distillers) and Bourbon Supreme, Four Roses and I W Harper. These are the nationally known brands, and behind them come a host of lesser brands ranging from the well known to labels popular only in one or two states and almost unknown elsewhere. Such brands include Old Stagg, Old Hickory, Virginia Gentleman, Kentucky Straight (Medley), Continental's Charter Oak, James E Pepper, Haller's County Fair, just plain County Fair and Medley USA. (Notice the number of distillers who use the adjectives Old and Kentucky to give a cachet to their bourbon.)

Two other whiskies that by legal definition come within the bourbon category but, according to at least one expert, are infinitely superior in taste, are the twin (legal) Tennessee sour mash whiskies – Jack Daniels and George Dickel. Jack Daniels ranks high among the popular brands and is one of the oldest American whiskies. As with George Dickel it derives its distinctive taste from the filtering of the young whiskey through activated charcoal which gives a nuttier, smoother taste.

Rye and corn whiskies hold only a relatively small amount of the straights market,

with the rye brands mainly accounted for by Old Overholt (the biggest), Wild Turkey, Jim Beam rye, Meadowbrook and Rittenhouse. Corn rests almost entirely on Medley's Mellow Corn for its reputation.

Most straights have a very well-defined character, aroma and body, a deeper colour from wood ageing, and a smoothness from longer maturation. They are the malts of America. The blends, which account for almost all of the remainder of the United States' whiskey production, are lighter in colour and taste, with a continuity of flavour, but a less distinctive character.

By far the best-known blend is Seagram's Seven Crown, the largest selling single spirits brand in the United States with, in 1976, sales of 6,525,000,000 cases. It is the linchpin of the vast Seagram empire. Other major blends include Kessler, Calvert Extra, Fleischmann Preferred, Corby's Reserve, Schenley Reserve, Sunny Brook, Carstairs, Wilson, Three Feathers, Four Roses, Bellows Partners Choice, P M Blended , Canadian Schenley OFC and many more.

In the early 1970s a third type of whiskey arrived on the American market with a great deal of fanfare – light whiskey and with it a white whiskey. The US government first permitted the production of light whiskies on January 26 , 1968, and the big companies began laying down stocks of this 'revolutionary' new whiskey type. They hoped to challenge the white spirits which, with the swing to lighter drinking, were taking an increasingly large amount of the total domestic spirits sales.

Light whiskey is defined as whiskey distilled to between 160° and 190° US proof, and stored in new or used uncharred barrels at greater than 125° US proof. It has much less intensity of flavour than those whiskies stored in charred barrels and, the higher the proof within the permitted limits, the less flavouring elements would be in the whiskey before maturation, an added means to lightness. These whiskies were designed to be an even sharper, less assertive drink than even the blends and the imported Canadians, a new concept in whiskey drinking. To give everybody a fair chance in the market, the US government decreed a starting day, July 1, 1972, when the new whiskey could be marketed.

But the light whiskies were one enormous and expensive failure. After just two years there were only four of the original 50 labels still surviving, and Crow Light and Four Roses Light were the only two that sold consistently. Most distillers withdrew their brands and used their stocks in their standard blends.

White whiskey, basically uncoloured but with the whiskey taste, was an even more curious spin-off of this experiment, and attracted even less interest than the lights. The only surviving brand seems to be Publicker's White Duck.

WHISKEY SOUR

Frost a large goblet by dipping the rim into a saucer of grenadine and then into one of caster sugar. Place 2½ oz Wild Turkey bourbon whiskey, 1½ oz fresh lemon juice, 1 dash Angostura Bitters, 1 barspoon caster sugar, or to taste, and 1 dash egg white in a cocktail shaker with ice. Shake well. Strain into the prepared glass and add a few lumps of ice from the shaker, and garnish with a slice of orange and a cocktail cherry.

MANHATTAN

Pour 2oz Wild Turkey bourbon whiskey, 1 oz red vermouth and 1 dash Angostura Bitters into a mixing glass. Stir and strain into a cocktail glass, and garnish with a cocktail cherry.

THE MOST FAMOUS COCKTAIL IN THE WORLD

One drink has done more to popularise the image of the cocktail than any other – the Dry Martini. It deserves its place as the king among cocktails. Dry Martini devotees are legion, each devotee has their own recipe, and each treats its preparation almost as a fetish.

Like most other cocktails, the Dry Martini originated in the United States, where its popularity among cocktail drinkers has remained unchallenged. The Dry Martini, says John Doxat, who has written a book about this single drink, most probably originated at the Waldorf-Astoria in New York before Prohibition. Its creator was a bartender called Martini (or possibly Martinez) who, says Doxat,

'recognised that some of the greatest innovations are the simplest, and took what had previously been just a gin and French vermouth and, by the alchemy of stirring the mixture in a separate container, transmogrified it into Dry Martini'.

It seems that the Martini has changed its character over the years, apparently becoming drier and drier. Before 1914 the Martini contained two parts gin to one part vermouth. Between 1933 and 1944 this had changed to 4:1, and subsequently this has moved to 15:1 although, according to one expert, there has been some reversion to the 4:1 ratio. Not everyone agrees with these proportions. The actor and

singer Dean Martin, one of the better-known Dry Martini drinkers, reputedly waves the vermouth bottle over his glass of gin while chanting very softly 'vermouth, vermouth'.

Some Dry Martini drinkers dress the drink up with a dash of orange bitters, Pernod, even sherry. But this is not, as John Doxat insists, a true Dry Martini. And he is not alone in this opinion, as witnessed by the American who watched a bartender expertly mixing his Dry Martini. When the bartender reached for a slice of lemon rind, the customer stopped him. 'When I want fruit salad, I'll ask for it,' he said. The olive, the other optional adornment, has many followers although the purists ignore it.

Opinions differ about the amount of vermouth that should be used in a Dry Martini. The less vermouth used, the drier the Martini.

It is essential that all the ingredients and utensils are extremely cold before beginning to mix the drink, so the gin and vermouth should be chilled, all glassware filled with ice cubes, and the barspoon and strainer stored in ice. Fill the mixing glass with fresh, clear ice, add 3 oz London gin and 2 or 3 drops of dry vermouth to taste. Stir gently, and strain into a stemmed glass. A sliver of lemon peel can be squeezed over the drink to release it oils, and then dropped in, or lime peel can be used if desired. An olive may also be added.

Mexico and the Caribbean

The scattered islands of the Caribbean are the world's major producers of rum. Each island produces its own distinctive variety, but all are distilled from sugar cane or molasses and they can very broadly be divided into either dark, richer bodied rums or the light rums.

The rums associated with the colourful history of the region, with piracy and the slave trade, are the rich, full-bodied varieties, produced exclusively on Jamaica or Guyana. Light-bodied rums, since the Cuban revolution, are principally distilled on Puerto Rico. Light rums are also the most popular of the rums produced on the South American mainland.

One other major international spirit comes from this region – tequila. This bitter-flavoured spirit, made in Mexico from the fermented juice of the agave plant, has grown considerably in popularity in recent years.

Mexico/Tequila

THE PRINCIPAL SPIRIT of Mexico – tequila – is recommended by Mexicans 'as a remedy for everything bad and to celebrate all good as well'. Tequila has its own special character – a fresh, almost tart flavour that leaves the tongue clean and tingling, and, as the saying suggests, the whole sensation is uplifting.

Just as vodka was the spirit of the sixties, tequila has become the spirit of the seventies. Within two decades it has become an international spirit drunk neat or as cocktails. Its commercialisation outside Mexico has been helped by among others the American writer Ernest Hemingway, and above all the erroneous belief that the drink is mildly hallucinatory, which arose because the drug *mescalin* is obtained from a similar cactus.

The Aztecs fermented the sap of the wild *blue maguey* or *mezcal azul* cactus to make a potent quasi-spirit they called *pulque*. The semi-religious place the drink had in their culture is evident in a surviving sacramental mural, carved more than 1,300 years ago.

The Spanish Conquistadors first brought the art of distilling to Mexico. In the absence of grapes and grain they turned to the native pulque. In crude stills they produced a rough spirit, now called *mescal* or *mezcal*. Later, more sophisticated techniques were introduced by a group of mescal producers in and around

MARGERITA

This cocktail is served in a glass frosted with salt – an unusual decoration for a cocktail, but the traditional accompaniment for tequila.

Frost a medium-size cocktail glass by rubbing the rim with a slice of lemon, and then dipping it into a saucer of salt. Place several lumps of ice in a cocktail shaker and add 1½ oz tequila, ½–¾ oz Cointreau, 1 oz fresh lemon juice, and a little caster sugar to taste. Shake and strain into the prepared glass.

In the Jalisco province, near Tequila, fields of the blue agave are cultivated for tequila. After the long spiky leaves have been cut off, the 'pineapples' are transported to the distillery, where they are baked and pulped to extract their juices for fermentation and distilling.

the small town of Tequila, among them the Cuervo family.

But, as a name, tequila only appeared in this century. At the Chicago World Fair in 1893 a prize was given to 'mescal brandy'. In 1910 when 'tequila wine' won a medal in San Antonio, the name had just started to establish itself. Nowadays it is used only for the spirit made in a small area of central-west Mexico, and the Mexican government is trying to protect the name against the 'tequilas' produced in Spain and Japan.

True tequila is made only from cactus plants grown in the volcanic soils around the tiny towns of Tequila and Tepatitlán near Guadalajara in the province of Jalisco. A sub-species of the agave cactus, the *Agave tequilana*, has been extensively cultivated on the slopes of the Sierra Madre by shippers of tequila. They say that this sub-species makes the best tequila, better than could be made from the maguey (also called Mexican Century), used for mescal.

The cactus takes between twelve and thirteen years to reach maturity and its spiky leaves stand above head height. The spikes are hacked off for harvesting to leave the bulbous central core called the *pina* (literally the pineapple). The pinas, weighing anything from 80 to 175 pounds each, are taken to the distilleries where they are cooked in giant steam ovens for several hours. Then the pinas are cooled and shredded, and the juice pressed free. This liquid and some of the fibrous pulp are mixed with sugar and the mash is fermented for about four days.

When the fermentation has finished, the wash is distilled in pot stills to give low grade alcohol which can be sold as mescal. To make tequila, the spirit is redistilled to give the pure, colourless 'silver' tequila. Before bottling, the tequila goes into large (20,000-litre) white oak vats to mellow for between 35 and 45 days.

Left for nine months or more in smaller, 50-gallon white oak barrels it takes on a light gold colour and sells at a higher price. Less scrupulous producers use artificial colouring to give their product a veneer of quality.

The best tequilas are left in the same barrels for three years or more to gain a deeper gold colour. These golden varieties are called *tequila anejo*, and the price varies according to the anejo (years) they have had in barrel. In Mexico the oldest ones sell at prices equal to those for fine cognacs in France. Tequila improves in taste with the length of time in the cask, but after ten years it begins to take a harsh and bitter woody taste from the oak.

Within Mexico connoisseurs have strong brand loyalties and claim they can distinguish between one tequila label and another. Different parts of the country also have their leading brands, so a southerner could find tequilas he has not seen before in the north. However, outside Mexico most major brands are similar in taste. This similarity increased when tequila became popular in the United States in the late 1960s and shippers were

Pulque, the forerunner of tequila, is the product of a single distillation of a mash made from the mezcal plant, and not, as this early French lithograph suggests, extracted rather unhygienically from the plant itself. The modern tequila industry is based at Tequila, right.

persuaded to refine their tequilas to a more international, delicately flavoured taste while still retaining its essential character. For export the normal tequila strength has been fixed at 70° proof, but in Mexico several examples are available at 77° and higher.

The production of tequila is concentrated in the hands of three dozen main producers with their distilleries around Tequila and Tepatitlán, and their offices in Guadalajara. Among the leading brands are Jose Cuervo, Sauza, Olmeca, El Viejo, San Matias, Orendain, Eucario Gonzalez, Vuida de Romero, Rosales, Rio Plata, Virreyes, Herradura, de Martinez, Tres Magueyes, Ruiz, and Amatitan.

Each is available in the silver variety as well as several grades of tequila anejo.

Other spirits and liqueurs

Mescal, which can be made from magueys grown anywhere in Jalisco or even outside the state, is potent and rough. Imbibed in sufficient quantity it would no doubt induce some kind of hallucinatory effect on the drinker. That, coupled with the similarity in name to mescalin, has led to the false idea that it and tequila can have a similar but much lesser effect. Mescalin comes from the small buds of the *peyote* cactus, not the giant hearts of the spiky maguey.

For stronger stomachs the best mescal is reputedly that in a bottle or earthenware crock containing, apart from the spirit, a dead worm as a seal of authenticity.

Pulque, the least sophisticated of Mexican drinks, is simply fermented cactus juice, and is still widely drunk in Mexico because it is so cheap. Invariably outsiders find the taste revolting. Since it is not unheard of for the fermentation vats to be covered with manure to heat the juice and speed up the process, these opinions are understandable.

Despite their tequila-drinking image, the Mexicans are not devoted to it. The tequilas lining the bar shelves are there more for the tourists than the locals. The middle class Mexican who can afford a good tequila is more likely to spend the same money on a bottle of Scotch whisky, and even mescal and pulque are losing ground to beer and cheap spirits such as rum.

After tequila, there are few other locally made spirits in Mexico, although production of both rum and brandy is growing. Both dark and light rums are distilled locally, the Castillo label, for example, is reputed to be of high quality. Increasingly, brandy is being distilled for local consumption and export – Domecq of Spain, with their Don Pedro labels, have invested heavily in Mexican-made brandy.

Mexican flavoured liqueurs, such as Xanath cream of vanilla from Montini and Vreez Vanilla de Mexico, are made from vanilla (another favourite Aztec drink) and coffee beans. Vreez also have several other flavours, such as chocolate, strawberry and peach, and Montini also make Camino Real coffee liqueur.

TEQUILA SUNRISE

This is a fairly new cocktail, and currently quite fashionable.

Place a few lumps of ice in a long glass, add 1½ oz tequila, and 6 oz fresh orange juice, and stir. Pour in ½ oz grenadine, and allow to diffuse through the drink.

The Caribbean/Rum

LEMON HART RUM
FOUNDED 1804

All rum is produced from sugar cane, either from the juice itself or, more likely, from fermented molasses. But different methods of production and climates on the islands create very different rums. Lemon Hart, with its rich full body and golden colour distinguishes it as a Jamaican blend.

HOT RUM GROG

A warming drink for a cold day.

Dissolve 2 barspoons demerara sugar in a little boiling water in a heavy goblet. Add 1½ oz dark aromatic rum, ½ oz fresh lemon juice, 2 or 3 cloves and a sprinkling of freshly-grated nutmeg. Stir well, top up with boiling water and serve with a cinnamon stick.

HISTORIANS BELIEVE SUGAR CANE was introduced to the Caribbean by Christopher Columbus, who brought cuttings from the Azores and planted them on the islands during his second voyage of discovery.

The cane proliferated in the ideal growing climate and, as cane replaced honey as the source of sweetness in their diet, the natives spread new cuttings throughout the islands.

The Spanish explorers and colonists who followed Columbus, brought with them the art of distilling, and rum, the juice of the sugar cane mixed with water and heated in a primitive still, became the major source of alcohol in the New World.

The first written reference to rum, from Barbados, dates around 1600, when the spirit was sufficiently established to have acquired a name. There are many theories about the derivation of the word. Most authors believe it comes from the old words *rumbullion* (rumpus) or *rumbustion* (uproar) – descriptive reference to the effects of the first rums on their drinkers. The name may come from an abbreviation of *saccharum* (Latin for the sugar cane); or by French from the Malay word *brum*, used by the French to describe a fermented drink. It may even be a corruption of the word *aroma*.

Rum had a host of other names besides – among them 'kill-devil' and 'Barbados water'. (Kill-devil may come from the natives' habit of using rum to heal blood clots, cuts, bruises and various ills.) These names were commonly used in the seventeenth century, one contemporary account of Barbados states 'the chief fudling they make in the islands is rumbullion, alias kill-devil, and this is made of sugar canes distilled, a hot, hellish and terrible liquor.'

With the end of Spanish dominance in the Caribbean, and the growth of British influence during the seventeenth and eighteenth centuries, rum spread abroad, first to the American Colonies, and then to England and the Continent.

At this time the Caribbean was one corner of the Triangular Trade. Slaves were transported from Africa to work the sugar cane fields, in turn molasses was brought from the islands to New England to make rum for the colonists, and this was re-exported to Africa in exchange for more slaves.

Before 1775 rum was being consumed by the American colonists at the annual rate of four gallons per head. New England built its fortunes on rum, George Washington was elected to the Virginia House of Burgesses after distributing free rum to the voters. Paul Revere is said to have only found his voice after two cups of Medford rum at the last stop on his historic ride. When the British Crown taxed molasses imported into the Colonies it caused great unrest and contributed to the feelings that led to the Boston Tea Party in 1773 and the American Revolution. Rum running from the islands into New England, past the British Navy, was commonplace.

A DAILY TOT OF GROG

Duty on the Spanish Main produced one principal benefit for the British Jack Tar in the 18th century – a daily ration of rum. The effects of the raw spirit on discipline led Admiral Vernon, in a bold and unpopular move, to order that the rum be diluted and served in half issues twice a day. The sailors disparagingly dubbed the new mixture 'grog', after the Admiral's rough coat, but the ruling was upheld.

In the islands themselves the sugar planters flourished. Alexis Lichine records the scene at one gracious party of the eighteenth century: 'A marble basin, built in the middle of the garden especially for the occasion, served as a bowl. Into it were poured 1,200 bottles of rum, 1,200 bottles of Málaga wine, and 400 quarts of boiling water. Then 600 pounds of the best cane sugar and 200 powdered nutmegs were added. The juice of 2,600 lemons was squeezed into the liquor.

'Onto the surface was launched a handsome mahogany boat, piloted by a boy of twelve who rowed about a few moments then coasted to the side and began to serve the assembled company of 600, which gradually drank up the ocean on which he floated.'

Rum first came back to England as ballast in the slaving ships returning from a westward trip. The missionaries sharing space with the rum earned these ships the nickname 'rum and bible ships'. By the mid-seventeenth century a taste for rum had been brought to England by the traders, and the sailors of the British Navy, who received a daily ration of half a pint of raw rum before noon.

Then in 1740 Admiral Vernon, on the advice of his officers, ordered that the ration must be watered down with four parts water to one of the spirit, and served in half rations twice a day. Vernon, known as Old Grog because of the rough *grogum* (silk and mohair) coat he always wore, had his nickname immortalised by the resentful sailors who dubbed the new mixture 'grog'.

After the Battle of Trafalgar the Navy rum had a second nickname – Nelson's Blood – as the admiral's body was reportedly preserved in a cask of rum for shipment back to England and burial. The traditional tot of grog persisted in the Royal Navy for almost two centuries. It was finally abolished in 1969 when the order was given to end the daily grog ration.

How Rum is Made

RUM IS THE SPIRIT of sugar cane, and its raw ingredient, molasses, is a by-product of the sugar industry. Throughout the Caribbean the commercial varieties of the sugar cane (*saccharum officinarum*) are used both for sugar and molasses in a cycle that begins with the arduous, labour intensive harvesting of the cane.

The freshly cut cane is taken to the sugar mills where, wet or dry, it is crushed between rollers to extract the juice. The residual pulp, called the *bagasse*, is again crushed several times more to extract any remaining liquid, and is then very often used as fuel in the factory's boilers. The liquid sugar extract is heated almost to boiling point, cooled, and the deposits removed, then heated and cooled again so that a rich, dark syrup is left, relatively free from impurities.

The syrup is placed in a centrifuge and spun until the sugar crystals are separated. These are removed to make commercial sugar, leaving a very dark, treacly mother liquor – the molasses.

As rum is one of the few spirits that retains much of the character of its base ingredient, each rum will vary according to the variety of cane used, its mineral content and sugar level, climatic and soil conditions and so on. But, to produce good rum, the molasses extracted from the cane should have a fresh and sweet smell, and should taste sweet and sound, with none of the fustiness or staleness that results from long storage in bad conditions. Ideally, it should be stored in clean, well aired tanks for three to four months after it is made. The 'cooled' molasses gives the rum a better fragrance, lets it ferment more readily, and leaves it easier to distil through complex changes.

At this point it is worth saying that not all rum is made from good molasses. Some of the rums from the French Antilles, particularly Martinique, are made from unrefined cane juice with its sugar intact (what they call *pur sucre de canne*), and similar rums are made in Haiti. Occasionally rums are also made from cane juice which has been concentrated into syrup form. But the vast majority of rums come from molasses, or *blackstrap*, as it is called locally.

Fermentation is the next step in the rum cycle. After the molasses has been cleaned, it is diluted with water to reduce the viscosity and the sugar content to a point where it is receptive to the yeasts which will convert the natural sugar to alcohol. Usually these are special yeast strains developed for the local conditions. But some rum producers, particularly in Guiana and Jamaica, use wild yeasts and allow them to act naturally on molasses which has been strengthened with the addition of *bagaese* (in which the wild yeasts will still be present).

Fermentation takes place in cooled vats

The process of producing rum, from the picking of the sugar cane to the final exportation of the barrels, is illustrated left. Old inn signs, above, advertising rum.

of around 20,000 gallons capacity. For the darker, heavier rums *dunder* (the residue left in the still after the previous distillation) and *limings* (the scum that forms on the surface of the molasses as the sugar is being extracted) will be added to the molasses at this point to give a more pungent flavour to the spirit.

The lighter rum types are fermented rapidly. Some only need 24 hours, but the majority need about 36 hours before the sugar in the molasses is converted to alcohol. For darker rums the molasses is fermented more slowly, twelve days is typical. With the additions of dunder and limings, the resulting *dead wash* (the distilling mash) has more depth and fragrance, through a higher ester content. The Jamaican Wedderburn and Plummer dark rums are two made by this method.

Next comes the distillation of the dead wash. Again, there are two ways of distilling, each having a determining effect on the style and character of the rum. From the time when rum was first made in the Caribbean until almost the turn of the century, pot stills were commonly used as the easiest way of separating the alcohol from the wash. They yielded heavy, aromatic rums that are still made, mainly in Jamaica, and which are an acquired taste for all but seasoned rum drinkers.

Around 1900 the continuous still was introduced into the West Indies and it has rapidly replaced the pot still in most of the rum islands as it can be used to make just about every type of rum except the rich pot

still type. Modern distilleries now invariably use three- to five-column continuous stills to make their white and light rums – the two styles which have soared in popularity in most of the major rum markets.

The pot still is used in the same way as for whisky or cognac – with only the middle run retained and the heads and tails run off for redistillation. Out of the still, the young spirit will only be around 50°.

In the continuous still, the dead wash goes in at the top and is vaporised by ascending steam, the alcohol is stripped out and condensed, then redistilled in the next column and so on, for greater purity. Rum made in a continuous still will emerge at about 68° proof – almost the required strength for most international markets – and will have a much greater purity. All white rums, for example, which by comparison with a pot still dark rum are very light in flavour, are made in this way as well as many high volume dark rums.

The raw colourless rum (any colour from the molasses is stripped out during the distillation cycle) then goes into new oak barrels and is left to mature. The best rums are left for at least three years, and a good pot still rum will continue to improve in the wood for up to twelve, depending on its original quality and the quality of the cask. The new spirit takes colour from the oak wood, and a small part of its flavour, while mellowing and losing its harsh new taste. The colour from the wood can be extracted by charcoal filtering, enhanced with caramel or left at its natural colour.

The Rum Islands

An old sugar mill, above, where the sugar cane was pressed after picking to extract the juice. Right, a china figure used to advertise Lemon Hart Rum.

RUM IS PRODUCED wherever sugar cane grows. A domestic variety is produced in countries as varied as the United States, South Africa and Australia. Even Russia produces its own rum. However, only the Caribbean, the world's major rum producer, exports rum in any quantity.

Each Caribbean island produces its own distinctive style of rum, the variations result from the base material used (cane juice, molasses, and so on), the method of distillation, and the length of maturation.

Barbados

Barbados, the garden island, makes lighter-bodied rums tending to medium, often with a slight smokiness. Fine, aged Barbados rums can almost be drunk as a liqueur.

Cane is the island's main crop. Because of the lack of fresh water supplies, most of the cane fields have to be irrigated. The rums are made from molasses, in pot or continuous stills, to fairly high strength. The island has three main distillers – Mount Gay, the West Indian Rum Refinery, and Barbados Distilleries. Most Barbados rum is shipped to Britain for further ageing and bottling under importers' names. Mount Gay sell under their own label as well as exporting in bulk.

Cuba

Cuba, once the home of Ron Bacardi, is the largest of the Caribbean islands, and was the major supplier of light rums. However, under the Castro government, exports ended, and most of the major distillers moved to other parts of the Caribbean.

Sugar cane is still a principal crop in the central area of the island, and molasses is used as the spirit base. Distillation in con-

tinuous stills gives a very light rum with a fragrant, refreshing taste.

In Cuba, the two main rums are Carta Blanca, and Carta Oro (a golden rum coloured with caramel). Recently there has been a slight revival of export shipments through the state-run Cuba export. French Guiana produces an indifferent white rum at two distilleries – Mirande and Prévot – almost totally for domestic consumption.

Guadeloupe

Guadeloupe is one of the two major suppliers of French rums, usually of the full-bodied pot still style. Most of its production is shipped in bulk to France for further maturation and bottling under the importers' brand names. However, Guadeloupe's reputation for rum, although good, is overshadowed by neighbouring Martinique.

A selection of the colourful labels which appear on bottles of Caribbean rum.

Among the distilleries on Guadeloupe producing rums are Fort Ille, Tabanon, Longueteau, Routa, Bourdon, Bologne Lassere, Néron and Péres Blancs.

Guyana

Guyana, formerly British Guiana, is part of the Latin American mainland, but its rums are classified as Caribbean. Its famous rum is Demerara, named after the river which irrigates most of the sugar cane fields. Like demerara sugar, it is dark and rich, although not as heavy as its colour suggests.

Demerara rum is made from the molasses left after the production of demerara sugar, which are fermented very rapidly (48 hours is the maximum) to give a lightness to the spirit. The rapid fermentation also gives the rum less depth of flavour than a longer fermented rum. Distillation, in pot or continuous stills, takes the spirit to a high strength. Pot stills are regarded as giving the better tasting rum.

Guyana is the largest of the four Caribbean producers that have British links. Apart from local sales nearly all Demerara rum is shipped to Britain for bottling under various brand names. It is one of the two most popular of the dark rum styles in Britain.

Four of the main distilleries clustered around the capital, Georgetown, are Uitvlugt, Enmore, Diamond and Versailles – a reflection of the diversity of the population.

Haiti

Haiti, once part of the French colonial empire, has emerged as a major Caribbean rum producer since the decline of Cuba as an exporter.

The best cane is grown in the shelter of high mountains on the northern hook of the island. The cane is immediately crushed and the juice distilled without being allowed to ferment. The continuing French influence on Haiti is evident in the double pot still distillation – the 'cognac' process – which gives medium- to full-bodied rums with considerable fragrance and medium alcoholic strength.

The first distillation gives a clear rum known on the island as *clairin*. Still a very rough spirit, it is sold cheaply to locals and plays an important part in voodoo rites as the libation offered to the spirits.

The second distillation of the clairin gives the true Haitian rum – a medium, very full-flavoured aromatic spirit.

France remains the major market for these rums, or *rhum(s)* as the French call them. The main distilleries are around Port-au-Prince, among them the renowned Damien distillery of rhum Barbancourt, considered by experts to be one of the best Caribbean rums. Other brands include rhum Nazon and rhum Tesserot: rhum Champion from the Croix des Bouquets distillery; rhum Marie Colas from the Cazeau distillery; and rhum Tropical from the Manègue distillery.

Jamaica

Jamaica has been described as the Bordeaux of the Caribbean. It is the oldest commercial rum producer in the Caribbean, and the best known British supplier since the seventeenth century, although Guyana surpasses it in quantity.

The traditional Jamaican rums are made from cane grown on the southern strip of the island. Full-flavoured, dark with a rich aroma, they supplied the British Navy for two hundred years. These rums, commonly called *Wedderburn* and *Plummer*, have recently given way to the more commercial lighter styles.

Today, Jamaican rums are made from molasses and are distilled in three main ways to produce three distinctive rums. Distilling in continuous stills, after a short fermentation to give a high alcohol, gives a light but well-flavoured style called common clean. Medium-bodied pot still rums are made from cane juice mixed with molasses to give a fine aroma. Heavy, slow fermented pot stilled Wedderburn and Plummer rums have a dark, rich fragrance.

Most of the rum produced in Jamaica goes to Britain, where it is matured in the damp British cellars (ideal for spirit maturation because of the low evaporation rate) and then bottled under brand names such as Lambs Navy, Old Charlie, Captain Morgan, Woods, Rope & Anchor, Black Heart, and Myer's.

Jamaican white rums sell under such names as Appleton's (one of the island's biggest producers) and Caroni.

Martinique

The island of Martinique is the home of the major French-based rum companies. The prosperity of the capital, Fort de France, is founded on the several dozen rum companies whose warehouses rim the town.

Fort de France is the capital and the most affluent town on Martinique by default. Until St Pierre was destroyed by volcanic eruption it was the major rum town and capital of Martinique. A few rum companies are returning to the site of the former capital, however, among them Rhum St James, who have their plantations nearby.

Most Martinique rums are made from cane juice, and are sold either without cask ageing, as *grappe blanche*, or are matured to take on the wood colour. Grappe blanche is the prime ingredient of Martinique rum punch, the popular island drink which the French company Duquesne also sell in France.

Duquesne also make white rum from cane

OTHER CARIBBEAN LIQUEURS

Apart from rum, the Caribbean also contributes two distinctive but entirely different drinks to the world's liquor cabinet.

Angostura bitters, essential to the good cocktail mixer and the wardrooms of the British Navy, has been made on Trinidad by the Angostura company since the early nineteenth century. Angostura bitters is made from a secret recipe using Trinidad rum flavoured with herbs and spices devised by a Frenchman, Dr Siegert, as a pick-me-up for residents of the tropical Caribbean islands.

The worldwide recognition of the drink has largely arisen from the British Navy's habit of adding a few drops to their gin to make the famous pink gin.

The recipe for Tia Maria was rediscovered by another doctor – Kenneth Evans. With Kahlua, Tia Maria now ranks as the best-known and most enjoyed of the coffee liqueurs. It is made from Jamaican rum flavoured with Blue Mountain coffee essences and other ingredients. Drier than Kahlua, it has a rich coffee aroma and colouring.

Other Caribbean drinks include Coffee House liqueur made from Virgin Islands rum; Puerto Rican anisette, called Tres Castillos; and Martinique orange-flavoured drinks, known as maduva, messica or maitina. Cuba used to make Aldabo orange liqueur and Ron Coco coconut liqueur, but whether production continues is uncertain.

BACARDI

This cocktail uses white rum as its main ingredient, thus achieving the delicate pink colour of the drink when mixed with grenadine.

Frost a medium-size cocktail glass by dipping the rim into a saucer of grenadine, and then into a saucer of caster sugar. Place several lumps of ice in a cocktail shaker and add 2 oz Bacardi rum, 1 oz fresh lime juice, 1 barspoon caster sugar and a few drops of grenadine. Shake well and strain into the prepared glass.

CUBA LIBRE

A most refreshing cocktail, the lime juice taking the edge off the sweetness of the Coca Cola.

Place several lumps of ice in a long glass and squeeze the juice of half a lime over the cubes, and then drop the lime into the glass. Add 2 oz Bacardi rum and top up with Coca Cola. Garnish with a thin slice of lime.

juice (which they sell under the brand name Genippa), and the dark three-year-old Grand Case and the ten-year-old Val d'Or.

The rival to Duquesne is Rhum Clement, both white and tawny, which is highly regarded by rum connoisseurs. It is made at the Clement distillery just north of the Duquesne plant on the east side of the island.

Rhum St James, distilled from cane juice syrup heavily strengthened with dunder, is the darkest and most aromatic of the Martinique rums, and is very popular in France.

The largest of the French rum importers is Bardinet who have their own distillery on the northwest side of the island. Based in Bordeaux, Bardinet import and mature a large amount of white and dark rum from their Dillon distillery, which is sold as Old Nick (white), Negrita and Très Vieux Dillon (dark).

Other Bardinet labels – St James, Bardinet dark and Vive (made only from molasses) – have something of the heavy Jamaican flavour and aroma.

Puerto Rico

Puerto Rico has taken over Cuba's mantle as the leading producer of white rums, largely thanks to the Bacardi company, now one of the largest distilling companies in the world.

The island, although smaller than Jamaica, is now the world's biggest rum producer, with most of its output going to the United States, to which it is linked.

Puerto Rican rums are traditionally distilled from molasses in a continuous still to a high strength, but retaining a lightness and good aroma. As most are intended to be clear,

Puerto Rican rums are very rarely stored in barrels.

Bacardi is the predominant brand, followed by a host of others, the 'rons'. Ronrico is probably second most important, followed by Ron Viejo (lightly coloured), Maraca, Carioca, Don Q and Merito.

Trinidad

Trinidad, the smallest of the three British influenced islands, produces good quality medium-bodied rums from quick-fermented

molasses distilled in continuous stills. Their high alcoholic content and weak body and aroma make them very suitable for blending with heavier rums.

The Virgin Islands

The Virgin Islands – St Thomas, St John and St Croix – all make a little rum, but St Croix dominates the other two. Its rums are very similar to Trinidad's. All production is in the hands of the government-run distillery and are sold with the name *cruzan* on the label.

A late 19th-century engraving of a sugar plantation in Havana, Cuba.

South America

THE TYPE OF SPIRIT consumed in Latin American countries can very broadly be determined by dividing the continent into two regions – the tropical lowlands, mainly to the north and east, and the temperate Andean areas, to the west and south.

In the tropical lowlands, sugar cane is invariably the base of the local drink. Abundant and cheap, it is used to make what could be described as white rum. In many instances there is a distinct local character to the spirit, in the same way as the South African cane spirit differs from Bacardi.

In the temperate Andean areas, particularly Argentina and Chile, grapes are used to make local spirits, but compared to the distribution of cane spirits it is a modest industry. Even in countries like Ecuador, where most of the population lives in the temperate highlands, sugar cane spirit from the nearby lowlands is the preferred drink.

Rums and rum-like drinks are cheap. In Brazil, one of the most affluent South American countries, a bottle costs only seven to eight British pence and is either drunk neat or as a mixer. The only rival drink is beer which in countries such as Bolivia and Peru challenges spirits as the drink of the poor.

Brazil

The spirit of Brazil is *cachaca*, distilled from fermented sugar cane in continuous stills. It is something like a white rum but with a distinct taste of its own, and regular drinkers find it drier than a rum. Cheaper examples are very fiery, and in some instances are sweetened with sugar syrup to ease the taste.

The best cachaca is the heads – the first spirit out of the still – and Brazilians identify it by shaking the bottle and seeing if bubbles form on the surface of the spirit. If so it is the best, and they call it *cachaca de cabeca*.

Cachaca is found only in Brazil (although white rums, such as Maroni from neighbouring French Guiana, have a similar taste). Unlike other Latin American spirits there is a proliferation of cachaca brands, two of the best-known brands are Pitú and Sao Francisco; many have odd names, such as Tatizinho, which means 'little armadillo'.

Most cachacas are colourless, but some labels, such as Ypiocha, can have a slight yellow colour from ageing in wood.

Normally cachaca is drunk neat in small, one-shot glasses; among the richer circles it is commonly mixed with lemon, *maracuja* (passion fruit), *tamarind*, sugar and ice to make a *batida*. In northern Brazil (the Amazons) it is also drunk in the same way as tequila, but substituting *caju* (the fruit of the cashew) for lemon. Caju has a strong drying effect on the throat, and the combination of a shot of cachaca followed by a lick of salt and a squeeze of caju is an acquired taste.

Several liqueurs are also produced in Brazil, with Conhaques and Bahia (a bittersweet blend of coffee and grain spirit) the most important.

Bolivia and Chile

In Bolivia, beer is normally drunk, but pisco is the principal spirit, served straight or with orange juice.

In Chile pisco is also the principal spirit, served neat or with water, or mixed as a pisco sour. There is some domestic brandy and gin production, and *aguardiente* is distilled from sugar cane and sold flavoured with anis.

At Christmas it is mixed with coffee, milk and vanilla and served cold as a traditional festive drink called the *Cola de Mono*.

Colombia

Colombia has two main spirits, both made from sugar cane – *ron* (white rum) and *aguardiente*. One distillery will make both. For example, the state-owned Industria Licorera de Bolivar at Cartagena distils molasses once to make a cheap rum under the Ron Popular label, or twice to make a better grade rum, Tres Esquinas (three corners), which is sold in a triangular bottle. For aguardiente the distillery adds an anis extract; for gin it adds a juniper extract.

The Colombian poor drink rum neat in a single-shot known as a *trago*, and most bottles come complete with a small blue plastic cup for holding a single measure. Even higher up the social scale it is drunk neat by the men, and the women mix it with soft drinks, or Coca Cola to make a Cuba Libre. On the coast a

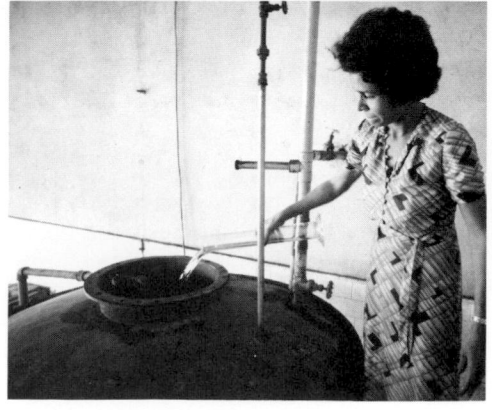

The New Year's Fair in the Colombian ranching town of Turbaco lasts three days. Celebrations include bull fighting (*corraleja*), gambling and, of course, the local rum, Ron Popular.

Aguardiente is a popular drink in the temperate Andean countries of South America. Its distinctive flavour comes from the measured quantities of anis which are added to the base spirit in the still.

speciality is *ron con agua de coco*, drunk straight from a fresh coconut – a little of the coconut water is poured away, then rum, a little sugar and crushed ice is added and stirred.

In the cooler areas around Medellin, the rum is sometimes aged to give a yellowish or dark colour and then sold under such brand names as Ron Medellin or Ron Viejo de Caldas.

Colombian aguardiente is the drink of the poor, who prefer it to rum. It is always drunk neat, although water is sometimes served as a chaser.

Ecuador
Aguardiente is also the principal spirit of Ecuador, although some pisco and cana is produced locally. A popular brand of aguardiente is Paico, and it is usually drunk in the same manner as the Colombians.

Paraguay
In Paraguay the main spirit is *cana*, distilled from sugar cane. It is a colourless spirit which falls between white rum and cachaca in taste, although the imperfect distillation methods usually produce a stronger, more fiery spirit. Cana is usually drunk neat, sometimes with ice, or as a mixer with fruit juices by the more affluent Paraguayans. But wine is the predominant Paraguayan drink, reducing the importance of cana.

Uruguay
Cana is also the main spirit of Uruguay. It is drunk in exactly the same way as in Paraguay, and again wine drinking detracts from its importance. Cana also has a rival in *grappa* – a clear brandy, which is made locally from grapes.

Venezuela
Venezuela is another rum drinking country, but in this instance mostly dark rum. As everywhere else in Latin America, rum is typically drunk neat in one-shot glasses or with fruit juice. Rum is also used to make a punch called Ponche de Crema where milk, eggs and sugar are mixed with the spirit. In the south of Venezuela it is mixed with fruit juice to make a *guarapita*.

Venezuela also produced a crude spirit called *cocui* from fermented cactus juice, which is high in alcohol and similar to a harsh tequila. Another spirit, *chicha*, is made by the Indians from fermented corn and is exceptionally coarse. Some aguardiente is made as well as *Pansgue*, a cordial based on rum and flavoured with cherry juice. Around Caracas *chouao*, named after the Chouao district once renowned for the quality of its cacao beans, is the local equivalent of crème de cacao (chocolate liqueur).

Argentina
Curiously Argentina, despite its importance as a wine producer, has no really significant domestic spirit, not even a national brandy.

Some domestic brandy is produced for local consumption, but it is only a localised drink. Beer and wine are the main drinks, and spirits sales are dominated by imported or locally-made gins and vodkas and imported Scotch whisky. Probably the most Europeanised country of South America, Argentina is an important Scotch whisky market. As with most of the other Latin American countries, Scotch is the status symbol, and it is served to important guests in all but the poorest homes.

Peru
Peru's famous spirit is *pisco* brandy. It was first made at Pisco, chief port for the vineyards of the southern valleys, in particular the Ica valley where most of the grapes for the spirit are grown. It is a water-white spirit, similar to the *aguardiente* of Portugal or the *marc* of France, which is sometimes aged to give it a pale lemon colour.

Good piscos have a slight oiliness and a strong, but not overpowering, flavour. Larate is one well-known brand, but Inca Pisco, in black bottles moulded to the shape of an Indian head, is the brand most widely known outside South America.

Within Peru, pisco takes a second place to beer. But pisco is often drunk with a fruit juice chaser, or mixed with lemon, sugar syrup and crushed ice and egg white as a *pisco sour*.

At the large Cartagena distillery in Colombia the alcohol content of the new spirit is carefully measured. Three labels produced at this distillery are shown next to the map.

Australia/Brandy

AUSTRALIAN SPIRITS LIVE in the shadow of domestic lagers, both in reputation and output. Rum, the first spirit to be distilled in Australia, has diminished in popularity during this century.

Australian brandy production has grown from an offshoot of the substantial wine and dried fruit industries to a significant industry in its own right.

Brandy production started in the last century along the Murray River. At that time, the main grape product in that area was the dried raisin, produced from the *doradillo* and *muscat gordo blanco* grape varieties. When the raisin industry switched to the seedless *sultana* it left a glut of doradillo and muscat grapes which were used for the first Australian brandies. Domestic brandy sales boomed after the last war when it became fashionable as a long drink (with dry ginger ale or lime and soda) and as a straight drink. From 1954 to 1975 the Federal Government helped to encourage grape growing with preferential duty rates on Australian brandy. The resulting lower retail prices pushed brandy into second place, behind Scotch whisky, as the preferred Australian spirit, overtaking domestic gin and rum.

Australia produces two distinct types of brandy. The majority, 60 percent and more, comes from the irrigated upper Murray River, and the Riverina district of the Murrumbidgee River in New South Wales. The grapes used are the doradillo, the Thompson Seedless sultana (rapidly becoming the predominant variety), and some muscat gordo blanco. The continuous still is widely used and makes a light-bodied, light-flavoured brandy that forms the backbone of most Australian blends.

In the non-irrigated or dry areas – the Barossa Valley and McLaren Vale in South Australia – the pot still is preferred, usually the *Bergstrom* designed by a South Australian coppersmith of that name and first used at the Horndale distillery near McLaren in the 1890s. The predominant grape varieties are the *grenache*, *Pedro Ximénez* and *palomino* (the sherry grapes) and *white hermitage* (the same grape as the St Emilion used for cognac and also known as white shiraz, trebbiano and ugni blanc). Dry area brandies made from these grapes tend to be fatter, heavier and fuller-flavoured.

When blended, the standard Australian brandy is lighter in body and flavour than a cognac. It is closer to a good French grape brandy, but has a smoother, softer flavour and lacks the so-called 'stalky' taste of a grape brandy. It is often sweetened slightly with cane sugar after maturation.

The main Australian brandies are St Agnes Château Tanunda, Tolleys TST, Mildara, Reynella, Remy (blended locally by a Remy Martin subsidiary) and Hennessy (in association with Jas Hennessy of Cognac). Several brands are labelled *hospital brandy*, a term as meaningless as *napoleon brandy*.

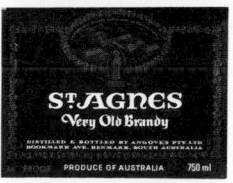

Of the several different Australian grapes, the majority grow in the irrigated Upper Murray River, far left. Among those growing in the dry areas is the Pedro Ximénez grape, above. Also in the dry Barossa Valley is the Chateau Tanunda Winery, top, and Seppelts brandy distillery.

235

Fortified Wines

THE MAIN GRAPES used for making Australian port are the *grenache*, *shiraz*, *cabernet sauvignon* and *mataro*. Producers use them to make the ruby and tawny styles, a few true vintage styles, and, in recent years, private bin, single year and other variations of the basic port types.

Most Australian vintage ports are vintage tawnies. Because of the confusion over vintage, the term is gradually falling out of use save for the very few bottle-aged vintage wines. Even the renowned Para Liqueur is a tawny, and in its squat bottle could not possibly be laid down to develop a crust.

The best Australian ports have a soft palate and sweet, luscious grapey aftertaste compared to the rounded flavour and dry spiritiness of Douro ports. Some of the best examples are Hardys Show Port, Penfolds Grandfather, and Lindemans RF1. Other popular examples include Hardys Fine Old Tawny, Penfolds Private Bin Old Tawny, Seaview Tawny, Angoves Special Vintage Ruby and McWilliams Rich Ruby.

Australian sherries at the top end of the market suffer little from comparison with their Spanish counterparts. The best brands are made in the same way as Jerez sherries, and while a discerning palate would find a slightly sweeter touch to the dry Australian styles, the established producers take as many pains over their wines as the big Spanish sherry makers.

Sweeter sherries, once the dominant style, are often very full and heavy without the finesse of an oloroso. In most cases they resemble Spanish cream sherries, and the cheaper brands can suffer from shortcuts in production. But with the drier varieties finding a bigger domestic market, the trend is away from these fuller, muscular wines.

Australian sherry is made in each of the wine growing states, with the classic Spanish palamino and Pedro Ximénez grape varieties predominating. Others used include the sultana, albillo and madeleine, with muscat, verdelho, tokay and madeira used for sweetening in tiny amounts.

Among the leading Australian sherry labels are Hamiltons Pale Fino and Oloroso, Reynella Flor and Del Pedro, Seppelts Dry, Medium, and Sweet Solero, Angoves Fino Dry, Hardys Dry Flor, Penfolds, George and Chestnut Teal and McWilliams Dry Friar.

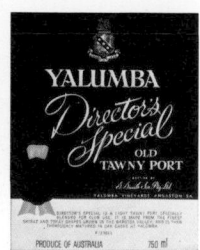

Australian ports are not always treated in such a lighthearted manner as at the grape treading championship shown left. Vast areas of land are irrigated by the Murray River, above.

Whisky

WHEN SUPPLIES OF Scotch whisky, one of Australia's favourite spirits, were drastically curtailed during the last war the way was opened for production of a domestic whisky.

The first blends rushed out to meet the demand were harsh and immature, giving Australian whisky a reputation that still lingers on, although most of the blends today have a greater average age than their Scottish counterparts.

The Australian distillers consciously set out to produce a domestic version of Scotch using the standard Scotch whisky process. By the mid–1950s, when Scottish whisky was freely available again in Australia, the local whisky brands were firmly established as lower-priced, acceptable alternatives to the well-known imported brands.

The four big Australian whiskies are Bond 7 (Gilbeys), Corio (United Distillers), Gilt Edge (Gilbeys), which dominates the South Australian market, and Four Seasons (United Distillers). Gilbeys and United Distillers both distil and blend their whiskies within the environs of Melbourne, where the water is suitable for distillation and the local barley and maize is said to be the best in Australia.

Bond 7 and Corio each control about 40 percent of the Australian market for domestic whisky, with Gilt Edge, Four Seasons, and one or two other brands, such as the much publicised Ned Kelly, bringing up the rear. Alongside these brands are scores of private-label Scotch whiskies, promoted by liquor retailers with their firm recommendations at prices that now undercut the Australian brands – giving a third tier to the whisky market in Australia.

At its peak in 1973 the Australian whisky industry supplied two out of every nine bottles of whisky sold domestically. Now this ratio has dropped to two out of every fifteen, largely because of the increasing sales of private-label Scotch.

The very slight difference between a standard Australian and Scotch whisky comes from the different microclimate in the maturation warehouses. Australian whiskies generally have a softer after-taste compared to the crisper style of most Scotch whisky blends. However, at a recent major blind tasting, no regular whisky drinkers could consistently identify Scotch from Australian whisky.

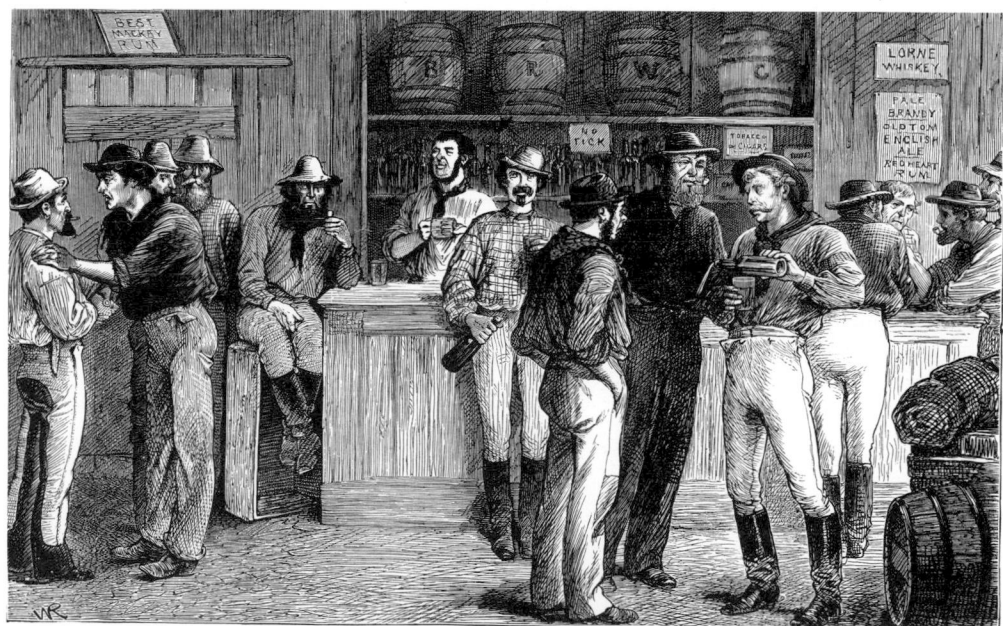

The world over, religious orders produce spirits and wines. Pictured left is the Mission Vineyards, run by the Marist Brothers.

Time for another round of drinks – known as a 'shout' in Australian circles – in a bush tavern. Two of Australia's best-selling whiskies, Gilt Edge and Bond 7, left.

AUSTRALIA
Rum

FROM THE COLONY'S inception, rum was the stable beverage of the settlers. Unlike gin, then the most popular spirit in Britain, which suffered at sea, it improved in cask during the long voyage. The Napoleonic wars meant that cognac was unavailable to the settlers. Scotch whisky did not become popular in Australia for another hundred years, and what little beer was brewed for private consumption neither kept nor travelled well. Rum from the West Indies, cheaper than brandy and longer lasting than gin, became the national drink of the new settlers.

During the late eighteenth and early nineteenth centuries the trade in illicit rum flourished and the inflated price of the spirit established it as a major form of currency. Various measures were introduced to counteract this, including, in 1796, the restriction by Governor Hunter of the distribution of rum to the licensed vendors. He called in the police, known as the New South Wales Corps, to enforce the ban. Instead, they took advantage of their position quickly to grab a stranglehold on the rum trade, earning themselves the nickname *The Rum Corps*.

Governor King, who succeeded Hunter in 1800, partially broke the hold of the Rum Corps, and severely restricted the import of all spirits.

Matters came to a head in 1808 with the Rum Rebellion when the Governor of New South Wales was arrested, and martial law declared. A new governor – Lachlan Macquarie – was sent out to the colony in 1810, and it was he who effectively ended the illicit rum trade.

His ultimate achievement of this campaign was to use rum to build Sydney's first major hospital. The building contractors were granted a monopoly to import 45,000 gallons of rum over three years in lieu of cash for their work. The building became known as the *Rum Hospital*. Its centre section has now been replaced by the present Sydney Hospital, but the original southern sections still stand.

In the latter part of the last century, reasonably-priced cognac and Irish whiskey made inroads into rum consumption, and the industry began to switch from the high ester, full-flavoured West Indies' rums to lighter-flavoured varieties made in Queensland as by-products of its sugar milling industry.

The Australian rum industry has the third largest share of the Australian market for potable spirits. Scotch whisky leads with 32 percent, then Australian brandy with 16 percent, followed by rum with 9 percent.

The largest rum distiller is the Colonial Sugar Refining Company (CSR) who produce rum at Pyrmont in Sydney from Queensland molasses. CSR supply most of the bulk rum bought by Australia's many independent regional wholesalers who bottle under their own labels.

Sugar harvesting in Queensland, left. The Rum Hospital in Sydney, above, was so-named because it was built on the proceeds of the sale of rum. It is now known as Sydney Hospital.

Fields of sugar cane stretching into the distance, right, at Bundaberg, Queensland.

Other Drinks

The Australian gin market is dominated by two domestic brands – Gilbeys and Vickers – which between them account for more than 60 percent of all gin sales.

Domestic gin distilling was pioneered in the 1920s by United Distillers (the Australian subsidiary of the British-based Distillers Company Ltd) with their Vickers brand. Gilbeys, made by the subsidiary of the International Distillers and Vintners Company (IDV), is also British-based.

Gilbeys was first imported into Australia in bottle at still-strength from London. To compete with Vickers on price IDV changed to domestic distilling but used the same recipe as their London-produced gin.

United and Gilbeys both operate from Melbourne, buying their botannicals from the same sources as the London distillers. The other major gins on the Australian market are imported – Gordons, Tanqueray and Beefeater.

Vodka sales are dominated by Smirnoff, distilled in Australia under licence from the American parent to the same 'vatted with activated charcoal' process. Karloff and Robka are two other national brands selling at lower prices than Smirnoff.

Liqueur compounding, based on imported essences, is a growing industry. Unaged liqueurs, such as cherry brandy, crème de menthe and advocaat, account for the majority of sales.

VOK are the principal liqueur producers, followed by Continental, Baitz, West End (owned by United Distillers), Gilbeys, Frangos and Fesq.

One Australian speciality is passion fruit liqueur made from the sweet yellow pulp and seeds of the passion fruit. Grand Cumberland is one well known brand. A second Australian liqueur is made from Queensland bananas.

THE SPIRITS OF NEW ZEALAND

New Zealand's period of prohibition, from 1914 through to the early 1930s, discouraged the local grape growers from following their Australian counterparts and distilling their surpluses for brandy. (The threat of prohibition has also stopped any moves to distil other spirits.) Despite a substantial production of table wines, no New Zealand brandy has yet appeared.

New Zealand's reputation for domestic distilled spirits rests on one company – Wilson Distillers of Dunedin who began making whisky in 1969 and launched two blends in February 1974 – 45 South and Wilsons Matured Blend. Both are made in the same way as Scotch, but are aged in old American bourbon casks.

Otherwise only gins, such as Gordons, and vodkas, like Smirnoff, distilled locally under licence, are made domestically, but there is one native liqueur made from the Kiwi fruit.

Sherry of good average quality is made in New Zealand by such wine producers as Penfolds, SYC, Cooks, Pleasant Valley, Mazuran, Mayfair Wines and Glenvale. Acceptable ports are made by Babich Wines and Montana Wines. In 1974 Penfolds (an offshoot of the Australian company) launched the first New Zealand vintage port, made from pinotage grapes, to a mixed reception from the wine critics. Only time will tell if the quality will encourage others to follow suit.

New Zealand produces several spirits, including a liqueur made from kiwi fruits harvested on the islands (left). The more conventional spirits of whisky, sherry and port are also made. Below is a vineyard in the Auckland Province.

Japan and the Far East

The Far East includes one major distilling nation, Japan. Most of the spirits produced in the other countries are almost unknown internationally. In Hindu and Moslem countries, such as India and Pakistan, domestic spirits have been banned or severely restricted, whilst in other countries no significant tradition of distilling exists.

Sake, the national drink of Japan, has until recently remained the preserve of the Japanese people. Exports of sake have grown in recent years, although they are overshadowed by the burgeoning Japanese whisky industry, which has grown to challenge the sales of Scotch internationally.

Arrack, a type of rum, is the only other well-known international spirit produced in this region. Its two main markets are Sweden, where it is used to make a punch, and The Netherlands.

Japan/Whisky

Japan is fast emerging as one of the world's major distilling nations. Currently, sales of Japanese spirits are still largely confined to the domestic market, but a Japanese presence is being increasingly felt in other countries.

Behind this rapid growth is an astonishing turnabout in Japanese drinking habits over the last twenty years. The traditional sake has been ousted as the country's leading spirits drink by whisky.

Suntory, the country's largest whisky company and the company behind the growth of the industry, dominate the domestic whisky market with an almost 75 percent share. They sell annually about 25,000,000 cases of their own whisky brands which, they say, puts them ahead of even the giant Distillers Company Limited.

Suntory was founded by Shinjiro Torii. He first sold other people's wines then, in 1907, launched Japan's first sweet wine made from local grapes. The wine was called Akadama (the symbol of the Rising Sun) and is still made and sold by Suntory.

Torii used the profits from the popular Akadama for a new project – Japan's first domestic whisky. In 1923 Torii built his first distillery in the Vale of Yamazaki, chosen for its fine water, and after seven years of experimenting launched Suntory Whisky White Label in 1929. But it took another ten years for White Label really to start selling. In the interim Torii bought a large vineyard at the foot of Mount Fuji to expand his wine production and to start making domestic brandy.

After a gap during the Second World War White Label reappeared, followed by Torys and Old Suntory labels. In 1957 the Yamazaki distillery was expanded to meet the growing demand for whisky, in part generated through the string of Suntory bars (Torys Bars) set up from the mid-1950s to the 1960s to sell mainly Suntory products.

The same period saw the company launch a range of new whiskies – Suntory Whisky Red (1964), Suntory Whisky Gold (1965) and Suntory Whisky Custom (1967), all blended to a lighter style to meet the changing Japanese whisky taste. In parallel, they introduced a series of premium whiskies – Suntory Whisky Royal (1960), Suntory Whisky Imperial (1964), Suntory Whisky Special Reserve (1969) and Suntory Whisky Excellence (1971).

In 1973 a second Suntory distillery was built at Hakushu and the company now ranks among the top five liquor companies in the world.

All the premium Suntory and other Japanese whiskies include an element of imported Scotch malt whisky, usually reflected in the price. The same applies to Japanese brandy. In both instances the imported spirit gives the blend an 'international' taste, although it has been used to improve inferior local whisky and hide a high grain content. The Scots have tried to counter this by preventing the export of bulk malt whisky, but so far with little success.

Suntory's top whiskies quite legitimately do have an element of fine malt whisky in them. Their foremost brand is The Whisky, of which only 6,000 bottles are made each year. Then follows Imperial (sold as Signature in the United States), Excellence, Royal, Special Reserve, Old (which sells over 10,000,000 cases in Japan alone), Kakubin, Gold Label, Gold 1000, White Label, Red Label, Torys Extra and Rawhide which has a 'bourbon' flavour.

Their brandies are led by Imperial (sold in a cut-glass decanter), XO (in a flat-sided bottle), VSOP (also in a cut-glass bottle), VSO and VO. Proofs of both whiskies and brandies range from 65° to 75°.

Suntory's rivals in whisky production are Nikka Distilleries, with G & G, Super Nikka, Black Nikka and Hi Nikka; Kirin Seagram with Robert Brown and Dunbar; and Sanraku Ocean with White Label. Several other distillers and blenders make Japanese whisky but none have greater than a one percent share of the market. Godo Shusei is perhaps the best-known of this group.

Sake, the country's oldest rice wine is the drink most associated with Japan by foreigners. It was mentioned as early as 712 AD when the first queen of Japan, Konohana Sakuya Hime, was said to brew her own. During the Heian period (794–1191) it was linked with the Mikado and court nobles and became the formal drink for festive and ceremonial events, religious events, weddings and banquets.

Its commercialisation began in the eighteenth century when professional distillers started to take over from the traditional family makers, and now most Japanese sake is made to the same process by one of the big companies.

The sake making process is similar to beer brewing except rice, instead of barley, is the basic ingredient. The freshly harvested rice is cleansed and steamed, then saccharified with a germ called *koji* (*Aspergillus oryzae*) which ferments the starch in the grain and converts it to alcohol, and the sake is drawn off for filtering and maturing. The average strength of sake is around 32° imperial proof and sake should be drunk within a year of its making to ensure the freshness is preserved.

Sake has a curious taste – sweet but with a dryness – and is colourless despite some maturing in wooden barrels. The Japanese traditionally serve it in small porcelain bottles called *tokkuri*, in which the sake is warmed to 100°F (38°C) then poured into small porcelain cups called *sakazuki* at the table.

The popular brands of sake in Japan are Hakutsuru, Ozeki, Gekkeikan, Sakura Masamune and Suntory Chiyoda.

Another traditional Japanese drink related to sake is *shochu*, which is basically distilled rice wine. Made in a continuous still, it retains more of its flavouring and usually higher strength of about 85°. Another shochu is also

made in the Okinawa Islands, where it is usually served cold.

There is no obligation for the distiller to use rice as the base material to make shochu although the leading brands do. At its best, shochu is a good white spirit similar to vodka, and after losing sales to whisky, it is now coming back into fashion because of its mixability, lightness, lower price, sharp flavour and associations with traditional Japan. There are hundreds of different brands, with perhaps the best-known being Takara.

The other distinctively Japanese drink is plum wine blended from white wine and the juice of the green *ume shu* plums. Plum wine has a brownish colour and a sour taste. It is usually about 23° proof and resembles a fortified wine. Suntory's Akadama, introduced about 1965, and Gekkeikan are the two main brands.

Plum wine is usually served at the end of a meal rather like a port or cognac. The other Japanese spirits – whisky and shochu – are

The modern Suntory Company was founded in 1899 by Shinjiro Torii. Now famous for its whiskies, Suntory began by producing a domestic sweet wine – Akadama.

Claimed to be the largest malt whisky distillery in the world, Suntory's Hakushu plant was opened in 1973. Twelve giant copper pot stills produce malt whisky for some of the 13 Suntory labels, including Royal. Suntory's distilleries also produce a range of other spirit such as brandy, and liqueurs, like the vivid green Midori melon liqueur, right.

usually served before, during, and after a meal as the Japanese do not change drinks when sitting down to eat.

Suntory also produce two typically Japanese liqueurs, one of which was launched in the United States in 1978 specifically for that market. It is Midori (meaning *green*) melon liqueur. Its base is the Japanese melon, from which Suntory extract an essence to ship to the United States where it is added to domestic spirit. Midori is a distinctive vivid green colour, and comes at 40° proof.

The second Japanese liqueur is Green Tea liqueur made from the essence of *matcha* powdered tea and *gyokuro* rolled tea. It is often referred to as *ocha* (meaning tea) liqueur in Japan and has a delicate tea fragrance. Suntory market it in a ceramic bottle.

Suntory also make a delicate pink Cherry Blossom liqueur, Crème de Kobai from Japanese plums, and an assortment of local versions of European liqueurs such as crème de moka and curaçao.

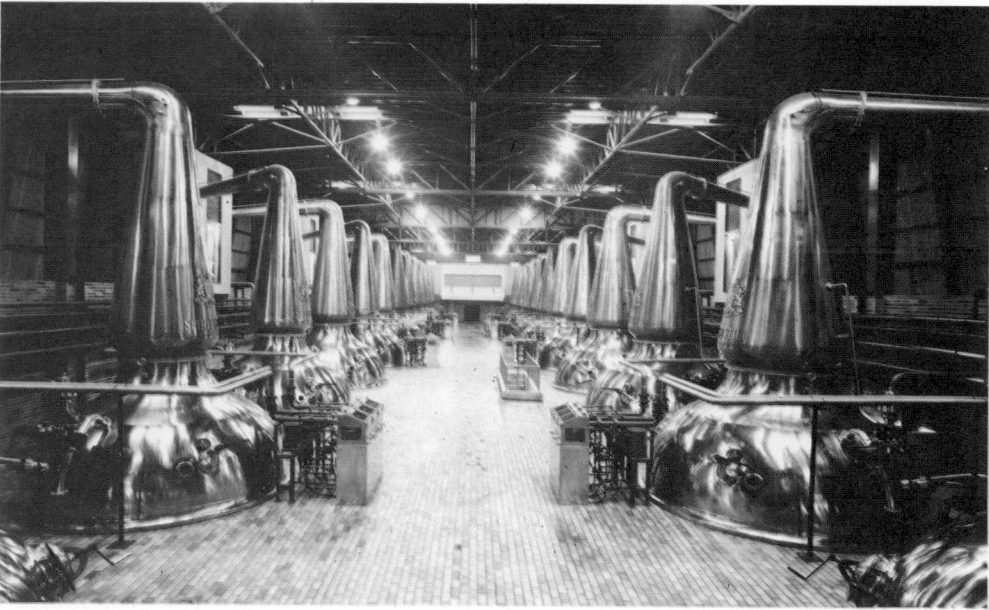

China

CHINA PRODUCES A VARIETY of grain, sorghum and grape-based drinks that, to Western eyes at least, look and sound as exotic as the country itself.

Many are medicinal or have medicinal properties and it is common practice to add 'beneficial ingredients' such as glucose, amino acids, vitamins or pectin to the base drink. Their consumption is confined to meal times, and rarely would they be consumed on their own other than for medicinal reasons.

Most of these drinks are made from grapes and have an alcoholic content of about 12° to 14° (slightly under sherry strength). Examples include Kao Liang Chiew (a general tonic), Tincture of Tiger Bone (for those with bone problems), Hung Mei Chinese port wine (a digestive and tonic), and Hwato brand Sze Chuan Dah Poo Chiew (said to be especially beneficial for pregnant women).

The production of all Chinese drinks is controlled by the China National Cereals, Oils and Foodstuffs Import and Export Corp – a state monopoly that is subdivided into nine branches: Peking, T'ien-chin (with its Golden Star brand), Shantung (using the Sunflower brand), Dairen (Hung Mei brand), Kwantung (Pearl River brand), Hupeh, Kwangsi, Fukien and Shanghai.

These branches produce various grape wines, medicinal wines, rice wines and specialities such as Lychee Chiew (a lychee wine with a strength and taste resembling sherry), Glutinous Rice Chiew, Pineapple wine and Bamboo Leaf Green Chiew. The Peking branch makes a Chinese champagne, and the Dairen and Shantung branches both produce Chinese cider.

The most common drink throughout China is rice wine, made by fermenting (and usually sweetening) glutinous rice or , in some cases, millet. It ranges in strength from normal wine levels up to that of a full-bodied sherry. While still a cottage industry in many parts of China, a number of commercial brands are made. These include Cheng Nien Feng Kang Chiew (Kwantung branch), Shao-Hsing Shan Niang Chiew, Chia Fan, Hua Tiao and Hsiang Hsueh (Shanghai branch, which specialises in rice wine) and Tsen Gon (Fukien).

The production of higher strength spirits in China is relatively small. The Shantung branch makes and sells whisky, dry gin and vodka under the Sunflower brand; Kwantung makes Pearl River brand rum; and Peking and Shantung both produce 'Special Fine' brandy.

The best-known Chinese spirit is Mou-Tai Chiew. It is fermented from the best wheat and millet to about 50° proof, then, according to one Chinese description, it is 'stored in cellars for a considerable long time before bottling, thus to bring out its characteristic delicious savour with its nutritious food value'. A contrary Western opinion describes it as having a 'fetid aroma and an unattractive, part-fermented taste'. The nearest equivalent, thought the taster, was the Mexican *pulque*.

Mou-Tai takes its name from Mou-Tai

Chen, a town near Jen Hwai city in northern Kweichow province, which has been the main production centre for the spirit over the last two centuries. The 'clear, pure local fountain water' is said to be ideal for Mou-Tai production.

In late 1976 China made its first step into world spirits marketing with the Great Wall Chinese vodka in the United States. Great Wall vodka is made near Ch'ing-tao, where vodka has been made for several decades using techniques learnt from Russian emigrés who fled to China. It is said to be made from 'golden wheat' and the mineral-rich water from 'deep artesian wells'. It is a pure grain spirit diluted to normal 70° proof, and in the United States it was launched as 'the world's most expensive vodka'.

The Far East

Most Chinese drinks have both alcoholic and medicinal virtues, but to the Western eye the contents of most bottles remain inscrutable. Mout-tai, a clear spirit distilled from wheat and millet, is the Chinese equivalent of sake.

Taiwan and Korea
Taiwan, through its Tobacco and Wine Monopoly, produces many of the mainland Chinese drinks, including rice wine and shokushu rice spirit, lychee and other fruit-based wines. It is also in the market with ginseng liqueur, more commonly associated with Korea, land of the Morning Calm, the major ginseng root producer.

Korean Ginseng Ju traditionally comes with a large ginseng root, looking like a parsnip, in every bottle. Jinro of Seoul are the main producers of Ginseng Ju.

India
India has verged on the brink of total prohibition since its independence, in 1947, and official government policy aims towards that goal despite the substantial taxes derived from drink and the opinions of a large section of the population.

The traveller is faced with an anomaly: some states are totally dry, some allow only permit holders to buy alcohol, and some are avowedly wet, although restrictions on drinking times still exist. In Gujarat state, for example, only 450 out of a population of 30,000,000 had permits to drink in 1976. Those who did not had to keep a public image of abstinence even if they indulged in alcohol in the privacy of their homes.

Big cities such as Calcutta, Hyderabad, Goa and Bangalore, all wet, only permitted drink-ing on about 200 days of the year. Specific days, including religious and national holidays, are set aside as dry days. The dry states, deprived of normal supplies of alcohol, were and still are, fighting against an increasing business in smuggled domestic and imported spirits.

In 1976 India has something like 50 distilleries producing domestic whisky, gin, rum, vodka and brandy ranging in quality from the palatable to the barely tolerable. These Western-style drinks have been added to traditional native drinks produced from indigenous materials. One, *toddy*, is produced from palm juice. The *palmyra* (*Borassus flabellifer*) is tapped like a rubber tree in many parts of India and Sri Lanka for its sweet palm sap which is left to evaporate into dark brown sugar syrup called *jaggery*. Jaggery is then fermented, or latterly distilled into toddy, a fearsome drink for all but the initiated.

Sri Lanka
In Sri Lanka, toddy usually means palm spirit, but in India the name has taken on a wider use and is often applied to drinks that are more properly called *arrack*, or *raki*. Arrack is a common drink throughout the East, and in India (and to a lesser extent Sri Lanka) it can be made from fermented coconut palm juice, rice, molasses, the flowers of the mahua (also called the *madhvi* or *daru* spirit),

the flowers of the deciduous butter tree, dates and cashew nuts. The ingredients depend very much on what is available – in Bengal and Cochin, for instance, both rice and toddy are combined to make arrack.

Cereals were also used as a base for arrack, particularly wheat and barley. *Kohala*, or barley, is alleged to be derived from the Sanskrit words *kru* (earth) and *hala* (poison) which passed into Arabic to become *al kohl* and hence *alcohol*.

The East Indies
Arrack or raki is commonly thought of as a Middle Eastern and Balkan drink, but it is also the drink of the East Indies (or the Batavias, as they were called in colonial days). Indeed, the popularity of arrack in Germany, Holland and the Low Countries stems more from their colonial links with the Batavias rather than any contact with the Middle East or the Balkans.

In the East Indies the common arrack was, and to a certain extent still is, crudely distilled from either coconut palm juice or sugar cane molasses. A common practice is to add rice, or partly malted rice, to the fermenting base juice. In Java, for instance, the rice is compressed into balls called *ragi* to give the resulting spirit extra alcohol.

The spirit, particularly when made from molasses, bears a strong resemblance to rum, and is often sold to tourists as such.

Africa/Brandy

Brandy is the national drink of South Africa. Almost half the domestic spirits consumption, and more than half of the production, is brandy.

The first successful South African wine harvest was recorded by Jan van Riebeeck in 1659, and within fifteen years brandy production was underway in the Cape province. It was the natural drink for the South African pioneers because it travelled well. In 'butt, barrel and medicine box' it was carried in the ox carts of the early scouts, hunters, trekkers, soldiers and missionaries as they colonised the new country.

The first South African brandies were rough spirits, made for their effect only. They were normally made from the grape husks, left after the juice had been pressed free, and water. After fermentation, the resulting bitter, malodorous brew was distilled in a crude pot still.

The primitive version of *marc* that resulted had such a distinctive taste that the locals dubbed it *Kaapse Smaak* or *Cape Smaak* (meaning 'Cape taste'). This later became *Cape Smoke,* which sometimes is still used to describe an inferior brandy.

The English settlers called it *Boor brandy* (brandy drunk by the Boer farmers); while the Afrikaaners often called it *dop* (from drop-brandewyn or 'husk' brandy), or even more aptly *witblits* (white lightning) – an equivalent name to moonshine and poteen.

From 1886 successive laws brought South African brandy distilling under governmental supervision, establishing a set of regulations that guaranteed minimum standards. The equipment and techniques used are similar to those in Cognac and Jarnac, although the grape varieties – palomino, hermitage (also known as cinsaut), steen and canaan – are different.

Once distilled, the young brandy goes into casks for at least three years. It will then be tasted by officers of the Government Brandy Board, and if acceptable will earn the distiller a customs rebate – hence the vernacular name *rebate brandy*.

If the distiller blends and bottles his three-year-old brandy, it will be regarded as a drink for mixing rather than drinking neat. Younger brandies lack grape taste, and are less nutty and fruity in flavour than their older equivalent.

As a result, the best casks are set aside and matured further to give liqueur brandies, designed for drinking neat. Oude Molen from Gilbey's South Africa, for example, is between ten and 15 years old, with some brandy in the blend that exceeds 20 years. KWV Ten-Year-Old is the other recognised label that on average contains brandies which are ten or more years old.

Most of the premium labels are about five years old, the best-known being Oude Meester Liqueur, KWV, VO, Bertrams VO, Hennessy Fine Liqueur and Martell VO (the last two being licensed brand names).

The hot Cape summers concentrate the sugar in the grapes, yielding full-flavoured brandies. In the early days these brandies were distilled in crude copper stills like those in the Oude Meester Wyn Museum.

There are two dozen companies that market South African brandies, but the Oude Meester Group dominates, accounting for nearly 70 percent of the market. Stellenbosch Farmers' Winery, Gilbeys South Africa and the Ko-operatieve Wijnbouwers Vereniging (Co-operative Winegrower's Association), the semi-governmental group, are also important.

There are about 60 different labels. Apart from those already mentioned, some of the better-known include Richlieu, Royal Oak and Louis XIV from Oude Meester; Limosin, Viceroy, Klipdrift and Commando from Castle Wine & Green; Santy's and Malamed's from Gilbeys SA; Tayler's VO and Mellowwood from Sedgewick Tayler; Old Chalet from Uniewyn; Huguenac and Viking from the Huguenot Wine Farmers; and KWV Three Star.

The law has ended the distilling of *mampoer* (mum-poor) in the northern states where grapes are not cultivated. Once widely made from the berries of the Kareeboom tree, and *moepels* and *maroelas* fruits, this potent spirit of the Free State, Natal and Transvaal was described as 'white and soft to look at, and the smoke that comes from it as you pull the cork is pale and rises in slow curves!'

One relic of pioneering days that has survived is *Buchu brandy*, made from ordinary brandy that has been allowed to draw on the leaves of the Buchu plant (*Barosma betulina*). Now cultivated in the northern Cape wine areas, this herb has been used to cure everything from snakebite to housemaid's knee. Modern Buchu brandy is still treated as a medicine for digestive upsets rather than for ordinary drinking, and is made commercially by Bosman & Company, Douglas Green, Huguenot Wine Farmers, Saxenburg Wines and Uniewyn.

South Africa's only commercially successful indigenous spirit is Cane, a white spirit closely related to vodka.

Cane originated in the sugar cane fields of Natal in the 1860s. The Indian settlers working the sugar fields took the raw cane residue and turned it into molasses. A large tub of the molasses was boiled over a fire and the droplets of condensation on the lid were run off into a bottle. The resulting raw spirit, called *gavine*, was sold illegally in cane field *shebeens*.

The moonshine spirit was not commercially made until the 1950s, when it was introduced as a Natal 'mystery' spirit, made from molasses in modern stills under proper supervision. In just over 25 years cane has become the second biggest-selling spirit in South Africa, with more than two dozen different labels, and a rapidly growing market share. It is now distilled twice for absolute purity and neutrality of taste, and it is used as a mixer for long drinks in much the same way as vodka. Leading brands include Mainstay, Seven Seas, Bengal, Collison's, Calypso and White Diamond.

In 1974 a cane flavoured with pure lemon juice was introduced under the brand name Limbo by Union Wine, under licence from H C König of West Germany. A rival brand, Lemon Breeze, has since appeared.

Van der Hum, which in old Dutch means something like 'what's its name' is the principal South African liqueur. It was first produced by the early Dutch settlers from the *naartjie*, a cousin of the tangerine and mandarine, as an alternative to the curaçao they could no longer obtain from Holland. Orange-flavoured, coloured and scented, it is drunk as a liqueur, in long drinks, and with a dash of brandy as a *brandy-hum*. Bertram's are the best-known producers, but most of the large spirits companies have their own brand.

Gin, vodka and rum are all distilled in South Africa, with Old Buck gin enjoying an advantage over its competitors through the supposed aphrodisiac properties associated with the horn of the buck.

South Africa has developed a thriving domestic sherry and port industry with the growth of its table wine trade. Sherries such as Cavendish Cape, Monis, Mymering and Drostdy are recognised for their quality and, within South Africa, sell below their true worth.

The Africans found alcohol rather overpowering when they were first introduced to it by pioneers in the 17th century, but they soon began making their own *Cape Smaak*.

OTHER AFRICAN SPIRITS

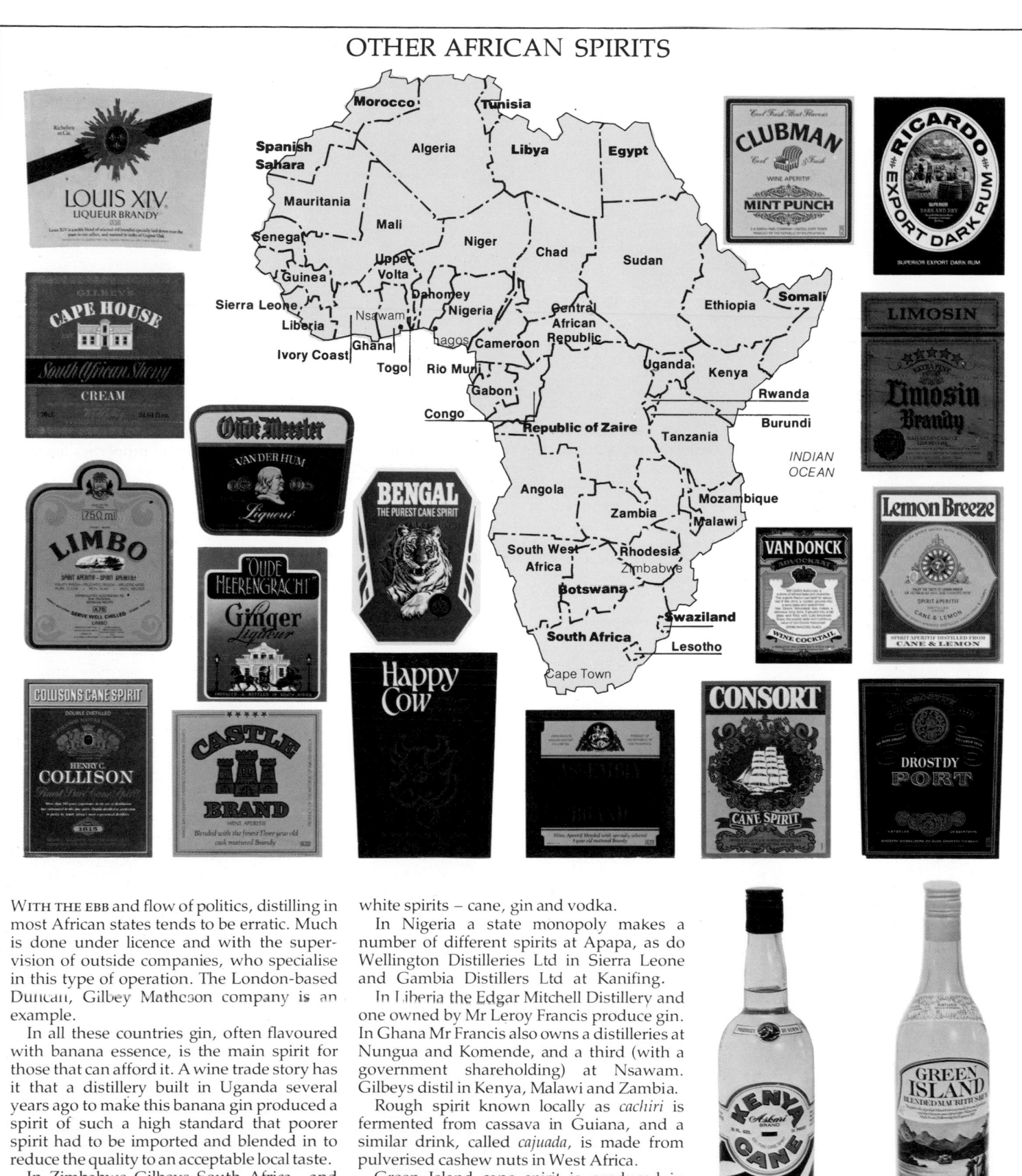

With the ebb and flow of politics, distilling in most African states tends to be erratic. Much is done under licence and with the supervision of outside companies, who specialise in this type of operation. The London-based Duncan, Gilbey Matheson company is an example.

In all these countries gin, often flavoured with banana essence, is the main spirit for those that can afford it. A wine trade story has it that a distillery built in Uganda several years ago to make this banana gin produced a spirit of such a high standard that poorer spirit had to be imported and blended in to reduce the quality to an acceptable local taste.

In Zimbabwe Gilbeys South Africa and Allied Distributors (a South African Distillers Corporation subsidiary) both produce mainly white spirits – cane, gin and vodka.

In Nigeria a state monopoly makes a number of different spirits at Apapa, as do Wellington Distilleries Ltd in Sierra Leone and Gambia Distillers Ltd at Kanifing.

In Liberia the Edgar Mitchell Distillery and one owned by Mr Leroy Francis produce gin. In Ghana Mr Francis also owns a distilleries at Nungua and Komende, and a third (with a government shareholding) at Nsawam. Gilbeys distil in Kenya, Malawi and Zambia.

Rough spirit known locally as *cachiri* is fermented from cassava in Guiana, and a similar drink, called *cajuada*, is made from pulverised cashew nuts in West Africa.

Green Island cane spirit is produced in Mauritius and, as in other countries, illegal distilling is widespread.

Index

This index, although comprehensive, does not have separate entries for every brand name of drink detailed in the text. For names of companies, distilleries, individuals, processes and associations which do not have a separate entry, look under the type of drink concerned, eg Malt whisky (Scotland): malting process. If the drink does not have a separate entry, look next under country of origin; if it is not specifically included, it can be found under 'other drinks'.

A

Absinthe 64—7
  as aphrodisiac 64
  bans on manufacture and
    sale 67
  popularity in 19th century 64
  potential dangers of 67
Absinthe drip *203*
Adam, Edouard 11
Advocaat 120
  producers 120
Africa 246—9
  brandy 246—8
  cane spirit 248
  gin and other spirits 249
  liqueurs 248
  mampoer 248
  map *249*
  spirits labels *249*
Aguardente (Portugal) 99
Aguardiente (Columbia) 232, 233
Aguardiente (Spain) 91
Akvavit (*see also Aquavit and Brannvin*) 106—9
  brands 108—9

distilling process 108
history of 106
how to drink 108
Maltese cross on labels 109
Akvavit labels *109*
Alambic still 8, 11
  armagnaçais 50
  charentais 40
Alcohol:
  origin of word 8
  to produce 14
Alcoholic content *see Proof systems*
Alexander (cocktail) 61
Amaretto di Saronno 78
American proof system 17
Amontillado sherry 89
Amoroso sherry 89
Angelica 19
Angostura bitters 230
Anis (France) 64—7
  difference from pastis 67
  distilling process 67
  origin of name 67
  Pernod 64, 67
Anis (Spain) 91—2
Aniseed, star *80*
Anisette 59, 67
Aperitifs 18
Apple brandy *see Calvados*
Aqua vitae 8
Aquavit (Germany) 139
Aquavit (Iceland) 112
Aquavit (Norway) 113
  Linie 113
Argentina 233
Armagnac 46—51
  area 46—9, *46*
  Bas zone 49
  base wine 49
  blending of 50
  casks 50
  character compared to

cognac 46
château Ravignon *49*
cognac houses with interests in 49
designations 51
distilling process 50
evaporation in cask 50
fully mature 50
grape varieties 46, 49
Haut zone 49
history of 49
maturation of 50
producers 49
sale and distribution 51
sales compared to cognac 49
'spinster' 51
still *46*,—7, 50
Ténareze zone 49
vintage 51
Arrack *see Raki*
Asbach coffee 133
Australia 234—9
  brandy 234—5
  fortified wines 236
  map *238*
  other drinks 239
  rum 238
  whisky 237
Austria, liqueurs 139

B

Bacardi (cocktail) 231
Barbados 228
Barley, two-rowed *15*
Beer consumption, top twenty nations 28
Beer production, top twenty nations 26
Belgium 124—7
  Filliers distillers 124
  Fourcroy company 126

Fryns company 127
Geens company 127
jenever (gin) 124—7
liqueurs 126, 127
major distillers 124
map *119*
Smeets company 127
stills at Fourcroy *124*
the south 127
Van Damme distillery 124—6, *124*
Bénédictine 59—60
Bitters (Germany) 135
  Underberg 135
Bitters (Italy) 73, 76—7
  Fernet Branca 76—7
  Unicum 3
Bitters (Netherlands) 123
Bitters (Trinidad):
  Angostura 230
Blended whisky (Scotland) 182—3
  blending and maturation 182
  component whiskies 182
  the art of blending 182
Bloody Mary (cocktail) 150
Blue Lady (cocktail) 123
Bolivia 232
Bourbon whiskey 214—15
  brands 215
  George Dickel 215
  history of 214
  Jack Daniels 215
Brandy:
  base ingredients 14
  mixers 24
Brandy (Africa) 246—8
  Buchu 248
  distilling and maturation 246
  history of 246
  liqueur brandies 246
  major companies and brands 248

Bibliography

Bradford, Sarah: The Story of Port, Christie's Wine Publications, London 1978
Brander, Michael: The Original Scotch, Hutchinson, London 1974
Brink, Andre P: Brandy in South Africa, Buren, Cape Town 1973
'Charles' and 'Carlos': The Cocktail Bar, Foulsham, London 1977
Croft-Cooke, Rupert: Madeira, Putnam & Co, London 1966
Daiches, David: Scotch Whisky, Fontana, London 1977
Decanter Magazine: Vol 1, No 1, September, London 1975
Dejay, Marie: Victorian Cups and Punches, Cassell, London 1974
Delamain Robert: Histoire du Cognac, Paris 1974
Doxat, John: Booth's Handbook of Cocktails and Mixed Drinks, Pan, London 1977
Doxat, John: Stirred—Not Shaken: The Dry Martini, Hutchinson, London 1976
Embury, David A: The Art of Mixing Drinks, Faber & Faber, London 1975
Encyclopedia Britannica: 1969 edition
Evans, Len: Australia and New Zealand Complete Book of

Wine, Hamlyn, Sydney 1974
Gold, Alec: Wines and Spirits of the World, Virtue, London 1968
Gonzalez Gordon, Manuel: Sherry, Cassell, London 1972
Grossman, Harold: Guide to Wines, Spirits and Beers, Frederick Muller, London 1974
Gunn, Neil: Whisky and Scotland, Souvenir Press, London 1977
Gunyon, RE: The Wines of Central and South-Eastern Europe, Duckworth, London 1971
Hallgarten, Peter: Liqueurs, Wine and Spirit Publications, London 1973
Hannum, Hurst and Blumberg: Brandies and Liqueurs of the World, Doubleday, New York 1976
Hogg, Anthony: Guide to Visiting Vineyards, Michael Joseph, London 1976
Isasi, Enrique de: Con una Copa de Jerez, Hauser y Menet, Madrid 1972
Jeffs, Julian: Sherry, Faber, London 1970
Johnson, Hugh: The World Atlas of Wine, Mitchell Beazley, London 1971
Johnson, Hugh: Wine, Mitchell Beazley, London 1974
Kirkeby, Henning: Danish Akvavit, Host & Sons Forlag, Copenhagen 1975
Lichine, Alexis: Encyclopedia of Wines and Spirits, Cassell, London 1967
Marrison, LW: Wines and Spirits, Penguin Books, London 1976

McDowall, RJS: The Whiskies of Scotland, John Murray, London 1975
McGuffin, John: In Praise of Poteen, Appletree, Belfast 1978
McGuire, EB: Irish Whiskey, Gill & Macmillan, Dublin 1973
Mederic, Louis: La Revolte de Paul Ricard, Plon, Paris 1969
Rainbird, George: Sherry and the Wines of Spain, London 1966
Rannie, William: Canadian Whisky, WF Rannie, Ontario 1976
Ray, Cyril: Cognac, Peter Davies, London 1973
Ray, Cyril: The Complete Book of Spirits and Liqueurs, Cassell, London 1977
Read, Jan: Guide to the Wines of Spain and Portugal, Pitman, London 1977
Read, Jan and Manjon, Maite: Paradores of Spain, Macmillan, London 1977
Read, Jan: The Wines of Spain, London 1973
Revue Vinicole: Armagnac, Supplement to Revue Vinicole Magazine, Paris
Revue Vinicole: Cognac, Supplement to Revue Vinicole Magazine, Paris
Vandyke Price, Pamela: The Taste of Wine, Macdonald & Jane's, London 1975
White, Francesca: Cheers—a Spirited Guide to Liquors and Liqueurs, Paddington Press, London 1977
Wilson, Ross: Scotch, David & Charles, Devon 1973

Brandy (Australia) 234—5
  from non-irrigated or dry
    areas 234
  from upper Murray river
    234
  major brands 234
Brandy (California) 210—11
  additives permitted 210
  California Brandy Advisory
    Board 211
  effects of Prohibition on
    210
  grape varieties 210
  history of 210
  major producers and brands
    211
  production and maturation
    210
  styles 210—11
  vine-growing area 210
Brandy (Cyprus) 102
Brandy (Egypt) 103
Brandy (France) see Cognac
  and Armagnac
Brandy (Germany) 132—3
  Asbach distillery 132—3
  Asbach Uralt 132
  branntwein aus wein 132
  production controls 132
  well-known brands 132
Brandy (Greece) 102—3
  Metaxa company 103
Brandy (Italy) 81—3
  brands 81—3
Brandy (Spain) 90—1, 92
  Brande Conde 92
  brands 90—1
  production process 90
Brandy labels:
  California 211
  France 41, 45
  Germany 132—3
  Spain 92—3
Brannvin (see also Akvavit
  and Aquavit) 111—12
  brands 111—12
  flavoured styles 111—12
  history of 111
  production since early
    1970s 111
  with food 112
Braunschweig, H 11
  pot still (1519) 8
Brazil 232
  cachaca 232
British Isles 154—93
British (or Sykes) proof
  system 17
Bureau National Inter-professionel
  des Calvados et Eaux-de-vie de
  cidre et de poire (BNICE) 54
Bureau National Inter-professionel
  du Cognac 45

C

California Brandy Advisory

Board 211
Californian tokay 19
Calisay 92
  preparation of herbs for 91
Calvados 54—5
  designated area 54, 54
  designated sub-areas 54, 54
  designations 54
  evaporation in cask 54
  production cycle 54
  stills 54, 55
Campari 74—5
Canada 196—201
  Seagram Company Ltd 198—201
  whisky 196—7
Caribbean 224—31
  Angostura bitters 230
  liqueurs 230
  map 229
  rum 224—31
Cassis 58
  use in cocktails 59
Charente grape harvest 34—5, 40
Chartreuse 60—1
Cherry Heering 110
  history of 110
  production process 110
Cherry Rocher 58—9
Chile 232
China 244
  grape-based drinks 244
  Great Wall vodka 244
  higher strength spirits 244
  Mou-Tai Chiew 244
  rice wine 244
  state liquor monopoly 244
Cinchon 24
Cocktail:
  history of the 20
  theories on derivation of
    name 20
Cocktail cabinet 22—3
  contents of 'ideal' 22—3, 22—3
Cocktail recipes:
  Alexander 61
  Bacardi 231
  Bloody Mary 150
  Blue Lady (Marie Antoinette)
    123
  Collins 165
  Cuba Libre 231
  Dry Martini 217
  Grasshopper 61
  Harvey Wallbanger 78
  Manhattan 216
  Margerita 220
  Negroni 76
  Pimms 167
  pink gin 165
  Rose de Chambertin 59
  Tequila Sunrise 223
  Whiskey Sour 216
  White Lady 61
Coffey still 11
Cognac 34—45
  1909 law 36, 37
  acres under cultivation 38
  age of 45

area 36—9, 38
  blenders and bottlers 43
  blending 42
  Bois Communs area 39
  Bois Ordinaires area 39
  Bons Bois area 39
  Borderies area 39
  bouilleurs de cru 43
  bouilleurs de profession 43
  casking 40—2
  casks 40
  co-operative distillers 43
  designations 45
  distilling cycle 40—2
  early-landed 45
  evaporation in cask 42
  fine champagne 39
  Fins Bois area 39
  Grande Champagne area 37
  grape varieties 39
  history of 34—5
  late-bottled 45
  legal additions to spirit 42
  main vineyard areas 37—9, 38
  major houses 43
  minimum ages 45
  Napoleon (approx. 1811) 45
  Napoleon (Bureau National
    designation) 45
  number of vine growers 43
  Petite Champagne area 37—9
  pressing the grapes 40
  still 40
  town of 36—7, 37
  town of Jarnac 36
  vintage 45
Cognac consumption, top
  twenty nations 38
Cognac labels 41, 45
  meaning of letters on 44
Cointreau 61
Collins (cocktail) 165
Colombia 232—3
  aguardiente 232, 233
  Cartagena distillery 233
  ron (white rum) 232—3
Conac 90
Congeners 14
Continuous still:
  alambic armagnaçais 50
  Coffey or patent 11
  distilling process 11, 11
Cordials, alcoholic (England) 169
Cork, world's largest producer 99
Crème de menthe 60
Cuba 228—9
  Cuba Libre (cocktail) 231
Curaçao 120
Cyprus 102
  brandy 102
  Commanderia 102
  sherry 102

D

Daniel, Jack 208—9
Danziger liqueurs 141

Dark rum, mixers 24
De la Boe, Franciscus 116
De Vilanova, Arnaud 8
Denmark 106—10
  akvavit 106—9
  De Danske Spritfabrikker
    (Danish Distilleries) 106—8,
    109
  liqueurs 110
Digestifs 19
Digestion (flavouring process) 12
Distillation 6—11
  basic principle of 8
  by continuous still 11, 11
  by pot still 10, 10
  history of 8—11
  origin of word 8
  rectification (redistillation) 11
  to produce eau-de-vie 9
Distilleries see Whiskey
  (Ireland): Old Bushmills
  distillery, etc
Distillers see Gin (Belgium):
  distillers, etc
Distillers Company Ltd 185
Drambuie 185
Dry Martini (cocktail) 217
Dubied, Major Henri 64
Dubonnet 68—9

E

East Indies 245
Eastern Europe 152
Eau-de-vie 8
  distilling process 9
Eau-de-vie (France) 52—7
  commercial varieties 52—7
  distillers 52
  distilling process 52
  fruit-flavoured varieties
    62—3
  kirsch 57
  storage of 57
  to distinguish from fruit
    liqueur 62
  varieties with dominant
    flower ingredient 63
Eau-de-vie (Germany)
  141
Eau-de-vie (Switzerland) 56
Eau-de-vie d'Andaye 68
Eau-de-vie de cidre 54
Eau-de-vie de Danzig 68
Eau-de-vie de Lie 68
Eau-de-vie de poire 54
Eau-de-vie labels (France)
  62
Ecuador 233
Egypt 103
England 156—69
  flavoured gins 164—7
  gin 156—61
  other drinks 168—9
  Plymouth gin 162—3
  Seagram Company interests in
    200

F

Far East 245
  map 245
Fernet Branca 76—7
  posters 77
Finland 112
  independent companies 112
  Oy Alko Ab (state liquor
    monopoly) 112
Fino sherry 88, 89
Flavourings 12—13, 12—13
  to introduce into base alcohol
    12
  to obtain from raw ingredients
    12
Flor 88
Fortified wines 18—19
  angelica 19
  Californian tokay 19
  moscato 19
  muscatel 19
  Pineau de Charente 19
  port 19
  sherry 18
  vin jaune 19
  vins doux naturels 19
Fortified wines (Australia) 236
France 32—69
  alcools blancs 52
  anis 64—7
  armagnac 46—51
  citrus-flavoured liqueurs 63
  cognac 34—45
  Dubonnet 68—9
  eau-de-vie 52—7
  eau-de-vie d'Andaye 68
  eau-de-vie de Danzig 68
  eau-de-vie de Lie 68
  Gay Lussac proof system 17
  'grape brandy' 68
  liqueurs 58—63
  marc 68
  Pernod 64, 67
  Pineau de Charente 68
  pousse rapière 49—50
  ratafia 68
  rum importers 69
  vermouth 68
Fruit brandy see Eau-de-vie
Fruit liqueur, to distinguish
  from eau-de-vie 62

G

Galliano 78
Gay Lussac proof system 17
Genever see Gin (Netherlands)
Germany 128—41
  Asbach coffee 133
  aufgesetzter 139
  enzian 139
  korn 130—1
  other drinks and liqueurs
    138—41
  Schladerer company 140—1

Grand Marnier 61
Grape harvest, Charente 34—5, 40
Grapes:
  armagnac 49
  cognac 39
  Pedro Ximènez 235
  St Emilion 36, 39
  Ugni Blanc 14
Grappa 81—3
  production process 81, 81
  verschnitt 139
  wacholder (gin) 134—7
  weinbrand (brandy) 132—3
Gin:
  base ingredients 14
  mixers 24
Gin (Australia) 239
Gin (Belgium) 126—7
  city of Hasselt 126—7
  distillers 127
Gin (England) 156—67
  Acts of Parliament concerning
    156—9
  appearance of 'dry' gin 159
  checking density of 161
  Coates & Co 162—3
  cold mix system of flavouring
    160—1
  distillation of 160
  final stages of preparation 161
  flavoured 164—7
  gin palace 158, 159
  Gladstone's bill, 1871 159
  history of 156—9
  Hogarth's Gin Lane 158, 159
  infusion of flavourings 160
  ingredients 160, 162, 162
  'London dry' 159, 160
  modern distillery 160—1
  'nosing' 160, 161, 161
  Old Tom 165—7
  Pimms No 1 Cup 167
  pink 162
  Plymouth 162—3
  spirits safes 161
  Tanqueray 164
  traditional system of
    flavouring 160
Gin (German equivalent) 134—7
  Original Schlichte Steinhäger
    136
  Schlichte company 134, 136—7
  Schlichte distillery 134—5, 136
  steinhäger 134—7
Gin (Netherlands) 116—19
  distillers 116—18
  jonge 118
  oude 116—17
  production process 116
Gin (Spain) 92
Gin labels:
  Belgium 126—7
  England 164—5
  Netherlands 119
Glossary of basic terms 16—19
Grain whisky (Scotland) 182
  distilleries 182
  still 182

Grappa labels 83
Grasshopper (cocktail) 61
Greece 102—3
  brandy 102—3
  other spirits 103
  ouzo 103
Green ginger wine 168—9
Grog, hot rum 224
Groupement des Grandes Liqueurs
  de France 58
Guadeloupe 229—30
Guyana 230

H

Haiti 230
Harvey Wallbanger (cocktail) 78
Heering, Peter F 110
Henriot, Mme 64
Hollands see Gin (Netherlands)
Hungary 152
  fruit brandies 152
  tokay 152

I

Iceland 112
  state liquor monopoly 112
Impurities 14
India 245
Ingredients, raw 14—15
  a selection 14—15
  for brandy 14
  for gin and vodka 14
  for whisky 14
  two-rowed barley 15
  Ugni Blanc grape 14
Ireland 186—93
  bars 190
  liqueurs and other spirits
    192—3
  Seagram Company interests in
    200
  whiskey 186—92
Irish coffee 193
  Danish version 108
  Swedish version 112
Irish Distillers Group Ltd 189, 190
Irish whiskey see Whiskey
  (Ireland)
Israel 103
Italy 70—83
  bitters and other aperitifs 74—7
  brandy and grappa 81—3
  liqueurs 78—80
  vermouth 72—4
Izarra 59

J

Jack Daniels Tennessee sour
  mash whisky 208—9
  charcoal mellowing of 208
  distillery at Lynchburg 208,

    208, 209
  history of 208
  maturation of 208
Jamaica 230
Japan 240—3
  brandy 242
  liqueurs 243
  plum wine 242—3
  sake 242
  shochu 242
  whisky 242—3
Jarnac, town of 36—7
Jenever see Gin (Belgium)

K

Kirsch (France) 57
  grades 57
Kirsch (Switzerland) 56
Kirsch labels 56—7
Korea 245
Korn 130—1
  Doornkat 130, 131
  flavoured 130
  Furst Bismarck 130
Korn labels 130—1
Kornbrannt (Kornbranntwein)
  see Korn

L

Labels see Cognac labels, etc
Lanfray, Jean 64
Liqueur:
  derivation of name 19
Liqueur labels:
  Belgium 126—7
  Denmark 110
  France 62
  Italy 79
  Netherlands 123
  Poland 147
  US 212—13
Liqueurs 19
  ingredients 19
Liqueurs (Africa) 248
  Van der Hum 248
Liqueurs (Australia) 239
Liqueurs (Belgium) 126—7
  Elixir D'Anvers 126
  Mandarine Napoleon 126
  specialist 127
Liqueurs (Caribbean) 230
  Tia Maria 230
Liqueurs (Denmark) 110
Liqueurs (England) 169
  Hallgarten 169
Liqueurs (Finland) 112
  brands 112
Liqueurs (France) 58—63
  anisette 59
  Bénédictine 59—60
  cassis 58
  Chartreuse 60—1
  Cherry Rocher 58—9
  citrus-flavoured 63

Cointreau 60
Eau de Melisse des Carmes
Boyer 58
flavoured with beans, kernels,
etc 63
Grand Marnier 60
Groupement des Grandes
Liqueurs de France 58
herb-based 58, 63
homemade 58
Izarra 59
major producers 58
Pippermint Get 60
regional 58
strawberry 59
Syndicat National des
Fabricants de Liqueurs 58
Verveine du Velay 59
Vieille Curé 58
Liqueurs (Germany) 139—41
Danziger Goldwasser 141
Danziger Silberwasser 141
Friesengeist 141
fruit 139—41
herb-flavoured 141
Swedenpunsch 141
Liqueurs (Greece) 103
Liqueurs (Ireland) 192—3
Bailey's Irish Cream 193
Irish Mist 192—3
Liqueurs (Italy) 78—80
Amaretto di Saronno 78
certosa 78
Galliano 78
Gra-Car 78
homemade 79
Sambuca 80
Strega 78
Liqueurs (Japan) 243
Liqueurs (Mexico) 223
Liqueurs (Netherlands)
120—3
advocaat 120
curaçao 120
producers 120, 122
proprietary brands 123
regional styles 123
'ship's' 123
traditional 120
Liqueurs (Portugal):
Escarchado 99
Liqueurs (Scotland) 185
Drambuie 185
Glayva 185
Glen Mist 185
Lochan Ora 185
Liqueurs (Spain) 92
Calisay 92
Liqueurs (Sweden) 112
Liqueurs (Turkey) 103
Liqueurs (US) 212—13
Forbidden Fruit 213
Rock and Rye 212
Southern Comfort 212
Wild Turkey 212
London dry gin 159, 160
Lullio, Raimundo 8
Luxemburg 127

M

Maceration 12
Madeira 100—1
bual 101
dated solera 101
history of 100
malmsey 101
production process 100
rainwater 101
sercial 101
verdelho 101
vintage 101
Madeira labels *101*
Màlaga 93
Malt whisky (Scotland) 172—81
blends of single malts 181
brand names 178—81
Campbeltown malts 181
Cardow distillery c. 1900 *181*
casks 176
classification by area 178—81
distillation 175—7
distilleries 178—81
green malt 175
Highland malts 181
individuality of each malt 178
Islay malts 178—81
Laphroaig distillery *178*
Lowland malts 181
malting process 172—3
mash tun 175, *175*
maturation of 176
peat reek 175
residue after distillation 176
separation of impure spirit
175—7
spirits safe 176, *177*
stills 175
wash tun 175, *175*
Manhattan (cocktail) 216
Manzanilla sherry 89
Marc 68
crus bourgeois 68
first growth 68
Marie Antoinette (cocktail) 123
Margerita (cocktail) 220
Marsala 79
production process 79
qualities 79
Martini and Rossi 72, 73
Martinique 230—1
Mead 169
Mediterranean 102—3
map *102—3*
Mexico 218—23
liqueurs 223
mescal 223
other spirits 223
pulque 222, 223
tequila 220—3
Mixers 24, *25*
for brandy 24
for dark rum 24
for gin 24
for North American whiskey 24
for schnapps 24

for vermouth 24
for vodka 24
for whisky 24
for white rum 24
soda water 24
story of Indian tonic water 24
Morocco 103
Moscato wines 19
Muscatel wines 19

N

Napoleon brandy 45
Negroni (cocktail) 76
Netherlands 114—23
best-known inns 119
brandewijn 118
corenwyn 118
drinking habits 119
genever 116—17
half and half 122, 123
liqueurs 120—3
map *119*
other drinks 118
vieux 118
New Zealand 239
North America 194—217
Norway 113
aquavit 113
Vinmonopolet (state liquor
monopoly) 113

O

Old Tom flavoured gin 165—7
Oloroso sherry 88, 89
Oporto 96
Ordinaire, Pierre 64
Ouzo 103

P

Palo cortado sherry 88
Paraguay 233
Pastis 67
brands 67
difference from anis 67
distilling process 67
Ricard 67
Patent still 11
Percolation 12
Pernod 64, 67
origin of name 64
popularity in 19th century 64
Peru 233
Pimms 167
cocktail recipe 167
Pineau de Charente 19
Pink gin 162, 165
Pippermint Get 60
Plymouth gin 162—3
Black Friars distillery 163
character of 162
Coates & Co 162—3
history of 162

protection of name 162
Poland 142—7
Polmos (state liquor monopoly)
145
vodka 144—7
Port (Australia) 236
some best brands 236
Port (New Zealand) 239
Port (Portugal) 94—9
crusted 99
declared vintages 97
history of 94
late-bottled vintage 97
production process 94—7
production region 94, *96*
quinta wines 97
ruby 97
tawny 97
to decant 97, *97*
vintage 97
vintage character 99
white 97
wood 99
Port labels:
Australia *236*
Portugal *96*
Port-style wine (England) 169
Portugal 94—9
liqueurs and other drinks 99
port 94—8
Pot still 10, 11
16th-century illustration *8*
alambic charentais 40
distilling process 10, *10*
early *6*
Poteen 188—9
Prohibition (US) 202, 204—5
18th Amendment 204
21st Amendment 205
American temperance
movement 204
bootlegging 205
consequences of 205
Proof systems:
American 17
British or Sykes 17
French (Gay Lussac) 17
Puerto Rico 231
Punch:
Alpine 81
Swedish 112

Q

Quinine 24
Quinine-based drinks (Spain) 92

R

Raki (Far East) 245
Raki (Mediterranean) 103
Ratafia 68
Raya sherry 88
Ricard, Paul 67
Rose de Chambertin
(cocktail) 59

Rum (Australia) 238
    Colonial Sugar Refining
        Company 238
    history of 238
    'Rum Hospital' 238, *238*
Rum (Barbados) 228
Rum (Caribbean) 224—31
    British Navy grog ration 225
    distillation of 226
    fermentation of 226
    history of 225
    maturation of 226
    molasses 226
    production process 226
    stills 226
    sugar cane 226
Rum (Colombia) 232—3
Rum (Cuba) 228—8
Rum (English-matured) 168
Rum (Guadeloupe) 229—30
Rum (Guyana) 230
Rum (Haiti) 230
Rum (Jamaica) 230
Rum (Martinique) 230—1
Rum (Puerto Rico) 231
Rum (Trinidad) 231
Rum (Virgin Islands) 231
Rum grog 224
Rum labels (Caribbean) *229*
Russia 148—53
    Prodintorg (state liquor
        monopoly) 148
    Tartars' milk alcohol 149
    vodka 148—53

S

Saintonge wines (Middle Ages)
    34
Sake 242
Sambuca 80
Scandinavia 104—13
    illegal distilling 112
    map *111*
Schiedam *see Gin (Netherlands)*
Schnapps *(see also Akvavit,
    Aquavit, Brannvin and
    Korn)*:
    mixers 24
Schnapsteufel 10
Scotland 170—85
    blended whisky 182—3
    major companies 184—5
    malt whisky 172—81
    Seagram Company interests in
        200
    whisky liqueurs 185
Seagram Company Ltd 197,
    198—201
    brands owned 198—200
    company with a conscience 199
    history of 200—1
    interests in US 198—200
    interests outside the Americas
        200
    Joseph Seagram 200
    Sam Bronfman 201

Seven Crown American
    whiskey 198
VO Canadian whisky 198
Waterloo distillery 201, *201*
White Wheat label *200*
Sherry:
    cream 89
    old landed 89
Sherry (Australia) 236
    main brands 236
Sherry (Cyprus) 102
    main producers 102
Sherry (England) 169
    brand names 169
Sherry (New Zealand) 239
Sherry (Spain) 86—9
    blending 88—9
    criadera 88, 89
    flor 88
    grapes 86, *86*
    growing area 86
    'Inocente' vineyard 87
    map of production area *88*
    production process 86—8
    solera system 88—9
Slivovitz 103
Sherry labels:
    Australia *236*
    England *168*
    Spain *88*
Sloe gin 164—5
    commercial recipes 164—5
    producers 164
Snaps *see Akvavit, Aquavit,
    Brannvin and Korn*
Soda water 24
South America 232—3
    map *233*
Southern Comfort 212
Spain 84—93
    aguardiente 91
    anis drinks 91—2
    brandy 90—1
    gins and vodkas 92
    liqueurs 92
    malaga 93
    ponche 92
    queimada 91
    quinine-based drinks 92
    sherry 86—9
Spirits:
    addition of mixers 24
    definition of 19
    Polish consumption 28
    Russian consumption 28
    Russian output 26
    world consumption 28—9
    world production 26—7
Spirits safe *6—7*
Sri Lanka 245
Stein, Robert 11
Steinhäger 134—7
Still:
    16th-century pot *8*
    alambic armagnaçais 46—7, *50*
    alambic charentais 40
    Coffey or patent 11
    continuous 11, *11*

early pot *6*
pot 10, *10*
Strega 78
Suntory Company 242, 243
Sweden 111—12
    Aktiebolaget Vin & Sprit-
        centralem (state liquor
        monopoly) 111
    brannvin 111—12
    other drinks 112
Switzerland 56—7
    eau-de-vie 56
    kirsch 56
Sykes (or British) proof
    system 17
Sylvius, Doctor 116
Syndicat National des Fabricants
    de Liqueurs 58

T

Taiwan 245
Tanqueray gin 164
Temperance movement (Britain)
    159
Temperance movement (US) 204
Tequila 220—3
    agave cactus *220, 221, 222*
    maturation of 222
    producers and brands 223
    production process 222
    Tequila labels 222
    Tequila Sunrise (cocktail) 223
Tokay (California) 19
Tokay (Hungary) 152
Tonic water, Indian 24
Torii, Shinjiro 243
Trinidad 231
Tunisia 103
Turkey 103

U

United States 202—17
    Californian brandy 210—11
    history of distilling industry 202
    Jack Daniels Tennessee sour
        mash 207—8
    liqueurs and other drinks
        212—13
    Prohibition 202, 204—5
    Seagram Company interests in
        198—200
    whiskey 202—9
    whiskey, brands 214—16
    'whiskey belt' 202
    Whiskey Rebellion 202
Uruguay 233
Usquebaugh 8
USSR *see Russia*

V

Venecia 89, *89*
Venezuela 233

Vermouth:
    composition of 73
    derivation of name 72
    dry white 73
    mixers 24
    origins of modern patent
        varieties 72
    production process 72—3
    red 73
    sweet white 73
Vermouth (France) 68
Vermouth (Italy) 72—5
    map of production area *72*
    Martini 72
    producers 74
    Verveine du Velay 59
Vieille Curé 58
Vin jaune 19
Vins doux naturels 19
Virgin Islands 231
Vodka:
    base ingredients 14
    mixers 24
    Russian output 26
Vodka (Australia) 239
Vodka (China) 244
Vodka (England) 168
    distillers and brands 168
Vodka (Finland) 112
    brands 112
Vodka (Poland) 144—7
    character of 145
    clear 145
    clear, brands 145
    distilling process 145
    flavoured 145
    flavoured, brands 145
    history of 144—5
    homemade 145—6
    main distilling centres 145
    serving and drinking 146
    Starka 145
    state monopoly 145
    Zubrowka 145, 146
Vodka (Russia) 148—53
    drinking habits 153
    flavoured 149—53
    history of 148
    home and export 149
    ingredients 148—9
    international brands 150—3
    main distilling areas 148
    Moskovskaya 26
    nastoika (heavily-flavoured) 153
    pepper-flavoured 150
    state monopoly 148
    Stolichnaya 26
Vodka (Spain) 92
Vodka labels:
    international *153*
    Poland *147*
    Russia *148*

W

*Wacholder see Gin (German
    equivalent)*

Weinbrand see Brandy (Germany)
Whiskey (Ireland) 186—92
  brands 190—2
  companies and distilleries 190
  famous companies now defunct
    189
  history of 186—9
  illegal distilling 186—9, *188—9*
  Irish Distillers Group Ltd
    189, 190
  maturation of 189—90
  Old Bushmills distillery *187*
  poteen 188—9
  production of 189
  taxes and controls, from
    17th century 186—9
Whiskey (US) 202—9
  38th Congress coda 206
  blended 207
  'bottled in bond' 207
  bourbon 206, 214—15
  corn 206, 215—16
  legal definition of 206
  light 216
  light, definition of 216
  mixers 24
  quality tests 206—7
  rye 206, 215—16
  'spirit' 207
  'straight' 206—7
  styles 206—7
  two main categories 206
  white 216
Whiskey labels (Ireland) *193*
Whiskey Sour (cocktail) 216
Whisky:
  base ingredients 14
  mixers 24
Whisky (Australia) 237
  brands and producers 237
  compared to Scotch 237
Whisky (Canada) 196—201
  Canada Pure Drug Company
    201
  companies and brands 196—201
  definition of 196
  Distillers Corporation Ltd 201
  Distillers Corporation-Seagram
    Ltd 201
  distilling cycle 196
  Gilbey Canada Ltd 197
  Hiram Walker & Sons 197
  Liquor Control Boards 197
  maturation of 196
  mixers 24
  Schenley Distilleries Ltd 197
  Seagram Company 197,
    198—201
Whisky (Japan) 242—3
  brands 242
  history of Suntory Company
    242
Whisky (New Zealand) 239
Whisky (Scotland) *(see also Malt
    whisky, Grain whisky and
    Blended whisky)* 170—85
  compared to Australian 237
  Distillers Company Ltd 185

  excise taxes, 17th to 19th
    century 170
  history of 170
  illegal distilling 170
  independent companies 185
  major companies 184—5
Whisky mac 169
Whisky labels:
  Canada *197*
  Scotland *184*
White Lady (cocktail) 61
White rum, mixers 24
Wine consumption, top twenty
  nations 29
Wine production, top twenty
  nations 27
Wines:
  Cyprus 102
  fortified 18—19
  Saintonge (Middle Ages) 34
Worcestershire sauce 151

Y

Yugoslavia 103

Picture Credits